The Seven Great Monarchies of The Ancient Eastern World by George Rawlinson

Volume V (of VII) The Fifth Monarchy: Persia

George Rawlinson was born on 23rd November 1812 at Chadlington, Oxfordshire. He was the younger brother to the eminent Assyriologist, Sir Henry Rawlinson.

Rawlinson took his degree at Trinity College, Oxford in 1838. Here he also enjoyed playing cricket and was considered to have been a rare talent at the sport. In 1840 he was elected to a fellowship at Exeter College, Oxford. After being ordained in 1841 he became, from 1842 to 1846, a tutor there as well.

In 1846 Rawlinson married Louisa, the daughter of Sir RA Chermside.

His progress continued to be rapid and varied in acknowledgement of his undoubted talents. In 1859 he was made a Bampton lecturer, and was Camden Professor of Ancient History from 1861 to 1889.

By 1872 Rawlinson was appointed canon of Canterbury, and after 1888 he was rector of All Hallows, Lombard Street.

In 1873, he was made proctor in Convocation for the Chapter of Canterbury.

As a scholar he produced, either on his own or in collaboration, several works which are greatly thought of even to this day. His translation of the History of Herodotus (in collaboration with Sir Henry Rawlinson and Sir John Gardiner Wilkinson), 1858–60; The Five Great Monarchies of the Ancient Eastern World, 1862–67; which was later expanded to include The Sixth Great Oriental Monarchy (Parthian), 1873; and The Seventh Great Oriental Monarchy (Sassanian), 1875. Among his other works were Manual of Ancient History, 1869; Historical Illustrations of the Old Testament, 1871; The Origin of Nations, 1877; History of Ancient Egypt, 1881; Egypt and Babylon, 1885; History of Phoenicia, 1889; Parthia, 1893; Memoir of Major-General Sir HC Rawlinson, 1898.

His lectures to an audience at Oxford University on the topic of the accuracy of the Bible in 1859 were published as the apologetic work The Historical Evidences of the Truth of the Scripture Records Stated Anew in later years.

Despite this somewhat prodigious output and alongside his other clerical and family duties he contributed to the Speaker's Commentary, the Pulpit Commentary, Smith's Dictionary of the Bible, and various similar publications.

George Rawlinson died on 7th October, 1902 in Canterbury.

Index of Contents

Index of Illustrations

In the following pages appear a large number of symbols and tables of the original language. For reasons of clarity we have decided in this instance to represent the text with facsimiles from the original book.

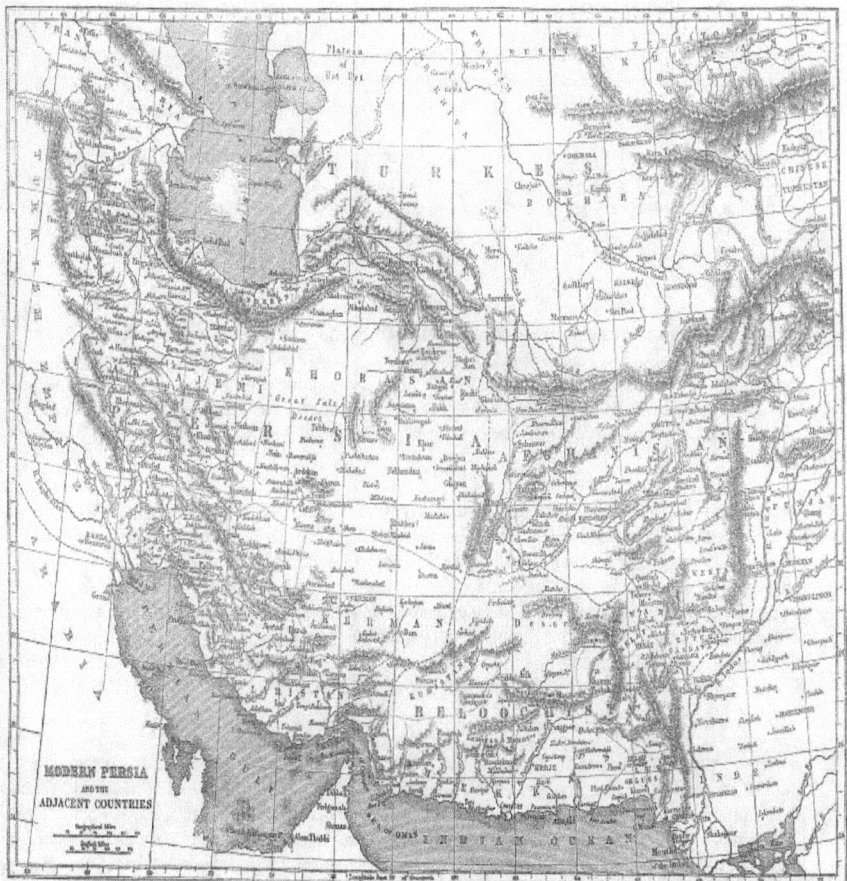

THE FIFTH MONARCHY

CHAPTER I

EXTENT OF THE EMPIRE

The geographical extent of the Fifth Monarchy was far greater than that of any one of the four which had preceded it. While Persia Proper is a comparatively narrow and poor tract, extending in its greatest length only some seven or eight degrees (less than 500 miles), the dominions of the Persian kings covered a space fifty-six degrees long, and in places more than twenty degrees wide. The boundaries of their empire were the desert of Thibet, the Sutlej, and the Indus, on the east; the Indian Sea, the Persian Gulf, the Arabian and Nubian deserts, on the south; on the west, the Greater Syrtis, the Mediterranean, the Egean, and the Strymon river; on the north, the Danube, the Black

Sea, the Caucasus, the Caspian, and the Jaxartes. Within these limits lay a territory, the extent of which from east to west was little less than 3000 miles, while its width varied between 500 and 1500 miles. Its entire area was probably not less than, two millions of square miles—or more than half that of modern Europe. It was thus at least eight times as large as the Babylonian Empire at its greatest extent, and was probably more than four times as large as the Assyrian.

The provinces included within the Empire may be conveniently divided into the Central, the Western, and the Eastern. The Central are Persia Proper, Susiana, Babylonia, Assyria, Media, the coast tract of the Caspian, and Sagartia, or the Great Desert. The Western are Paeonia, Thrace, Asia Minor, Armenia, Iberia, Syria and Phoenicia, Palestine, Egypt, and the Cyrenaica. The Eastern are Hyrcania, Parthia, Aria, Chorasmia, Sogdiana, Bactria, Scythia, Gandaria, Sattagydia, India, Paricania, the Eastern AEthiopia, and Mycia.

Of these countries a considerable number have been already described in these volumes. Susiana, Babylonia, Assyria, Media, the Caspian coast, Armenia, Syria, Phoenicia, and Palestine, belong to this class; and it may be assumed that the reader is sufficiently acquainted with their general features. It would therefore seem to be enough in the present place to give an account of the regions which have not yet occupied our attention, more especially of Persia Proper—the home of the dominant race.

Persia Proper seems to have corresponded nearly to that province of the modern Iran, which still bears the ancient name slightly modified, being called Farsistan or Fars. The chief important difference between the two is, that whereas in modern times the tract called Herman is regarded as a distinct and separate region, Carmania anciently was included within the limits of Persia. Persia Proper lay upon the gulf to which it has given name, extending from the mouth of the Tab (Oroatis) to the point where the gulf joins the Indian Ocean. It was bounded on the west by Susiana, on the north by Media Magna, on the east by Mycia, and on the south by the sea. Its length seems to have been about 450, and its average width about 250 miles. It thus contained an area of rather more than 100,000 square miles.

In modern times it is customary to divide the province of Fars into the ghermsir, or, "warm district," and the serdsir, or "cold region"—and the physical character of the country must have made such a division thoroughly appropriate at every period. The "warm district" is a tract of sandy plain, often impregnated with salt, which extends between the mountains and the sea the whole length of the province, being a continuation of the flat region of Susiana, but falling very much short of that region in all the qualities which constitute physical excellence. The soil is poor, consisting of alternate sand and clay—it is ill-watered, the entire tract possessing scarcely a single stream worthy of the name of river—and, lying only just without the northern Tropic, the district is by its very situation among the hottest of western Asia. It forms, however, no very large portion of the ancient Persia, being in general a mere strip of land, from ten to fifty miles wide, and thus not constituting more than an eighth part of the territory in question.

The remaining seven eighths belong to the serdsir, or "cold region." The mountain-range which under various names skirts on the east the Mesopotamian lowland, separating off that depressed and generally fertile region from the bare high plateau of Iran, and running continuously in a direction parallel to the course of the Mesopotamian streams—i.e. from the north-west to the south-east—changes its course as it approaches the sea, sweeping gradually round between long. 50° and 55°, and becoming parallel to the coast-line, while at the same time it broadens out, till it covers a space of nearly three degrees, or above two hundred miles. Along the high tract thus created lay the bulk of the ancient Persia, consisting of alternate mountain, plain, and narrow valley, curiously intermixed, and as yet very incompletely mapped. This region is of varied character. In places richly, fertile, picturesque, and romantic almost beyond imagination, with lovely wooded dells, green mountain-sides, and broad plains suited for the production of almost any crops, it has yet on the whole a predominant character of sterility and barrenness, especially towards its more northern and eastern portions. The supply of water is everywhere scanty. Scarcely any of the streams are strong enough to reach the sea. After short courses they are either absorbed by the sand or end in small salt lakes, from which the superfluous water is evaporated. Much of the country is absolutely without streams, and would be uninhabitable were it not for the kanats, or karizes, subterranean channels of spring-water, described at length in a former volume.

The only rivers of the district which deserve any attention are the Tab (or Oroatis), whereof a description has been already given, the Kur or Bendamir (called anciently Araxes), with its tributary, the Pulwar (or Cyrus), and the Khoonazaberni or river of Khisht.

The Bendamir rises in the mountains of the Bakhtiyari chain, in lat. 30° 35′, long. 51° 50′ nearly, and runs with a course which is generally south-east, past the ruins of Persepolis, to the salt lake of Neyriz or Kheir, which it enters in long. 53° 30′. It receives, where it approaches nearest to Persepolis, the Pulwar or Kur-ab, a small stream coming from the north-east and flowing by the ruins of both Pasargadae and Persepolis. A little below its junction with this stream the Bendamir is crossed by a bridge of five arches, and further down, on the route between Shiraz and Herman, by another of twelve. Here its waters are to a great extent drawn off by means of canals, and are made to fertilize a large tract of rich flat country on either bank, after which the stream pursues its course with greatly diminished volume to the salt lake in which it ends. The entire course, including only main windings, may be estimated at 140 or 150 miles.

The Khoonazaberni or river of Khisht rises near the ruins of Shapur, at a short distance from Kazerun, on the route between Bushire and Shiraz, and flows in a broad valley between lofty mountains towards the south-west, entering the Persian Gulf by three mouths, the chief of which is at Rohilla, twenty miles north of Bushire, where the stream has a breadth of sixty yards, and a depth of about four feet. Above Khisht the river is already thirty yards wide. Its chief tributary is the Dalaki stream, which enters it from the east, nearly in long. 51°. The entire course of the Khisht river may be about 95 or 100 miles. Its water is brackish except near the source.

The principal lakes are the Lake of Neyriz and the Deriah-i-Nemek. The Deriah-i-Nemek is a small basin distant about ten miles from Shiraz, which receives the waters of the streams that supply that town. It has a length of about fifteen and a breadth of about three or three and a half miles. The lake of Neyriz or Kheir is of far larger size, being from fifty to sixty miles long and from three to six broad, though in the summer season it is almost entirely dried up. Salt is then obtained from the lake in large quantities, and forms an important feature in the commerce of the district. Smaller lakes, also salt or brackish, exist in other parts of the country, as Lake Famur, near Kazerun, which is about six miles in length, and from half a mile to a mile across.

The most remarkable feature of the country consists in the extraordinary gorges which pierce the great mountain-chain, and render possible the establishment of routes across that tremendous barrier. Scarped rocks rise almost perpendicularly on either side of the mountain-streams, which descend rapidly with frequent cascades and falls. Along the slight irregularities of these rocks the roads are carried in zigzags, often crossing the streams from side to side by bridges of a single arch, which are thrown over profound chasms where the waters chafe and roar many hundred feet below.46 [PLATE XXVI.] The roads have for the most part been artificially cut in the sides of the precipices, which rise from the streams sometimes to the height of 2000 feet. In order to cross from the Persian Gulf to the high plateau of Iran, no fewer than three or four of these kotuls, or strange gorge-passes, have to be traversed successively. Thus the country towards the edge of the plateau is peculiarly safe from attack, being defended on the north and east by vast deserts, and on the south by a mountain-barrier of unusual strength and difficulty.

Plate XXVI.

View in the mountain pass between Bushire and Shiraz.

PLATE XXVI

It is in these regions, which combine facility of defence with pleasantness of climate, that the principal cities of the district have at all times been placed. The earliest known capital of the region was Pasargadae, or Persagadae, as the name is sometimes written, of which the ruins still exist near Murgab, in lat. 30° 15′ long. 53° 17′. Here is the famous tomb of Cyrus, whereof a description will be given hereafter; and here are also other interesting remains of the old Persian architecture. Neither the shape nor the extent of the town can be traced. The situation was a plain amid mountains, watered by small streams which found their way to a river of some size (the Pulwar) flowing at a little distance to the west. [PLATE XXVII Fig. 1.]

Vol. II.   Plate. XXVII.

Fig. 1.

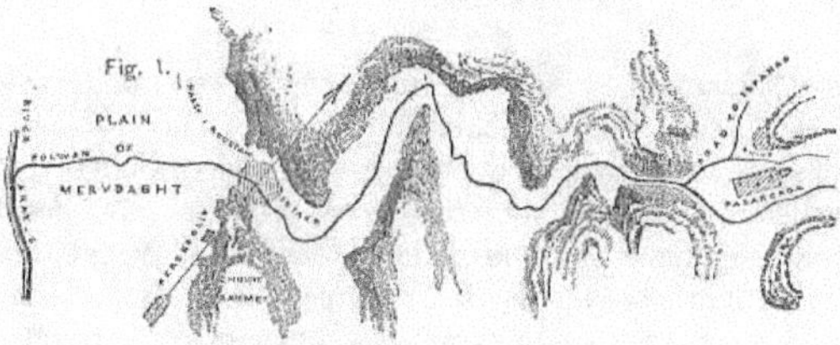

PLAIN OF MERVDASHT

Chart of the country between Pasargadae (Murgab) and Persepolis.

Fig. 2.

Ancient Shadoof.

Fig. 3.

View of Mount Demavend in the Elburz.

PLATE XXVII

At the distance of thirty miles from Pasargadae, or of more than forty by the ordinary road, grew up the second capital, Persepolis, occupying a more southern position than the primitive seat of power, but still situated towards the edge of the plateau, having the mountain-barrier to the south-west and the desert at no great distance to the north-east. Like its predecessor, Persepolis was situated in a plain, but in a plain of much larger dimensions and of far greater fertility. The plain of Merdasht is one of the most productive in Persia, being watered by the two streams of the Bendamir and the Pulwar, which unite a few miles below the site of the ancient city. From these two copious and unfailing rivers a plentiful supply of the precious fluid can at all times be obtained; and in Persia such a supply will always create the loveliest verdure, the most abundant crops, and the richest and thickest foliage. The site of Persopolis is naturally far superior to that in which the modern provincial capital, Shiraz, has grown up, at about the same distance from Persepolis as that is from Pasargadae. and in the same—i.e. in a south-west—direction.

Besides Persepolis and Pasargadse, Persia Proper contained but few cities of any note or name. If we include Carmania in Persia, Carmana, the capital of that country, may indeed be mentioned as a third Persian town of some consequence; but otherwise the names which occur in ancient authors are insignificant, and designate villages rather than towns of any size. Carmana, however, which is mentioned by Ptolemy and Ammianus as the capital of those parts, seems to have been a place of considerable importance. It may be identified with the modern Kerman, which lies in lat. 39° 55', long. 56° 13', and is still one of the chief cities of Persia. Situated, like Pasargadae and Persepolis, in a capacious plain surrounded by mountains, which furnish sufficient water for cultivation to be carried on by means of kanats in most parts of the tract enclosed by them, and occupying a site through which the trade of the country almost of necessity passes, Kerman must always be a town of no little consequence. Its inland and remote position, however, caused it to be little known to the Greeks; and, apparently, the great Alexandrian geographer was the first who made them acquainted with its existence and locality.

The Persian towns or villages upon the coast of the Gulf were chiefly Armuza (which gave name to the district of Ar-muzia), opposite the modern island of Ormuz; Sisidona, which must have been near Cape Jerd; Apostana, probably about Shewar; Gogana, no doubt the modern Kongoon; and Taoce on the Granis, famous as having in its neighborhood a royal palace, which we may perhaps place near Dalaki, Taoce itself occupying the position of Rohilla, at the mouth of the Khisht river. Of the inland towns the most remarkable, after Persepolis, Pasargadse, and Carmana, were Gabae, near Pasar-gadae, also the site of a palace; Uxia, or the Uxian city, which may have occupied the position of Mai-Amir, Obroatis, Tragonice, Ardea, Portospana, Hyrba, etc., which it is impossible to locate unless by the merest conjecture.

The chief districts into which the territory was divided were Paraetacene, a portion of the Bakhtiyari mountain-chain, which some, however, reckoned to Media; Mardyene, or the country of the Mardi, also one of the hill tracts; Taocene, the district about Taoce, part of the low sandy coast region; Ciribo, the more northern portion of the same region; and Carmania, the entire eastern territory. These districts were not divided from one another by any marked natural features, the only division of the country to which such a character attached being the triple one into the high sandy plains north of the mountains, the mountain region, and the Deshtistan, or low hot tract along the coast.

From this account it will be easy to understand how Persia Proper acquired and maintained the character of "a scant land and a rugged," which we find attaching to it in ancient authors. The entire area, as has been already observed was about 100,000 square miles—little more than half that of Spain, and about one fifth of the area of modern Persia. Even of this space nearly one half was uninhabitable, consisting either of barren stony mountain or of scorching sandy plain, ill supplied with water, and often impregnated with salt, the habitable portion consisted of the valleys and plains among the mountains and along their skirts, together with certain favored spots upon the banks of streams in the flat regions. These flat regions themselves were traversed in many places by rocky ridges of a singularly forbidding aspect. The whole appearance of the country was dry, stony, sterile. As a modern writer observes, "the livery of the land is constantly brown or gray; water is scanty; plains and mountains are equally destitute of wood. When the traveller, after toiling over the rocky mountains that separate the plains looks down from the pass he has won with toil and difficulty upon the country below, his eye wanders unchecked and unrested over an uniform brown expanse losing itself in distance."

Still this character, though predominant, is not universal. Wherever there is water, vegetation springs up. The whole of the mountain region is intersected by valleys and plains which are more or less fertile. The line of country between Bebahan and Shiraz is for above sixty miles "covered with wood and verdure," in East of Shiraz, on the route between that city and Kerman the country is said to be in parts "picturesque and romantic," consisting of "low luxuriant valleys or; plains separated by ranges of low mountains, green to their very summits with beautiful turf." The plains of Khubbes, Merdasht, Ujan, Shiraz, Kazerun, and others, produce abundantly under a very inefficient system of cultivation. Even in the most arid tracts there is generally a time of greenness immediately after the spring rains, when the whole country smiles with verdure.

It has been already remarked that the Empire, which, commencing from Persia Proper, spread itself towards the close of the sixth century before Christ, over the surrounding tracts, included a number of countries not yet described in these volumes, since they formed no part of any of the four Empires which preceded the Persian. To complete, therefore, the geographical survey proper to our subject, it will be necessary to give a sketch of the tracts in question. They will fall naturally into three groups, an eastern, a north-western, and a southwestern—the eastern extending from the skirts of Mount Zagros to the Indian Desert, the north-western from the Caspian to the Propontis, and the south-western from the borders of Palestine to the shores of the Greater Syrtis.

Inside the Zagros and Elburz ranges, bounded on the north and west by those mountain-lines, on the east by the ranges of Suliman and Hala, and on the south by the coast-chain which runs from Persia Proper nearly to the Indus, lies a vast tableland, from 3000 to 5000 feet above the sea-level, known to modern geographers as the Great Plateau of Iran. Its shape is an irregular rectangle, or trapezium, extending in its greatest length, which is from west to east, no less than twenty degrees, or above 1100 miles, while the breadth from north to south varies from seven degrees, or 480 miles (which is its measure along the line of Zagros), to ten degrees, or 690 miles, where it abuts upon the Indus valley. The area of the tract is probably from 500,000 to 600,000 square miles.

It is calculated that two thirds of this elevated region are absolutely and entirely desert. The rivers which flow from the mountains surrounding it are, with a single exception—that of the Etymandrus or Helmend—insignificant, and their waters almost always lose themselves, after a course proportioned to their volume, in the sands of the interior. Only two, the Helmend and the river of Ghuzni, have even the strength to form lakes; the others are absorbed by irrigation, or sucked up by the desert. Occasionally a river, rising within the mountains, forces its way through the barrier, and so contrives to reach the sea. This is the case, especially, on the south, where the coast chain is pierced by a number of streams, some of which have their sources at a considerable distance inland. On the north the Heri-rud, or River of Herat, makes its escape in a similar way from the plateau, but only to be absorbed, after passing through two mountain chains, in the sands of the Kharesm. Thus by far the greater portion of this region is desert throughout the year, while, as the summer advances, large tracts, which in the spring were green, are burnt up—the rivers shrink back towards their sources—the whole plateau becomes dry and parched—and the traveller wonders that any portion of it should be inhabited.

It must not be supposed that the entire plateau of which we have been speaking is to the eye a single level and unbroken plain. In the western portion of the region the plains are constantly intersected by "brown, irregular, rocky ridges," rising to no great height, but serving to condense the vapors held in the air, and furnishing thereby springs and wells of inestimable value to the inhabitants. In the southern and eastern districts "immense" ranges of mountains are said to occur; and the south-eastern as well as the north-eastern corners of the plateau are little else than confused masses of giant elevations. Vast flats, however, are found. In the Great Salt Desert, which extends from Kashan and Koum to the Deriah or "Sea" in which the Helmend terminates, and in the sandy desert of Seistan, which lies east and south-east of that lake, reaching from near Furrah to the Mekran mountains, plains of above a hundred miles in extent appear to occur, sometimes formed of loose sand, which the wind raises into waves like those of the sea, sometimes hard and gravelly, or of baked and indurated clay.

The tract in question, which at the present day is divided between Afghanistan, Beloochistan, and Iran, contained, at the time when the Persian Empire arose, the following nations: the Sagartians, the Cossseans, the Parthians, the Hariva or Arians, the Gandarians, the Sattagydians, the Arachotians, the Thamanseans, the Sarangae, and the Paricanians. The Sagartians and Cossseans dwelt in the western portion of the tract, the latter probably about the Siah-Koh mountains, the former scattered over the whole region from the borders of Persia Proper to the Caspian Gates and the Elburz range. Along its northern edge, east of the Sagartians, were the Parthians, the Arians, and the Gandarians. occurring in that order as we proceed from west to east. The Parthians held the country known now as the Atak or "Skirt," the flat tract at the southern base of the Elburz from about Shahrud to Khaff, together with a portion of the mountain region adjoining. This is a rich and valuable territory, well watered by a number of small streams, which, issuing from the ravines and valleys of the Elburz, spread fertility around, but lose themselves after a short, course in the Salt Desert. Adjoining the Parthians upon the east were the Haroyu, Hariva, or Arians, an Iranic race of great antiquity, who held the country along the southern skirts of the mountains from the neighborhood of Khaff to the point where the Heri-rud (Arius) issues from the Paropamisan mountains. The character of this country closely resembles that of Parthia, whereof it is a continuation; but the copious stream of the Heri-rud renders it even more productive.

The Gandarians held Kabul, and the mountain tract on both sides of the Kabul river as far as the upper course of the Indus, thus occupying the extreme north-eastern corner of the plateau, the region where its elevation is the greatest. Lofty mountain-ridges, ramifying in various directions but tending generally to run east and west, deep gorges, narrow and tremendous passes, like the Khyber, characterize this district. Its soil is generally rocky and barren; but many of the valleys are fertile, abounding with enchanting scenery and enjoying a delightful climate. More especially is this the case in the neighborhood of the city of Kabul, which is perhaps the Caspatyrus of Herodotus, where Darius built the fleet which descended the Indus.

South of Aria and Gandaria, in the tract between the Great Desert and the Indus valley, the plateau was occupied by four nations—the Thamanseans, the Sarangians, the Sattagydians, and the Arachotians. The Thamanaean country appears to have been that which lies south and south-east of Aria (Herat), reaching from the Haroot-rud or river of Subzawar to the banks of the Helmend about Ghirisk. This is a varied region, consisting on the north and the north-east of several high mountain chains which ramify from a common centre, having between them large tracts of hills and downs, while towards the south and the south-west the country is comparatively low and flat, descending to the level of the desert about the thirty second parallel. Here the Thamanseans were adjoined upon by the Sarangians, who held the land about the lake in which the Helmend terminates—the Seistan of Modern Persia. Seistan is mainly desert. One third of the surface of the soil is composed of moving sands, and the other two thirds of a compact sand, mixed with a little clay, but very rich in vegetable matter. It is traversed by a number of streams, as the Haroot-rud, the river of Furrah, the river of Khash, the Helmend, and others, and is very productive along their banks, which are fertilized by annual inundations; but the country between the streams is for the most part an arid desert.

The Sattagydians and Arachotians divided between them the remainder of Afghanistan, the former probably occupying south-eastern Kabul, from the Ghuzni river and its tributaries to the valley of the Indus, while the latter were located in the modern Candahar, upon the Urghand-ab and Turnuk rivers. The character of these tracts is similar to that of north-western Kabul, but somewhat less rugged and mountainous. Hills and downs alternate with rocky ranges and fairly fertile vales. There is a scantiness of water, but still a certain number of moderate-sized rivers, tolerably well supplied with affluents. The soil, however, is either rocky or sandy; and without a careful system of irrigation great portions of the country remain of necessity barren and unproductive.

The south-eastern corner of the plateau, below the countries of the Sarangians and the Arachotians, was occupied by a people, called Paricanians by Herodotus, perhaps identical with the Gedrosians of later writers. This district, the modern Beloochistan, is still very imperfectly known, but appears to be generally mountainous, to have a singularly barren soil, and to be deficient in rivers. The nomadic life is a necessity in the greater part of the region, which is in few places suitable for cultivation, but has good pastures in the mountains or the plains according to the season of the year. The rivers of the country are for the most part mere torrents, which carry a heavy body of water after rains, but are often absolutely dry for several months in succession. Water, however, is generally obtainable by digging wells in their beds; and the liquid procured in this way suffices, not only for the wants of man and beast, but also for a limited irrigation.

The Great Plateau which has been here described is bordered everywhere, except at its north-eastern and north-western corners, by low regions. On the north the lowland is at first a mere narrow strip intervening between the Elburz range and the Caspian, a strip which has been already described in the account given of the Third Monarchy. Where, however, the Caspian ends, its shore trending away to the northward, there succeeds to this mere strip of territory a broad and ample tract of sandy plain, extending from about the 54th to the 68th degree of east longitude—a distance of 760 miles—and reaching from the 36th to the 50th parallel of north latitude—a distance not much short of a thousand miles! This tract which comprises the modern Khanats of Khiva and Bokhara, together with a considerable piece of Southern Asiatic Russia, is for the most part a huge trackless desert, composed of loose sand, black or red, which the wind heaps up into hills. Scarcely any region on the earth's surface is more desolate. The boundless plain lies stretched before the traveller like an interminable sea, but dead, dull, and motionless. Vegetation, even the most dry and sapless, scarcely exists. For three or four hundred miles together he sees no running stream. Water, salt, slimy, and discolored, lies Occasionally in pools, or is drawn from wells, which yield however only a scanty supply. For anything like a drinkable beverage the traveller has to trust to the skies, which give or withhold their stores with a caprice that is truly tantalizing. Occasionally, but only at long intervals, out of the low sandy region there issues a rocky range, or a plateau of moderate eminence, where the soil is firm, the ground smooth, and vegetation tolerably abundant. The most important of the ranges are the Great and Little Balkan, near the Caspian Sea, between the 39th and 40th parallels, the Khalata and Urta Tagh, north-west, of Bokhara, and the Kukuth; still further to the north-west in latitude 42° nearly. The chief plateau is that of Ust-Urt, between the Caspian and the Sea of Aral, which is perhaps not more than three or four hundred feet above the sandy plain, but is entirely different in character.

This desolate region of low sandy plain would be wholly uninhabitable, were it not for the rivers. Two great streams, the Amoo or Jyhun (anciently the Oxus), and the Sir or Synuti (anciently the Jaxartes), carry their waters across the desert, and pour them into the basin of the Aral. Several others of less volume, as the Murg-ab, or river of Merv, the Abi Meshed or Tejend, the Heri-rud, the river of Maymene, the river of Balkh, the river of Khulm, the Shehri-Sebz, the Ak Su or river of Bokhara, the Kizil Deria, etc., flow down from the high ground into the plain, where their waters either become lost in the sands, or terminate in small salt pools. Along the banks of these streams the soil is fertile, and where irrigation is employed the crops are abundant. In the vicinity of Khiva, at Kermineh on the Bokhara river, at Samarcand, at Balkh—and in a few other places, the vegetation is even luxuriant; gardens, meadows, orchards, and cornfields fringe the river-bank; and the natives see in such favored spots resemblances of Paradise! Often, however, even the river-banks themselves are uncultivated, and the desert creeps up to their very edge; but this is in default, not in spite, of human exertion. A well-managed system of irrigation could, in almost every instance, spread on either side of the streams a broad strip of verdure.

In the time of the Fifth Monarchy, the tract which has been here described was divided among three nations. The region immediately to the east of the Caspian, bounded on the north by the old course of the Oxus and extending eastward to the neighborhood of Merv, though probably not including that city, was Chorasmia, the country of the Chorasmians. Across the Oxus to the north-east was Sogdiana (or Sugd), reaching thence to the Jaxartes, which was the Persian boundary in this direction. South of Sogdiana, divided from it by the Middle and Upper Oxus, was Bactria, the country of the Bakhtars or Bactrians. The territory of this people reached southward to the foot of the Paropamisus, adjoining Chorasmia and Aria on the west, and on the south Sattagydia and Gandaria.

East of the table-land lies the valley of the Indus and its tributaries, at first a broad tract, 350 miles from west to east, but narrowing as it descends, and in places not exceeding sixty or seventy miles, across. The length of the valley is not less than 800 miles. Its area is probably about a hundred thousand square miles. We may best regard it as composed of two very distinct tracts—one the broad triangular plain towards the north, to which, from the fact of its being watered by five main streams, he natives have given the name of Punj-ab, the other the long and comparatively narrow valley of the single Indus river, which, deriving its appellation from that noble stream, is known in modern geography as Sinde. The Punjab, which contains an area of above fifty thousand square miles, is mountainous towards the north, where it adjoins on Kashmeer and Thibet, but soon sinks down into a vast plain, with a soil which is chiefly either sand or clay, immensely productive under irrigation, but tending to become jungle or desert if left without human care. Sinde, or the Indus valley below the Punjab, is a region of even greater fertility. It is watered, not only by the main stream of the Indus, but by a number of branch channels which the river begins to throw off from about the 28th parallel. It includes, on the right bank of the stream, the important tract called Cutchi Gandava, a triangular plain at the foot of the Suliman and Hala ranges, containing about 7000 square miles of land which is all capable of being made into a garden. The soil is here for the most part rich, black, and loamy; water is abundant; and the climate suitable for the growth of all kinds of grain. Below Cutchi Gandava the valley of the Indus is narrow for about a hundred miles, but about Tatta it expands and a vast delta is formed. This is a third triangle, containing above a thousand square miles of the richest alluvium, which is liable however to floods and to vast changes in the river beds, whereby often whole fields are swept away. Much of this tract is moreover low and swampy; the climate is trying; and rice is almost the only product that can be advantageously cultivated.

The low region lying south of the Great Plateau is neither extensive nor valuable. It consists of a mere strip of land along the coast of the Indian Ocean, extending a distance of about nine degrees (550 miles) from the mouth of the Persian Gulf to Cape Monze, near Kurrachee, but in width not exceeding ten or, at the most, twenty miles. This tract was occupied in ancient times mainly by a race which Herodotus called Ethiopians and the historians of Alexander Ichthyophagi (Fish-Eaters). It is an arid, sultry, and unpleasant region, scarcely possessing a perennial stream, and depending for its harvests entirely upon the winter rains, and for its water during the summer on wells which are chiefly brackish. Tolerable pasturage is, however, obtainable in places even during the hottest part of the year, and between Cape Jask and Gwattur the crops produced are far from contemptible.

A small tract of coast, a continuation of the territory just described, intervening between it and Kerman, was occupied in the early Persian times by a race known to the Persians as Maka, and to the Greeks as Mycians. This district, reaching from about Cape Jask to Gombroon, is one of greater fertility than is usual in these regions, being particularly productive in dates and grain. This fertility seems, however, to be confined to the vicinity of the sea-shore.

To complete the description of the Eastern provinces two other tracts must be mentioned. The mountain-chain which skirts the Great Plateau on the north, distinguished in these pages by the name of Elburz, broadens out after it passes the south-eastern corner of the Caspian Sea till it covers a space of nearly three degrees (more than 200 miles). Instead of the single lofty ridge which separates the Salt Desert from the low Caspian region, we find between the fifty-fourth and fifty-ninth degrees of east longitude three or four distinct ranges, all nearly parallel to one another, having a general direction of east and west. Broad and rich valleys are enclosed between these latitudinal ranges which are watered by rivers of a considerable size, as more especially the Ettrek and the Gurgan. Thus a territory is formed capable of supporting a largish population, a territory which possesses a natural unity, being shut in on three sides by mountains, and on the fourth by the Caspian. Here in Persian times was settled a people called Hyrcani; and from them the tract derived the name of Hyrcania (Vehrkana), while the lake on which it adjoined came to be known as "the Hyrcanian Sea." The fertility of the region, its broad plains, shady woods and lofty mountains were celebrated by the ancient writers.

Further to the east, beyond the low sandy plain, and beyond the mountains in which its great rivers have their source—on the other side of the "Roof of the World," as the natives name this elevated region—lay a tract unimportant in itself, but valuable to the Persians as the home of a people from whom they obtained excellent soldiers. The plain of Chinese Tartary, the district about Kashgar and Yarkand, seems to have been in possession of certain Sacans or Scythians, who in the flourishing times of the empire acknowledged subjection to the Persian crown. These Sacans, who call themselves Huma-varga or Amyrgians, furnished some of the best and bravest of the Persian troops. Westward they bordered on Sogdiana and Bactria; northward they extended probably to the great mountain-chain of the Tien-chan; on the east they were shut in by the vast desert of Gobi or Shamoo; while southward they must have touched Gandaria and perhaps India. A portion of this country—that towards the north and west—was well watered and fairly productive; but the southern and eastern part of it must have been arid and desert.

From this consideration of the Eastern provinces of the Empire, we pass on naturally to those which lay towards the North-West. The Caspian Sea alone intervened between these two groups, which thus approached each other within a distance of some 250 or 260 miles.

Almost immediately to the west of the Caspian there rises a high table-land diversified by mountains, which stretches eastward for more than eighteen degrees between the 37th and 41st parallels. This highland may properly be regarded as a continuation of the great Iranean plateau, with which it is connected at its south-eastern corner. It comprises a portion of the modern Persia, the whole of Armenia, and most of Asia Minor. Its principal mountain-ranges are latitudinal or from west to east, only the minor ones taking the opposite or longitudinal direction. Of the latitudinal chains the most important is the Taurus, which, commencing at the southwestern corner of Asia

Minor in longitude 29° nearly, bounds the great table-land upon the south, running parallel with the shore at the distance of sixty or seventy miles as far as the Pylse Cilicise, near Tarsus, and then proceeding in a direction decidedly north of east to the neighborhood of Lake Van, where it unites with the line of Zagros. The elevation of this range, though not equal to that of some in Asia, is considerable. In Asia Minor the loftiest of the Taurus peaks seem to attain a height of about 9000 or 10,000 feet. Further to the east the elevation appears to be even greater, the peaks of Ala Dagh, Sapan, Nimrud, and Mut Khan in the tract about Lake Van being all of them considerably above the line of perpetual snow, and therefore probably 11,000 or 12,000 feet.

At the opposite side of the table-land, bounding it towards the north, there runs under various names a second continuous range of inferior elevation, which begins near Brusa, in the Keshish Dagh or Mysian Olympus, and proceeds in a line nearly parallel with the northern coast to the vicinity of Kars. Between this and Taurus are two other important ridges, which run westward from the neighborhood of Ararat to about the 34th degree of east longitude, after which they subside into the plain.

The heart of the mountain-region, the tract extending from the district of Erivan on the east to the upper course of the Kizil-Irmak river and the vicinity of Sivas upon the west, was, as it still is, Armenia. Amidst these natural fastnesses, in a country of lofty ridges, deep and narrow valleys, numerous and copious streams, and occasional broad plains—a country of rich pasture grounds, productive orchards, and abundant harvests—this interesting people has maintained itself almost unchanged from the time of the early Persian kings to the present day. Armenia was one of the most valuable portions of the Persian Empire, furnishing, as it did, besides stone and timber, and several most important minerals, an annual supply of 20,000 excellent horses to the stud of the Persian king.

The highland west of Armenia, the plateau of Asia Minor, from the longitude of Siwas (37° E.) to the sources of the Meander and the Hermus, was occupied by the two nations of the Cappadocians and Phrygians, whose territories were separated by the Kizil-Irmak or Halys river. This tract, though diversified by some considerable ranges, and possessing one really lofty mountain, that of Argseus, was, compared with Armenia, champaign and level. Its broad plains afforded the best possible pasturage for sheep, while at the same time they bore excellent crops of wheat. The entire region was well-watered; it enjoyed a delightful climate; and besides corn and cattle furnished many products of value.

Outside the plateau on the north, on the north-east, on the west, and on the south, lie territories which, in comparison with the high region whereon they adjoined, may be called lowlands. The north-eastern lowland, the broad and rich valley of the Kur, which corresponds closely with the modern Russian province of Georgia, was in the possession of a people called by Herodotus Saspeires or Sapeires, whom we may identify with the Iberians of later writers. Adjoining upon them towards the south, probably in the country about Erivan, and so in the neighborhood of Ararat, were the Alarodians, whose name must be connected with that of the great mountain. On the other side of the Sapeirian country, in the tracts now known as Mingrelia and Imeritia, regions of a wonderful beauty and fertility, were the Colchians—dependants, but not exactly subjects, of Persia.

The northern lowland, which consisted of a somewhat narrow strip of land between the plateau and the Euxine, was a rich and well-wooded region, 630 miles in length, and in breadth from forty to a hundred. It was inhabited by a large number of rude and barbarous tribes, each of whom possessed a small portion of the sea-board. These tribes, enumerated in the order of their occurrence from east to west, were the following: the Moschi, the Macrones (or Tzani), the Mosy-noeci, the Mares, the Tibareni, the Chalybes, the Paphlagones, the Mariandyni, the Bithyni, and the Thyni. The Moschi, Macrones, Mosynoeci, Mares, and Tibareni dwelt towards the east, occupying the coast from

Batoum to Ordou. The Chalybes inhabited the tract immediately adjoining on Sinope. The Paphlagonians held the rest of the coast from the mouth of the Kizil-Irmak to Cape Baba, where they were succeeded by the Mariandyni, who owned the small tract between Cape Baba and the mouth of the Sakkariyeh (Sangarius). From the Sangarius to the canal of Constantinople dwelt the Thynians and Bithynians intermixed, the former however affecting the coast and the latter the interior of the country. The entire tract was of a nearly uniform character, consisting of wooded spurs from the northern mountain-chain, with, valleys of greater or less width between them. Streams were numerous, and vegetation was consequently rich; but it may be doubted whether the climate was healthy.

The western lowland comprised the inland regions of Mysia, Lydia, and Caria, together with the coast-tracts which had been occupied by immigrant Greeks, and which were known as Juolis, Doris, and Ionia. The broad and rich plains, the open valleys, the fair grassy mountains, the noble trees, the numerous and copious rivers of this district are too well known to need description here. The western portion of Asia Minor is a terrestrial paradise, well deserving the praises which Herodotus with patriotic enthusiasm bestowed upon it. The climate is delightful, only that it is somewhat too luxurious; the soil is rich and varied in quality; the vegetable productions are abundant; and the mountains, at any rate anciently, possessed mineral treasures of great value.

The lowland upon the south is narrower and more mountainous than either of the others. It comprised three countries only—Lycia, Pamphylia, and Cilicia. The tract is chiefly occupied by spurs from Taurus, between which lie warm and richly wooded valleys. In Lycia, however, the mountain-ridges embrace some extensive uplands, on a level not much inferior to that of the central plateau itself, while in Pamphylia and Cilicia are two or three low alluvial plains of tolerable extent and of great fertility. Of these the most remarkable is that near Tarsus, formed by the three streams of the Cydnus, the Sarus, and the Pyramus, which extends along the coast a distance of forty miles and reaches inland about thirty, the region which gave to the tract where it occurs the name of Cilicia Campestris or Pedias.

The Persian dominion in this quarter was not bounded by sea. Opposite to Cilicia lay the large and important island of Cyprus, which was included in the territories of the Great King from the time of Cambyses to the close of the Empire. Further to the west, Rhodes, Cos, Samos, Chios, Lesbos, Tenedos, Lemnus, Imbrus, Samothrace, Thasos, and most of the islands of the Egean were for a time Persian, but were never grasped with such firmness as to be a source of real strength to their conquerors. The same may be said of Thrace and Pseonia, subjugated under Darius, and held for some twenty or thirty years, but not assimilated, not brought into the condition of provinces, and therefore rather a drain upon the Empire than an addition to its resources. It seems unnecessary to lengthen out this description of the Persian territories by giving an account of countries and islands, whose connection with the Empire was at once so slight and so temporary.

A few words must, however, be said respecting Cyprus. This island, which is 140 miles long from Bafa (Paphos) to Cape Andrea, with an average width for two thirds of its length of thirty-five, and for the remaining third of about six or seven miles, is a mountainous tract, picturesque and varied, containing numerous slopes, and a few plains, well fitted for cultivation. According to Eratosthenes it was in the more ancient times richly wooded, but was gradually cleared by human labor. Its soil was productive, and particularly well suited for the vine and the olive. It grew also sufficient corn for its own use. But its special value arose from its mineral products. The copper mines near Tamasus were enormously productive, and the ore thence derived so preponderated over all other supplies that the later Romans came to use the word Cyprium for the metal generally—whence the names by which it is even now known in most of the languages of modern Europe. On the whole Cyprus was considered inferior to no known island. Besides its vegetable and mineral products, it furnished a large number of excellent sailors to the Persian fleet.

It remains to notice briefly those provinces of the south-west which had not been included within any of the preceding monarchies, and which are therefore as yet undescribed in these volumes. These provinces are the African, and may be best considered under the three heads of Egypt, Libya, and the Cyrenaica.

Egypt, if we include under the name not merely the Nile valley and the Delta, but the entire tract interposed between the Libyan Desert on the one side and the Arabian Gulf or Red Sea on the other, is a country of nearly the size of Italy. It measures 520 miles from Elephantine to the Mediterranean, and has an average width of 150 or 160 miles. It must thus contain an area of about 80,000 square miles. Of this space, however, at least three fourths is valueless, consisting of bare rocky mountain or dry sandy plain. It is only along the course of the narrow valley in which the Nile flows from the Cataracts to beyond Cairo, in the tract known as the Faioum, and in the broad region of the Delta, that cultivation is possible. Even in the Delta itself there are large spaces which are arid, and others which are permanent marshes, so that considerable portions of its surface are unfitted for husbandry. But if the quantity of cultivable land is thus limited in Egypt, the quality is so excellent, in consequence of the alluvial character of the soil, that the country was always in ancient times a sort of granary of the world. The noble river, bringing annually a fresh deposit of the richest soil, and furnishing a supply of water, which is sufficient, if carefully husbanded, to produce a succession of luxuriant crops throughout the year, makes Egypt—what it is even at the present day—one of the most fertile portions of the earth's surface—a land of varied products, all excellent—but especially a land of corn, to which the principal nations of the world looked for their supplies, either regularly, or at any rate in times of difficulty.

West of Egypt was a dry and sandy tract, dotted with oases, but otherwise only habitable along the shore, which in the time of the Persian Empire was occupied by a number of wild tribes who were mostly in the lowest condition to which savage man is capable of sinking. The geographical extent of this tract was large, exceeding considerably that of Egypt; but its value was slight. Naturally, it produced nothing but dates and hides. The inhumanity of the inhabitants made it, however, further productive of a commodity, which, until the world is christianized, will probably always be regarded as one of high value—the commodity of negro slaves, which were procured in the Sahara by slave-hunts, and perhaps by purchase in Nigritia.

Still further to the west, and forming the boundary of the Empire in this direction, lay the district of the Cyrenaica, a tract of singular fertility and beauty. Between Benghazi, in east longitude 20°, and the Ras al Tynn (long. 23° 15'), there rises above the level of the adjacent regions an extensive table land, which, attracting the vapors that float over the Mediterranean, condenses them, and so abounds with springs and rills. A general freshness and greenness, with rich vegetation in places, is the consequence. Olives, figs, carobs, junipers, oleanders, cypresses, cedars, myrtles, arbutus-trees, cover the flanks of the plateau and the hollows which break its surface, while the remainder is suitable alike for the cultivation of cereals and for pasturage. Nature has also made the region a special gift in the laserpitium or silphium, which was regarded by the ancients as at once a delicacy and a plant of great medicinal power, and which added largely to the value of the country.

Such was the geographical extent of the Persian Empire, and such were the chief provinces which it contained besides those previously comprised in the empires of Media or Babylon. Territorially, the great mass of the Empire lay towards the east, between long. 50° and 75°, or between the Zagros range and the Indian Desert. But its most important provinces were the western ones. East of Persepolis, the only regions of much value were the valleys of the Indus and the Oxus. Westward lay

Susiana, Babylonia, Assyria, Media, Armenia, Iberia, Cappadocia, Asia Minor, Cyprus, Syria, Palestine, Egypt, the Cyrenaica—all countries of great, or at least considerable, productiveness. The two richest grain tracts of the ancient world, the best pasture regions, the districts which produced the most valuable horses, the most abundant of known gold-fields, were included within the limits of the Empire, which may be looked upon as self-sufficing, containing within it all that man in those days required, not only for his necessities, but even for his most cherished luxuries.

The productiveness of the Empire was the natural result of its possessing so many and such large rivers. Six streams of the first class, having courses exceeding a thousand miles in length, helped to fertilize the lands which owned the sway of the Great King. These were the Nile, the Indus, the Euphrates, the Jaxartes, the Oxus, and the Tigris. Two of the six have been already described in these volumes, and therefore will not need to detain us here; but a few words must be said with respect to each of the remaining four, if our sketch of the geography of the Empire is to make any approach to completeness.

The Nile was only in the latter part of its course a Persian stream. Flowing, as we now know that it does, from within a short distance of the equator, it had accomplished more than three fourths of its course before it entered a Persian province. It ran, however, through Persian territory a distance of about six hundred miles, and conferred on the tract through which it passed immeasurable benefits. The Greeks sometimes maintained that "Egypt was the gift of the river;" and, though this was very far from being a correct statement in the sense intended, there is a meaning of the words in which we may accept them as expressing a fact. Egypt is only what she is through her river. The Nile gives her all that makes her valuable. This broad, ample, and unfailing stream not only by its annual inundation enriches the soil and prepares it for tillage in a manner that renders only the lightest further labor necessary, but serves as a reservoir from which inexhaustible supplies of the precious fluid can be obtained throughout the whole of the year. The water, which rises towards the end of June, begins to subside early in October, and for half the year—from December till June—Egypt is only cultivable through irrigation. She produces, however, during this period, excellent crops—even at the present day, when there are few canals—from the facility with which water is obtained, by means of a very simple engine, out of the channel of the Nile. This unfailing supply enabled the cultivator to obtain a second, a third, and even sometimes a fourth crop from the same land within the space of a year.

The course of the Nile from Elephantine, where it entered Egypt, to Cercasorus, near Heliopolis, where it bifurcated, was in general north, with, however, a certain tendency westward. It entered Egypt nearly in long. 33°, and at Neapolis (more than two degrees further north) it was still within 15° of the same meridian; then, however, it took a westerly bend, crossed the 32nd and 31st meridians, and in lat. 28° 23 reached west as far as long. 30° 43'. After this it returned a little eastward, recrossed the 31st meridian, and having reached long. 31° 22' near Aphroditopolis (lat.29° 25), it proceeded almost due north to Cercasorus in lat. 30° 7'. The course of the river up to this point was, from its entry into the country, about 540 miles. At Cercasorus the Delta began. The river threw out two branches, which flowed respectively to the north-east and the north-west, while between them was a third channel, a continuation of the previous course of the stream, which pierced the Delta through its centre, flowing almost due north. Lower down, further branch channels were thrown out, some natural, some artificial, and the triangular tract between the two outer arms of the river was intersected by at least five, and (in later times) by fourteen large streams. The right and left arms appear to have been of about equal in length, and may be estimated at 150 or 160 miles; the central arm had a shorter course, not exceeding 110 miles. The volume of water which the Nile pours into the Mediterranean during a day and night is estimated at from 150,000 millions to 700,000 millions of cubic metres. It was by far the largest of all the rivers of the Empire.

The Indus, which was the next largest of the Persian rivers to the Nile, rose (like the Nile) outside the Persian territory. Its source is in the region north of the Himalaya range, about lat. 31°, long. 82° 30′. It begins by flowing to the north-west, in a direction parallel to that of the Western Himalayas, along the northern flank of which it continues in this line a distance of about 700 miles, past Ladak, to long. 75° nearly. Here it is met by the Bolor chain, which prevents its further progress in this direction and causes it to turn suddenly nearly at a right angle to the south-west. Entering a transverse valley, it finds a way (which is still very imperfectly known) through the numerous ridges of the Himalaya to the plain at its southern base, on which it debouches about thirty miles above Attock. It is difficult to say at what exact point it crossed the Persian frontier, but probably at least the first 700 miles of its course were through territory not Persian. From Attock to the sea the Indus is a noble river. It runs for 900 miles in a general direction of S.S.W. through the plain in one main stream (which is several hundred yards in width), while on its way it throws off also from time to time small side streamlets, which are either consumed in irrigation or rejoin the main channel. A little below Tatta its Delta begins—a Delta, however, much inferior in size to that of the Nile. The distance from the apex to the sea is not more than sixty miles, and the breadth of the tract embraced between the two arms does not exceed seventy miles. The entire course of the Indus is reckoned at 1960 miles, of which probably 1260 were through Persian territory. The volume of the stream is always considerable, while in the rainy season it is very great. The Indus is said then to discharge into the Indian ocean 446,000 cubic feet per second, or 4280 millions of cubic yards in the twenty-four hours.

The Oxus rises from an Alpine lake, lying on the western side of the Bolor chain in lat. 37° 40′, long. 73° 50′. After a rapid descent from the high elevation of the lake, during which it pursues a somewhat serpentine course, it debouches from the hills upon the plain about long. 69° 20′, after receiving the river of Fyzabad, and then proceeds, first west and afterwards north-west, across the Great Kharesmian Desert to the Sea of Aral. During the first 450 miles of its course, while it runs among the hills, it receives from both sides numerous and important tributaries; but from the meridian of Balkh those fail entirely, and for above 800 miles the Oxus pursues its solitary way, unaugmented by a single affluent, across the waste of Tartary, rolling through the desert a wealth of waters, which must diminish, but which does not seem very sensibly to diminish, by evaporation. At Kilef, sixty miles north-west of Balkh, the width of the river is 350 yards; at Khodja Salih, thirty miles lower down, it is 823 yards with a depth of twenty feet; at Kerki, seventy miles below Khodja Salih, it is "twice the width of the Danube at Buda-Pesth," or about 940 yards; at Betik, on the route between Bokhara and Merv, its width has diminished to 650 yards, but its depth has increased to twenty-nine feet. Finally, at Gorlen Hezaresp near Khiva, the breadth of the Oxus is so great that both banks are hardly distinguishable at the same time; but the stream is here comparatively shallow, ceasing to be navigable at about this point. The present course of the Oxus from its rise in Lake Sir-i-Kol to its termination in the Sea of Aral is estimated at 1400 miles. Anciently its course must have been still longer. The Oxus, in the time of the Achaemenian kings, fell into the Caspian by a channel which can even now be traced. Its length was thus increased by at least 450 miles, and, exceeding that of the Jaxartes, fell but little short of the length of the Indus.

The Oxus, like the Nile and the Indus, has a periodical swell, which lasts from May to October. It does not, however, overflow its hanks. Under a scientific system of irrigation it is probable that a considerable belt of land on either side of its course might be brought under cultivation. But at present the extreme limit to which culture is carried, except in the immediate vicinity of Khiva, seems to be four miles; while often, in the absence of human care, the desert creeps up to the very brink of the river.

The Jaxartes, or Sir-Deria, rises from two sources in the Thian-chan mountain chain, the more remote of which is in long. 79° nearly. The two streams both flow to the westward in almost parallel valleys, uniting about long. 71°. After their junction the course of the stream is still to the westward for two degrees; but between Khokand and Tashkend the river sweeps round in a semicircle and proceeds to run first due north and then north-west, skirting the Kizil Koum desert to Otrar, where it resumes its original westerly direction and flows with continually diminishing volume across the desert to the Sea of Aral. The Jaxartes is a smaller stream than the Oxus. At Otrar, after receiving its last tributary, it is no more than 250 yards wide. Below this point it continually dwindles, partly from evaporation, partly from the branch stream which it throws off right and left, of which the chief are the Cazala and the Kuvan Deria. On its way through the desert it spreads but little fertility along its banks, which are in places high and arid, in others depressed and swampy. The branch streams are of some service for irrigation; and it is possible that a scientific system might turn the water of the main channel to good account, and by its means redeem from the desert large tracts which have never yet been cultivated. But no such system has hitherto been applied to the Sir, and it is doubtful whether success would attend it. The Sir, where it falls into the Sea of Aral, is very shallow, seldom even in the flood season exceeding four feet. The length of the stream was till recently estimated at more than 1208 miles; but the latest explorations seem to require an enlargement of this estimate by at least 200 or 250 miles.

In rivers of the second class the Persian Empire was so rich that it will be impossible, within the limits prescribed for the present work, to do more than briefly enumerate them. The principal were, in Asia Minor, the Hermus (Ghiediz Chai), and the Maeander (Mendere) on the west, the Sangarius (Sakka-riyeh), the Halys (Kizil Irmak), and the Iris (Yechil Irmak) on the north, the Cydnus (Tersoos Chai), Sarus (Cilician Syhun), and Pyramus (Cilician Jyhun) on the south; in Armenia and the adjacent regions, the Araxes (Aras), Cyrus (Kur), and Phasis (Eion); on the Iranic plateau, the Sefid-rud, the Zenderud or river of Isfahan, the Etymandrus (Helmend), and the Arius (Heri-rud); in the low country east of the Caspian, the Gurgan and Ettrek, rivers of Hyrcania, the Margus Churghab (or river of Merv), the Delias or river of Balkh, the Ak Su or Bokhara river, and the Kizil Deria, a stream in the Khanat of Kokand; in Afghanistan and India, the Kabul river, the Hydaspes (Jelum), the Aoesines (Chenab), the Hydraotes (Ravee), and the Hyphasis (Sutlej or Gharra); in Persia Proper, the Oroatis (Hindyan or Tab), and the Bendamir; in Susiana, the Pasitigris (Kuran), the Hedypnus (Jerahi), the Choaspes (Kerkhah), and the Eulsenus (a branch of the same); in the Upper Zagros region, the Gyndes (Diyaleh), and the Greater and Lesser Zabs; in Mesopotamia, the Chaboras (Kha-bour), and Bilichus (Belik); finally, in Syria and Palestine, the Orontes or river of Antioch (Nahr-el-asy), the Jordan, and the Barada or river of Damascus. Thus, besides the six great rivers of the Empire, forty other considerable streams fertilized and enriched the territories of the Persian monarch, which, though they embraced many arid tracts, where cultivation was difficult, must be pronounced upon the whole well-watered, considering their extent and the latitude in which they lay.

The Empire possessed, besides its rivers, a number of important lakes. Omitting the Caspian and the Aral, which lay upon its borders, there were contained within the Persian territories the following important basins: the Urumiyeh, Lake Van, and Lake Goutcha or Sivan in Armenia; Lakes Touz-Ghieul, Egerdir, Bey-Shehr, Chardak, Soghla, Buldur, Ghieul-Hissar, Iznik, Abullionte, Maniyas, and many others in Asia Minor; the Sabakhah, the Bahr-el-Melak, and the Lake of Antioch in Northern Syria; the Lake of Hems in the Coele-Syrian valley; the Damascus lakes, the Lake of Merom, the Sea of Tiberias, and the Dead Sea in Southern Syria and Palestine; Lake Moeris and the Natron lakes in Egypt; the Bahr-i-Nedjif in Babylonia; Lake Neyriz in Persia Proper; the Lake of Seistan in the Iranic Desert; and Lake Manchur in the In dus valley. Several of these have been already described in these volumes. Of the remainder the most important were the Lake of Van, the Touz-Ghieul, the great lake of Seistan, and Lake Moeris. These cannot be dismissed without a brief description.

Lake Van is situated at a very unusual elevation, being more than 5400 feet above the sea level. It is a triangular basin, of which the three sides front respectively S.S.E., N.N.E., and N.W. by W. The sides are all irregular, being broken by rocky promontories; but the chief projection lies to the east of the lake, where a tract is thrown out which suddenly narrows the expanse from about fifty miles to less than five. The greatest length of the basin is from N.E. to S.W., where it extends a distance of eighty miles between Amis and Tadvan; its greatest width is between Aklat and Van, where it measures across somewhat more than fifty miles. The scenery which surrounds it is remarkable for its beauty. The lake is embosomed amid high mountains, picturesque in outline, and all reaching in places the level of perpetual snow. Its waters, generally placid, but sometimes lashed into high waves, are of the deepest blue; while its banks exhibit a succession of orchards, meadows, and gardens which have scarcely their equals in Asia. The lake is fed by a number of small streams flowing down from the lofty ridges which surround it, and, having no outlet, is of course salt, though far less so than the neighboring lake of Urumiyeh. Gulls and cormorants float upon its surface fish can live in it; and it is not distasteful to cattle. Set in the expanse of waters are a few small islets, whose vivid green contrasts well with the deep azure which surrounds them.

The Touz-Ghieul is a basin of a very different character. Situated on the upland of Phrygia, in lat. 39°, long. 33°, 30', its elevation is not more than 2500 feet. Low hills of sandstone and conglomerate encircle it, but generally at some distance, so that a tract of plain, six or seven miles in width, intervenes between their base and the shore. The shape of the lake is an irregular oval, with the greater axis running nearly due north and south. Its greatest length is estimated at forty-five miles, its width varies, but is generally from ten to sixteen miles. At one point, however, nearly opposite to Kodj Hissar, the lake narrows to a distance of no more than five miles; and here a causeway has been constructed from shore to shore, which, though ruined, still affords a dry pathway in the summer. The water of the Touz-Ghieul is intensely salt, containing at some seasons of the year no less than thirty-two per cent of saline matter, which is considerably more than the amount of such matter in the water of the Dead Sea. The surrounding plain is barren, in places marshy, and often covered with an incrustation of salt. The whole scene is one of desolation. The acrid waters support no animal organization; birds shun them; the plain grows nothing but a few stunted and sapless shrubs. The only signs of life which greet the traveller are the carts of the natives, which pass him laden with the salt that is obtained with ease from the saturated water.

The Zerreh or Sea of Seistan—called sometimes the Hamun, or "expanse"—is situated in the Seistan Desert on the Great Iranic plateau, and consequently at an elevation of (probably) 3000 feet. It is formed by the accumulation of the waters brought down by the Helmend, the Haroot-rud, the river of Khash, the Furrah-rud and other streams, which flow from the mountains of Afghanistan, with converging courses to the south-west. It is an extensive basin, composed of two arms, an eastern and a western. The western arm, which is the larger of the two, has its greatest length from N.N.E. to S.S.W., and extends in this direction about ninety miles. Its greatest width is about twenty-five miles. The eastern arm is rather more than forty miles long, and from ten to twenty broad. It is shaped much like a fish's tail. The two arms are connected by a strait seven or eight miles in width, which joins them near their northern extremities. The water of the lake, though not salt, is black and has a bad taste. Fish support life in it with difficulty, and never grow to any great size. The lake is shallow, not much exceeding a depth of three or four feet. It contracts greatly in the summer, at which time the strait connecting the two arms is often absolutely dry. The edges of the lake are clothed with tamarisk and other trees; and where the rivers enter it, sometimes by several branches, the soil is rich and cultivation productive; but elsewhere the sand of the desert creeps up almost to the margin of the water, clothed only with some sickly grass and a few scattered shrubs.

The Birket-el-Keroun, or Lake Moaris of the classical writers, is a natural basin—not, as Herodotus imagined, an artificial one—situated on the western side of the Nile valley, in a curious depression which nature has made among the Libyan hills. This depression—the modern district of the Faioom—is a circular plain, which sinks gradually towards the north-west, descending till it is more than 100 feet below the surface of the Nile at low water. The Northern and northwestern portion of the depression is occupied by the lake, a sheet of brackish water shaped like a horn (whence the modern name) measuring about thirty-five or thirty-six miles from end to end, and attaining in the middle a width of between five and six miles. The area of the lake is estimated roughly at 150 square miles, its circumference at about ninety miles. It has a depth varying from twelve to twenty-four feet. Though the water is somewhat brackish, yet the Birket contains several species of fresh-water fish; and in ancient times its fisheries are said to have been exceedingly productive.

The principal cities of the Empire were, besides Pesargadae and Persepolis, Susa—the chief city of Susiana—which became the capital; Babylon, Ecbatana, Rhages, Zadracarta, Bactra (now Balkh), Maracanda (now Samarcand), Aria, or Artacoana (Herat), Caspatyrus on the Upper Indus,Taxila (Attock?), Pura (perhaps Bunpoor), Carmana (Kerman), Arbela, Nisibis, Amida (now Diarbekr); Mazaca in Cappadocia; Trapezus (Trebizond), Sinope, Dascyleium, Sardis, Ephesus, Miletus, Gordium, Perga, and Tarsus in Asia Minor: Damascus, Jerusalem, Sidon, Tyre, Azotus or Ashdod, and Gaza in Syria; Memphis and Thebes in Egypt; Cyrene and Barca in the Cyrenaica. Of these, while Susa had from the time of Darius Hystaspis a decided pre-eminence as the main residence of the court, and consequently as the usual seat of government, there were three others which could boast the distinction of being royal abodes from time to time, either regularly at certain seasons, or occasionally at the caprice of the monarch. These were Babylon, Ecbatana, and Persepolis, the capitals respectively of Chaldaea, Media, and Persia Proper, all great and ancient cities, accustomed to the presence of Courts, and all occupying positions sufficiently central to render them not ill-suited for the business of administration. Next to these in order of dignity may be classed the satrapial residences, often the chief cities of old monarchies, such as Sardis, the capital city of Lydia, Dascyleium of Bithynia, Memphis of Egypt, Bactra of Bactria, and the like; while the third rank was held by the towns, where there was no Court, either royal or satrapial.

Before this chapter is concluded a few words must be said with respect to the countries which bordered upon the Persian Empire. The Empire was surrounded, for the most part, either by seas or deserts. The Mediterranean, the Egean, the Propontis, the Euxine, the Caspian, the Indian Ocean, the Persian Gulf, and the Arabian Gulf or Bed Sea washed its shores, bounding almost all its western, and much of its northern and southern sides; while the sands of the Sahara, the deserts of Arabia and Syria of India and Thibet, filled up the greater part of the intervening spaces. The only countries of importance which can be viewed as in any sense neighbors of Persia are European and Asiatic Scythia, Hindustan, Arabia, Ethiopia, and Greece.

Where the Black Sea, curving round to the north, ceased to furnish to the Empire the advantage of a water barrier, a protection of almost equal strength was afforded to it by the mountain-chain of the Caucasus. Excepting on the extreme east, where it slopes gently to the Caspian, this range is one of great elevation, possessing but few passes, and very difficult to traverse. Its fastnesses have always been inhabited by wild tribes, jealous of their freedom; and these tribes may have caused annoyance, but they could at no time have been a serious danger to the Empire. They were weak in numbers, divided in nationality and in interests, and quite incapable of conducting any distant expedition. Like their modern successors, the Circassians, Abassians, and Lesghians, their one and only desire was to maintain themselves in possession of their beloved mountains; and this desire would cause them to resist all attempts that might be made to traverse their country, whether proceeding from the north or from the south, from the inhabitants of Europe or from those of Asia. Persia was thus strongly protected in this quarter; but still she could not feel herself altogether safe. Once at least within historic memory the barrier of the Caucasus had proved to be surmountable. From the vast Steppe which stretches northwards from its base, in part salt, in part grassy, had crossed into Asia—through its passes or round its eastern flank—a countless host, which had swept all before it, and brought ruin upon flourishing empires. The Scythian and Samaritan hordes of the steppe-country between the Wolga and the Dnieper were to the monarchies of Western Asia a permanent, if a somewhat distant, peril. It could not be forgotten that they had proved themselves capable of penetrating the rocky barrier which would otherwise have seemed so sure a protection, or that when they swarmed across it in the seventh century before our era, their strength was at first irresistible. The Persians knew, what the great nations of the earth afterwards forgot, that along the northern horizon there lay a black cloud, which might at any time burst, carrying desolation to their homes and bringing ruin upon their civilization. We shall find the course of their history importantly affected by a sense of this danger, and we shall have reason to admire the wisdom of their measures of precaution against it.

It was not only to the west of the Caspian that the danger threatened. East of that sea also was a vast steppe-region—rolling plains of sand or grass—the home of nomadic hordes similar in character to those who drank the waters of the Don and Wolga. The Sacse, Massagetse, and Dahse of this country, who dwelt about the Caspian, the Aral, and the Lower Jaxartes, were an enemy scarcely less formidable than the Sarmatians and the Scyths of the West. As the modern Iran now suffers from the perpetual incursions of Uzbegs and Turcomans, so the north-eastern provinces of the ancient Persia were exposed to the raids of the Asiatic Scythians and the Massagetse, who were confined by no such barrier as the Caucasus, having merely to cross a river, probably often fordable during the summer, in order to be in Persia. Hyrcania and Parthia had indeed a certain amount of protection from the Kharesmian Desert; but the upper valleys of the great streams—the satrapies of Sogdiana and Bactria—must have suffered considerable annoyance from such attacks.

On the side of India, the Empire enjoyed a twofold security. From the shores of the Indian Ocean in the vicinity of the Runn of Cutch to the 31st parallel of north latitude—a distance of above 600 miles—there extends a desert, from one to two hundred miles across, which effectually shuts off the valley of the Indus from the rest of Hindustan. It is only along the skirts of the mountains, by Lahore, Umritsir, and Loodiana, that the march of armies is possible—by this line alone can the Punjabis threaten Central India, or the inhabitants of Central India attack the Punjab. Hence in this quarter there was but a very narrow tract to guard; and the task of defence was still further lightened by the political condition of the people. The Gangetic Indians, though brave and powerful, were politically weak, from their separation into a number of distinct states under petty Rajahs, who could never hope to contend successfully against the forces of a mighty Empire. Persia, consequently, was safe upon this side, in the division of her adversaries. Nor had she neglected the further security which was obtainable by an interposition between her own actual frontier and her enemies' dominions of a number of half-subject dependencies. Native princes were allowed to bear sway in the Punjab region, who acknowledged the suzerainty of Persia, and probably paid her a fixed tribute, but whose best service was that they prevented a collision between the Power of whom they held their crowns and the great mass of their own nation.

The Great Arabian Peninsula, which lay due south of the most central part of the Empire, and bordered it on this side for about thirteen degrees, or (if we follow the line of the boundary) for above a thousand miles, might seem to have been the most important of all the adjacent countries, since it contains an area of a million of square miles, and is a nursery of brave and hardy races. Politically, however, Arabia is weak, as has been shown in a former volume; while geographically she presents to the north her most arid and untraversable regions, so that it is rarely, and only under very exceptional circumstances, that she menaces seriously her northern neighbors. Persia seems never to have experienced any alarm of an Arab invasion; her relations with the tribes that came into closest contact with her were friendly; and she left the bulk of the nation in unmolested enjoyment of their independence.

Another country adjoining the Persian Empire on the south, and one which might have been expected to cause some trouble, was Ethiopia. To Egypt Ethiopia had always proved an unquiet, and sometimes even a dangerous, neighbor; she was fertile, rich, populous; her inhabitants were tall, strong, and brave; she had a ready means of marching into Egypt down the fertile valley of the Nile; and her hosts had frequently ravaged, and even held for considerable terms of years, that easily subjected country. It is remarkable that during the whole time of the Persian dominion Ethiopia seems to have abstained from any invasion of the Egyptian territory. Apparently, she feared to provoke the power which had seated itself on the throne of the Pharaohs, and preferred the quiet enjoyment of her own wealth and resources to the doubtful issues of a combat with the mistress of Asia.

On her western horizon, clearly discernible from the capes and headlands of the Asiatic coast, but separated from her, except in one or two places, by a tolerably broad expanse of sea, and so—as it might have seemed—less liable to come in contact with her than her neighbors upon the land, lay the shores and isles of Greece—lovely and delightful regions, in possession of a brave and hardy race, as yet uncorrupted by luxury, though in the enjoyment of a fair amount of civilization. As the eye looked across the Egean waters, resting with pleasure on the varied and graceful forms of Sporades and Cyclades, covetous thoughts might naturally arise in the beholder's heart; and the idea might readily occur of conquering and annexing the fair tracts which lay so temptingly near and possessed such numerous attractions. The entire region, continent and islands included, was one of diminutive size—not half so large as an ordinary Persian satrapy; it was well peopled, but its population could not have amounted to that of the Punjab or of Egypt, countries which Persia had overrun in a single campaign; its inhabitants were warlike, but they were comparatively poor, and the true sinews of war are money; moreover, they were divided amongst themselves, locally split up by the physical conformation of their country, and politically repugnant to anything like centralization or union. A Persian king like Cambyses or Darius might be excused if, when his thoughts turned to Greece, he had a complacent feeling that no danger could threaten him from that quarter—that the little territory on his western border was a prey which he might seize at any time that it suited his convenience or seemed good to his caprice; so opening without any risk a new world to his ambition. It required a knowledge that the causes of military success and political advance lie deeper than statistics can reach—that they have their roots in the moral nature of man, in the grandeur of his ideas and the energy of his character—in order to comprehend the fact, that the puny power upon her right flank was the enemy which Persia had most to fear, the foe who would gradually sap her strength, and finally deal her the blow that would lay her prostrate.

CHAPTER II

CLIMATE AND PRODUCTIONS

It is evident that an Empire which extended over more than twenty degrees of latitude, touching on the one hand the tropic of Cancer, while it reached upon the other to the parallel of Astrakan, and which at the same time varied in elevation, from 20,000 feet above to 1300 below the sea level, must have comprised within it great differences of climate, and have boasted an immense variety of productions. No general description can be applicable to such a stretch of territory; and it will therefore be necessary to speak of the various parts of the Empire successively in order to convey to the reader a true idea of the climatic influences to which it was subject, and the animals, vegetables, and minerals which it produced.

Commencing with Persia Proper, the original seat and home of the race with whose history we are specially concerned at present, we may observe that it was regarded by the ancients as possessing three distinct climates—one along the shore, dry and scorchingly hot; another in the mountain region beyond, temperate and delightful; and a third in the tract further inland, which was thought to be disagreeably cold and wintry. Moderns, on the contrary, find two climates only in Fars—one that of the Desbistan or "low country," extremely hot and dry, with frequent scorching and oppressive winds from the south and the south-east; the other, that of the highlands, which is cold in winter, but in summer pleasant and enjoyable. In the Deshistan snow never falls, and there is but little rain; heavy dews, however, occur at night, so that the mornings are often fresh and cool; but the middle of the day is almost always hot, and from March to November the temperature at noon ranges from 90° to 100° of Fahrenheit. Occasionally it reaches 125°, and is then fearfully oppressive. Fierce gusts laden with sand sweep over the plain, causing vegetation to droop or disappear, and the animal world to hide itself. Man with difficulty retains life at these trying times, feeling a languor and a depression of spirits which are barely supportable.10 All who can do so quit the plains and betake themselves to the upland region till the great heats are past, and the advance of autumn brings at any rate cool nights and mornings. The climate of the uplands is severe in winter. Much snow falls, and the thermometer often marks from ten to fifteen degrees of frost. From time to time there are furious gales, and, as the spring advances, a good deal of wet falls; but the summer and autumn are almost rainless. The heat towards midday is often considerable, but it is tempered by cool winds, and even at the worst is not relaxing. The variations of temperature are great in the twenty-four hours, and the climate is, so far, trying; but, on the whole, it seems to be neither disagreeable nor unhealthy.

A climate resembling that of the Deshtistan prevailed along the entire southern coast of the Empire, from the mouth of the Tigris to that of the Indus. It was exchanged in the lower valleys of the great streams for a damp close heat, intolerably stifling and oppressive. The upper valleys of these streams and the plains into which they expanded were at once less hot and less moist, but were subject to violent storms, owing to the near vicinity of the mountains. In the mountains themselves, in Armenia and Zagros, and again in the Elburz, the climate was of a more rigorous character—intensely cold in winter, but pleasant in the summer time. [PLATE XXVII., Fig. 3.] Asia Minor enjoyed generally a warmer climate than the high mountain regions; and its western and southern coasts, being fanned by fresh breezes from the sea, or from the hills of the interior, and cooled during the whole of the summer by frequent showers, were especially charming. In Syria and Egypt the heats of summer were somewhat trying, more especially in the Ghor or depressed Jordan valley, and in the parts of Egypt adjoining on Ethiopia; but the winters were mild, and the springs and autumns delightful. The rarity of rain in Egypt was remarkable, and drew the attention of foreigners, who recorded, in somewhat exaggerated terms, the curious meteorological phenomenon. In the Cyrenaica there was a delicious summer climate—an entire absence of rain, with cool breezes from the sea, cloudy skies, and heavy dews at night, these last supplying the moisture which through the whole of summer covered the ground with the freshest and loveliest verdure. The autumn and winter rains were, however, violent; and terrific storms were at that time of no unusual occurrence. The natives regarded it as a blessing, that over this part of Africa the sky was "pierced," and allowed moisture to fall from the great reservoir of "waters above the firmament;" but the blessing must have seemed one of questionable value at the time of the November monsoon, when the country is deluged with rain for several weeks in succession.

On the opposite side of the Empire, towards the north and the north-east, in Azerbijan, on the Iranian plateau, in the Afghan plains, in the high flat region east of the Bolor, and again in the low plain about the Aral lake and the Caspian, a severe climate prevailed during the winter, while the summer combined intense heat during the day with extraordinary cold—the result of radiation—at night. Still more bitter weather was experienced in the mountain regions of these parts—in the Bolor, the Thian Chan, the Himalaya, and the Paropamisus or Hindu Kush—where the winters lasted more than half the year, deep snow covering the ground almost the whole of the time, and locomotion being rendered almost impossible; while the summers were only moderately hot. On the other hand, there was in this quarter, at the very extreme east of the Empire, one of the most sultry and disagreeable of all climates—namely, that of the Indus valley, which is either intolerably hot and dry, with fierce tornadoes of dust that are unspeakably oppressive, or close and moist, swept by heavy storms, which, while they somewhat lower the temperature, increase the unhealthiness of the region. The worst portion of the valley is its southern extremity, where the climate is only tolerable during three months of the year. From March to November the heat is excessive; dust-storms prevail; there are dangerous dews at night; and with the inundation, which commences in April, a sickly time sets in, which causes all the wealthier classes to withdraw from the country till the stagnant water, which the swell always leaves behind it, has dried up.

Upon the whole, the climate of the Empire belonged to the warmer class of the climates which are called temperate. In a few parts only, indeed, as in the Indus valley, along the coast from the mouth of the Indus to that of the Tigris, in Lower Babylonia and the adjoining portion of Susiana, in Southern Palestine, and in Egypt, was frost absolutely unknown; while in many places, especially in the high mountainous regions, the winters were bitterly severe; and in all the more elevated portions of the Empire, as in Phrygia and Cappadocia, in Azerbijan, on the great Iranian plateau, and again in the district about Kashgar and Yarkand, there was a prolonged period of sharp and bracing weather. But the summer warmth of almost the whole Empire was great, the thermometer probably ranging in most places from 90° to 120° during the months of June, July, August, and September. The springs and autumns were, except in the high mountain tracts, mild and enjoyable; the Empire had few very unhealthy districts; while the range of the thermometer was in most of the provinces considerable, and the variations in the course of a single day and night were unusually great, there was in the climate, speaking generally, nothing destructive of human vigor—nothing even inimical to longevity.

The vegetable productions of Persia Proper in ancient times (so far as we have direct testimony on the subject) were neither numerous nor very remarkable. The low coast tract supplied dates in tolerable plenty, and bore in a few favored spots, corn, vines, and different kinds of fruit-trees; but its general character was one of extreme barrenness. In the mountain region there was an abundance of rich pasture, excellent grapes were grown, and fruit-trees of almost every sort, except the olive, flourished. One fruit-tree, regarded as indigenous in the country, acquired a special celebrity, and was known to the Romans as the persica, whence the German Pfirsche, the French peche, and our "peach." Citrons, which grew in few places, were also a Persian fruit. Further, Persia produced a coarse kind of silphium or assafoetida; it was famous for its walnuts, which were distinguished by the epithet of "royal"; and it supplied to the pharmacopeia of Greece and Rome a certain number of herbs.

The account of Persian vegetable products which we derive from antiquity is no doubt very incomplete; and it is necessary to supplement it from the observations of modern travellers. These persons tell us that, while Fars and Kerman are ill-supplied with forest-trees, they yet produce in places oaks, planes, chenars or sycamores, poplars, willows, pinasters, cypresses, acacias, fan-palms, konars, and junipers. Among shrubs, they bear the wild fig, the wild almond, the tamarisk, the myrtle, the box, the rhododendron, the camel's thorn, the gum tragacanth, the caper plant, the benneh, the blackberry, and the liquorice-plant. They boast a great abundance of fruit-trees—as date-bearing palms, lemons, oranges, pomegranates, vines, peaches, nectarines, apricots, quinces, pears, apples, plums, figs, cherries, mulberries, barberries, walnuts, almonds, and pistachio-nuts. The kinds of grain chiefly cultivated are wheat, barley, millet, rice, and Indian corn or maize, which has been imported into the country from America. Pulse, beans, sesame, madder, henna, cotton, opium, tobacco, and indigo, are also grown in some places. The three last-named, and maize or Indian corn, are of comparatively recent introduction; but of the remainder it may be doubted whether there is a single one which was unknown to the ancient inhabitants.

Among Persian indigenous animals may be enumerated the lion, the bear, the wild ass, the stag, the antelope, the ibex or wild goat, the wild boar, the hyena, the jackal, the wolf, the fox, the hare, the porcupine, the otter, the jerboa, the ichneumon, and the marmot. The lion appears to be rare, occurring only in some parts of the mountains. The ichneumon is confined to the Deshtistan. The antelope, the wild boar, the wolf, the fox, the jackal, the porcupine, and the jerboa are common. Wild asses are found only on the northern side of the mountains, towards the salt desert. In this tract they are frequently seen, both singly and in herds, and are hunted by the natives, who regard their flesh as a great delicacy.

The most remarkable of the Persian birds are the eagle, the vulture, the cormorant, the falcon, the bustard, the pheasant, the heath-cock, the red-legged partridge, the small gray partridge, the pin tailed grouse, the sand-grouse, the francolin, the wild swan, the flamingo, the stork, the bittern, the oyster-catcher, the raven, the hooded crow, and the cuckoo. Besides these, the lakes boast all the usual kinds of water-fowl, as herons, ducks, snipe, teal, etc.; the gardens and groves abound with blackbirds, thrushes, and nightingales; curlews and peewits are seen occasionally; while pigeons, starlings, crows, magpies, larks, sparrows, and swallows are common. The francolin is hunted by men on foot in the country between Shiraz and Kerman, and is taken by the hand after a few flights. The oyster-catcher, which is a somewhat rare bird, has been observed only on Lake Neyriz. The bustard occurs both in the low plain along the coast, and on the high plateau, where it is captured by means of hawks. The pheasant and the heath-cock (the latter a black species spotted with white) are found in the woods near Failyun. The sand-grouse and the pin-tailed grouse belong to the eastern portion of the country, the portion known anciently as Carmania or "the hot region." The other kinds are diffused pretty generally.

The shores and rivers of Persia Proper supplied the people very plentifully with fish. The ancient writers tell us that the inhabitants of the coast tract lived almost wholly on a fish diet. The Indian Sea appears in those days to have abounded with whales, which were not unfrequently cast upon the shores, affording a mine of wealth to the natives. The great ribs were used as beams in the formation of huts, while the jaws served as doors and the smaller bones as planking. Dolphins also abounded in the Persian waters; together with many other fish of less bulk, which were more easy to capture. On these smaller fish, which they caught in nets, the maritime inhabitants subsisted principally. They had also an unfailing resource in the abundance of oysters, and other shell-fish along their coast—the former of excellent quality.

In the interior, though the lakes, being salt or brackish, had no piscatory stores, the rivers were, for the most part, it would seem, well provided; at least, good fish are still found in many of the streams, both small and large; and in some they are exceedingly plentiful. Modern travellers fail to distinguish the different kinds; but we may presume that they are not very unlike those of the adjoining Media, which appear to be trout, carp, barbel, dace, bleak, and gudgeon.

The reptiles of Persia Proper are not numerous. They are chiefly tortoises, lizards, frogs, land-snakes, and water-snakes. The land-snakes are venomous, but their poison is not of a very deadly character; and persons who have been bitten by them, if properly treated, generally recover. The lizards are of various sizes, some quite small, others more than three feet long, and covered with a coarse rough skin like that of a toad. They have the character of being venomous, and even dangerous to life; but it may be doubted whether they are not, like our toads and newts, in reality perfectly harmless.

The traveller in Persia suffers less from reptiles than from insects. Scorpions abound in all parts of the country, and, infesting houses, furniture, and clothes, cause perpetual annoyance. Mosquitoes swarm in certain places and seasons, preventing sleep and irritating the traveller almost beyond endurance. A poisonous spider, a sort of tarantula, is said to occur in some localities; and Chardin further mentions a kind of centipede, the bite of which, according to him, is fatal. To the sufferings which these creatures cause, must be added a constant annoyance from those more vulgar forms of insect life which detract from the delights of travel even in Europe.

Persia, moreover, suffers no less than Babylonia and Media, from the ravages of locusts. Constantly, when the wind is from the south-east, there cross from the Arabian coast clouds of these destructive insects, whose numbers darken the air as they move, in flight after flight, across the desert to the spots where nature or cultivation has clothed the earth with verdure. The Deshtistan, or low country, is, of course, most exposed to their attacks, but they are far from being confined to that region. The interior, as far as Shiraz itself, suffers terribly from this scourge, which produces scarcity, or even famine, when (as often happens) it is repeated year after year. The natives at such times are reduced to feeding on the locusts themselves; a diet which they do not relish, but to which necessity compels them.

The locusts of Persia Proper are said to be of two kinds. One, which is regarded as bred in the country, bears the name of missri, being identified with the locust of Egypt. The other, which is thought to be blown over from Arabia, and thus to cross the sea, is known as the melelch deriai, or "sea-locust." The former is regarded as especially destructive to the crops, the latter to the shrubs and trees.

The domestic animals in use at the present day within the provinces of Fars and Kerman are identical with those employed in the neighboring country of Media, and will need only a very few words of notice here. The ordinary horse of the country is the Turcoman, a large, strong, but somewhat clumsy animal, possessed of remarkable powers of endurance; but in the Deshtistan the Arabian breed prevails, and travellers tell us that in this region horses are produced which fall but little short of the most admired coursers of Nejd. Cows and oxen are somewhat rare, beef being little eaten, and such cattle being only kept for the supply of the dairy, and for purposes of agriculture. Sheep and goats are abundant, and constitute the chief wealth of the inhabitants; the goat is, on the whole, preferred, and both goats and sheep are generally of a black or brown color. The sheep of Kerman are small and short-legged; they produce a wool of great softness and delicacy.

It is probable that in ancient times the domestic animals of the country were nearly the same as at the present day. The statement of Xenophon, that anciently a horse was a rarity in Persia Proper, is contradicted by the great bulk of the early writers, who tell us that the Persians were from the first expert riders, and that their country was peculiarly well fitted for the breeding of horses. Their camels, sheep, goats, asses, and oxen, are also expressly mentioned by the Greeks, who even indicate a knowledge of the fact that goats were preferred to sheep by the herdsmen of the country.

The mineral treasures of the country appear to have been considerable, though to what extent they were known and made use of in ancient times is open to some question. Mines of gold, silver, copper, iron, red lead, and orpiment are said to have been actually worked under the Persian kings; and some of the other minerals were so patent and obvious, that we can scarcely suppose them to have been neglected. Salt abounded in the region in several shapes. It appeared in some places as rock salt, showing itself in masses of vast size and various colors. In other places it covered the surface of the ground for miles together with a thick incrustation, and could be gathered at all seasons with little labor. It was deposited by the waters of several lakes within the territory, and could be collected round their edges at certain times of the year. Finally, it was held in solution, both in the lakes and in many of the streams; from whose waters it might have been obtained by evaporation. Bitumen and naphtha were yielded by sources near Dalaki, which were certainly known to the ancients. Sulphur was deposited upon the surface of the ground in places. Some of the mountains contained ordinary lead; but it is not unlikely that this metal escaped notice.

Ancient Persia produced a certain number of gems. The pearls of the Gulf, which have still so great a reputation, had attracted the attention of adventurers before the time of Alexander, whose naval captains found a regular fishery established in one of the islands. The Orientals have always set a high value on this commodity; and it appears that in ancient times the Gulf pearls were more highly esteemed than any others. Of hard stones the only kinds that can be distinctly assigned to Persia Proper are the iritis, a species of rock-crystal; the atizoe, a white stone which had a pleasant odor; the mithrax, a gem of many hues, the nipparene, which resembled ivory; and the the lycardios or mule, which was in special favor among the natives of the country.

From this account of the products of Persia Proper we have now to pass to those of the Empire in general—a wide subject, which it will be impossible to treat here with any completeness, owing to the limits to which the present work is necessarily confined. In order to bring the matter within reasonable compass, the reader may be referred in the first instance to the account which was given in a former volume of the products of the empire of Babylon; and the enquiry may then be confined to those regions which were subject to Persia, but not contained within the limits of the Fourth Monarchy.

Among the animals belonging to these regions, the following are especially noticeable:—The tiger, the elephant, the hippopotamus, the crocodile, the monitor, the two-humped camel, the Angora goat, the elk, the monkey, and the spotted hysena, or Felis chaus. The tiger, which is entirely absent from Mesopotamia, and unknown upon the plateau of Iran, abounds in the low tract between the Elburz and the Caspian, in the flat region about the Sea of Aral, and in the Indus valley. The elephant was, perhaps, anciently an inhabitant of Upper Egypt, where the island of Elephantine remained an evidence of the fact. It was also in Persian times a denizen of the Indus valley, though perhaps only in a domesticated state. The hippopotamus, unknown in India, was confined to the single province of Egypt, where it was included among the animals which were the objects of popular worship. The crocodile—likewise a sacred animal to the Egyptians—frequented both the Nile and the Indus. Monitors, which are a sort of diminutive crocodiles, were of two kinds: one, the Lacerta Nilotica, was a water animal, and was probably found only in Egypt; the other, Lacerta scincus, frequented dry and sandy spots, and abounded in North Africa and Syria, as well as in the Nile valley. The two-humped camel belonged to Bactria, where he was probably indigenous, but was widely spread over the Empire, on account of his great strength and powers of endurance.

The Angora goat is, perhaps, scarcely a distinct species. If not identical with the ordinary wild goat of Persia and Mesopotamia (Capra cegagrus), he is at any rate closely allied to it; and it is possible that all his peculiar characteristics may be the effect of climate. He has a soft, white, silky fleece, very long, divided down the back by a strong line of separation, and falling on either side in beautiful spiral ringlets; his fleece weighs from two to four pounds. It is of nearly uniform, length, and averages from five to five and a half inches.

The elk is said to inhabit Armenia, Affghanistan, and the lower part of the valley of the Indus; but it is perhaps not certain that he is really to be found in the two latter regions. Monkeys abound in Eastern Oabul and the adjoining parts of India. They may have also existed formerly in Upper Egypt. The spotted hyena, Felis chaus (Canis crocuta of Linnaeus), is an Egyptian animal, inhabiting principally the hills on the western side of the Nile. In appearance it is like a large cat, with a tuft of long black hair at the extremities of its ears—a feature which it has in common with the lynx.

Among the rarer birds of the Empire may be mentioned the ostrich, which occurred in Mesopotamia; parrots, which were found in Cabul and the Punjab; ibises, which abounded in Egypt, and in the Delta of the Indus, the great vulture (Vultur cinereus), which inhabited the Taurus, the Indian owl (Athena Indica), the spoonbill (Platalea nudifrons); the benno (Ardea bubulcus), and the sicsac (Charadrius melanocephalus).

The most valuable of the fish belonging to the Persian seas and rivers were the pearl oyster of the Gulf, and the murex of the Mediterranean, which furnished the famous purple dye of Tyre. After these may be placed the sturgeon and sterlet of the Caspian, the silurus of the Sea of Aral, the Aleppo eel, and the palla, a small but excellent fish, which is captured in the Indus during the flood season. The Indian Ocean and the Persian Gulf, as we have seen, were visited by whales; dolphins, porpoises, cod, and mullet abounded in the same seas; the large rivers generally contained barbel and carp; while some of them, together with many of the smaller streams, supplied trout of a good flavor. The Nile had some curious fish peculiar to itself, as the oxyrinchus, the lepidotus, the Perca Nilotica, the Silurus Schilbe Niloticus, the Silurus carmuth and others. Great numbers of fish, mostly of the same species with those of the Nile, were also furnished by the Lake Moeris; and from these a considerable revenue was derived by the Great Kings.

Among the more remarkable of the reptiles which the Empire comprised within its limits may be noticed—besides the great saurians already mentioned among the larger animals—the Nile and Euphrates turtles (Trionyx Egypticus and Trionyx Euphraticus), iguanas (Stellio vulgaris and Stellio spinipes), geckos, especially the Egyptian house gecko (O. lobatus), snakes, such as the asp (Coluber haje) and the horned snake (Coluber cerastes), and the chameleon. The Egyptian turtle is a large species, sometimes exceeding three feet in length. It is said to feed on the young of the crocodile. Both it and the Euphrates turtle are of the soft kind, i.e., of the kind which has not the shell complete, but unites the upper and under portions by a coriaceous membrane. The turtle of the Euphrates is of moderate size, not exceeding a a length of two feet. It lives in the river, and on warm days suns itself on the sandbanks with which the stream abounds. It is active, strong, violent, and passionate. When laid on its back it easily recovers itself. If provoked, it will snap at sticks and other objects, and endeavor to tear them to pieces. It is of an olive-green color, with large irregular greenish black spots.

Iguanas are found in Egypt, in Syria, and elsewhere. The most common kind (Stellio vulgaris) does not exceed a foot in length, and is of an olive color, shaded with black. It is persecuted and killed by the Mahometans, because they regard its favorite attitude as a derisive imitation of their own attitude of prayer. There is another species, also Egyptian, which is of a much larger size, and of a grass-green color. This is called Stellio spinipes: it has a length of from two to three feet.

The gecko is a kind of nocturnal lizard. Its eyes are large, and the pupil is extremely contractile. It hides itself during the day, and is lively only at nights. It haunts rooms, especially kitchens, in Egypt, where it finds the insects which form its ordinary food. Its feet constitute its most marked characteristic. The five toes are enlarged and furnished with an apparatus of folds, which, by some peculiar action, enable it to adhere to perfectly smooth surfaces, to ascend perpendicular walls, cross ceilings, or hang suspended for hours on the under side of leaves. The Egyptians called it the abu burs, or "father of leprosy," and there is a wide-spread belief in its poisonous character; but modern naturalists incline to regard the belief as unfounded, and to place the gecko among reptiles which are absolutely harmless. [PLATE XXVIII., Fig. 1.]

Plate XXVIII.

Fig. 1.

Fig. 2.

The Egyptian Asp, or *Coluber haje*.

Gecko, and feet of Gecko magnified.

Fig. 4.

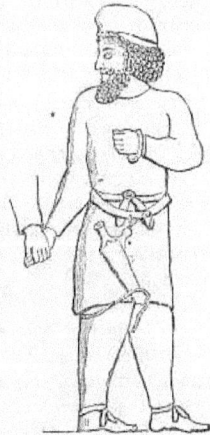

Fig. 3.

The " Cerastes."

Persian Foot-soldier in the
ordinary costume (Persepolis)

Fig. 5.

The Chameleon.

PLATE XXVIII

The asp of Egypt (Coluber haje) is a species of cobra. It is a large snake, varying from three to six feet in length, and is extremely venomous. It haunts gardens, where it is of great use, feeding on mice, frogs, and various small reptiles. It has the power of greatly dilating the skin of the neck, and this it does when angered in a way that is very remarkable. Though naturally irritable, it is easily tamed; and the serpent-charmers of the East make it the object of their art more often than any other species. [PLATE XXVIII., Fig. 2.] After extracting the fangs or burning out the poison-bag with a red-hot iron, the charmer trains the animal by the shrill sounds of a small flute, and it is soon perfectly docile.

The cerastes is also employed occasionally by the snake-charmers. It has two long and thin excrescences above the eyes, whereto the name of "horns" has been given: they stand erect, leaning a little backwards; no naturalist has as yet discovered their use. The cerastes is of a very pale brown color, and is spotted with large, unequal, and irregularly-placed spots. Its bite is exceedingly dangerous, since it possesses a virulent poison; and, being in the habit of nearly burying itself in the sand, which is of the same color with itself, it is the more difficult of avoidance. Its size also favors its escaping notice, since in length it rarely much exceeds a foot. [PLATE XXVIII., Fig. 3.]

The chameleon has in all ages attracted the attention of mankind. It is found in Egypt, and in many others parts of Africa, in Georgia, and in India. The power of changing color which it possesses is not really its most remarkable characteristic. Far more worthy of notice are its slow pace, extraordinary form, awkward movements, vivacity, and control of eye, and marvellous rapidity of tongue. It is the most grotesque of reptiles. With protruding and telescopic eyes, that move at will in the most opposite directions, with an ungainly head, a cold, dry, strange-looking skin, and a prehensile tail, the creature slowly steals along a branch or twig, scarcely distinguishable from the substance along which it moves, and scarcely seeming to move at all, until it has come within reach of its prey. Then suddenly, with a motion rapid as that of the most agile bird, the long cylindrical and readily extensile tongue is darted forth with unerring aim, and the prey is seized and swallowed in a single moment of time. The ordinary color of the chameleon is a pale olive-green. This sometimes fades to a sort of ashen-gray, while sometimes it warms to a yellowish-brown, on which are seen faint spots of red. Modern naturalists, for the most part, attribute the changes to the action of the lungs, which is itself affected chiefly by the emotions of anger, desire, and fear. [PLATE XXVIII., Fig. 5.]

The great extent of the Empire caused its vegetable productions to include almost all the forms known to the ancient world. On the one hand, the more northern and more elevated regions bore pines, firs, larches, oaks, birch, beech, ash, ilex, and junipers, together with the shrubs and flowers of the cooler temperate regions; on the other hand, the southern tracts grew palms of various kinds, mangoes, tamarind-trees, lemons, oranges, jujubes, mimosas, and sensitive plants. Between these extremes of tropical and cold-temperate products, the Empire embraced an almost infinite variety of trees, shrubs, and flowers. The walnut and the Oriental plane grew to avast size in many places. Poplars, willows, fig-mulberries, konars, cedars, cypresses, acacias, were common. Bananas, egg-plants, locust-trees, banyans, terebinths, the gum-styrax, the gum-tragacanth, the assafoetida plant, the arbor vitse, the castor-oil plant, the Judas-tree, and other somewhat rare forms, sprang up side by side with the pomegranate, the oleander, the pistachio-nut, the myrtle, the bay, the laurel, the mulberry, the rhododendron, and the arbutus. The Empire grew all the known sorts of grain, and almost all the known fruits. Among its various productions of this class, it is only possible to select for notice a few which were especially remarkable either for their rarity or for their excellent quality.

The ancients celebrated the wheat of AEolis, the dates of Babylon, the citrons of Media, the Persian peach, the grapes of Carmania, the Hyrcanian fig, the plum of Damascus, the cherries of Pontus, the mulberries of Egypt and of Cyprus, the silphium of Gyrene, the wine of Helbon, the wild-grape of Syria. It is not unlikely that to these might have been added as many other vegetable products of first-rate excellence, had the ancients possessed as good a knowledge of the countries included within the Empire as the moderns. At present, the mulberries of Khiva, the apricots of Bokhara, the roses of Mexar, the quinces and melons of Isfahan, the grapes of Kasvin and Shii-az, the pears of Natunz, the dates of Dalaki, have a wide-spread reputation, which appears in most cases to be well deserved. On the whole, it is certain that for variety and excellence the vegetable products of the Persian Empire will bear comparison with those of any other state or community that has as yet existed, either in the ancient or the modern world.

Two only of these products seem to deserve a longer description. The Cyrenaic silphium, of which we hear so much, as constituting the main wealth of that province, was valued chiefly for its medicinal qualities. A decoction from its leaves was used to hasten the worst kind of labors; its root and a juice which flowed from it were employed in a variety of maladies. The plant, which is elaborately described by Theophrastus, appears to have been successfully identified by modern travellers in the Cyrenaica, who see it in the drias or derias of the Arabs, an umbelliferous plant, which grows to a height of about three feet, has a deleterious effect on the camels that browse on it, and bears a striking resemblance to the representations of the ancient silphium upon coins and medals. This plant grows only in the tract between Merj and Derna—the very heart of the old silphium country, while that it has medicinal properties is certain from its effects upon animals; there can thus be little doubt that it is the silphium of the ancients, somewhat degenerated, owing to want of cultivation.

The Egyptian byblus or papyrus (Cyperus papyrus) was perhaps the most valuable of all the vegetables of the Empire. The plant was a tall smooth reed of a triangular shape. It grew to the height of ten or fifteen feet, and terminated in a tuft or plume of leaves and flowers. Though indigenous in the country, it was the subject of careful cultivation, and was grown in irrigated ground, or in such lands as were naturally marshy. The root of the plant was eaten, while from its stem was made the famous Egyptian paper. The manufacture of the papyrus was as follows; The outer rind having been removed, there was exposed a laminated interior, consisting of a number of successive layers of inner cuticle, generally about twenty. These were carefully separated from one another by the point of a needle, and thus were obtained a number of strips of the raw material, which were then arranged in rows, covered with a paste, and crossed at right angles by another set of strips placed over them, after which the whole was converted into paper by means of a strong pressure. A papyrus roll was made by uniting together a greater or less number of such sheets. The best paper was made from the inmost layers of cuticle. The outer rind of the papyrus was converted into ropes; and this fabric was found to be peculiarly adapted for immersion in water.

The mineral treasures of the Empire were various and abundant. It has been noticed already that Persia Proper, if we include in it Carmania, possessed mines of gold, silver, copper, iron, red lead, orpiment, and salt, yielding also bitumen, naphtha, sulphur, and most probably common lead. We are further informed by ancient writers that Drangiana, or Sarangia, furnished the rare and valuable mineral tin, without which copper could not be hardened into bronze; that Armenia yielded emery, so necessary for the working and polishing of gems; that the mountains and mines of the Empire supplied almost all the varieties of useful and precious stones; and that thus there was scarcely a mineral known to and required by the ancients for the purposes of their life which the Great King could not command without having recourse to others than his own subjects. It may be likewise noticed that the more important were very abundant, being found in many places and in large quantities. Gold was furnished from the mountains and deserts of Thibet and India, from the rivers of Lydia, and probably from other places where it is still found, as Armenia, Cabul, and the neighborhood of Meshed. Silver, which was the general medium of exchange in Persia, must have been especially plentiful. It was probably yielded, not only by the Kerman mines, but also by those of Armenia, Asia Minor, and the Elburz. Copper was obtained in great abundance from Cyprus, as well as from Carmania; and it may have been also derived, as it is now in very large quantities, from Armenia. Iron, really the most precious of all metals, existed within the Persian territory in the shape of huge boulders, as well as in nodules and in the form of ironstone. Lead was procurable from Bactria, Armenia, Korman, and many parts of Affghanistan; orpiment from Bactria, Kerman, and the Hazareh country; antimony from Armenia, Affghanistan, and Media; hornblende, quartz, talc, and asbestos, from various places in the Taurus.

Of all necessary minerals probably none was so plentiful and so widely diffused as salt. It was not only in Persia Proper that nature had bestowed this commodity with a lavish hand—there was scarcely a province of the Empire which did not possess it in superfluous abundance. Large tracts were covered by it in North Africa, in Media, in Carmania, and in Lower Babylonia. In Asia Minor, Armenia, Syria, Palestine, and other places, it could be obtained from lakes. In Kerman, and again in Palestine, it showed itself in the shape of large masses, not inappropriately termed "mountains." Finally, in India it was the chief material of a long mountain-range, which is capable of supplying the whole world with salt for many ages.

Bitumen and naptha were also very widely diffused. At the eastern foot of the Caucasus, where it subsides into the Caspian Sea, at various points in the great Mesopotamian plain, in the Deshtistan or low country of Persia Proper, in the Bakh-tiyari mountains, and again in the distant Jordan valley, these two inseparable products are to be found, generally united with indications of volcanic action, present or recent. The bitumen is of excellent quality, and was largely employed by the ancients. The naphtha is of two kinds, black naphtha or petroleum, and white naphtha, which is much preferred to the other. The bitumen-pits also, in some places, yielded salt.

Another useful mineral with which the Persians were very plentifully supplied, was sulphur. Sulphur is found in Persia Proper, in Carmania, on the coast of Mekran, in Azerbijan, in the Elburz, on the Iranian plateau, in the vicinity of the Dead Sea, and in very large quantities near Mosul. Here it is quarried in great blocks, which are conveyed to considerable distances.

Excellent stone for building purposes was obtainable in most parts of the Empire. Egypt furnished an inexhaustible supply of the best possible granite; marbles of various kinds, compact sandstone, limestone, and other useful sorts were widely diffused; and basalt was procurable from some of the outlying ranges of Taurus. In the neighborhood of Nineveh, and in much of the Mesopotamian region, there was abundance of grey alabaster, and a better kind was quarried near Damascus. A gritty silicious rock on the banks of the Euphrates, a little above Hit, was suitable for mill-stones.

The gems furnished by the various provinces of the Empire are too numerous for mention. They included, it must be remembered, all the kinds which have already been enumerated among the mineral products of the earlier Monarchies. Among them, a principal place must, one would think, have been occupied by the turquoise—the gem, par excellence, of modern Persia—although, strange to say, there is no certain mention of it among the literary remains of antiquity. This lovely stone is produced largely by the mines at Nishapur in the Elburz, and is furnished also in less abundance and less beauty by a mine in Kerman, and another near Khojend. It is noticed by an Arabian author as early as the twelfth century of our era. A modern writer on gems supposes that it is mentioned, though not named, by Theophrastus; but this view scarcely seems to be tenable.

Among the gems of most value which the Empire certainly produced were the emerald, the green ruby, the red ruby, the opal, the sapphire, the amethyst, the carbuncle, the jasper, the lapis lazuli, the sard, the agate, and the topaz. Emeralds were found in Egypt, Media, and Cyprus; green rubies in

Bactria; common or red rubies in Caria; opals in Egypt, Cyprus, and Asia Minor; sapphires in Cyprus; amethysts also in Cyprus, and moreover in Egypt, Galatia, and Armenia; carbuncles in Caria; jaspers in Cyprus, Asia Minor, and Persia Proper; the lapis lazuli in Cyprus, Egypt, and Media; the sard in Babylonia; the agate in Carmania, Susiana, and Armenia; and the topaz or chrysoprase in Upper Egypt.

The tales which are told of enormous emeralds are undoubtedly fictions, the material which passed for that precious substance being really in these cases either green jasper or (more probably) glass. But lapis lazuli and agate seem to have existed within the Empire in huge masses. Whole cliffs of the former overhang the river Kashkar in Kaferistan; and the myrrhine vases of antiquity which were (it is probable) of agate, and came mainly from Carmania, seem to have been of a great size.

We may conclude this review by noticing, among stones of less consequence produced within the Empire, jet, which was so called from being found at the mouth of the river Gagis in Lycia, garnets, which are common in Armenia, and beryl, which is a product of the same country.

CHAPTER III

CHARACTER, MANNERS AND CUSTOMS, DRESS, ETC., OF THE PEOPLE

"I lifted up mine eyes, and saw, and, behold, there stood before the river a ram which had two horns: and the two horns were high; but one was higher than the other, and the higher came up last."— *Dan. viii. 3.*

The ethnic identity of the Persian people with the Medes, and the inclusion of both nations in that remarkable division of the human race which is known to ethnologers as the Ipanic or Arian, have been maintained in a former volume. To the arguments there adduced it seems unnecessary to add anything in this place, since at the present day neither of the two positions appears to be controverted. It is admitted generally, not only that the Persians were of the same stock with the Medes, but that they formed, together with the Medes and a few other tribes and peoples of less celebrity, a special branch of the Indo-European family—a branch to which the name of Arian may be assigned, not merely for convenience sake, but on grounds of actual tradition and history. Undistinguished in the earlier annals of their race, the Medes and Persians became towards the eighth or seventh century before our era, its leading and most important tribes. Closely united together, with the superiority now inclining to one, now to the other, they claimed and exercised a lordship over all the other members of the stock, and not only over them, but over various alien races also. They had qualities which raised them above their fellows, and a civilization, which was not, perhaps, very advanced, but was still not wholly contemptible. Such details as could be collected, either from ancient authors, or from the extant remains, of the character, mode of life, customs, etc., of the Medes, have already found a place in this work.

The greater part of what was there said will apply also to the Persians. The information, however, which we possess, with respect to this latter people, is so much more copious than that which has come down to us with regard to the Medes, that, without repeating anything from the former place, our materials will probably enable us to give to the present chapter considerable dimensions.

The woodcuts of the preceding volume will have made the reader sufficiently familiar with the physiognomy of the Persians, or, at any rate, with the representation of it which has come down to us upon the Persian monuments. It may be remarked that the type of face and head is uniform upon all of them, and offers a remarkable contrast to the type assigned to themselves by the Assyrians, from whom the Arians evidently adopted the general idea of bas-reliefs, as well as their general mode of treating subjects upon them. The novelty of the physiognomy is a strong argument in favor of its truthfulness; and this is further confirmed by the evidence which we have, that the Persian artists aimed at representing the varieties of the human race, and succeeded fairly in rendering them. Varieties of, physiognomy are represented upon the bas-reliefs with much care, and sometimes with remarkable success, as the annexed head of a negro, taken from one of the royal tombs, will sufficiently indicate. [PLATE XXIX., Fig.1.]

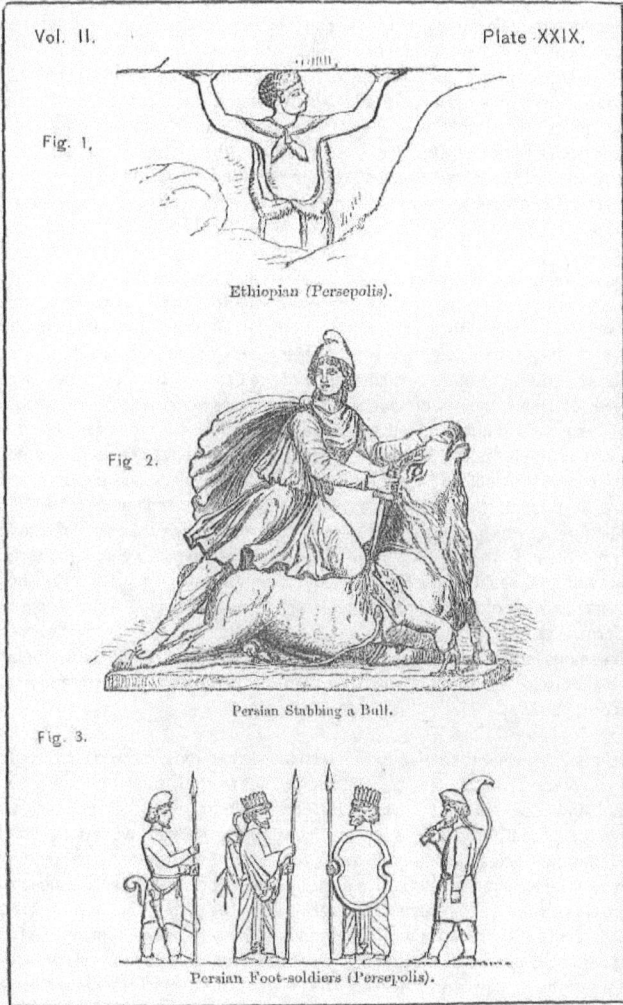

Vol. II.   Plate XXIX.

Fig. 1.

Ethiopian (Persepolis).

Fig 2.

Persian Stabbing a Bull.

Fig. 3.

Persian Foot-soldiers (Persepolis).

PLATE XXIX

According to Herodotus, the skulls of the Persians were extraordinarily thin and weak—a phenomenon for which he accounted by the national habit of always covering the head. There does not seem to be in reality any ground for supposing that such a practice would at all tend to produce such a result. If, therefore, we regard the fact of thinness as established, we can only view it as an original feature in the physical type of the race. Such a feature would imply, on the supposition that the heads were of the ordinary size, a large brain-cavity, and so an unusual volume of brain, which is generally a concomitant of high intellectual power.

The Persians seem, certainly, to have been quick and lively, keen-witted, capable of repartee, ingenious, and, for Orientals, far-sighted. They had fancy and imagination, a relish for poetry and art, and they were not without a certain power of political combination. But we cannot justly ascribe to them any high degree of intellectual excellence. The religious ideas which they held in common with the Medes were, indeed, of a more elevated character than is usual with races not enlightened by special revelation; but these ideas were the common stock of the Iranic peoples, and were inherited by the Persians from a remote ancestry, not excogitated by themselves. Their taste for art, though marked, was neither pure nor high. We shall have to consider, in a future chapter, the architecture and mimetic art of the people to weigh their merits in these respects, and, at the same time, to note their deficiencies.

Without anticipating the exact verdict then to be pronounced, we may say at once that there is nothing in the remains of the Persian architecture and sculpture that have come down to us indicative of any remarkable artistic genius; nothing that even places them on a par with the best works of the kind produced by Orientals. Again, if the great work of Firdausi represents to us, as it probably does, the true spirit of the ancient poetry of the Persians, we must conclude that, in the highest department of art, their efforts were but of moderate merit. A tone of exaggeration, an imagination exuberant and unrestrained, a preference for glitter over solid excellence, a love of far-fetched conceits, characterize the Shahnameh; and, though we may fairly ascribe something of this to the idiosyncrasy of the poet, still, after we have made all due allowance upon this score, the conviction presses upon us that there was a childish and grotesque character in the great mass of the old Persian poetry, which marks it as the creation of moderate rather than of high intellectual power, and prevents us from regarding it with the respect with which we view the labors of the Greeks and Romans, or, again, of the Hebrews, in this department. A want of seriousness, a want of reality, and, again, a want of depth, characterize the poetry of Iran, whose bards do not touch the chords which rouse what is noblest and highest in our nature. They give us sparkle, prettiness, quaint and ingenious fancies, grotesque marvels, an inflated kind of human heroism; but they have none of the higher excellencies of the poetic art, none of the divine fire which renders the true poet, and the true prophet, one.

Among moral qualities, we must assign to the Persians as their most marked characteristics, at any rate in the earlier times, courage, energy, and a regard for truth. The valor of their troops in the great combats of Platsea and Thermopylae extorted the admiration of their enemies, who have left on record their belief that, "in boldness and warlike spirit, the Persians were not a whit behind the Greeks," and that their defeat was "wholly owing to the inferiority of their equipment and training." Without proper shields, with little defensive armor, wielding only short swords and lances that were scarcely more than javelins, they dashed themselves upon the serried ranks of the Spartans, seizing the huge spear-shafts of these latter with their hands, striving to break them, and to force a way in. No conduct could have been braver than this, which the modern historian well compares with brilliant actions of the Romans and the Swiss. The Persians thoroughly deserved to be termed (as they are termed by AEschylus), a "valiant-minded people;" they had boldness, elan, dash, and considerable tenacity and stubbornness; no nation of Asia or Africa was able to stand against them;

if they found their masters in the Greeks, it was owing, as the Greeks themselves tell us, to the superiority of Hellenic arms, equipment, and, above all, of Hellenic discipline, which together rendered the most desperate valor unavailing, when it lacked the support of scientific organization and united simultaneous movement.

The energy of the Persians during the earlier years of their ascendancy is no less remarkable than their courage. AEschylus speaks of a mysterious fate which forced them to engage continually in a long series of wars, to take delight in combats of horse, and in the siege and overthrow of cities. Herodotus, in a tone that is not very different, makes Xerxes, soon after his accession, represent himself as bound by the examples of his forefathers to engage his country in some great enterprise, and not suffer the military spirit of his people to decay through want of employment. We shall find, when we come to consider the history of the Empire, that, for eighty years, under four sovereigns, the course indicated by these two writers was in fact pursued—that war followed on war, expedition on expedition—the active energy of sovereign and people carrying them on, without rest or pause, in a career of conquest that has few parallels in the history of Oriental nations. In the subsequent period, this spirit is less marked; but, at all times, a certain vigor and activity has characterized the race, distinguishing it in a very marked way from the dreamy and listless Hindus upon the one hand, and the apathetic Turks upon the other.

The Persian love of truth was a favorite theme with the Greeks, who were, perhaps, the warmer in their praises from a latent consciousness of their own deficiency in the virtue. According to Herodotus, the attention of educators was specially directed to the point, and each young Persian was taught by his preceptors three main things:—"To ride, to draw the bow, and to speak the truth." We find that, in the Zendavesta, and more especially in its earliest and purest portions, truth is strenuously inculcated. Ahura-Mazda himself is "true," "the father of all truth," and his worshippers are bound to conform themselves to his image. Darius, in his inscriptions, protests frequently against "lies," which he seems to regard as the embodiment of all evil. A love of finesse and intrigue is congenital to Orientals; and, in the later period of their sway, the Persians appear to have yielded to this natural inclination, and to have used freely in their struggle with the Greeks the weapons of cunning and deception; but, in the earlier period, a different spirit prevailed; lying was then regarded as the most disgraceful act of which a man could possibly be guilty truth was both admired and practised; Persian kings, entrapped into a promise, stood to it firmly, however much they might wish it recalled; foreign powers had never to complain that the terms of a treaty were departed from; the Persians thus form an honorable exception to the ordinary Asiatic character, and for general truthfulness and a faithful performance of their engagements compare favorably with the Greeks and Romans.

The Persian, if we may trust Herodotus, was careful to avoid debt. He had a keen sense of the difficulty with which a debtor escapes subterfuge and equivocation—forms, slightly disguised, of lying. To buy and sell wares in a market place, to chaffer and haggle over prices, was distasteful to him, as apt to involve falsity and unfairness. He was free and open in speech, bold in act, generous, warm-hearted, hospitable. His chief faults were an addiction to self-indulgence and luxury, a passionate abandon to the feeling of the hour, whatever that might happen to be; and a tameness and subservience in all his relations towards his prince, which seem to moderns almost incompatible with real self-respect and manliness.

The luxury of the Persians will be considered when we treat of their manners. In illustration of the two other weak points of their character, it may be observed that, in joy and in sorrow, they were alike immoderate; in the one transported beyond all reasonable bounds, and exhibiting their transports with entire unreserve and openness; in the other proportionately depressed, and quite unrestrained in the expression of their anxiety or misery. AEschylus' tragedy of the "Persae" is, in this respect, true to nature, and represents with accuracy the real habits of the nation. The Persian was a stranger to the dignified reserve which has commonly been affected by the more civilized among Western nations. He laughed and wept, shouted and shrieked, with the unrestraint of a child, who is not ashamed to lay bare his inmost feelings to the eyes of those about him. Lively and excitable, he loved to give vent to every passion that stirred his heart, and cared not how many witnessed his lamentations or his rejoicings.

The feeling of the Persian towards his king is one of which moderns can with difficulty form a conception. In Persia the monarch was so much the State, that patriotism itself was, as it were, swallowed up in loyalty; and an absolute unquestioning submission, not only to the deliberate will, but to the merest caprice of the sovereign, was, by habit and education, so engrained into the nature of the people that a contrary spirit scarcely ever manifested itself. In war the safety of the sovereign was the first thought, and the principal care of all. The tales told of the self-devotion of individuals to secure the preservation of the monarch may not be true, but they indicate faithfully the actual tone of men's sentiments about the value of the royal person. If the king suffered, all was lost; if the king escaped, the greatest calamities seemed light, and could be endured with patience. Uncomplaining acquiescence in all the decisions of the monarch—cheerful submission to his will, whatever it might chance to be—characterized the conduct of the Persians in time of peace. It was here that their loyalty degenerated into parasitical tameness, and became a defect instead of a virtue. The voice of remonstrance, of rebuke, of warning, was unheard at the Court; and tyranny was allowed to indulge unchecked in the wildest caprices and extravagances. The father, whose innocent son was shot before his eyes by the king in pure wantonness, instead of raising an indignant protest against the crime, felicitated him on the excellence of his archery. Unfortunates, bastinadoed by the royal orders, declared themselves delighted, because his majesty had condescended to recollect them. A tone of sycophancy and servility was thus engendered, which, sapping self-respect, tended fatally to lower and corrupt the entire character of the people.

In considering the manners and customs of the Persians, it will be convenient to follow the order already observed in treating of Assyria and Media—that is to say, to treat, in the first instance, of their warlike, and subsequently of their peaceful usages. On the latter the monuments throw considerable light; on the former, the information which they supply is comparatively scanty.

The Persians, like the Medes, regarded chariots with disfavor, and composed their armies almost entirely of foot and horse. The ordinary dress of the foot-man was, in the earlier times, a tunic with long sleeves, made of leather, and fitting rather tightly to the frame, which it covered from the neck to the knee. Under this was worn a pair of trousers, also of leather, and tolerably tight-fitting, especially at the ankles, where they met a sort of high shoe, or low boot. The head was protected by a loose round cap, apparently of felt, which projected a little in front, and rose considerably above the top of the head. Round the waist was worn a double girdle or belt, from which depended a short sword. [PLATE XXVIII Fig. 4.]

The offensive arms of the foot-man were, a sword, a spear, and a bow. The sword, which was called by the Persians akinaces, appears to have been a short, straight weapon, suited for stabbing rather than for cutting, and, in fact, not very much better than a dagger. [PLATE XXIX., Fig. 2.] It was carried in a sheath, and was worn suspended from the girdle on the right side. From the Persepolitan sculptures it would seem not to have hung freely, but to have been attached to the right thigh by a thong which passed round the knee. The handle was short, and generally unprotected by a guard; but, in some specimens, we see a simple cross-bar between the hilt and the blade.

The spear carried by the Persian foot-man was also short, or, at any rate, much shorter than the Greek. To judge by the representations of guardsmen on the Persepolitan sculptures, it was from six to six and a half or seven feet in length. The Grecian spear was sometimes as much as twenty-one feet. The Persian weapon had a short head, which appears to have been flattish, and which was strengthened by a bar or ridge down the middle. The shaft, which was of cornel wood, tapered gradually from bottom to top, and was ornamented at its lower extremity with a ball, sometimes carved in the shape of an apple or a pomegranate. [PLATE XXIX., Fig. 3.]

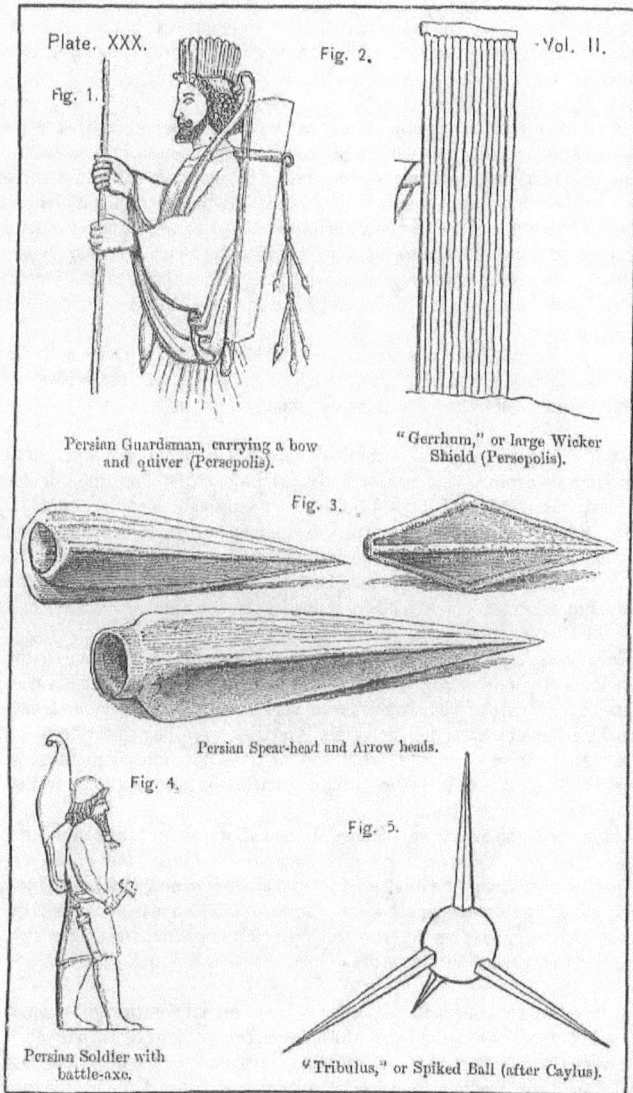

Plate. XXX.

Fig. 1.

Fig. 2.

Vol. II.

Persian Guardsman, carrying a bow and quiver (Persepolis).

"Gerrhum," or large Wicker Shield (Persepolis).

Fig. 3.

Persian Spear-head and Arrow heads.

Fig. 4.

Fig. 5.

Persian Soldier with battle-axe.

"Tribulus," or Spiked Ball (after Caylus).

PLATE XXX

The Persian bow, according to Herodotus and Xenophon, was of unusual size. According to the sculptures, it was rather short, certainly not exceeding four feet. It seems to have been carried strung, either on the left shoulder, with the arm passed through it, or in a bow-case slung at the left side. It was considerably bent in the middle, and had the ends slightly turned back. [PLATE XXX., Fig. 1.] The arrows, which were of reed, tipped with metal, and feathered, were carried in a quiver, which hung at the back near the left shoulder. To judge from the sculptures, their length must have been about two feet and a half. The arrow-heads, which were either of bronze or iron, seem to have been of various shapes, the most common closely resembling the arrow-heads of the Assyrians. [PLATE XXX., Fig. 3.]

Other offensive weapons carried occasionally by the Persian foot-men were, a battle-axe, a sling, and a knife. The battle-axe, which appears in the sculptures only in one or two instances, is declared to have been a common Persian weapon by Xenophon, who, upon such a point, would seem to be trustworthy. The use of the sling by the Persian light-armed is quite certain. It is mentioned by Curtius and Strabo, no less than by Xenophon; and the last-named writer speaks with full knowledge on the subject, for he witnessed the effect of the weapon in the hands of Persian slingers during his return with the Ten Thousand. The only missiles which the Persian slingers threw were stones; they did not, like the Rhodians, make use of small lumps of lead.

The knife seems also to have been a Persian weapon. Its blade appears to have been slightly curved, like that of a pruning-hook. It was worn in a sheath, and was probably thrust into the belt or girdle like the similar weapon, half knife, half dagger, of a modern Persian.

The ordinary defence of the Persian against the weapons of his enemy was a shield of wicker-work, which covered him almost from head to foot, and which probably differed little from the wattled shield of the Assyrians. [PLATE XXX., Fig. 2.] This he commonly planted on the ground, supporting it, perhaps, with a crutch, while he shot his arrows from behind it. Occasionally, he added to this defence the protection of a coat of mail, composed either of scale armor, or of quilted linen, like the corselets of the Egyptians. Armor of the former kind was almost impenetrable, since the scales were of metal—iron, bronze, or sometimes gold—and overlapped one another like those of a fish.

The Persian cavalry was armed, in the early times of the monarchy, almost exactly in the same manner as their infantry. Afterwards, however a considerable change seems to have been made. In the time of the younger Cyrus cavalry soldiers were very fully protected. They wore helmets on their heads, coats of mail about their bodies, and greaves on their legs. Their chief offensive arms seem, then, to have been the short sword, the javelin, and the knife. It is probable that they were without shields, being sufficiently defended by their armor, which (as we have seen) was almost complete.

The javelin of the horseman, which was his special weapon, was a short strong spear or pike, with a shaft of cornel-wood, and an iron point. It was common for him to carry two such weapons, one of which he used as a missile, while he retained the other in order to employ it in hand-to-hand combat with the enemy. It was a stout manageable weapon, and though no match for the longer and equally strong spear of the Macedonian cavalry, was preferred by Xenophon to the long weak reed-lance commonly carried by horse-soldiers in his day.

It was the practice of the later Persians to protect with armor, not only the horseman, but the horse. They selected for the service large and powerful animals, chiefly of the Nisaean breed, and cased them almost wholly in mail. The head was guarded by a frontlet, and the neck and chest by a breast-piece; the sides and flanks had their own special covering and cuisses defended the thighs. These defences were not merely, like those of the later Assyrian heavy cavalry, of felt or leather, but consisted, like the cuirasses worn by the riders, of some such material covered with metal scales. The weight which the horse had to sustain was thus very great, and the movements of the cavalry force were, in consequence, slow and hesitating. Flight was difficult; and, in a retreat, the weaker animals were apt to sink under their burdens, and to be trampled to death by the stronger ones.

There can be no doubt that, besides these heavy horsemen, the Persians employed, even in the latest times, and much more in the earlier, a light and agile cavalry force. Such were the troops which, under Tissaphernes, harassed the Ten Thousand during their retreat; and such, it may be conjectured, was really at all times the great body of their cavalry. The education of the Persian, as we shall see hereafter, was directed to the formation of those habits of quickness and agility in the mounting and managing of horses, which have a military value only as furnishing a good training for the light-cavalry service; and the tendency of the race has at all times been, not to those forms of military organization which are efficient by means of solidity and strength, but to those lighter, more varied, and more elastic branches which compensate for a want of solidity by increased activity, readiness, and ease of movement.

Though the Persians did not set any great store by chariots, as an arm of the military service, they nevertheless made occasional use of them. Not only were their kings and princes, when they commanded their troops in person, accustomed to direct their movements, both on the march and even inaction, from the elevation of a war-chariot, but now and then, in great battles, a considerable force of them was brought into the field, and important consequences were expected from their employment. The wheels of the war-chariots were armed with scythes; and these, when the chariot was set in motion, were regarded as calculated to inflict great damage on the ranks of opponents. Such hopes seem, however, to have been generally disappointed. As every chariot was drawn by at least two horses, and contained at least two persons—the charioteer and the warrior—a large mark was offered by each to the missiles of the light troops who were commonly stationed to receive them; and, as practically it was found that a single wound to either horse or man threw the whole equipage into confusion, the charge of a scythed chariot was commonly checked before it reached the line of battle of the enemy. Where this was not the case, the danger was escaped by opening the ranks and letting the chariots pass through them to the rear, a good account being speedily given of any adventurer who thus isolated himself from the support of his own party.

The Persian war-chariot was, probably, somewhat loftier than the Assyrian. The wheels appear to have been from, three to four feet in diameter; and the body rose above them to a height from the ground of nearly five feet. The person of the warrior was thus protected up to his middle by the curved board which enclosed the chariot on three sides. The axle-tree is said to have been broad, since breadth afforded a security against being overturned, and the whole construction to have been strong and solid. The wheels had twelve spokes, which radiated from a nave of unusual size. The felloes were narrower than the Assyrian, but were still composed, like them, of two or three distinct layers of wood. The tires were probably of metal, and were indented like the edge of a saw. [PLATE XXXI., Fig. 1.]

No great ornamentation of the chariot appears to have been attempted. The body was occasionally patterned with a chequer-work, which maybe compared with a style common in Assyria, and the spokes of the wheels were sometimes of great elegance, but the general character of the workmanship was massive and plain. The pole was short, and terminated with a simple curve. From the evidence of the monuments it would seem that chariots were drawn by two horses only; but the classical writers assure us that the ordinary practice was to have teams of four. The harness used was exceedingly simple, consisting of a yoke, a belly-band, a narrow collar, a head-stall, a bit, and reins. When the charioteer left his seat, the reins could be attached to a loop or bar which projected from the front of the chariot-board.

Chariots were constructed to contain two, or perhaps, in some instances, three persons. These consisted of the warrior, his charioteer, who stood beside him, and an attendant, whose place was behind, and whose business it was to open and shut the chariot doors. The charioteer wore a visor and a coat of mail, exposing nothing to the enemy but his eyes.

Vol. II.   Plate XXXI.

Fig. 1

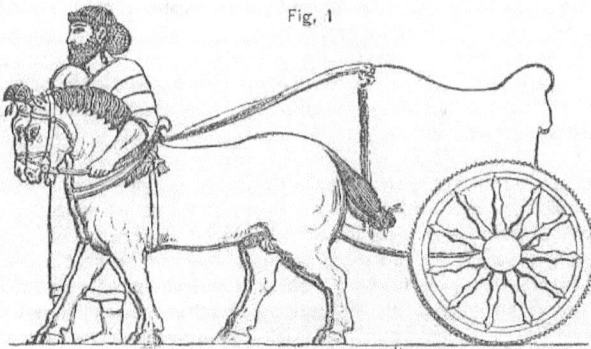

Persian Chariot (from Persepolis).

Fig. 2

Fig. 3.

Greek Triaconter, after Montfaucon.

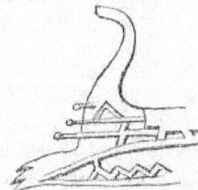

Beak of Persian War-galley (enlarged from a Coin).

Fig. 4

Fig. 5.

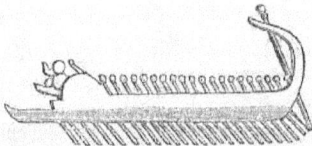

Persian Penteconter (enlarged from a Coin).

Head of Persian King (from a Daric).

PLATE XXXI

The later Persians made use also of elephants in battle, but to a very small extent, and without any results worth mentioning.

The chief points of Persian tactics were the following. The army was organized into three distinct services—those of the chariots, the horse, and the foot. In drawing up the line of battle, it was usual, where chariots were employed, to place them in the front rank, in front of the rest of the army. Behind the chariots were stationed the horse and the foot; the former generally massed upon the wings; the latter placed in the middle, drawn up according to nations, in a number of oblong squares, which touched, or nearly touched, one another. The bravest and best armed troops were placed in front; the ranks towards the rear being occupied by those of inferior quality. The depth of the ranks was usually very great, since Oriental troops cannot be trusted to maintain a firm front unless they are strongly supported from behind. No attempt, however, seems to have been made at forming a second line of battle in the rear of the first, nor does there even seem to have been any organized system of reserves. When the battle began, the chariots were first launched against the enemy, whose ranks it was hoped they would confuse, or, at any rate, disturb. After this the main line advanced to the attack, but without any inclination to come at once to close quarters. Planting their shields firmly on the ground in front of them, the Persian heavy-armed shot flight after flight of arrows against their foe, while the slingers and other light-armed in the rear sent clouds of missiles over the heads of their friends into the adverse ranks beyond them. It was usually the enemy which brought this phase of the battle to an end, by pressing onward and closing with the Persian main line in a hand:to-hand combat. Here the struggle was commonly brief—a very few minutes often decided the engagement. If the Persian line of battle was forced or broken, all was immediately regarded as lost—flight and rout followed. The cavalry, from its position on the wings, might attempt, by desperate charges on the flanks of the advancing foe, to stay his progress, and restore the fortune of the day, but such efforts were usually unavailing. Its line of battle once broken, a Persian army lost heart; its commander commonly set the example of flight, and there was a general rush of all arms from the battle-field.

For success the Persians trusted mainly to their numbers, which enabled them, in some cases, to renew an attack time after time with fresh troops, in others to outflank and surround their adversary. Their best troops were undoubtedly their cavalry, both heavy and light. The heavy, armed in the old times with bows, and in the later with the javelins, highly distinguished itself on many important occasions. The weight of its charge must have been great; its offensive weapons were good; and its armor made it almost invulnerable to ordinary weapons. The light cavalry was celebrated for the quickness and dexterity of its manoeuvres. It had the loose organization of modern Bashi-Bazouks or Cossacks; it hung in clouds on the enemy—assailed, retreated, rallied, re-advanced—fled, and even in flight was formidable, since each rider was trained to discharge his arrows backwards with a sure aim. against the pursuing foe. The famous skill of the Parthians in their horse-combats was inherited from their Persian predecessors, who seem to have invented the practice which the later people carried to perfection.

Though mainly depending for success on their numbers, the Persians did not wholly despise the use of contrivance and stratagem. At Arbela, Darius Codomannus had spiked balls strewn over the ground where he expected the Greek cavalry to make its attacks. [PLATE XXX., Fig. 5]; and, at Sardis, Cyrus obtained his victory over the Lydian horse by frightening them with the grotesque and unfamiliar camel. Other instances will readily occur to the reader, whereby it appears that the art of war was studied, and ingenuity allowed its due place in military matters, by this people, who showed a fair share of Oriental subtlety in the devices which they employed against their enemies.

It is doubtful whether we are to include among these devices the use of military engines. On the one hand, we have several distinct statements by the author of the "Cyrpoasdia," to the effect that engines were well known to the Persians; on the other, we remark an entire absence from the works of other ancient writers of any notice that they actually employed them, either in their battles or their sieges. The silence of Scripture, of Herodotus, of the inscriptions, of Quintus Curtius, of Arrian, may fairly be regarded as outweighing the unsupported authority of the romance-writer, Xenophon; and though it would be rash to decide that such things as siege-towers, battering rams, and balistce—all of which are found to have been in constant use under the Assyrian and Babylonian monarchies—were wholly discarded by, or unknown to, their successors in the government of Asia, yet a wise criticism will conclude, that they were, at any rate, unfamiliar to the Persians, rarely and sparingly (if at all) employed by them, other methods of accomplishing the ends whereto they served having more approved themselves to this ingenious people. In ordinary sieges it would seem that they trusted to the bank or mound, while sometimes they drove mines under the walls, and sought in this way to effect a breach. Where the place attacked was of great strength, they had recourse in general either to stratagem or to blockade. Occasionally they employed the destructive force of fire, and no doubt they often succeeded by the common method of escalade. On the whole, it must certainly be said that they were successful in their sieges, exhibiting in their conduct of them courage, activity, and considerable fertility of resource.

A Persian army was usually, though not always, placed under a single commander. This commander was the monarch, if he was present; if not, it was a Persian, or a Mede, nominated by him. Under the commander-in-chief were a number of general officers, heads of corps or divisions, of whom we find, in one instance, as many as nine. Next in rank to these were the chiefs of the various ethnic contingents composing the army, who were, probably, in general the satraps of the different provinces. Thus far appointments were held directly from the crown; but beyond this the system was changed. The ethnic or satrapial commanders appointed the officers next below themselves, the captains over a thousand, and (if their contingent was large enough to admit it) the captains over ten thousand; who, again, nominated their subordinates, commanders of a hundred, and commanders of ten. Thus, in the main, a decimal scale prevailed. The lowest rank of officers commanded each ten men, the next lowest a hundred, the next to that a thousand, the next ten thousand. The officer over ten thousand was sometimes a divisional chief; sometimes he was subject to the commander of an ethnic contingent, who was himself under the orders of the head of a division. Altogether there were six ranks of officers, exclusive of the commander-in-chief.

The proper position of the commander-in-chief was considered to be the centre of the line of battle. He was regarded as safer there than he would have been on either wing; and it was seen that, from such a position, his orders would be most rapidly conveyed to all parts of the battlefield. It was not, however, thought to be honorable that he should keep aloof from the fight, or avoid risking his own person. On the contrary, he was expected to take an active part in the combat; and therefore, though his place was not exactly in the very foremost ranks, it was towards the front, and the result followed that he was often exposed to imminent danger. The consequences of this arrangement were frequently disastrous in the extreme, the death or flight of the commander producing universal panic, stopping the further issue of any general order, and thus paralyzing the whole army.

The numbers of a Persian army, though no doubt exaggerated by the Greeks, must have been very great, amounting, probably, on occasions, to more than a million of combatants. Troops were drawn from the entire empire, and were marshalled in the field according to nations, each tribe accoutred in its own fashion. Here were seen the gilded breastplates and scarlet kilts of the Persians and Medes; there the woollen shirt of the Arab, the leathern jerkin of the Berber, or the cotton dress of the native of Hindustan. Swart savage Ethiops from the Upper Nile, adorned with a war-paint of white and red, and scantily clad with the skins of leopards or lions, fought in one place with huge clubs, arrows tipped with stone, and spears terminating in the horn of an antelope. In another, Scyths, with their loose spangled trousers and their tall pointed caps, dealt death around from their unerring blows; while near them Assyrians, helmeted, and wearing corselets of quilted linen, wielded the tough spear, or the still more formidable iron mace. Rude weapons, like cane bows, unfeathered arrows, and stakes hardened at one end in the fire, were seen side by side with keen swords and daggers of the best steel, the finished productions of the workshops of Phoenicia and Greece. Here the bronze helmet was surmounted with the ears and horns of an ox; there it was superseded by a fox-skin, a leathern or wooden skull-cap, or a head-dress fashioned out of a horse's scalp. Besides horses and mules, elephants, camels, and wild asses, diversified the scene, and rendered it still more strange and wonderful to the eye of a European. One large body of cavalry was accustomed to enter the field apparently unarmed; besides the dagger, which the Oriental never lays aside, they had nothing but a long leathern thong. They used this, however, just as the lasso is used by the natives of Brazil, and the wretch at whom they aimed their deadly noose had small chance of escape. The Persians, like the Assyrians, usually avoided fighting during the winter, and marched out their armies against the enemy in early spring. With the great hosts which they moved a fixed order of march was most necessary; and we find evidence of so much attention being paid to this point that confusion and disorder seem scarcely ever to have arisen. When the march lay within their own country, it was usual to send on the baggage and the sumpter-beasts in advance, after which came about half the troops, moving slowly in a long and continuous column along the appointed line of route. At this point a considerable break occurred, in order that all might be clear for the most important part of the army, which was now to follow. A guard, consisting of a thousand horse and a thousand foot, picked men of the Persian people, prepared the way for what was most holy in the eyes of the nation—the emblems of their religion, and their king. The former consisted of sacred horses and cars; perhaps, in the later times, of silver altars also, bearing the perpetual and heaven-kindled fire, which was a special object of Persian religious regard, and which the superstition of the people viewed as a sort of palladium, sure to bring the blessings of heaven upon their arms. Behind the sacred emblems followed the Great King himself, mounted on a car drawn by Nissean steeds, and perhaps protected on either side by a select band of his relatives. Behind the royal chariot came a second guard, consisting, like the first, of a thousand foot and a thousand horse. Then followed ten thousand picked foot, probably the famous "Immortals;" then came a body of ten thousand picked Persian horsemen. After these a space of four hundred yards (nearly a quarter of a mile) was left vacant; then marched, in a second continuous column, the remainder of the host.

On entering an enemy's country, or drawing near a hostile force in their own, certain alterations in these dispositions became necessary, and were speedily effected. The baggage-train was withdrawn, and instead of moving before the army, followed at some little distance in the rear. Horsemen were thrown out in front, to feel for the enemy and notify his arrival. Sometimes, if the host was large, a division of the troops was made, and several corps d'armee advanced against the foe simultaneously by distinct routes. When this took place, the commander-in-chief was careful to accompany the central force, so as to find himself in his proper position if he was suddenly compelled to give battle.

Night movements were seldom attempted by the Persians. They marched from sunrise to sunset, halting, probably, during the midday heat. In their most rapid marches they seldom accomplished more than from twenty to twenty-five miles in the day; and when this rate was attempted for any continuance, it was necessary to rest the men at intervals for as much as three days at a time. The great drag upon rapidity of movement was the baggage-train, which consisted ordinarily of a vast multitude of camels, horses, asses, mules, oxen, etc., in part carrying burthens upon their backs, in part harnessed to carts laden with provisions, tents, and other necessaries. The train also frequently comprised a number of litters, in which the wives or female companions of the chief men were luxuriously conveyed, amid a crowd of eunuchs and attendants, and with all the cumbrous paraphernalia of female wardrobes. Roads, it must be remembered, did not exist; rivers were not bridged, except occasionally by boats; the army marched on the natural ground along an established line of route which no art had prepared for the passage of man or beast. Portions of the route would often be soft and muddy; the carts and litters would become immovable, their wheels sinking into the mire up to the axles; all the efforts of the teams would be unavailing; it must have been imperative to halt the main line, and employ the soldiers in the release of the vehicles, which had to be lifted and carried forward till the ground was sufficiently firm to bear them. When a river crossed the line of route, a ford had to be sought, boats procured, or rafts extemporized. The Persians were skilful in the passage of streams, to which they became accustomed in their first campaigns under Cyrus; but the march was necessarily retarded by these and similar obstacles, and we cannot be surprised that the average rate of movement was slow.

As evening approached the Persians sought a suitable place for their camp. An open plain was preferred for the purpose, and the vicinity of water was a necessity. If an enemy was thought to be at hand, a ditch was rapidly dug, and the earth thrown up inside; or if the soil was sandy, sacks were filled with it, and the camp was protected with sand-bags. Immediately within the rampart were placed the gerrhophori, or Persians armed with large wicker shields. The rest of the soldiers had severally their appointed places, the position assigned to the commander-in-chief being the centre. All the army had tents, which were pitched so as to face the east. The horses of the cavalry were tethered and hobbled in front of the tents of their owners.

The Persians disliked encamping near to their enemy. They preferred an interval of seven or eight miles, which they regarded as a considerable security against a surprise. As their most important arm was the cavalry, and as it was impossible for the cavalry to unfasten and unhobble their steeds, to equip them properly, to arm themselves, and then to mount in a short space of time, when darkness and confusion reigned around, a night attack on the part of an enterprising enemy would have been most perilous to a Persian army. Hence the precaution which they observed against its occurrence—a precaution which was seldom or never omitted where they felt any respect for their foe, and which seems to have been effective, since we do not hear of their suffering any disaster of the kind which they so greatly feared.

The Persians do not seem to have possessed any special corps of pioneers. When the nature of the country was such as to require the felling of timber or the removal of brushwood, the army was halted, and the work was assigned to a certain number of the regular soldiers. For the construction of bridges, however, in important places, and for other works on a grand scale intended to facilitate an expedition, preparations were made beforehand, the tasks being entrusted either to skilled workmen, or to the crews of ships, if they were tolerably easy of performance.

Commissariat arrangements were generally made by the Persians on a large scale, and with the best possible results. An ample baggage-train conveyed corn sufficient to supply the host during some months and in cases where scarcity was apprehended, further precautions were taken. Ships laden with corn accompanied the expedition as closely as possible, and supplemented any deficiency that might arise from a failure on the part of the land transport department. Sometimes, too, magazines were established at convenient points along the intended line of march previously to the setting forth of the army, and stores were thus accumulated at places where it was probable they would be found of most service.

Requisitions for supplies were also made upon the inhabitants of the towns and villages through which lay the route of the army. Whenever the host rested for a night at a place of any consequence, the inhabitants seem to have been required to furnish sufficient bread for a meal to each man, and, in addition, to provide a banquet for the king (or general) and his suite, which was always very numerous. Such requisitions, often intolerably burthensome to those upon whom they were laid, must have tended greatly to relieve the strain upon their own resources, which the sustentation of such enormous hosts as the Persian kings were in the habit of moving, cannot have failed to produce in many cases.

The effectiveness of these various arrangements for the provisioning of troops upon a march was such that Persian armies were rarely, if ever, in any difficulty with respect to their subsistence. Once only in the entire course of their history do we hear of the Persian forces suffering to any considerable extent from a want of supplies. According to Herodotus, Cambyses, when he invaded Ethiopia, neglected the ordinary precautions and brought his army into such straits that his men began to eat each other. This caused the total failure of his expedition, and the loss of a great proportion of the troops employed in it. There is, however, reason to suspect that, even in this case, the loss and difficulty which occurred have been much exaggerated.

The Persians readily gave quarter to the enemy who asked it, and generally treated their prisoners of war with much kindness. Personages of importance, as monarchs or princes, either preserved their titles and their liberty, with even a certain nominal authority, or received appanages in other parts of the Persian territory, or, finally, were retained about the Court as friends and table-companions of the Great King. Those of less rank were commonly given lands and houses in some province remote from their own country, and thenceforth held the same position as the great mass of the subject races. Exchanges of prisoners do not seem to have been thought of. In a few cases, persons, whom we should regard as prisoners of war, experienced some severities, but probably only when they were viewed by the Persians, not as fair enemies, but as rebels. Rebels were, of course, liable to any punishment which the king might think it right to inflict upon them, and there were occasions after a revolt when sentences of extreme rigor were passed upon the persons considered to have been most in fault. According to Herodotus, three thousand Babylonians were crucified by order of Darius, to punish their revolt from him; and, though this is probably an exaggeration, it is certain that sometimes, where an example was thought to be required, the Persians put to death, not only the leader of a rebellion, but a number of his chief adherents. Crucifixion, or, at any rate, impalement of some sort, was in such cases the ordinary punishment. Sometimes, before a rebel was executed, he was kept for a while chained at the king's door, in order that there might be no doubt of his capture.

Among the minor punishments of rebellion were branding, and removal of the rebels en masse from their own country, to some remote locality. In this latter case, they were merely treated in the same way as ordinary prisoners of war. In the former, they probably became royal slaves attached to the household of the monarch.

Though the Persians were not themselves a nautical people, they were quite aware of the great importance of a navy, and spared no pains to provide themselves with an efficient one. The conquests of Phoenicia, Cyprus, Egypt, and the Greek islands were undertaken, it is probable, mainly with this object; and these parts of the Empire were always valued chiefly as possessing skilled seamen, vessels, and dockyards, from which the Great King could draw an almost inexhaustible supply of war-ships and transports. Persia at times had the complete command of the Mediterranean Sea, and bore undisputed sway in the Levant during almost the whole period of her existence as an empire.

The war-ship preferred by the best naval powers during the whole period of the Persian rule was the trireme, or decked galley impelled by rowers sitting in three tiers, or banks, one above another. This vessel, the invention of the Corinthians, had been generally adopted by the nations bordering on the Mediterranean in the interval between B.C. 700 and B.C. 525, when by the reduction of Phoenicia, Cyprus, and Egypt, the Persians obtained the command of the sea. Notwithstanding the invention of quadriremes by the Carthaginians before B.C. 400, and of quinqueremes by Dionysius the Elder soon after, the trireme stood its ground, and from first to last the Persian fleets were mainly composed of this class of vessels.

The trireme was a vessel of a considerable size, and was capable of accommodating two hundred and thirty persons. Of these, two hundred constituted the crew, while the remaining thirty were men-at-arms, corresponding to our own "marines." By far the greater number of the crew consisted of the rowers, who probably formed at least nine-tenths of the whole, or one hundred and eighty out of the two hundred. The rowers sat, not on benches running right across the vessel, but on small seats attached to its side. They were arranged, as before stated, in three tiers, not, however, directly one over the head of another, but obliquely, each at once above and behind his fellow. Each rower had the sole management of a single oar, which he worked through a hole pierced in the side of the vessel. To prevent his oar from slipping he had a leathern strap, which he twisted round it, and fastened to the thole, probably by means of a button. The remainder of the crew comprised the captain, the steersman, the petty officers, and the sailors proper, or those whose office it was to trim the sails and look to the rigging. The trireme of Persian times had, in all cases, a mast, and at least one sail, which was of a square shape, hung across the mast by means of a yard or spar, like the "square-sail" of a modern vessel. The rudder was composed of two broad-bladed oars, one on either side of the stern, united, however, by a cross-bar, and managed by a single steersman. The central part of a trireme was always decked, and on this deck, which was generally level with the bulwarks, stood and fought the men-at-arms, whose business it was to engage the similar force of the enemy.

The weapon of the trireme, with which she was intended chiefly to attack her foe, was the beak. [PLATE XXXI., Fig. 3.] This consisted of a projection from the prow of the ship, either above or below the water-line, strongly shod with a casting of iron, and terminating either in the head of an animal, or in one or more sharp points. A trireme was expected, like a modern "ram," to use this implement against the sides of her adversary's vessels, so as to crush them in and cause the vessels to sink. Driven by the full force of her oars, which impelled her almost at the rate of a modern steamer, she was nearly certain, if she struck her adversary full, to send ship and men to the bottom. She might also, it is true, greatly damage herself; but, to preclude this, it was customary to make the whole prow of a trirene exceedingly strong, and, more particularly, to support it with beams at the side which tended to prevent the timbers from starting.

Besides triremes, which constituted the bulk of the Persian navy, there were contained in their fleet various other classes of vessels, as triaconters, penteconters, cercuri, and others. Triaconters were long, sharp-keeled ships, shaped very much like a trireme, rowed by thirty rowers, who sat all upon a level, like the rowers in modern boats, fifteen on either side of the vessel. [PLATE XXXI., Fig. 2.] Penteconters were very similar, the only difference being in the number of the oars and oarsmen. [PLATE XXXI., Fig. 4.] Both these classes of vessels seem to have been frequently without sails. Cercuri were light boats, very long and swift. They are said to have been invented by the Cyprians, and were always peculiar to Asia.

The transports of the Persians were either for the conveyance of horses or of food. Horse-transports were large clumsy vessels, constructed expressly for the service whereon they were used, possessing probably a special apparatus for the embarkation and disembarkation of the animals which they were built to carry. Corn-transports seem to have been of a somewhat lighter character. Probably, they varied very considerably in their size and burthen, including huge and heavy merchantmen on the one hand, and a much lighter and smaller craft on the other.

The Persians used their ships of war, not only for naval engagements, but also for the conveyance of troops and the construction of bridges. Accustomed to pass the great streams which intersect Western Asia by bridges of boats, which were permanently established wherever an unfordable river crossed any of the regular routes connecting the provinces with the capital, the Persians, when they proceeded to carry their arms from Asia into Europe, conceived the idea of bridging the interval between the continents, which did not much exceed the width of one of the Mesopotamian streams, by constructions similar in principle and general character to those wherewith long use had made them familiar in their own country. Ranging a number of vessels side by side, at no great distance one from another, parallel with the course of the stream, which ran down the straits, anchoring each vessel stem and stern to keep it in place, and then laying upon these supports a long wooden platform, they made a floating bridge of considerable strength, reaching from the Asiatic to the European coast, on which not only men, but horses, camels, chariots, and laden carts passed over safely from the one continent to the other. Only, as the water which they had to cross was not a river, but an arm of the real salt sea, and might, therefore, in case of a storm, show a might and fury far beyond a river's power, they thought it necessary to employ, in lieu of boats, the strongest ships which they possessed, namely, triremes and pentecon-ters, as best capable of withstanding the force of an angry sea. Bridges of this kind were intended sometimes for temporary, sometimes for permanent constructions. In the latter case, great care and much engineering skill was lavished on their erection. The shore cables, which united the ships together, and sustained the actual bridge or platform, were made of most carefully selected materials, and must have been of enormous strength; the ships were placed in close proximity one to another; and by the substitution of a double for a single line—of two bridges, in fact, for one—the solidity of the work was very largely augmented. Yet, rare as was the skill shown, solid and compact as were the causeways thus thrown by human art over the sea, they were found inadequate to the end desired. The great work of Xerxes, far the most elaborate of its class, failed to withstand the fury of the elements for a single year; the bridge, constructed in one autumn, was utterly swept away in the next; and the army which had crossed into Europe by its aid had to embark as it best could, and return on board ship to Asia.

As the furnishing of the Persian fleet was left wholly to the subject nations of the Empire, so was its manning intrusted to them almost entirely. Phoenicians, Syrians, Egyptians, Cypriots, Cilicians, Lycians, Pamphylians, Carians, Greeks, equipped in the several costumes of their countries, served side by side in their respective contingents of ships, thereby giving the fleet nearly the same motley appearance which was presented by the army. In one respect alone did the navy exhibit superior uniformity to their sister service—the epibatae, or "marines," who formed the whole fighting force of the fleet while it kept the sea, was a nearly homogeneous body, consisting of three races only (two of which were closely allied), namely, Persians, Medes, and Sacse. Every ship had thirty such men on board; all, it is probable, uniformly armed, and all animated by one and the same spirit. To this force the Persians must have owed it mainly that their great fleets were not mere congeries of mutually repellant atoms, but were capable of acting against an enemy with a fair amount of combination and singleness of purpose.

When a fleet accompanied a land army upon an expedition, it was usually placed under the same commander. This commander, however, was not expected to adventure himself on board much less to take the direction of a sea-fight. He intrusted the fleet to an officer, or officers, whom he nominated, and was content himself with the conduct of operations ashore. Occasionally the land and sea forces were assigned to distinct commanders of co-ordinate authority—an arrangement which led naturally, to misunderstanding and quarrel.

The tactics of a Persian fleet seem to have been of the simplest kind Confident in their numbers, until experience had taught them the fallaciousness of such a ground of hope, they were chiefly anxious that their enemy should not escape. To prevent this they endeavored to surround the ships opposed to them, advancing their line in a crescent form, so as to enclose their adversary's wings, or even detaching squadrons to cut off his retreat. They formed their line several ships deep and when the hour of battle came, advanced directly at their best speed against the enemy, endeavoring to run down his vessels by sheer force, and never showing any acquaintance with or predilection for manoeuvres of a skilful antagonist, who avoided or successfully withstood this first onset, they were apt through their very numbers to be thrown into disorder: the first line would become entangled with the second, the second with the third, and inextricable confusion would be the result. Confusion placed them at the mercy of their antagonist, who, retaining complete command over his own vessels, was able to strike theirs in vulnerable parts, and, in a short time, to cover the sea with shattered and sinking wrecks. The loss to the Persians in men as well as in material, was then sure to be very great; for their sailors seldom knew how to swim, and were consequently drowned, even when the shore was but a few yards distant.

When, from deficiency in their numbers, or distrust of their own nautical skill in comparison with that of their enemy, the commanders of a Persian fleet wished to avoid an engagement, a plan sometimes adopted was to run the ships ashore upon a smooth soft beach, and, after drawing them together, to surround them with such a rampart as could be hastily made, and defend this rampart with the sailors. The crews of the Persian vessels were always more or less completely armed, in order that, if occasion arose, they might act as soldiers ashore, and were thus quite capable of fighting effectively behind a rampart. They might count, too, under such circumstances, upon assistance from such of their own land forces as might happen to be in the neighborhood, who would be sure to come with all speed to their aid, and might be expected to prove a sure protection.

The subject nations who furnished the Persians with their fleet were, in the earlier times, the Phoenicians, the Egyptians, the Cypriots, the Cilicians, the Syrians of Palestine, the Pamphylians, the Lycians, the Carians, and the Greeks of Asia Minor and the islands. The Greeks seem to have furnished the largest number of ships; the Phoenicians, the next largest; then the Egyptians; after them the Cypriots; then the Cilicians; then the Carians; next the Lycians; while the Pamphylians furnished the least. The best ships and the best sailors were the Phoenicians, especially those of Sidon. In later times, ships were drawn either from Phoenicia alone, or from Phoenicia, Cilicia, and Cyprus.

The limits assigned to the present work forbid the further prosecution of this branch of our inquiry, and require us now to pass on from the consideration of the Persian usages in war, to that of their manners and customs, their habits and proceedings, in time of peace. And here it will once more be convenient to follow a division of the subject with which the reader is familiar, and to treat first of the public life of the King and Court, and next of the private life of the people.

The Persian king held the same rank and position in the eyes of his subjects which the great monarch of Western Asia, whoever he might be, had always occupied from time immemorial. He was their lord and master, absolute disposer of their lives, liberties, and property; the sole fountain of law and right, incapable himself of doing wrong, irresponsible irresistable—a sort of God upon earth; one whose favor was happiness, at whose frown men trembled, before whom all bowed themselves down with the lowest and humblest obeisance.

To a personage so exhalted, a state and pomp of the utmost magnificence was befitting. The king's ordinary dress in time of peace was the long flowing "Median garment," or candys—made in his case (it is probable) of richest silk, which, with its ample folds, its wide hanging sleeves, and its close fit about the neck and chest, gave dignity to almost any figure, and excellently set off the noble presence of an Achaemenian prince. The royal robe was either of purple throughout, or sometimes of purple embroidered with gold. It descended below the ankles; resting on the foot even when the monarch was seated. A broad girdle confined it at the waist. Under it was worn a tunic, or shirt, which reached from the neck to the knee, and had tight-fitting sleeves that covered the arm to the wrist. The tunic was purple in color, like the candys, or robe, but striped or mixed with white. The lower limbs were encased in trousers of a crimson hue. On his feet the the king wore shoes like those of the Medes, long and taper at the toe buttoned in front, and reaching very high up the instep: their color was deep yellow or saffron. [PLATE XXXII., Fig.1.]

Plate. XXXII.

Vol. II.

Fig. 1.

Fig. 2.

King seated on his Throne (Persepolis).

Head of Persian King
(Persepolis).

Fig. 3

Fig. 4.

As of Persian Kings (from Cylinders).

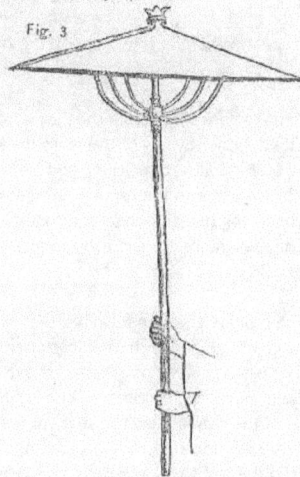

Royal Parasol (Persepolis).

PLATE XXXII

Thus far the monarch's costume, though richer in material than the dress of the Persian nobles, and in some points different in color, was on the whole remarkably like that of the upper class of his subjects. It was, however, most important that his dress should possess some distinguishing feature, and that that feature should be one of very marked prominency. In an absolute monarchy the king must be unmistakable, at almost any distance, and almost in any light. Consequences of the gravest kind may follow from any mistake of the royal identity; and it is therefore essential to the comfort both of prince and subject that some very conspicuous badge shall mark and notify the monarch's presence. Accordingly, it appears that the Persian ruler was to be known by his headdress, which was peculiar alike in shape and in color, and was calculated to catch the eye in both respects. It bore the name kitaris or hidaris, and was a tall stiff cap, slightly swelling as it ascended, flat at top, and terminating in a ring or circle which projected beyond the lines of the sides. Round it, probably near the bottom, was worn a fillet or band—the diadem proper—which was blue, spotted with white.

As the other Persians wore either simple fillets round their heads, or soft, rounded, and comparatively low caps, with no band round them, the king's headdress, which would tower above theirs and attract attention by its color, could readily be distinguished even in the most crowded Court.

It has been asserted that the kidaris, or tiara of the Persian kings, was "commonly adorned with gold and jewelry;" and this may possibly have been the case, but there is no evidence that it was so. Its material was probably either cloth or felt, and it was always of a bright color, though not (apparently) always of the same color. Its distinguishing features were its height, its stiffness, and the blue and white fillet which encircled it.

Among other certain indications of the royal presence may be mentioned the golden sceptre, and the parasol. The sceptre, which is seen frequently in the king's hands, was a plain rod, about five feet in length, ornamented with a ball, or apple, at its upper end, and at its lower tapering nearly to a point. The king held it in his right hand, grasping it near, but not at, the thick end, and rested the thin end on the ground in his front. When he walked, he planted it upright before him, as a spearman would plant his spear. When he sate, he sloped it outwards, still, however, touching the ground with its point.

The parasol, which has always been in the East a mark of dignity, seems in Persia, as in Assyria, to have been confined, either by law or usage, to the king. The Persian implement resembled the later Assyrian, except that it was not tasselled, and had no curtain or flap. It had the same tent-like shape, the same long thick stem, and the same ornament at the top. It only differed in being somewhat shallower, and in having the supports, which kept it open, curved instead of straight. It was held over the king's head on state occasions by an attendant who walked immediately behind him. [PLATE XXXII., Fig. 3.]

The throne of the monarch was an elevated seat, with a high back, but without arms, cushioned, and ornamented with a fringe, and with moldings or carvings along the back and legs. The ornamentation consisted chiefly of balls and broad rings, and contained little that was artistic or elaborate. The legs, however, terminated in lions' feet, resting upon half balls, which were ribbed or fluted. The sides of the chair below the seat appear to have been panelled, like the thrones of the Assyrians, but were not adorned with any carving. The seat of the throne was very high from the ground, and without a rest the legs would have dangled. A footstool consequently was provided, which was plain, like the throne, but was supported on legs terminating in the feet of bulls. Thus the lion and the bull, so frequent in the symbolism of the East, were here again brought together, being represented as the supports of the throne.

With respect to the material whereof the throne was composed, there can be no doubt that it was something splendid and costly. Late writers describe it as made of pure gold; but, as we hear of its having silver feet, we may presume that parts at least were of the less precious metal. Ivory is not said to have been used in its composition. We may, perhaps, conjecture, that the frame of the throne was wood, and that this was overlaid with plates of gold or silver, whereby the whole of the woodwork was concealed from view, and an appearance of solid metal presented.

The person of the king was adorned with golden ornaments. He had earrings of gold in his ears, often inlaid with jewels he wore golden bracelets upon his wrists; and he had a chain or collar of gold about his neck. [PLATE XXXIII., Fig. 1.] In his girdle, which was also of gold, he carried a short sword, the sheath of which was formed of a single precious stone. The monuments, unfortunately, throw little light on the character and workmanship of these portions of the royal costume. We may gather from them, perhaps, that the bracelets had a large jewel set in their centre, and that the collars were of twisted work, worn loosely around the neck. The sword seems to have differed little from that of the ordinary Persians. It had a short straight blade, a mere crossbar for a guard, and a handle almost devoid of ornament. This plainness was compensated, if we may trust Curtius, by the magnificence of the sheath, which was, perhaps, of jasper, agate, or lapis lazuli. [PLATE XXXIII., Fig. 2.]

Plate XXXIII

Fig. 3.

Persian King in his Chariot
(from a daric).

PLATE XXXIII

The officers in most close attendance on the monarch's person were, in war, his charioteer, his stool-bearer, his bow-bearer, and his quiver-bearer; in peace, his parasol-bearer, and his fan bearer, who was also privileged to carry what has been termed "the royal pocket-handkerchief."

The royal charioteer is seemingly unarmed. His head is protected merely by a fillet. He sits in front of his master, and both his hands are fully occupied with the management of the reins. He has no whip, and seems to urge his horses forward simply by leaning forward himself, and slackening or shaking the reins over them. He was, no doubt, in every case a Persian of the highest rank, such near proximity to the Royal person being a privilege to which none but the very noblest could aspire. [PLATE XXXIII., Fig. 2.]

The office of the stool-bearer, was to assist the king as he mounted his chariot or dismounted from it. He carried a golden stool, and followed the royal chariot closely, in order that he might be at hand whenever his master felt disposed to alight. On a march, the king was wont to vary the manner of his travelling, exchanging, when the inclination took him, his chariot for a litter, and riding in that more luxurious vehicle till he was tired of it, after which he returned to his chariot for a space. The services of the stool-bearer were thus in constant requisition, since it was deemed quite impossible that his Majesty could ascend or descend his somewhat lofty war-car without such aid.

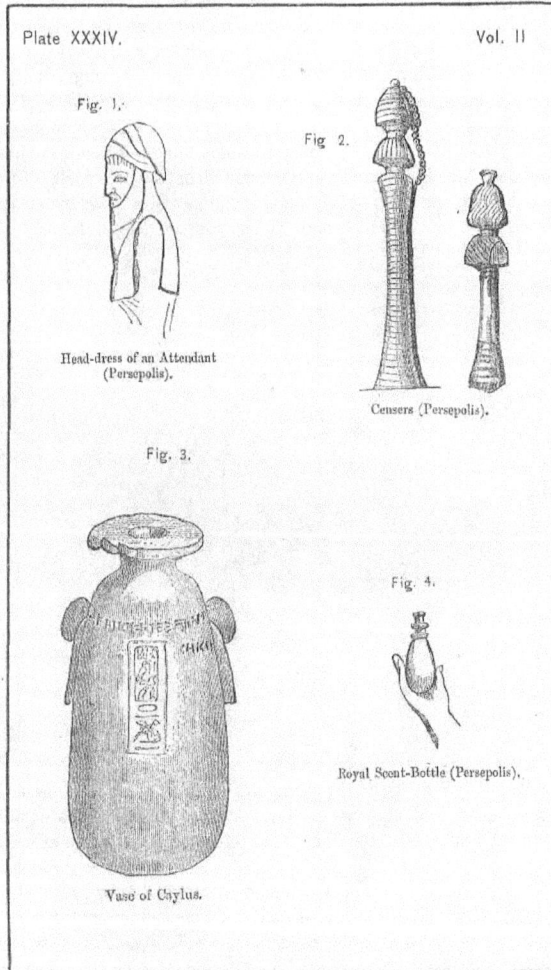

Plate XXXIV.   Vol. II

Fig. 1.

Fig 2.

Head-dress of an Attendant
(Persepolis).

Censers (Persepolis).

Fig. 3.

Fig. 4.

Royal Scent-Bottle (Persepolis).

Vase of Caylus.

PLATE XXXIV

The rank of the bow-bearer was probably nearly as great as that of the driver of the chariot. He was privileged to stand immediately behind the monarch on grand occasions, so carrying in his left hand the weapon from which he derived his appellation. The quiver-bearer had the next place. Both wore the Median costume—the candys, or flowing robe, the girdle, the high shoe, and the stiff fluted cap, or, perhaps, occasionally the simple fillet. Sometimes the two offices would seem to have been held by the same person, unless we are to attribute this appearance, where it occurs, to the economy of the artist, who may have wished to save himself the trouble of drawing two separate figures. [PLATE XXXIII., Fig. 5.]

The parasol-bearer was attired as the bow and quiver bearers, except that he was wholly unarmed, and had the fillet for his proper head-dress. Though not a military officer, he accompanied the monarch in his expeditions, since in the midst of war there might be occasions of state when his presence would be convenient. The officer who bore the royal fan and handkerchief had generally the same costume; but sometimes his head was enveloped in a curious kind of cowl or muffler, which covered the whole of it except the forehead, the eyes, the nose, the mouth, and the upper portion of the cheeks. [PLATE XXXIV., Fig. 1.]

The fan, or fly-chaser, had a long straight handle, ornamented with a sort of beading, which held a brush of some springy fibrous matter. [PLATE XXXIII., Fig. 4.] The bearer, whose place was directly behind the monarch, held his implement, which bent forward gracefully, nearly at arm's length over his master's head.

It would seem that occasionally the bearer of the handkerchief laid aside his fly-chaser, and assumed in lieu of it a small bottle containing perfumery. [PLATE XXXIV., Fig. 4.] In a sculptured tablet at Persepolis, given by Ker Porter, an attendant in the Median robe, with a fillet upon his head, who bears the handkerchief in the usual way in his left hand, carries in the palm of his right what seems to be a bottle, not-unlike the scent-bottle of a modern lady. It has always been an Oriental custom to wash the hands before meals, and the rich commonly mix some perfumery or other with the water. We may presume that this was the practice at the Persian Court, and that the Great King therefore took care to have an officer, who should at all times be ready to provide his guests, or himself, with the scent which was most rare or most fashionable.

The Persians seem to have been connoisseurs in scents. We are told that, when the royal tiara was not in wear, it was laid up carefully with a mixture of myrrh and labyzus, to give it an agreeable odor. Unguents were thought to have been a Persian invention, and at any rate were most abundantly used by the upper classes of the nation. The monarch applied to his own person an ointment composed of the fat of lions, palm wine, saffron, and the herb helianthes, which was considered to increase the beauty of the complexion. He carried with him, even when he went to the wars, a case of choice unguents; and such a treasure fell into the hands of Alexander, with the rest of Darius's camp equipage, at Arbela. It may be suspected that the "royal ointment" of the Parthian kings, composed of cinnamon, spikenard, myrrh, cassia, gum styrax, saffron, cardamum, wine, honey, and sixteen other ingredients, was adopted from the Persians, who were far more likely than the rude Parthians to have invented so recondite a mixture. Nor were scents used only in this form by the ingenious people of whom we are speaking. Arabia was required to furnish annually to the Persian crown a thousand talents' weight of frankincense; and there is reason to believe that this rare spice was largely employed about the Court, since the walls of Persepolis have several representations of censers, which are sometimes carried in the hands of an attendant, while sometimes they stand on the ground immediately in front of the Great King.321 [PLATE XXXIV., Fig. 2.]

The box or vase in which the Persians commonly kept their unguents was of alabaster. This stone, which abounded in the country, was regarded as peculiarly suited for holding ointments, not only by the Persians, but also by the Egyptians, the Greeks, and (probably) the Assyrians. The Egyptian variety of stone seems to have been especially valued; and vases appear to have been manufactured in that country for the use of the Persian monarch, which were transmitted to the Court, and became part of the toilet furniture of the palace.330 [PLATE XXXIV., Fig. 3.]

Among the officers of the Court, less closely attached to the person of the monarch than those above enumerated, may be mentioned the steward of the household; the groom or master of the horse; the chief eunuch, or keeper of the women; the king's "eyes" and "ears," persons whose business it was to keep him informed on all matters of importance; his scribes or secretaries, who wrote his letters and his edicts; his messengers, who went his errands; his ushers, who introduced strangers to him; his "tasters," who tried the various dishes set before him lest they should be poisoned; his cupbearers who handed him his wine, and tasted it; his chamberlains, who assisted him to bed; and his musicians, who amused him with song and harp. Besides these, the Court comprised various classes of guards, and also doorkeepers, huntsmen, grooms, cooks, and other domestic servants in great abundance, together with a vast multitude of visitors and guests, princes, nobles, captives of rank, foreign refugees, ambassadors, travellers. We are assured that the king fed daily within the precincts of his palace as many as fifteen thousand persons, and that the cost of each day's food was four hundred talents. A thousand beasts were slaughtered for each repast, besides abundance of feathered game and poultry. The beasts included not only sheep, goats, and oxen, but also stags, asses, horses, and camels. Among the feathered delicacies were poultry, geese, and ostriches.

The monarch himself rarely dined with his guests. For the most part he was served alone. Sometimes he admitted to his table the queen and two or three of his children. Sometimes, at a "banquet of wine," a certain number of privileged boon companions were received, who drank in the royal presence, not, however, of the same wine, nor on the same terms.

The monarch reclined on a couch with golden feet, and sipped the rich wine of Helbon; the guests drank an inferior beverage, seated upon the floor. At a great banquet, it was usual to divide the guests into two classes. Those of lower degree were entertained in an outer court or chamber to which the public had access, while such as were of higher rank entered the private apartments, and drew near to the king. Here they were feasted in a chamber opposite to the king's chamber, which had a curtain drawn across the door, concealing him from their gaze, but not so thick as to hide them from their entertainer. Occasionally, on some very special occasion, as, perhaps, on the Royal birthday, or other great festival, the king presided openly at the banquet, drinking and discoursing with his lords, and allowing the light of his countenance to shine freely upon a large number of guests, whom, on these occasions, he treated as if they were of the same flesh and blood with himself. Couches of gold and silver were spread for all, and "royal wine in abundance" was served to them in golden goblets. On these, and, indeed, on all occasions, the guests, if they liked, carried away any portion of the food set before them which they did not consume at the time, conveying it to their homes, where it served to support their families.

The architecture of the royal palace will be discussed in another chapter; but a few words may be said in this place with respect to its furniture and general appearance. The pillared courts and halls of the vast edifices which the Achaemenian monarchs raised at Susa and Persepolis would have had a somewhat bare and cold aspect, if it had not been for their internal fittings. The floors were paved with stones of various hues, blue, white, black, and red, arranged doubtless into patterns, and besides were covered in places with carpeting. The spaces between the pillars were filled with magnificent hangings, white green, and violet, which were fastened with cords of fine linen (?) and purple to silver rings and pillars of marble, screening the guests from sight, while they did not too much exclude the balmy summer breeze. The walls of the apartments were covered with plates of gold. All the furniture was rich and costly. The golden throne of the monarch stood under an embroidered canopy or awning supported by four pillars of gold inlaid with precious stones. [PLATE

XXXV.] Couches resplendent with silver and gold filled the rooms. The private chamber of the monarch was adorned with a number of objects, not only rich and splendid, but valuable as productions of high art. Here, impending over the royal bed, was the golden vine, the work of Theodore of Samos, where the grapes were imitated by means of precious stones, each of enormous value. Here, probably, was the golden plane-tree, a worthy companion to the vine, though an uncourtly Greek declared it was too small to shade a grasshopper. Here, finally, was a bowl of solid gold, another work of the great Samian metallurgist, more precious for its artistic workmanship than even for its material.

Canopy of Persian Throne (Persepolis).

PLATE XXXV

Nothing has hitherto been said of the Royal harem or seraglio, which, however, as a feature of the Court always important, and ultimately preponderating over all others, claims a share of our attention. In the early times, it would appear that the Persian kings were content with three or four wives, and a moderate number of concubines. Of the wives there was always one who held the most exalted place, to whom alone appertained the title of "Queen," and who was regarded as "wife" in a different sense from the others. Such was Atossa to Darius Hystaspis, Amestris to Xerxes, Statira to Darius Codomannus. Such, too, were Vashti and Esther to the prince, whoever he was, whose deeds are recorded in Scripture under the name of Ahasuerus. The chief wife, or Queen-Consort, was privileged to wear on her head a royal tiara or crown. She was the acknowledged head of the female apartments or Gynaeceum, and the concubines recognized her dignity by actual prostration. On great occasions, when the king entertained the male part of the Court, she feasted all the females in her own part of the palace. She had a large revenue of her own, assigned her, not so much by the will of her husband, as by an established law or custom. Her dress was splendid, and she was able to indulge freely that love of ornament of which few Oriental women are devoid. Though legally subject to her husband as much as the meanest of his slaves, she could venture on liberties which would have been fatal to almost any one else, and often, by her influence over the monarch, possessed a very considerable share of power.

The status of the other wives was very inferior to this; and it is difficult to see how such persons were really in a position much superior to that of the concubines. As daughters of the chief nobles— for the king could only choose a wife within a narrow circle—they had, of course, a rank and dignity independent of that acquired by marriage; but otherwise they must have been almost on a par with those fair inmates of the Gynaeceum who had no claim even to the name of consort. Each wife had probably a suite of apartments to herself, and a certain number of attendants—eunuchs, and tirewomen—at her disposal; but the inferior wives saw little of the king, being only summoned each in their turn to share his apartment, and had none of the privileges which made the position of chief wife so important.

The concubines seem to have occupied a distinct part of the Gynaeceum, called "the second house of the women." They were in the special charge of one of the eunuchs, and were no doubt kept under strict surveillance. The Empire was continually searched for beautiful damsels to fill the harem, a constant succession being required, as none shared the royal couch more than once, unless she attracted the monarch's regard very particularly. In the later times of the Empire, the number of the concubines became enormous, amounting (according to one authority) to three hundred and twenty-nine, (according to another) to three hundred and sixty. They accompanied the king both in his wars and in his hunting expeditions. It was a part of their duty to sing and play for the royal delectation; and this task, according to one author, they had to perform during the whole of each night. It is a more probable statement that they entertained the king and queen with music while they dined, one of them leading, and the others singing and playing in concert.

The Gynaeceum—in the Susa palace, at any rate—was a building distinct from the general edifice, separated from the "king's house" by a court. It was itself composed of at least three sets of apartments—viz. apartments for the virgins who had not yet gone into the king, apartments for the concubines, and apartments for the Queen-Consort and the other wives. These different portions were under the supervision of different persons. Two eunuchs of distinction had the charge respectively of the "first" and of the "second house of the women." The Queen-Consort was, at any rate nominally, paramount in the third, her authority extending over all its inmates, male and female.

Sometimes there was in the Gynaeceum a personage even more exalted than any which have as yet been mentioned. The mother of the reigning prince, if she outlived his father, held a position at the Court of her son beyond that even of his Chief Wife. She kept the ensigns of royalty which she had worn during the reign of her husband; and wielded, as Queen-Mother, a far weightier and more domineering authority than she ever exercised as Queen-Consort. The habits of reverence and obedience, in which the boy had been reared, retained commonly their power over the man; and the monarch who in public ruled despotically over millions of men, succumbed, within the walls of the seraglio, to the yoke of a woman, whose influence he was too weak to throw off. The Queen-Mother had her seat at the royal table whenever the king dined with his wife; and, while the wife sat below, she sat above the monarch. She had a suite of eunuchs distinct from those of her son. Ample revenues were secured to her, and were completely at her disposal. She practically exercised—though she could not perhaps legally claim—a power of life and death. She screened offenders from punishment, procuring for them the royal pardon, or sheltering them in her own apartments; and she poisoned, or openly executed, those who provoked her jealousy or resentment.

The service of the harem, so far as it could not be fitly performed by women, was committed to eunuchs. Each legitimate wife—as well as the Queen-Mother—had a number of these unfortunates among her attendants; and the king intrusted the house of the concubines, and also that of the virgins, to the same class of persons. His own attendants seem likewise to have been chiefly eunuchs. In the later times, the eunuchs acquired a vast political authority, and appear to have then filled all the chief offices of state. They were the king's advisers in the palace, and his generals in the field. They superintended the education of the young princes, and found it easy to make them their tools. The plots and conspiracies, the executions and assassinations, which disfigure the later portion of the Persian annals, maybe traced chiefly to their intrigues and ambition. But the early Persian annals are free from these horrors; and it is clear that the power of the eunuchs was, during this period, kept within narrow bounds. We hear little of them in authentic history till the reign of Xerxes. It is remarkable that the Persepolitan sculptures, abounding as they do in representations of

Court life, of the officers and attendants who approached at all closely to the person of the monarch, contain not a single figure of a eunuch in their entire range. We may gather from this that there was at any rate a marked difference between the Assyrian and the early Persian Court in the position which eunuchs occupied at them respectively: we should not, however, be justified in going further and questioning altogether the employment of eunuchs by the Persian monarchs during the early period, since their absence from the sculptures may be accounted for on other grounds.

It is peculiarly noticeable in the Persian sculptures and inscriptions that they carry to excess that reserve which Orientals have always maintained with regard to women. The inscriptions are wholly devoid of all reference to the softer sex, and the sculptures give us no representation of a female. In Persia, at the present day, it is regarded as a gross indecorum to ask a man after his wife; and anciently it would seem that the whole sex fell under a law of taboo, which required that, whatever the real power and influence of women, all public mention of them, as well as all representations of the female form, should be avoided. If this were so, it must of course still more have been the rule that the women—or, at any rate, those of the upper classes—should not be publicly seen. Hence the indignant refusal of Vashti to obey the command of King Aha-suerus to show herself to his Court. Hence, too, the law which made it a capital offence to address or touch one of the royal concubines or even to pass their litters upon the road. The litters of women were always curtained; and when the Queen Statira rode in hers with the curtains drawn, it was a novelty which attracted general attention, as a relaxation of the ordinary etiquette, though only females were allowed to come near her. Married women might not even see their nearest male relatives, as their fathers and brothers; the unmarried had, it is probable, a little more liberty.

As the employment of eunuchs at the Persian Court was mainly in the harem, and in offices connected therewith, it is no wonder that they shared, to some extent, in the law of taboo, which forbade the representation of women. Their proper place was in the female courts and apartments, or in close attendance upon the litters, when members of the seraglio travelled, or took the air—not in the throne-room, or the antechambers, or the outer courts of the palace, which alone furnished the scenes regarded as suitable for representation.

Of right, the position at the Persian Court immediately below that of the king belonged to the members of certain privileged families. Besides the royal family itself—or clan of the Achaemenidae—there were six great houses which had a rank superior to that of all the other grandees. According to Herodotus these houses derived their special dignity from the accident that their heads had been fellow-conspirators with Darius Hystaspis; but there is reason to suspect that the rank of the families was precedent to the conspiracy in question, certain families conspiring because they were great, and not becoming great because they conspired. At any rate, from the time of Darius I., there seem to have been seven great families, including that of the Achaemenidae, whose chiefs had the privilege of free communication with the monarch, and from which he was legally bound to choose his legitimate wives. The chiefs appear to have been known as "the Seven Princes," or "the Seven Counsellors," of the king. They sat next to him at public festivals; they were privileged to tender him their advice, whenever they pleased; they recommended important measures of state, and were, in part, responsible for them; they could demand admission to the monarch's presence at any time, unless he were in the female apartments; they had precedence on all great occasions of ceremony, and enjoyed a rank altogether independent of office. Sometimes—perhaps most commonly—they held office; but they rather conferred a lustre on the position which they consented to fill, than derived any additional splendor from it.

It does not appear that the chiefs of the seven great families had any peculiar insignia. Officers of the Court, on the contrary, seem to have always carried, as badges marking their position, either wands about three feet in length, or an ornament resembling a lotos blossom, which is sometimes seen in the hands of the monarch himself. Such officers wore, at their pleasure, either the long Median robe and the fluted cap, or the close-fitting Persian tunic and trousers, with the loose felt [Greek name]. All had girdles, in which sometimes a dagger was placed; and all had collars of gold about their necks, and earrings of gold in their ears. The Median robes were of various colors—scarlet, purple, crimson, dark gray, etc. Over the Persian tunic a sleeved cloak, or great coat, reaching to the ankles, was sometimes worn; this garment was fastened by strings in front, and descended loosely from the shoulders, no use being commonly made of the sleeves, which hung empty at the wearer's side. [PLATE XXXVI., Fig. 1.]

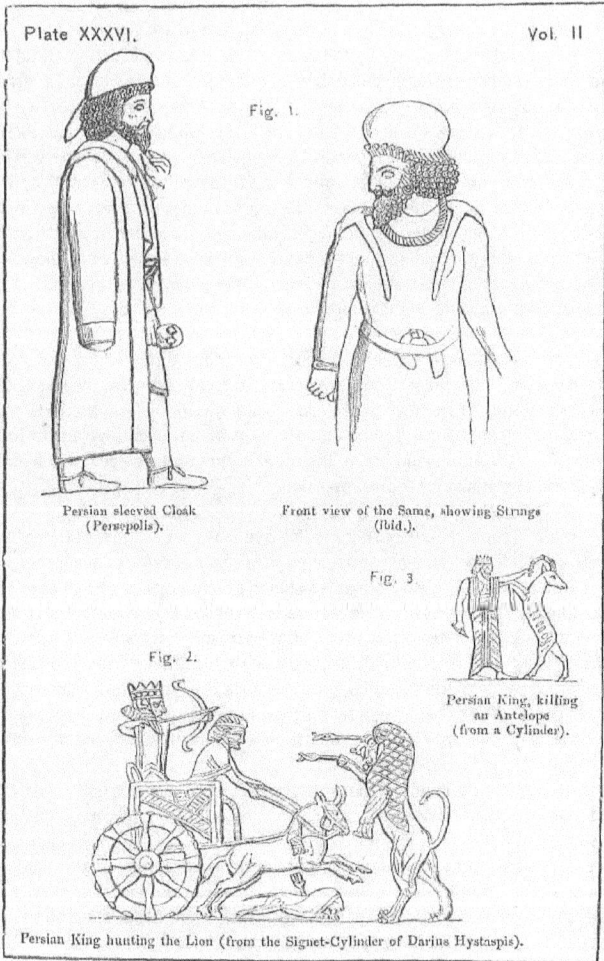

Plate XXXVI.   Vol. II

Fig. 1.

Persian sleeved Cloak   Front view of the Same, showing Strings
(Persepolis).   (ibid.).

Fig. 3

Fig. 2.

Persian King, killing
an Antelope
(from a Cylinder).

Persian King hunting the Lion (from the Signet-Cylinder of Darius Hystaspis).

PLATE XXXVI

An elaborate Court ceremonial was the natural accompaniment of the ideas with respect to royalty embodied in the Persian system. Excepting the "Seven Princes," no one could approach the royal person unless introduced by a Court usher, Prostration—the attitude of worship—was required of all as they entered the presence. The hands of the persons introduced had to be hidden in their sleeves so long as their audience lasted. In crossing the Palace Courts it was necessary to abstain carefully from touching the carpet which was laid for the king to walk on. Coming into the king's presence unsummoned was a capital crime, punished by the attendants with instant death, unless the monarch himself, as a sign that he pardoned the intrusion, held out towards the culprit the golden sceptre which he bore in his hands. It was also a capital offence to sit down, even unknowingly, upon the royal throne; and it was a grave misdemeanor to wear one of the king's cast-off dresses. Etiquette was almost as severe on the monarch himself as on his subjects. He was required to live chiefly in seclusion; to eat his meals, for the most part, alone; never to go on foot beyond the palace walls; never to revoke an order once given, however much he might regret it; never to draw back from a promise, whatever ill results he might anticipate from its performance. To maintain the quasi-divine character which attached to him it was necessary that he should seem infallible, immutable, and wholly free from the weakness of repentance.

As some compensation for the restrictions laid upon him, the Persian king had the sole enjoyment of certain luxuries. The wheat of Assos was sent to the Court to furnish him with bread, and the vines of Helbon were cultivated for the special purpose of supplying him with wine. Water was conveyed to Susa for his use from distant streams regarded as specially sweet and pure; and in his expeditions he was accompanied, by a train of wagons, which were laden with silver flasks, filled from the clear stream of the Choaspes. The oasis of Ammon contributed the salt with which he seasoned his food. All the delicacies that the Empire anywhere produced were accumulated on his board, for the supply of which each province was proud to send its best and choicest products.

The chief amusements in which the Great King indulged were hunting and playing at dice. Darius Hystaspis, who followed the chase with such ardor as on one occasion to dislocate his ankle in the pursuit of a wild beast, had himself represented on his signet-cylinder as engaged in a lion-hunt. From this representation, we learn that the Persian monarchs, like the Assyrian, pursued the king of beasts in their chariots, and generally despatched him by means of arrows. Seated in a light car, and attended by a single unarmed charioteer, they invaded the haunts of these fiercest of brutes, rousing them from their lairs—probably with Indian hounds, and chasing them at full speed if they fled, or, if they faced the danger, attacking them with arrows or with the javelin. [PLATE XXXVI., Fig. 2.] Occasionally the monarch might indulge in this sport alone; but generally he was (it seems) accompanied by some of his courtiers, who shared the pleasures of the chase with him on the condition that they never ventured to let fly their weapons before he had discharged his. If they disregarded this rule they were liable to capital punishment, and might esteem themselves fortunate if they escaped with exile.

Besides lions, the Persian monarch chased, it is probable, stages, antelopes, wild asses, wild boars, bears, wild sheep, and leopards. [PLATE XXXVI., Fig. 3.] These animals all abounded in the neighborhood of the royal palaces, and they are enumerated by Xenophon among the beasts hunted by Cyrus. The mode of chasing the wild ass was for the horsemen to scatter themselves over the plain, and to pursue the animal in turns, one taking up the chase when the horse of another was exhausted. The speed of the creature is so great that no horse with a rider on his back can long keep pace with him; and thus relays were necessary to tire him out, and enable the hunters to bring him within the range of their weapons.

When game was scarce in the open country, or when the kings were too indolent to seek it in its native haunts, they indulged their inclination for sport by chasing the animals which they kept in their own "paradises." These were walled enclosures of a large size, well wooded, and watered with sparkling streams, in which were bred or kept wild beasts of various kinds, chiefly of the more harmless sorts, as stags, antelopes, and wild sheep. These the kings pursued and shot with arrows, or brought down with the javelin; but the sport was regarded as tame, and not to be compared with hunting in the open field.

Within the palace the Persian monarchs are said to have amused themselves with dice. They played, it is probable, chiefly with their near relatives, as their wives, or the Queen-Mother. The stakes, as was to be expected, ran high, as much as a thousand darics (nearly L 1100.) being sometimes set on a single throw. Occasionally they played for the persons of their slaves, eunuchs, and others, who, when lost, became the absolute property of the winner.

Another favorite royal amusement was carving or planing wood. According to AElian, the Persian king, when he took a journey, always employed himself, as he sat in his carriage, in this way; and Ctesias speaks of the occupation as pursued also within the walls of the palace. Manual work of this kind has often been the refuge of those rulers, who, sated with pleasure and devoid of literary tastes, have found time hang heavy upon their hands.

In literature a Persian king seems rarely to have taken any pleasure at all. Occasionally, to beguile the weary hours, a monarch may have had the "Book of the Chronicles of the Kings of Persia and Media" read before him; but the kings themselves never opened a book, or studied any branch of science or learning. The letters, edicts, and probably even the inscriptions, of the monarch were the composition of the Court scribes, who took their orders from the king or his ministers, and clothed them in their own language. They did not even call upon their master to sign his name to a parchment; his seal, on which his name was engraved, sufficiently authenticated all proclamations and edicts.

Among the more serious occupations of the monarch were the holding of councils, the reviewing of troops, the hearing of complaints, and the granting or refusing of redress, the assignment of rewards, perhaps, in some cases, the trying of causes, and, above all, the general direction of the civil administration and government of the Empire. An energetic king probably took care to hear all the reports which were sent up to the Court by the various officials employed in the actual government of the numerous provinces, as well as those sent in by the persons who from time to time inspected, on the part of the Crown, the condition of this or that satrapy. Having heard and considered these reports, and perhaps taken advice upon them, such a monarch would give clear directions as to the answers to be sent, which would be embodied in despatches by his secretaries, and then read over to him, before he affixed his seal to them. The concerns of an empire so vast as that of Persia would have given ample employment for the greater part of the day to any monarch who was determined not only to reign, but to govern. Among the Persian sovereigns there seems to have been a few who had sufficient energy and self-denial to devote themselves habitually to the serious duties of their office. Generally, however, the cares of government were devolved upon some favorite adviser, a relative, or a eunuch, who was entrusted by the monarch with the entire conduct of affairs, in order that he might give himself up to sensual pleasures, to the sports of the field, or to light and frivolous amusements.

The passion for building, which we have found so strong in Assyria and Babylonia, possessed, but in a minor degree, a certain number of the Persian monarchs. The simplicity of their worship giving little scope for architectural grandeur in the buildings devoted to religion, they concentrated their main efforts upon the construction of palaces and tombs. The architectural character of these works will be considered in a later chapter. It is sufficient to note here that a good deal of the time and attention of many monarchs were directed to these objects; and particularly it is interesting to remark, that, notwithstanding their worldly greatness, and the flattering voices of their subjects, which were continually bidding them "live for ever," the Persian kings were quite aware of the frail tenure by which man holds his life, and, while they were still in vigorous health, constructed their own tombs.

It was an important principle of the Magian religion that the body should not after death be allowed to mingle with, and so pollute, any one of the four elements. Either from a regard for this superstition, or from the mere instinctive desire to preserve the lifeless clay as long as possible, the Persians entombed their kings in the following way. The body was placed in a golden coffin, which was covered with a close-fitting lid, and deposited either in a massive building erected to serve at once as a tomb and a monument, or in a chamber cut out of some great mass of solid rock, at a considerable elevation above its base. In either case, the entrance into the tomb was carefully closed, after the body had been deposited in it, by a block or blocks of stone. [PLATE XXXVII., Fig. 1.] Inside the tomb were placed, together with the coffin, a number of objects, designed apparently for the king's use in the other world, as rich cloaks and tunics, trousers, purple robes, collars of gold, earrings of gold, set with gems, daggers, carpets, goblets, and hangings. Generally the tomb was ornamented with sculptures, and sometimes, though rarely, it had an inscription (or inscriptions) upon it, containing the name and titles of the monarch whose remains reposed within.

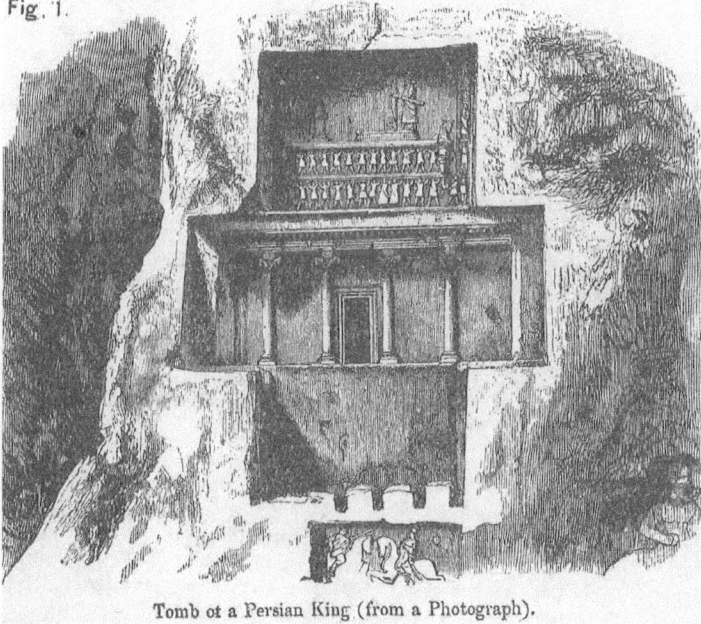

Fig. 1.

Tomb of a Persian King (from a Photograph).
PLATE XXXVII

If the tomb were a building, and not rock-hewn, the ground in the vicinity was formed into a park or garden, which was planted with all manner of trees. Within the park, at some little distance from the tomb, was a house, which formed the residence of a body of priests, who watched over the safety of the sepulchre.

Plate XXXVIII.   Vol. II.

Fig. 1

Fragment of Two-Horse Chariot (from Persepolis).

Fig 2

Ordinary Persian Costume.

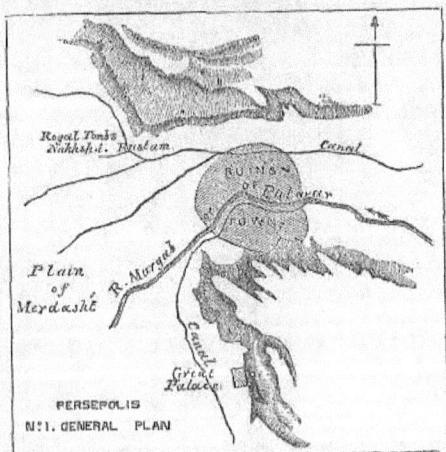

Fig. 3.

PLATE XXXVIII

The Greeks seem to have believed that divine honors were sometimes paid to a monarch after his decease; but the spirit of the Persian religion was so entirely opposed to any such observance that it is most probable the Greeks were mistaken. Observing that sacrifices were offered once a month in the vicinity of some of the royal tombs, they assumed that the object of the cult was the monarch himself, whereas it was no doubt really addressed either to Ormazd or to Mithras. The Persians cannot rightly be accused of the worship of dead men, a superstition from which both the Zoroastrian and the Magian systems were entirely free.

From this account of the Persian monarchs and their Court, we may now turn to a subject which moderns regard as one of much greater interest—the general condition, manners, and customs of the Persian people. Our information on these points is unfortunately far less full than on the subject which we have been recently discussing, but still it is perhaps sufficient to give us a tolerably complete notion of the real character of the nation.

The Persians, according to Herodotus, were divided into ten tribes, of which four were nomadic and three agricultural. The nomadic were the Dai, the Mardi, the Dropici, and the Sagartii; the agricultural were the Panthilaei, the Derusisei, and the Germanii, or Carmanians. What the occupation of the other three tribes was Herodotus does not state; but, as one of them—the Pasargadae—was evidently the ruling class, consisting, therefore (it is probable), of land owners, who did not themselves till the soil, we may perhaps assume that all three occupied this position, standing in Persia somewhat—as the three tribes of Dorians stood to the other Greeks in the Peloponnese. If this were the case, the population would have been really divided broadly into the two classes of settled and nomade, whereof the former class was subdivided into those who were the lords of the soil, and those who cultivated it, either as farmers or as laborers, under them.

The ordinary dress of the poorer class, whether agricultural or nomade, was probably the tunic and trousers of leather which have been already mentioned as the true national costume of the people. The costume was completed by a loose felt cap upon the head, a strap or belt round the waist, and a pair of high shoes upon the feet, tied in front with a string. [PLATE XXXVIII., Fig. 2.] In later times a linen or muslin rag replaced the felt cap, and the tunic was lengthened so as to reach half way between the knee and the ankle.

The richer classes seem generally to have adopted the Median costume which was so prevalent at the Court. They wore long purple or flowered robes with loose hanging sleeves, flowered tunics reaching to the knee, also sleeved, embroidered trousers, tiaras, and shoes of a more elegant shape than the ordinary Persian. Nor was this the whole of their dress. Under their trousers they wore drawers, under their tunics shirts, on their hands gloves, and under their shoes socks or stockings—luxuries these, one and all, little known in the ancient world. The Persians were also, like most Orientals, extremely fond of ornaments. Men of rank carried, almost as a matter of course, massive chains or collars of gold about their necks, and bracelets of gold upon their arms. The sheaths and handles of their swords and daggers were generally of gold, sometimes, perhaps, studded with gems. Many of them wore earrings. Great expense was lavished on the trappings of the horses which they rode or drove; the bridle, or at least the bit, was often of solid gold, and the rest of the equipment was costly. Among the gems which were especially affected, the pearl held the first place. Besides being set in the ordinary way, it was bored and strung, in order that it might be used for necklaces, bracelets, and ankles. Even children had sometimes golden ornaments, which were preferred when the gold was of a reddish color.

Very costly and rich too was the furniture of the better class of houses. The tables were plated or inlaid with silver and gold. Splendid couches, spread with gorgeous coverlets, invited the inmates to repose at their ease; and, the better to insure their comfort, the legs of the couches were made to rest upon carpets, which were sufficiently elastic to act as a sort of spring, rendering the couches softer and more luxurious than they would otherwise have been. Gold and silver plate, especially in the shape of drinking-cups, was largely displayed in all the wealthy mansions, each household priding itself on the show which it could make of the precious metals.

In respect of eating and drinking, the Persians, even better sort, were in the earlier times noted for their temperance and sobriety. Their ordinary food was wheaten bread, barley-cakes, and meat simply roasted or boiled, which they seasoned with salt and with bruised cress-seed, a substitute for mustard. The sole drink in which they indulged was water. Moreover, it was their habit to take one meal only each day. The poorer kind of people were contented with even a simpler diet, supporting themselves, to a great extent, on the natural products of the soil, as dates, figs, wild pears, acorns, and the fruit of the terebinth-tree. But these abstemious habits were soon laid aside, and replaced by luxury and self-indulgence, when the success of their arms had put it in their power to have the full and free gratification of all their desires and propensities. Then, although the custom of having but one meal in the day was kept up, the character of the custom was entirely altered by beginning the meal early and making it last till night. Not many sorts of meat were placed on the board, unless the occasion was a grand one; but course after course of the lighter kinds of food flowed on in an almost endless succession, intervals of some length being allowed between the courses to enable the guests to recover their appetites. Instead of water, wine became the usual beverage; each man prided himself on the quantity he could drink; and the natural result followed that most banquets terminated in general intoxication. Drunkenness even came to be a sort of institution. Once a year, at the feast of Mithras, the king of Persia, according to Duris, was bound to be drunk. A general practice arose of deliberating on all important affairs under the influence of wine, so that, in every household, when a family crisis impended, intoxication was a duty.

The Persians ate, not only the meats which we are in the habit of consuming, but also the flesh of goats, horses, asses, and camels. The hump of the last-named animal is considered, even at the present day, a delicacy in many parts of the East; but in ancient Persia it would seem that the entire animal was regarded as fairly palatable. The horse and ass, which no one would touch in modern Persia, were thought, apparently, quite as good eating as the ox; and goats, which were far commoner than sheep, appeared, it is probable, oftener at table. The dietery of a grand house was further varied by the admission into it of poultry and game—the game including wild boars, stags, antelopes, bustards, and probably partridges; the poultry consisting of geese and chickens. Oysters and other fish were used largely as food by the inhabitants of the coast-region.

Grades of society were strongly marked among the Persians; and the etiquette of the Court travelled down to the lowest ranks of the people. Well-known rules determined how each man was to salute his equal, his inferior, or his superior; and the observance of these rules was universal. Inferiors on meeting a decided superior prostrated themselves on the ground; equals kissed each other on the lips; persons nearly but not quite equals kissed each other's cheeks. The usual Oriental rules prevailed as to the intercourse of the sexes. Wives lived in strict seclusion within the walls of the Gynaeceum, or went abroad in litters, seeing no males except their sons, their husbands, and their husbands' eunuchs. Concubines had somewhat more freedom, appearing sometimes at banquets, when they danced, sang, and played to amuse the guests of their master.

The Persian was allowed to marry several wives, and might maintain in addition as many concubines as he thought proper. Most of the richer class had a multitude of each, since every Persian prided himself on the number of his sons, and it is even said that an annual prize was given by the monarch to the Persian who could show most sons living. The concubines were not unfrequently Greeks, if we may judge by the case of the younger Cyrus, who took two Greek concubines with him when he made his expedition against his brother. It would seem that wives did not ordinarily accompany their husbands, when these went on military expeditions, but that concubines were taken to the wars by most Persians of consideration. Every such person had a litter at her disposal, and a number of female attendants, whose business it was to wait upon her and execute her orders.

All the best authorities are agreed that great pains were taken by the Persians—or, at any rate, by those of the leading clans—in the education of their sons. During the first five years of his life the boy remained wholly with the women, and was scarcely, if at all, seen by his father. After that time his training commenced. He was expected to rise before dawn, and to appear at a certain spot, where he was exercised with other boys of his age in running, slinging stones, shooting with the bow, and throwing the javelin. At seven he was taught to ride, and soon afterwards he was allowed to begin to hunt. The riding included, not only the ordinary management of the horse, but the power of jumping on and off his back when he was at speed, and of shooting with the bow and throwing the javelin with unerring aim, while the horse was still at full gallop. The hunting was conducted by state-officers, who aimed at forming by its means in the youths committed to their charge all the qualities needed in war. The boys were made to bear extremes of heat and cold, to perform long marches, to cross rivers without wetting their weapons, to sleep in the open air at night, to be content with a single meal in two days, and to support themselves occasionally on the wild products of the country, acorns, wild pears, and the fruit of the terebinth-tree. On days when there was no hunting they passed their mornings in athletic exercises, and contests with the bow or the javelin, after which they dined simply on the plain food mentioned above as that of the men in the early times, and then employed themselves during the afternoon in occupations regarded as not illiberal—for instance, in the pursuits of agriculture, planting, digging for roots, and the like, or in the construction of arms and hunting implements, such as nets and springes. Hardy and temperate habits being secured by this training, the point of morals on which their preceptors mainly insisted was the rigid observance of truth. Of intellectual education they had but little. It seems to have been no part of the regular training of a Persian youth that he should learn to read. He was given religious notions and a certain amount of moral knowledge by means of legendary poems, in which the deeds of gods and heroes were set before him by his teachers, who recited or sung them in his presence, and afterwards required him to repeat what he had heard, or, at any rate, to give some account of it. This education continued for fifteen years, commencing when the boy was five, and terminating when he reached the age of twenty.

The effect of this training was to render the Persian an excellent soldier and a most accomplished horseman. Accustomed from early boyhood to pass the greater part of every day in the saddle, he never felt so much at home as when mounted upon a prancing steed. On horseback he pursued the stag, the boar, the antelope, even occasionally the bear or the lion, and shot his arrows, or slung his stones, or hurled his javelin at them with deadly aim, never pausing for a moment in his career. [PLATE XXXVII., Fig. 2.] Only when the brute turned on his pursuers, and stood at bay, or charged them in its furious despair, they would sometimes descend from their coursers, and receive the attack, or deal the coup de grace on foot, using for the purpose a short but strong hunting-spear. [PLATE XXXVII., Fig. 3.] The chase was the principal delight of the upper class of Persians, so long as the ancient manners were kept up, and continued an occupation in which the bolder spirits loved to indulge long after decline had set in, and the advance of luxury had changed, to a great extent, the character of the nation.

At fifteen years of age the Persian was considered to have attained to manhood, and was enrolled in the ranks of the army, continuing liable to military service from that time till he reached the age of fifty. Those of the highest rank became the body-guard of the king, and these formed the garrison of the capital. They were a force of not less than fourteen or fifteen thousand men. Others, though liable to military service, did not adopt arms as their profession, but attached themselves to the

Court and looked to civil employment, as satraps, secretaries, attendants, ushers, judges, inspectors, messengers. A portion, no doubt, remained in the country districts, and there followed those agricultural pursuits which the Zoroastrian religion regarded as in the highest degree honorable. But the bulk of the nation must, from the time of the great conquests, have passed their lives mainly, like the Roman legionaries under the Empire, in garrison duty in the provinces. The entire population of Persia Proper can scarcely have exceeded two millions. Not more than one fourth of this number would be males between the ages of fifteen and fifty. This body of 500,000 men, besides supplying the official class at the Court and throughout the provinces, and also furnishing to Persia Proper those who did the work of its cultivation, had to supply to the whole Empire those large and numerous garrisons on whose presence depended the maintenance of the Persian dominion in every province that had been conquered. According to Herodotus, the single country of Egypt contained, in his day, a standing army of 120,000 Persians; and, although this was no doubt an exceptional case, Egypt being more prone to revolt than any other satrapy, yet there is abundant evidence that elsewhere, in almost every part of the Empire, large bodies of troops were regularly maintained; troops which are always characterized as "Persians." We may suspect that under the name were included the kindred nation of the Medes, and perhaps some other Arian races, as the Hyrcanians, and the Bactrians, for it is difficult to conceive that such a country as Persia Proper could alone have kept up the military force which the Empire required for its preservation; but to whatever extent the standing army was supplemented from these sources, Persia must still have furnished the bulk of it; and the demands of this service must have absorbed, at the very least, one third if not one half of the adult male population.

For trade and commerce the Persians were wont to express extreme contempt. The richer classes made it their boast that they neither bought nor sold, being supplied (we must suppose) from their estates, and by their slaves and dependents, with all that they needed for the common purposes of life. Persians of the middle rank would condescend to buy, but considered it beneath them to sell; while only the very lowest and poorest were actual artisans and traders. Shops were banished from the more public parts of the towns; and thus such commercial transactions as took place were veiled in what was regarded as a decent obscurity. The reason assigned for this low estimation of trade was that shopping and bargaining involved the necessity of falsehood.

According to Quintus Curtius, the Persian ladies had the same objection to soil their hands with work that the men had to dirty theirs with commerce. The labors of the loom, which no Grecian princess regarded as unbecoming her rank, were despised by all Persian women except the lowest; and we may conclude that the same idle and frivolous gossip which resounds all day in the harems of modern Iran formed the main occupation of the Persian ladies in the time of the Empire.

With the general advance of luxury under Xerxes and his successors, of which something has been already said, there were introduced into the Empire a number of customs of an effeminate and demoralizing character. From the earliest times the Persians seem to have been very careful of their beards and hair, arranging the latter in a vast number of short crisp curls, and partly curling the former, partly training it to hang straight from the chin. After a while, not content with this degree of care for their personal appearance, they proceeded to improve it by wearing false hair in addition to the locks which nature had given them, by the use of cosmetics to increase the delicacy of their complexions, and by the application of a coloring matter to the upper and lower eyelids, for the purpose of giving to the eye an appearance of greater size and beauty. They employed a special class of servants to perform these operations of the toilet, whom the Greeks called "adorners". Their furniture increased, not merely in splendor, but in softness; their floors were covered with carpets, their beds with numerous and delicate coverlets; they could not sit upon the ground unless a cloth was first spread upon it; they would not mount a horse until he was so caparisoned that the seat on his back was softer even than their couches. At the same time they largely augmented the number and variety of their viands and of their sauces, always seeking after novel delicacies, and offering rewards to the inventors of "new pleasures." A useless multitude of lazy menials was maintained in all rich households, each servant confining himself rigidly to a single duty, and porters, bread-makers, cooks, cup-bearers, water-bearers, waiters at table, chamberlains, "awakers," "adorners," all distinct from one another, crowded each noble mansion, helping forward the general demoralization. It was probably at this comparatively late period that certain foreign customs of a sadly lowering character were adopted by this plastic and impressible people, who learnt the vice of paederasty from the Greeks, and adopted from the Assyrians the worship of Beltis, with its accompaniment of religious prostitution.

On the whole the Persians may seem to have enjoyed an existence free from care, and only too prosperous to result in the formation of a high and noble character. They were the foremost Asiatic people of their time, and were fully conscious of their pre-eminency. A small ruling class in a vast Empire, they enjoyed almost a monopoly of office, and were able gradually to draw to themselves much of the wealth of the provinces. Allowed the use of arms, and accustomed to lord it over the provincials, they themselves maintained their self-respect, and showed, even towards the close of their Empire, a spirit and an energy seldom exhibited by any but a free people. But there was nevertheless a dark side to the picture—a lurking danger which must have thrown a shadow over the lives of all the nobler and richer of the nation, unless they were utterly thoughtless. The irresponsible authority and cruel dispositions of the kings, joined to the recklessness with which they delegated the power of life and death to their favorites, made it impossible for any person of eminence in the whole Empire to feel sure that he might not any day be seized and accused of a crime, or even without the form of an accusation be taken and put to death, after suffering the most excruciating tortures. To produce this result, it was enough to have failed through any cause whatever in the performance of a set task, or to have offended, even by doing him too great a service, the monarch or one of his favorites. Nay, it was enough to have provoked, through a relation or a connection, the anger or jealousy of one in favor at Court; for the caprice of an Oriental would sometimes pass over the real culprit and exact vengeance from one quite guiltless—even, it may be, unconscious—of the offence given. Theoretically, the Persian was never to be put to death for a single crime; or at least he was not to suffer until the king had formally considered the whole tenor of his life, and struck a balance between his good and his evil deeds to see which outweighed the other. Practically, the monarch slew with his own hand any one whom he chose, or, if he preferred it, ordered him to instant execution, without trial or inquiry. His wife and his mother indulged themselves in the same pleasing liberty of slaughter, sometimes obtaining his tacit consent to their proceedings, sometimes without consulting him. It may be said that the sufferers could at no time be very many in number, and that therefore no very wide-spread alarm can have been commonly felt; but the horrible nature of many of the punishments, and the impossibility of conjecturing on whom they might next fall, must be set against their infrequency; and it must be remembered that an awful horror, from which no precautions can save a man, though it happen to few, is more terrible than a score of minor perils, against which it is possible to guard. Noble Persians were liable to be beheaded, to be stoned to death, to be suffocated with ashes, to have their tongues torn out by the roots, to be buried alive, to be shot in mere wantonness, to be flayed and then crucified, to be buried all but the head, and to perish by the lingering agony of "the boat." If they escaped these modes of execution, they might be secretly poisoned, or they might be exiled, or transported for life. Their wives and daughters might be seized and horribly mutilated, or buried alive, or cut into a number of fragments. With these perils constantly impending over their heads, the happiness of the nobles can scarcely have been more real than that of Damocles upon the throne of Dionysius.

In conclusion, we may notice as a blot upon the Persian character and system, the cruelty and barbarity which was exhibited, not only in these abnormal acts of tyranny and violence, but also in the regular and legal punishments which were assigned to crimes and offences. The criminal code, which—rightly enough—made death the penalty of murder, rape, treason, and rebellion, instead of stopping at this point, proceeded to visit with a like severity even such offences as deciding a cause wrongfully on account of a bribe, intruding without permission on the king's privacy, approaching near to one of his concubines, seating oneself, even accidentally, on the throne, and the like. The modes of execution were also, for the most part, unnecessarily cruel. Poisoners were punished by having their heads placed upon a broad stone, and then having their faces crushed, and their brains beaten out by repeated blows with another stone. Ravishers and rebels were put to death by crucifixion. The horrible punishment of "the boat" seems to have been no individual tyrant's cruel conception, but a recognized and legal form of execution. The same may be said also of burying alive. Again the Persian secondary punishments were for the most part exceedingly barbarous. Xenophon tells us, as a proof of the good government maintained by the younger Cyrus, in his satrapy, that under his sway it was common to see along all the most frequented roads numbers of persons who had had their hands or feet cut off, or their eyes put out, as a punishment for thieving and rascality. And other writers relate that similar mutilations were inflicted on rebels, and even on prisoners of war. It would seem, indeed, that mutilation and scourging were the ordinary forms of secondary punishment used by the Persians, who employed imprisonment solely for the safe custody of an accused person between his arrest and his execution, while they had recourse to transportation and exile only in the case of political offenders.

CHAPTER IV

LANGUAGE AND WRITING

It has been intimated in the account of the Median Empire which was given in a former-volume that the language of the Persians, which was identical, or almost identical, with that of the Medes, belonged to the form of speech known to moderns as Indo-European. The characteristics of that form of speech are a certain number of common, or at least widely spread, roots, a peculiar mode of inflecting, together with a resemblance in the inflections, and a similarity of syntax or construction. Of the old Persian language the known roots are, almost without exception, kindred forms to roots already familiar to the philologist through the Sanscrit, or the Zend, or both; while many are of that more general type of which we have spoken—forms common to all, or most of the varieties of the Indo-European stock. To instance in a few very frequently recurring words—"father" is in old Persian (as in Sanscrit) pitar, which differs only in the vocalization from the Zendic patar, the Greek [ ], and the Latin pater, and of which cognate forms are the Gothic fadar, the German voter, the English father, and the Erse athair.

CHAPTER IV.

LANGUAGE AND WRITING.

Τῆς Περσίδος γλώσσης ὅσα ἠδύνατο.—Thucyd. i. 38.

It has been intimated in the account of the Median Empire which was given in a former volume that the language of the Persians, which was identical, or almost identical, with that of the Medes, belonged to the form of speech known to moderns as Indo-European.[1] The characteristics of that form of speech are a certain number of common, or at least widely spread, roots, a peculiar mode of inflecting, together with a resemblance in the inflections, and a similarity of syntax or construction. Of the old Persian language the known roots are, almost without exception, kindred forms to roots already familiar to the philologist through the Sanscrit, or the Zend, or both; while many are of that more general type of which we have spoken—forms common to all, or most of the varieties of the Indo-European stock. To instance in a few very frequently recurring words—"father" is in old Persian (as in Sanscrit) *pitar*, which differs only in the vocalization from the Zendic *patar*, the Greek πατήρ, and the Latin *pater*, and of which cognate forms are the Gothic *fadar*, the German *vater*, the English *father*, and the Erse *athair*. "Name" is in old Persian (as in both Zend and Sanscrit) *nâma*, for which we have in Greek, ὄνομα, in Latin *nomen*, in German *nahme* or *name*, in English *name*. "Man" is *martiya*, for which we have in Greek βρότος, in Latin *mortalis*, in English *mortal*, in modern Persian, *merd*. "Horse" is *açpa*, the same as in Zend, with which may be compared the Sanscrit *açva*, the modern Persian *asp*, the Greek ἵππ-ος, the Welsh *osw*, and even the Latin *equus*.[2]

The following table (pp. 366, 367) exhibits a number of similar instances.

With respect to inflections, we may observe first, that the original masculine nominatival ending (as was long ago observed by Herodotus[3]) was *sh* or *s*—the same as in Latin and

Old Persian.	Sanscrit.	Zend.	Greek.	Latin.	German.	English.	Mod. Persian.
Aj (to drive)	aj	az	ἀγ-ειν	ag-ere		to act.	
Api (water)	áp	ap		aqua (?)	aue	av (in Av-on	ab.
Amiya (I am)	asmi	ahmi	εἰμί	sum		am	am.
Arika (hostile)	ari		ἔρις	rixa (?)			
Bad (to bind)	bandh	bahd			binden	bind	bas-tan (band).
Bar (to carry)	bhri	bere	φέρειν	ferre	fuhren	bear	bur-dan.
Bu (to be)	bhu	bu			bin	be	bu-dan.
Bumi (earth)	bhumi	bumi		humus			bumi.
Brâtar (brother)	bhrâtar	brâtar		frater	bruder	brother	birader.
Cha (and)	ka	ka	καί	que			
Cta (to stand)	sthâ	çta	ἵστημι	sto	stehen	stand	ista-dan.
Dâ (to give)	dhâ	dâ	δίδωμι	da-re			da-dan.
Dâ (to know)	dâ, dô	dao	δάω	doc-eo (?)			dan-istan.
Darsh (to dare)		dars	θαρσ-εῖν	au-dere	dürfen	dare.	
Duvarâ (door)	dvara	dvara	θύρα	(fores) (?)	thüre	door	dar.
Duvitiya (second)	dvitiyâ	bitya	δεύτερος	duo	zweite	two	du.
Fratama (first)	prathamâ	frathema	πρῶτος	primus	frum's (Goth)	first.	
Garma (warm)		gharemo	θερμός (?)		warm	warm	gherm.
Garb (to take)	gribh, grabh	gerev	ἁρπ-άζω	rapio	greifen	gripe	girif-tan.
Gausha (the ear)		gaosha	οὖς	auris, ausculto	ohr	ear	gush.
Gub (to speak)	gup			jubeo (?)		gab, gabble	guf-tan.
Had-ish (a seat)		hadhis	ἕδος κ. τ. λ	sed-es	sitz	seat.	
Hama (together)		hama	ἁμά	cum			ham.
I (to go)	i	i	ἰέναι	i-re			
Jan (to strike, kill)	han	zan, jan	θέν-ω				zan.
Jiv (to live)	jiv	jiv, jvo	ζάΓω	vivo			zis-tan.
Ka (who)	ka	ka		quis	hva (O. G.)	who	ki.
Khshnas (to know)			γιγνώσ-κω	gnos-co	kennen	know	shinâs.
Mâm (me)	mâm	manm	ἐμέ, με	me	mich	me	man.

Old Persian.	Sanscrit.	Zend.	Greek.	Latin.	German.	English.	Mod. Persian.
Man (to think)	man	man	μένος	mens	meinen	mean.	
Man (to wait)		mann	μένω	maneo			man-dan.
Mar (to die)	mri	mere	(βρότος)	morior			mur-dan.
Matar	mâtar	mâtar	μήτηρ	mater	mutter	mother	mader.
Mathista (greatest)	mazista		{ μείζων / μέγιστος }			mightiest, most.	
Mâha (month)	mas	mâogha	μήν	mensis	monat	month	mah.
Nâha (nose)	nâsâ	naogha		nasus	nase	nose.	
Napat (grandson)	napât	napô	(ἀνεφιός)	nepos	neffe	nephew	nava.
Navama (ninth)	navamâ	nâuma	ἐννέΓα	novem	neun	nine	navam.
Nâvi (ship)	naus	naviya	ναῦς	navis	nacho (O. G.)		nau.
Niya (not)	na, nih	naedha	νη-	ne-	ni-cht	nay, not	na.
Pad (foot, footstep)	pâda	pndhu	πόδ-α	ped-em	fuss	foot	pâ.
Paça (after)		paç-kat		post			pas.
Pathi (path)	panthan	pâtha	πάτος	pons (?)	pfad	path.	
Raçta (right)	raj	raz		rectus	richtig	right	rast.
Shim (him)		him	ὅν		ihn	him	ash.
Tars (to fear)	tras	tereç	τρέ-ω	tre-mo		tremble	tars.
Tigra (an arrow, sharp)	tigma	tighra			degen (?)	dagger (?)	tir.
Taumâ (family)	tokma	taokhma	(τέκω)	stemma	stamm	stem	tukhm.
Thah (to say)	ças	çagh			sagen	say	sukhn(speech).
Tritiya (third)	tritiyâ	thritya	τρίτος	tertius	dritte	third.	
Tuvam (thou)	twam	tum	τύ, σύ	tu	du	thou	tu.
Vaj (to bring)	vah	vaz		veho.			
Vâ (or, enclit.)	vâ	vâ		ve			vâ.
Vayam (we)	vayam	vaêm			wir	we.	
U (good)	su	hu	εὖ	euge			khub.
Utâ (and)	utâ	uta		et	und (?)	and (?).	

Greek;[4] and this ending is found whenever the final vowel of the root is *i* or *u;* as in *Kurush, Daryavush, Fravartish*, and the like. When, however, the final root-vowel happened to be *â*, the *s* was dropped, first, perhaps, passing into a breathing, and then becoming absorbed in the vowel.[5] Thus we have *Auramazdâ, Artakhshatrâ, khshatrapâ* (satrap), etc. Where the root ended in a consonant, the final consonant was sometimes dropped, and the preceding vowel sound elongated—as *brâtar*, nom. *brâtâ*, "brother" *pitar*, nom. *pitâ*, "father;" *jatar*, nom. *jatâ*, "enemy;" *napat*, nom. *napâ*, "grandson;" while at other times the consonant was retained, either with or without the light *a;* e.g. *açpa*, "a horse," *martiya*, "a man," *kauf*, "a mountain," *daraug*, "a lie," etc. Feminine nominatives usually ended in *-â* long; a few had *-i* as their final vowel; and these seem to have taken the masculine nominatival sign *-sh;* e.g. *shiyatish*, "happiness."[6] Neuters appear to have ended only in *-am*, a form analogous to the Latin *-um* and Greek *-ov*; examples are *avahanam*, "dwelling;" *hamaranam*, "battle;" *vardanam*, "city, state."

Besides the nominative, the ancient Persians recognized five other cases. These were the genitive, the accusative, the vocative, the ablative, and the locative.[7] The dative was wanting, and its force was expressed through the genitive.

The genitive singular of nouns masculine in *â* was formed ordinarily by the addition of *hya*, with which we may compare the Sanscrit *-sya* and the Greek *-oio*.[8] Other masculine nouns formed the genitive by adding to the root *-a*,[9] which probably stood for *-ah*, the Old Persian equivalent of the Sanscrit genitival *-as*. Masculines in *-ish* and *-ush* made the genitive in *-aish* and *-aush*, as *Kur-ush*, *Kur-aush*; *Fravart-ish*, *Fravart-aish*. Feminines in *â* formed the genitive by adding *-yâ*, as *taumâ*, "a family," gen. *taumâyâ;* those in *-ish* changed *-ish* into *-iya*, as *bumish*, "the earth," gen. *bumiya*. The genitive of neuter nouns does not occur in the inscriptions.

The universal sign of the accusative singular was *-m*.[10] Nouns whose nominative ended in *-sh* made the accusative by changing *-sh* into *-m*. Nouns in *-â* or *-â* took *-m* in addition. The closest analogy to this is furnished by the Latin; but we may compare also the Greek *-v*, the German *-n* ("den ihn"), and our own *-m* in "him," and "whom."

The vocative seems to have ended, as in Sanscrit, with the root-vowel of the word, which, if not already long, was elongated; e.g. *martiyâ*, "man," voc. *martiyâ*, "O man."

The ablative is thought to have terminated originally in -*at;*[11] but the *t* fell away, and the regular sign of the case became the long -*â*. (Compare the Latin ablative of nouns in -*a* and -*as*.)

The ordinary sign of the locative (which in Sanscrit and Zend is -*i*) was in the Old Persian -*ya* or -*iya*. Masculine nouns in -*ă* took the full form -*iya*, as *Armina*, loc. *Armina-iya*. Feminines in -*â* took -*yá*, as *Athura*, loc. *Athuráyá; Arbirá*, loc. *Arbiráyá*. Feminines in -*i* took sometimes simply -*yá*, as *api*, "water," loc. *apiyá;* sometimes they changed -*i* into *aiyá*, as *Bakhtri*, loc. *Bakhtraiyá; Harauvati*, loc. *Harauva-taiyá*. Themes in -*u* took *v* as the characteristic of the locative instead of *y*,[12] the masculines changing -*u* into *auva* (with a short final ă), and the feminines changing -*u* or -*au* into -*auvá* (with the long *á*). Examples of masculines are *Babiru*, loc. *Babirauva; Margu*, loc. *Margauva;* of feminines, *dahyâu*, "a province," loc. *dahyauvá; Ufratu*, "the Euphrates," loc. *Ufra-tauvá*.

The nominative plural of roots in -*ă* seem to have been origi- nally formed by changing ă into *áha*—the proper Persian equivalent of the Vedic -*ásas*—and this ending is found in the plural of one word, viz. *baga*, "God," which makes nom. pl. *bagáha*. The termination -*áha* was, however, in most in- stances contracted into -*á;*[13] e.g. *martyá*, "men;" *khshaya-thiyá*, "kings," and the like. The nominative plural of roots in -*â*, -*i* and -*u* is unknown, the inscriptions furnishing no ex- amples.

The sign of the genitive plural was the suffix -*nám*[14] (compare the Latin -*rum*), which was preceded by -*á*, *i* (?) or -*u*, accord- ing to the characteristic vowel of the theme; e.g. *baga*, gen. pl. *bagánám; khshayathiya*, gen. pl. *khshayathiyánám; dahyâu*, gen. pl. *dahyunám*. The accusative plural[15] of roots in -*a* and -*am* was the same as the nominative plural, e.g. *martiya*, "a man," acc. pl. *martiyá*, "men;" *hamaranám*, "a battle," acc. pl. *hamaraná*, "battles."

No vocatives plural have been found. The ablative plural was formed by the addition of -*bish* or -*ibish* (compare the Latin -*ibus*[16] to the root of the word, as *baga*, *bagaibish; vith*, *vithibish; rauca*, *raucabish*, etc.

The sign of the locative plural was the suffix -*shuva*,[17] which in themes with the light -ă became -*ishuva*, as *Mada*, "a Mede," *Madaishuva*, "among the Medes."

The following are examples of the declensions so far as they are known to us:

Declension of Nouns ending in ă.

Sing.		Plural.	
N. Mada...............	a Mede.	Madâ..................	Medes.
G. Madahyâ..	of a Mede.	Madânam.............	of Medes.
Ac. Madam........	a Mede	Madâ..............	Medes.
V. Madâ..	O Mede.	Madâ (?)	O Medes.
Abl. Madâ...............	by a Mede.	Madaibish............	by Medes.
Loc. Madaiya...........	with a Mede.	Madaishuva..........	with the Medes

Declension of Nouns masculine ending in â.

Sing.	Plural.
N. Auramazdâ.	Wanting.
G. Auramazdâha.	
Ac. Auramazdâm.	
V. Auramazdâ.	
Abl. Auramazdâ,	
Loc. Auramazdayâ (?)	

Declension of Nouns feminine ending in â.

Sing.		Plural.
N. Taumâ........	a family.	Unknown.
G. Taumâyâ......	of a family.	
Ac. Taumân (?)...	a family.	
V. Taumâ........	O family.	
Abl. Taumâyâ	by a family.	
Loc. Taumâyâ.....	in a family.	

Declension of Nouns ending in i and ish.

Sing.		Plural.
N. Apish...................	water.	Unknown.
G. Apâish	of water.	
Ac. Apim..................	water.	
V. Unknown, prob. Api.		
Abl. Unknown.		
Loc. Apiya.................	in water.	

Declension of Nouns ending in ush.

Sing.		Plural.	
N. Dahyâ-ush.........	a province.	Dahyâ-va...........	provinces.
G. Dahyâ-âush (?)	of a province.	Dahy-unâm..........	of provinces.
Ac. Dahyâ-um.........	a province.	Dahyâ-va............	provinces.
V. Unknown		Unknown.	
Abl. Unknown		Unknown.	
Loc. Dahyâ-uva.........	in a province.	Dahy-ushuvâ........	in provinces.

Declension of Nouns neuter ending in am.

Sing.		Plural.	
N. Hamaranam.......	a battle.	Hamaranâ...........	battles.
G. Unknown.		Unknown.	
Ac. Hamaranam........	a battle.	Hamaranâ...........	battles.
V. Unknown.		Unknown.	
Abl. Unknown.		Unknown.	
Loc. Unknown.		Unknown.	

ADJECTIVES.

Adjectives appear to have followed in all respects the inflections of nouns. They ended generally in the weak -a; but one
theme in -u has been found (paru, "much"), and there may
also have been themes in -i.

The following is an example of an ordinary adjective in -*a*. (Forms of the adjective not actually found are printed in italics.)

Sing.

M.	F.	N.
N. vazark-a.	vazark-â.	*vazark-am.*
G. vazark-ahyâ.	vazark-âyâ.	(unknown).
Ac. vazarg-am.	*vazark-âm.*	vazark-am.
V. vazark-â.	(unknown).	(unknown).
Abl. vazark-â.	*vazark-âyâ.*	(unknown).
Loc. vazark-aiya.	vazark-âyâ.	(unknown).

Plural.

M.	F.	N.
N. vazark-â.	vazark-â.	*vazark-â.*
G. vazark-ânâm.	vazark-ânâm.	(unknown).
Ac. vazark-â.	vazark-â.	*vazark-â.*
V. vazark-â (?).	(unknown).	(unknown).
Abl. vazark-aibish.	(unknown).	(unknown).
Loc. vazark-aishuva.	vazark-auva.	(unknown).

As in Sanscrit,[18] the comparative degree of adjectives seems to have been formed by adding -*tara* to the positive, e.g. *apa*, "distant," *apa-tara*, "the more distant;" the superlative by adding -*tama*, e.g. *fra*, *fra-tama*, "the first." There was also a superlative in -*ista* (compare the Greek ιστος), which would seem to imply a comparative in -*iyas*.[19] The only known example of this superlative is *mathista*, "greatest."

NUMERALS.

The numerals are but little known to us, owing to the practice which prevailed of writing them by the means of signs. A single wedge, placed perpendicularly, marked one (Ỿ); two such signs marked two, and so on up to nine; the sign of ten was the double wedge, or arrow head (ᐸ), and this was used for the tens up to ninety. To mark a hundred the horizontal wedge was probably used (ᐳ—).

A few numerals only, and those, in every case, ordinals, have reached us through the inscriptions. They are *fratama*, "the first," *duvitiya*, "the second," *tritiya*, "the third," and *navama*, "the ninth."[20] *Fratama*, for which the Zend has *fratema*, combines the formative letters which we find separately in πρῶτος and *pri-mus*. Its root *fra* is cognate with προ. *Duvitiya* corresponds closely with δεύτερος, as *tritiya* does

with τρίτος and *tertius. Navama,* "ninth," implies a car-
dinal number, very closely resembling *novem.*

<h2 style="text-align:center">PRONOUNS.</h2>

The personal pronouns in Old Persian, as in most Indo-
European tongues, were declined very irregularly—the different
cases really belonging to completely distinct roots. The roots
themselves are without exception such as occur in other cognate languages,[21] and approach very closely indeed to the
forms used in the Zend, as will appear by the subjoined
declensions.

Declension of âdam," I."

Sing.		Plural.	
Old Persian.	Zend.	Old Persian.	Zend.
N. âdam	azem.	vayam.................	vaem.
G. manâ	mana.	amâkham.... ....ahmâkem.	
Ac. { mâm	mana.	(unknown).	
{ -maiya (*encl.*).			
Abl. ma (*encl.*).	....	(unknown).	

The pronoun of the second person is known to us only in the
singular, in which it is declined as follows :—

Nom. Tuvam................." thou " (comp. Sans. *tvam* and Zend *tum*).
Gen. -taiya or -taya (*encl.*).
Acc. Thuvâm (compare Sans *tvâm* and Zend *thwañm*).
Voc. Tuvam.

The ordinary pronoun of the third person is *hauva,* which is
declined as follows :—

Sing.

M.	F.	N.
N. Hauva.	Hauva.	Ava.
G. Avahyâ.	(Unknown.)	(Unknown.)
Ac. { Avam.	(Unknown.)	Ava.
{ -shim (*enclitic*).		
Abl. -shaiya (*encl.*).	(Unknown.)	(Unknown.)

Plural.

M.	F.	N.
N. Avaiya.	Avâ	(Unknown.)
G. { Avaishâm.	(Unknown.)	(Unknown.)
{ -shâm (*encl.*).		
Ac. { Avaiyâ.	(Unknown.)	(Unknown.)
{ -shim, -shish (*encl.*).	-shim (*encl.*).	
Abl. -âhâm (*encl.*).	-shâm (*encl.*).	

Strictly speaking, *hauva* is the more remote demonstrative,
equivalent to our "that;" but practically its use is personal.

There appear to have been originally three such demonstratives in the Old Persian, *hauva*, *ava*, and *shi* or *shish*, from the surviving cases of which the above declension is made up.

Hauva is probably identical with the Sanscrit *sas* (*sa*, *so*) and the Zend *hau* (*hô*).[22] *Ava* has no exact equivalent in Sanscrit or Zend; but its inflections have mostly their Zendic representatives—the gen. *avahyá* corresponding to *avaghê*, the acc. *avam* to *aom*, the nom. masc. pl. *avaiya* to *avâ*, the nom. fem. pl. *avâ* to *avâo*, and the gen. pl. *avaishâm* to *avaêshâm*. The third element, *shi*, which has furnished the pronominal suffixes, *shish*, *shim*, *shâm*, and *shaiya*, corresponds to the Zend *hoi*, *hê*, and *shê*, which are used for the genitive and dative singular of the third person in all genders.[23]

The nearer demonstrative, "this," is expressed by *iyam*, which is declined as follows :—

Sing.

	M.	F.	N.
N.	Iyam.	Iyam.	Ima.
G.	(Unknown.)	Ahyâyâ.	(Unknown,)
Ac.	Imam.	Imâm.	Ima.
Abl. or *Instr.*	Anâ.	(Unknown.)	(Unknown.)

Plural.

	M.	F.	N.
N.	ImaIya.	Imâ.	(Unknown.)
G.	(Unknown.)	(Unknown.)	(Unknown.)
Ac.	Imaiya.	Imâ.	Imâ.
Abl. or *Instr.*	(Unknown.)	(Unknown.)	(Unknown.)

Here again the agreement with the Zend, and also with the Sanscrit, is very complete.[24]

The relative, "who," "which," is rendered by *hya*. Its declension, so far as we can trace it out, is the following:—

Sing.

	M.	F.	N.
N.	Hya.	Hyâ.	Tya.
G.	(Unknown.)	(Unknown.)	(Unknown.)
Ac.	Tyam.	Tyâm.	Tya.
Voc.	Hyâ.	(Unknown.)	(Unknown.)
Abl.	Tyanâ.	(Unknown.)	(Unknown.)

Plural.

	M.	F.	N.
N.	Tyaiya.	Tyâ.	Tyâ.
G.	Tyanisâm.	Tyaisâm.	(Unknown.)
Ac.	Tyaiya.	Tyâ.	Tyâ.
Abl.	(Unknown.)	(Unknown.)	(Unknown.)

Other pronouns are *ka*, "who" (interrog.);[25] *aita*, "it;" *aniya*, "another;" *uvá*, "self," "own" (compare Lat. *suus*), which is found only in composition; *kashchiya*, "any one" (compare Lat. *quisque*); *hama*, "all" (compare Lat. *omnis*); *haruva*, "all," etc.

VERBS.

The verb in old Persian had three voices, Active, Middle, and Passive; but of these the middle differed in form very slightly from the Passive. The moods recognized were the Indicative, the Imperative, the Subjunctive or Potential, and the Infinitive. The tenses seem to have been the present, the imperfect, the aorist, and the perfect. There was no future, the deficiency being supplied by the present subjunctive, which had a future force.

Of the verb substantive *amiya* (= sum), the conjugation, so far as we know it, is the following:

INDICATIVE.

Present.

Amiya............ "I am."   Amahya........ ..... "we are."
Ahya .... "Thou art." (Unknown.)
Astiya............ "He is."   Hatiya[26] .... "they are."

Imperfect.

Aham .... "I was."   (Unknown.)
(Unknown.)   (Unknown.)
Aha................ "He was."   Aha ... . "they are."

Imperfect Middle.

Ahata or Ahatâ.............. "they became."

CONJUNCTIVE.

Present.

Ahatiya...................... "He may be."

It is impossible to give anything like a complete example of the conjugation of a regular verb. The inscriptions are so similar in their character, and run so much in the same groove, that, while we have abundant examples of certain forms, the great majority of the forms are wanting. Suffice it to notice a few points in which the conjugation resembled the Greek or the Latin, or both, such as the following.

Past time was usually marked by prefixing an augment, the augment used being the long *á*, which was regularly attached to the imperfect and aorist tenses, as *jan*, imperf. *ájanam;* *thah*, imperf. *áthaham;* *dá*, imperf. *ádadá;* aor. *ádá*. The perfect tense, which occurs but rarely, seems to have had, instead of the augment, a reduplication; as *kar*, *chakhriyá*.

The ordinary sign of the first person singular was -*mi* or -*m* (compare Greek, εἰμί τίθημι. Latin su*m*, era*m*, si*m*, esse*m*, etc.); of the first person plural, -*mahya* or *mâ* (Latin, -*mus*; Æol. Greek, -*μες*); of the third person singular, -*sh* (Greek, τίθησι; English, "ha*s*," "i*s*"); but this sign was commonly dropped; of the third person plural, -*tiya* or (according to Spiegel) -*ñtiy* (compare Greek, τύπτονται; Latin, "su*nt*").

The past participle ended in -*ta*, as *karta*, neut. *kartam* "done;" *dâta*, "given," from *dâ*; *pâta*, "protected," from *pâ*; *basta*, "bound" from *bad*, etc. (Compare the Sanscrit and Latin past participles.)

ADVERBS.

Of adverbs, the most important are those of time and place. Among adverbs of time the old Persian had the following: *yathâ*, "when;" *thakatâ*, "then;" *pasâva*, "afterwards;" *aparam*, "hereafter;" *paruvam*, "before;" *daragam*, "long;" *duvaistam*, "long ago;" and *duvitatâranam*, "for a length of time." Among those of places were *idâ*, "here;" *avadâ*, "there;" *apataram*, "elsewhere;" and *amutha*, "thence."

The ordinary negative was *niya*,[27] "not;" but besides this there was a negative of prohibition, *mâ*, corresponding exactly to the Greek μή and the Latin *ne*, in such phrases as μή γένοιτο *ne facias*, and the like.[28]

Among adverbs of quality may be mentioned *vasiya*, "much," "greatly," "often;" and *darsham*, "wholly," "entirely;" the former of which occurs very frequently in the inscriptions.

PREPOSITIONS.

Among prepositions the following have been satisfactorily identified: *hachâ*, "from;" *abiya*, *patiya*, "to;" *abish*, "by;" *ni*, "in;" *hadâ*, "with;" *upa*, "near;" *ayasta*, "near" or "by;" *patish*, "before" (= Latin *coram*); *pasâ*, "behind," "after;" *pariya*, "concerning;" *atara*, "among;" *anuva*, "along;" *atiya*, "across;" *upariya*, "over," "above;" and *athiya*, "over against." Of these, *abiya* may be compared with the Greek ἐπί, *ni* with ἐνί, *pariya* with περί, *upariya* with Greek ὑπέρ, Latin *super*, *athiya* with ἀντί, *upa* with Latin *apud*, *pasa* with *post*, *ayasta* with *juxta*, and *atara* with *inter*. *Hachâ*, *hadâ*, *patiya*, and *anuva*, have close correspondents in the Zend,[29] but none in languages with which the ordinary reader is familiar.

Two or three other prepositions, which are not found separately, are indicated by compound words, in which they occur as an element. Thus *hama*[30] seems to have had the sense of the Greek ἀνά or ὁμοῦ, and *tara* that of the Latin *trans*, with which they are etymologically connected. *Parâ* had also apparently the sense of "from" or "away."[31]

CONJUNCTIONS.

Of conjunctions the most common were *uta* and *·cha* (enclitic), "and;" which corresponded respectively to the Latin *et* and *que; va*, "or" (compare Latin *ve*); *avathâ*, "thus," "so" (compare Greek οὔτω); *yatha*, "as," its correlative; *tya*, "that;" *aivam*, "both—and" (used like the Latin *tum—tum*); *avâ*, "so long"—*yava*, "as;" *chitâ*, "all the while"—*yâtâ*, "until;" *yadiya*, "if;" and *matiya*, "lest" (compare the Greek μήτι).

SYNTAX.

The ordinary rules of Indo-European syntax were (as might be supposed) observed in the old Persian. Adjectives agreed with their substantives in gender, number, and case. Thus we have *kara Parsa* "the Persian people," in the nominative, but *karam Parsam uta Madam*, "the Persian and Median people," in the accusative; *imâm bumim*, "this earth" (accus.); *ahyayâ bumiyâ vazarkayâ*, "of this great earth" (gen.); *Baga vazarka*, "a great God" (nom.); *hadâ vithaibish Bagaibish*, "with the tutelary Gods" (abl.), etc. Relative pronouns agreed with their antecedents in number, gender, and person, but their case depended on the verb accompanying them; as *iyam dahyavush*, tyâm *manâ Auramazdâ frâbara*, "this province which Ormazd has given me"—*ima dahyâva*, tyâ *adam adarshiya*, "these provinces which I have possessed"—*avam kâram*, hya *manâ niya gaubatiya*, "that people which is not called mine," etc.

The latter of two substantives was placed in the genitive case; as, *khshâyathiya khshayathiyanâm*, "king of kings"—*Vishtaspahyâ putra*, "son of Hystaspes," and the like. The genitive case also followed the superlative; as *mathishta Bagânâm* "the greatest of the Gods."

Verbs commonly governed the accusative, as *mâm khshâyathiyam akunaush*, "he made me king;" *khshatram hauva agarbayatâ*, "he seized the empire," etc. When the force of the verb passed on to a second object, that object was expressed by the genitive-dative case; as *Auramazdâ khshatram manâ frâbara*, "Ormazd granted me the empire;" *manâ bajim abaratâ*, "they brought me tribute." Occasionally a verb governed a double accusative, as *khshatramshim adinam*, "I took the empire from him."

Prepositions generally governed the accusative or the ablative. The accusative followed *abiya*, "to," "after;" *athiya*, "over," "against," "near;" *atara*, "among;" *pariya* "concerning;" *patiya*, "to," "for;" *patish*, "in face of;" *upa*, "near;" and *upariya*, "over," "above." *Hadâ*, "with," and *hachâ*, "from," took the ablative. The locative followed *anuva*, "along," and perhaps sometimes *patiya* and *abish*.[32] *Pasâ*, "after," took a genitive.

Among the peculiarities of old Persian syntax may be mentioned the following: (1.) The pronouns had in certain cases an enclitic form, wherein they could be attached to almost any kind of word:[33] e.g. *Auramazdâ-maiya upastam abara*, "Oromasdes mihi opem tulit"—*adam*shim *avajanam*, "Ego eum occidi"—*hachâ*ma, "a me"—*mâm Auramazdâ patuva*, *utâ*maiya *khshatram*, *utâ tya*maiya *kartam*, "Me Oromazdes protegat, et mihi imperium, et quod a me factum." (2.) Adjectives, instead of simply accompanying their substantives, were often joined to them by the relative pronoun *hya*, the relative being in such cases attracted into the case of the noun, e.g. *kâra* hya *hamitriya*, *kâram* tyam *Mâdam*, *pathim* tyam *raçtam*, etc. (3.) The genitive of the personal pronoun was usually employed in the place of a possessive pronoun: e.g. manâ *badaka* "meus servus" (lit. "*mei* servus"); amâkham *taumâ*, "nostra familia" (lit. "*nostrûm* familia"), etc. Sometimes a redundant relative accompanied these expressions; as, hyâ *amâkham taumâ*, "quæ nostrûm familia," *i.e.* "familia nostra." (4.) The substantive verb was most commonly omitted from a sentence,[34] as *Adam Kurush*, "Ego Cyrus"—*i.e.* "Ego *sum* Cyrus."

In conclusion, a passage is subjoined, accompanied by an interlinear Latin translation, whereby the close similarity of the syntactical construction, and order of the words, in the Latin and the Old Persian will be apparent.

Baga	*vazarka*	*Auramazdâ*,	*hya*	*imâm*	*bumim*	*adâ*,	*hya*	*avam*
Deus	magnus	Oromasdes,	qui	hanc	terram	dedit,	qui	istud
asmânam	*adâ*,	*hya*	*mortiyam*	*adâ*,	*hya*	*shiyâtim adâ*		*martiyahyâ*,
cœlum	dedit,	qui	hominem	dedit,	qui	felicitatem dedit		homini,
hya	*Dâryavum*	*khshâyathiyam*		*akunaush*,		*aivam*		*paruvanâm*
qui	Darium	regem		fecit,		tum		multorum
khshâyathiyam,	*aivam*	*paruvanâm*		*framâtaram.*	*Adam*		*Dâryavush*	
regem,	tum	multorum		dominum.	Ego (sum)		Darius,	

khshâyathiya rex	*vazarka,* magnus,	*khshâyathiya* rex	*khshâyathiyânâm,* regum,	*khshâyathiya* rex
dahyunâm provinciarum	*vizpazanânâm,* a-multis-gentibus-habitatarum,	*khshâyathiya* rex	*ahyâyâ* hujus	*bumiya* terræ
vazarkâya magnæ	*duriâpiya,* latò-patentis,	*Vishtâspahyâ* Hystaspis	*putra,* filius,	*Hakhâmanishiya;* Achœmenius; *Pârsa,* Persa,
Pârsahyâ Persæ	*putra,* filius,	*Ariya,* Arius,	*Ariya chitra.* ex Aria stirpe.	*Thâtiya* Dicit *Dâryavush* Darius
khshâyathiya: rex:	*Vashnâ* Gratiâ	*Auramazdâhâ* Oromazdis	*imâ* hæ (sunt) provinciæ	*dahyâra* quas *tyâ* *adam* ego
agarbâyam obtinui	*apataram* longiùs	*hachâ* a	*Pârsâ.* Perside.	*Adamsham* Ego illas *patiyakhshaiya* rexi. *Manâ* Mihi
bajim tributum	*abara......ha.* tulerunt......		*Tyahsâm* Quod illis	*hachâma* à me *athahya,* dictum est, *ava* illud
akunava. fecerunt.	*Dâtam* Jussum	*tya* quod	*manâ,* à me,	*aita* id *adâri.* servatum est.

The ordinary Persian writing was identical with that which has been described in the second volume of this work as Median. A cuneiform alphabet, consisting of some thirty-six or thirty-seven forms, expressive of twenty-three distinct sounds, sufficed for the wants of the people, whose language was simple and devoid of phonetic luxuriance. Writing was from left to right, as with the Arian nations generally. Words were separated from one another by an oblique wedge; and were divided at any point at which the writer happened to reach the end of a line. Enclitics were joined without any break to the words which they accompanied.

The Persian writing which has come down to us is almost entirely upon stone. It comprises various rock tablets, a number of inscriptions upon buildings, and a few short legends upon vases and cylinders. It is in every case incised or cut into the material. The letters are of various sizes, some (as those at Elwend) reaching a length of about two inches, others (those, for instance, on the vases) not exceeding the sixth of an inch. The inscriptions cover a space of at least a hundred and eighty years, commencing with Cyrus, and terminating with Artaxerxes Ochus, the successor of Mnemon. The style of the writing is, on the whole, remarkably uniform, the latter inscriptions containing only two characters unknown to the earlier times. Orthography, however, and grammar are in these later inscriptions greatly changed, the character of the changes being indicative of corruption and decline, unless, indeed, we are to ascribe them to mere ignorance on the part of the engravers.

There can be little doubt that, besides the cuneiform character, which was only suited for inscriptions, the Persians employed a cursive writing for common literary purposes. Ctesias informs us that the royal archives were written on parchment; and there is abundant evidence that writing was an art perfectly familiar to the educated Persian. It might have been supposed that the Pehlevi, as the lineal descendant of the Old Persian language, would have furnished valuable assistance towards solving the question of what character the Persians employed commonly; but the alphabetic type of the Pehlevi inscriptions is evidently Semitic; and it would thus seem that the old national modes of writing had been completely lost before the establishment by Ardeshir, son of Babek, of the new Persian Empire.

CHAPTER V

ARCHITECTURE AND OTHER ARTS

Ἱδρυτο [ὁ μέγας βασιλεύς] ἐν Σούσοις ἢ Ἐκβατάνοις . . . θαυμαστὸν ἐπέχων βασίλειον οἶκον, καὶ περίβολον, χρυσῷ καὶ ἠλέκτρῳ καὶ ἐλέφαντι ἀστράπτοντα· πυλῶνές τε πολλοὶ καὶ συνεχεῖς, πρόθυρά τε συχνοῖς εἰργόμενα σταδίοις ἀπ' ἀλλήλων, θύραις τε χαλκαῖς καὶ τείχεσι μεγαλοῖς ὠχύρωτο.—De Mundo, vi. p. 637.

If in the old world the fame of the Persians, as builders and artists, fell on the whole below that of the Assyrians and Babylonians—their instructors in art, no less than in letters and science—it was not so much that they had not produced works worthy of comparison with those which adorned Babylon and Nineveh, as that, boasting less antiquity and less originality than those primitive races, they did not strike in the same way the imagination of the lively Greeks, who moreover could not but feel a certain jealousy of artistic successes, which had rewarded the efforts of a living and rival people. It happened, moreover, that the Persian masterpieces were less accessible to the Greeks than the Babylonian, and hence there was actually less knowledge of their real character in the time when Greek literature was at its best. Herodotus and Xenophon, who impressed on their countrymen true ideas of the grandeur and magnificence of the Mesopotamian structures, never penetrated to Persia Proper, and perhaps never beheld a real Persian building. Ctesias, it is true, as a resident at the Achaemenian Court for seventeen years, must certainly have seen Susa and Ecbatana, if not even Persepolis, and he therefore must have been well acquainted with the character of Persian palaces; but, so far as appears from the fragments of his work which have come down to us, he said but little on the subject of these edifices. It was not until Alexander led his cohorts across the chain of Zagros to the high plateau beyond, that a proper estimate of the great Persian buildings could be made; and then the most magnificent of them all was scarcely seen before it was laid in ruins. The barbarous act of the great Macedonian conqueror, in committing the palace of Persepolis to the flames, tended to prevent a full recognition of the real greatness of Persian art even after the Greeks had occupied the country; but we find from this time a certain amount of acknowledgment of its merits—a certain number of passages, which, like that which forms the heading to this chapter, admit alike its grandeur and its magnificence.

If, however, the ancients did less than justice to the efforts of the Persians in architecture, sculpture, and the kindred arts, moderns have, on the contrary, given them rather an undue prominence. From the middle of the seventeenth century, when Europeans first began freely to penetrate the East, the Persian ruins, especially those of Persepolis, drew the marked attention of travellers; and in times when the site of Babylon had attracted but scanty notice, and that of Nineveh and the other great Assyrian cities was almost unknown, English, French, and German savans measured, described, and figured the Persian remains with a copiousness and exactness that left little to desire. Chardin, the elder Mebuhr, Le Brun, Ouseley, Ker Porter, exerted themselves with the most praiseworthy zeal to represent fully and faithfully the marvels of the Chehl Minar; and these persevering efforts were followed within no very lengthy period by the splendid and exhaustive works of the Baron Texier and of MM. Flandin and Coste. Persepolis rose again from its ashes in the superb and costly volumes of these latter writers, who represented on the grandest scale, and in the most finished way, not only the actual but the ideal—not only the present but the past—placing before our eyes at once the fullest and completest views of the existing ruins, and also restorations of the ancient structures, some of them warm with color and gilding, which, though to a certain extent imaginary, probably give to a modern the best notion that it is now possible to form of an old Persian edifice.

It is impossible within the limits of the present work, and with the resources at the author's command, to attempt a complete description of the Persian remains, or to vie with writers who had at their disposal all the modern means of illustration. By the liberality of a well-known authority on architecture, he is able to present his readers with certain general views of the most important structures; and he also enjoys the advantage of illustrating some of the most curious of the details with engravings from a set of photographs recently taken. These last have, it is believed, an accuracy beyond that of any drawings hitherto made, and will give a better idea than words could possibly do of the merit of the sculptures. With these helps, and with the addition of reduced copies from some of MM. Flandin and Coste's plates, the author hopes to be able to make his account fairly intelligible, and to give his readers the opportunity of forming a tolerably correct judgment on the merit of the Persian art in comparison with that of Babylon and Assyria.

Persian architectural art displayed itself especially in two forms of building—the palace and the tomb. Temples were not perhaps unknown in Persia, though much of the worship may always have been in the open air; but temples, at least until the time of Artaxerxes Mnemon, were insignificant, and neither attracted the attention of contemporaries, nor were of such a character as to leave traces of themselves to after times. The palaces of the Persian kings, on the other hand, and the sepulchres which they prepared for themselves, are noticed by many ancient writers as objects of interest; and, notwithstanding certain doubts which have been raised in recent years, it seems tolerably certain that they are to be recognized in the two chief classes of ancient ruins which still exist in the country.

The Persian palatial buildings, of which traces remain, are four in number. One was situated at Ecbatana, the Median capital, and was a sort of adjunct to the old residence of the Median kings. Of this only a very few vestiges have been hitherto found; and we can merely say that it appears to have been of the same general character with the edifices which will be hereafter described. Another was built by Darius and his son Xerxes on the great mound of Susa; and of this we have the ground-plan, in a great measure, and various interesting details. A third stood within the walls of the city of Persepolis, but of this not much more is left than of the construction at Ecbatana. Finally, there was in the neighborhood of Persepolis, but completely distinct from the town, the Great Palace, which, as the chief residence, at any rate of the later kings, Alexander burnt, and of which the remains still to be seen are ample, constituting by far the most remarkable group of buildings now existing in this part of Asia.

It is to this last edifice, or group of edifices, that the reader's attention will be specially directed in the following pages. Here the greatest of the Persian monarchs seem to have built the greatest of their works. Here the ravages of time and barbarism, sadly injurious as they may have been, have had least effect. Here, moreover, modern research has spent its chief efforts, excavations having been made, measurements effected, and ground-plans laid down with accuracy. In describing the Persepolitan buildings we have aids which mostly fail us elsewhere—charts, plans, drawings in extraordinary abundance and often of high artistic value, elaborate descriptions, even photographs. [PLATE XXXVIII., Fig. 3.] If the describer has still a task of some difficulty to perform, it is because an overplus of material is apt to cause almost as much embarrassment as too poor and scanty a supply.

Plate XXXVIII.   Vol. II.

Fig. 1

Fragment of Two-Horse Chariot (from Persepolis).

Fig. 2

Ordinary Persian Costume.

Fig. 3.

Royal Tombs
Nakhshi-Rustam   Canal

RUINS
of Palavar
TOWN

Plain
of
Merdashté   R. Murgat

Canal

Great
Palace

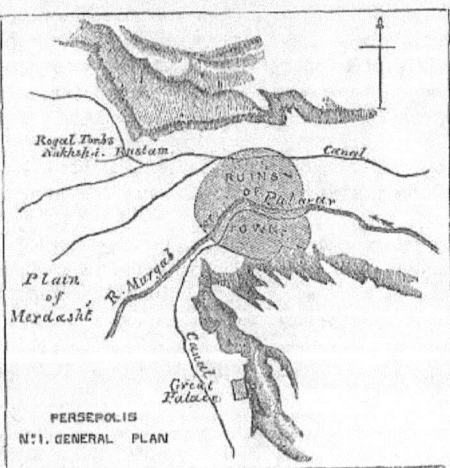

PERSEPOLIS
N°1. GENERAL PLAN

PLATE XXVIII

The buildings at Persepolis are placed upon a vast platform. It was the practice of the Persians, as of the Assyrians and Babylonians, to elevate their palaces in this way. They thus made them at once more striking to the eye, more dignified, and more easy to guard. In Babylonia an elevated habitation was also more healthy and more pleasant, being raised above the reach of many insects, and laid open to the winds of heaven, never too boisterous in that climate. Perhaps the Assyrians and Persians in their continued use of the custom, to some extent followed a fashion, elevating their royal residences, not so much for security or comfort, as because it had come to be considered that a palace ought to have a lofty site, and to look down on the habitations of meaner men; but, however this may have been, the custom certainly prevailed, and at Persepolis we have, in an almost perfect condition, this first element of a Persian palace. [PLATE XXXIX.]

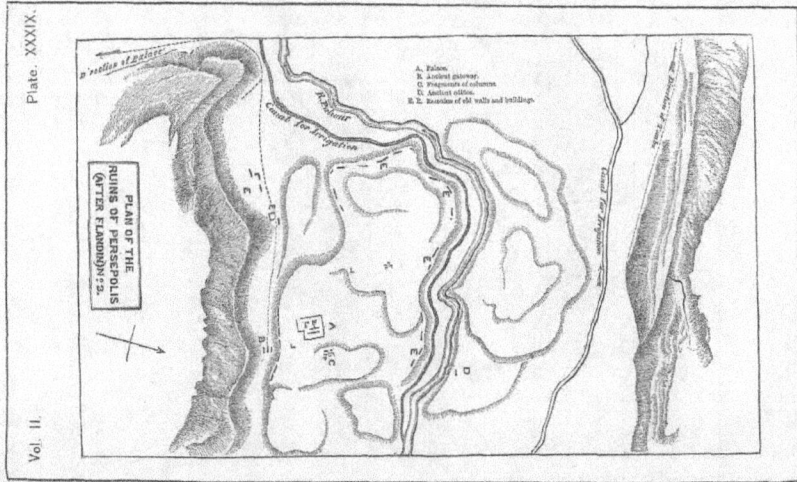

Plate. XXXIX.

Vol. II.

PLAN OF THE
RUINS OF PERSEPOLIS
(AFTER FLANDIN)??.

A. Palace.
B. Ancient gateway.
C. Fragments of columns.
D. Ancient edifice.
E. E. Remains of old walls and buildings.

PLATE XXXIX

The platform at Persepolis is built at the foot of a high range of rocky hills, on which it abuts towards the east. It is composed of solid masses of hewn stone, which were united by metal clamps, probably of iron or lead. The masses were not cut to a uniform size, nor even always to a right angle, but were fitted together with a certain amount of irregularity, which will be the best understood from the woodcut overleaf. Many of the blocks were of enormous size; and their quarrying, transport, and elevation to their present places, imply very considerable mechanical skill. They were laid so as to form a perfectly smooth perpendicular wall, the least height of which above the plain below is twenty feet. The outline of the platform was somewhat irregular. Speaking roughly, we may call it an oblong square, with a breadth about two thirds of its length; but this description, unless qualified, will give an idea of far greater uniformity than actually prevails. [PLATE XL., Fig. 1.] The most serious irregularity is on the north side, the general line of which is not parallel to the south side, nor at right angles with the western one, but forms with the general line of the western an angle of about eighty degrees. The cause of this deviation lay probably in the fact that, on this side, a low rocky spur ran out from the mountain-range in this direction, and that it was thought desirable to accommodate the line of the structure to the natural irregularities of the ground. In addition to the irregularity of general outline thus produced, there is another of such perpetual occurrence that it must be regarded as an essential element of the original design, and therefore probably as approving itself to the artistic notions of the builder. This is the occurrence of frequent angular projections and indentations, which we remark on all three sides of the platform equally, and which would therefore seem to have been regarded in Persia, no less than in Assyria, as ornamental.

Plate XL.   Vol II.

Fig. 1.

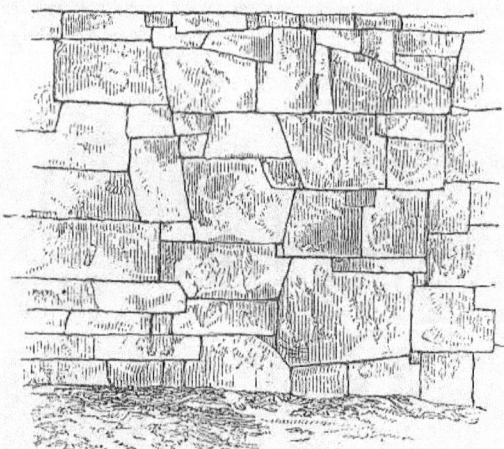

Masonry of Great Platform, Persepolis.

Fig. 2.

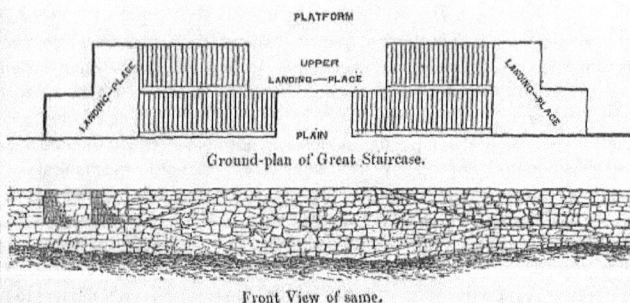

Ground-plan of Great Staircase.

Front View of same.

PLATE XL

The whole of the platform is not of a uniform height. On the contrary, it seems to have been composed, as originally built, of several quite distinct terraces. Three of these still remain, exhibiting towards the west a very marked difference of elevation. The lowest of the three is on the south side, and it may therefore be termed the Southern Terrace. It extends from east to west a distance of about 800 feet, with a width of about 170 or 180, and has an elevation above the plain of from twenty to twenty-three feet. Opposite to this, on the northern side of the platform, is a second terrace, more than three times the breadth of the southern one, which may be called, by way of distinction, the Northern Terrace. This has an elevation above the plain of thirty-five feet. Intermediate between these two is the great Central or Upper Terrace, standing forty-five feet above the plain, having a length of 770 feet along the west face of the platform, and a width of about 400. Upon this Upper Terrace were situated almost all the great and important buildings.

The erection of a royal residence on a platform composed of several terraces involved the necessity of artificial ascents, which the Persian architects managed by means of broad and solid staircases. These staircases constitute one of the most remarkable features of the place, and seem to deserve careful and exact description. [PLATE XLI., Fig. 2.]

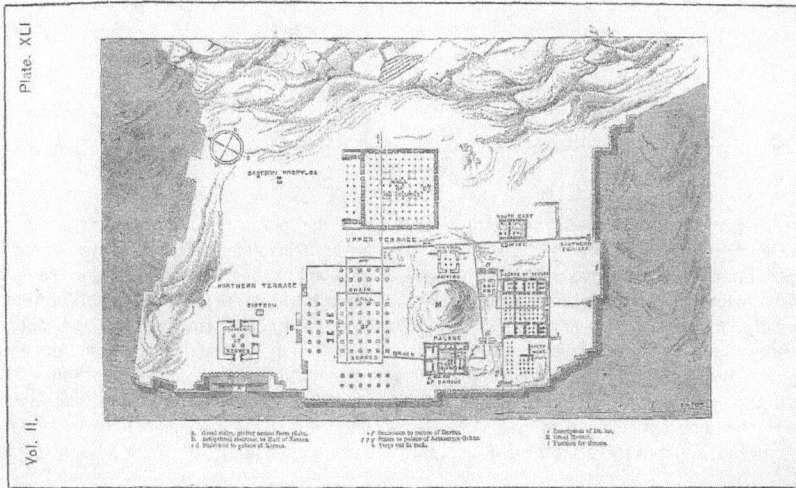

PLATE XLI

The first, and grandest in respect of scale, is on the west front of the platform towards its northern end, and leads up from the plain to the summit of the northern terrace, furnishing the only means by which the platform can even now be ascended. It consists of two distinct sets of steps, each composed of two flights, with a broad landing-place between them, the steps themselves running at right angles to the platform wall, and the two lower flights diverging, while the two upper ones converge to a common landing-place on the top. The slope of the stairs is so gentle that, though each step has a convenient width, the height of a step is in no case more than from three to four inches. It is thus easy to ride horses both up and down the staircase, and travellers are constantly in the habit of ascending and descending it in this way.

The width of the staircase is twenty-two feet—space sufficient to allow of ten horsemen ascending each flight of steps abreast. Altogether this ascent, which is on a plan unknown elsewhere, is pronounced to be the noblest example of a flight of stairs to be found in any part of the world. It does not project beyond the line of the platform whereto it leads, but is, as it were, taken out of it. [PLATE XLII.]

Propylæa, Chehl Minar and Palace of Darius, from top of Great Stairs, Persepolis. From Fergusson.

PLATE XLII

The next, and in some respects the most remarkable of all the staircases, conducts from the level of the northern platform to that of the central or upper terrace. This staircase fronts northward, and opens on the view as soon as the first staircase (A on the plan) has been ascended, lying to the right of the spectator at the distance of about fifty or sixty yards. It consists of four single flights of steps, two of which are central, facing one another, and leading to a projecting landing-place (B), about twenty feet in width; while the two others are on either side of the central flights, distant from them about twenty-one yards. The entire length of this staircase is 212 feet; its greatest projection in front of the line of the terrace whereon it abuts, is thirty-six feet. The steps, which are sixteen feet wide, rise in the same gentle way as those of the lower or platform staircase. The height of each is under four inches; and thus there are thirty-one steps in an ascent of ten feet.

The feature which specially distinguishes this staircase from the lower one already described is its elaborate ornamentation. The platform staircase is perfectly plain. The entire face which this staircase presents to the spectator is covered with sculptures. In the first place, on the central projection, which is divided perpendicularly into three compartments, are represented, in the spandrels on either side, a lion devouring a bull, and in the compartment between the spandrels eight colossal Persian guardsmen, armed with spears and either with sword or shield. Further, above the lion and bull, towards the edge of the spandrel where it slopes, forming a parapet to the steps, [PLATE XLIII., Fig. 1.] there was a row of cypress trees, while at the end of the parapet and along the whole of its inner face were a set of small figures, guardsmen habited like those in the central compartment, but carrying mostly a bow and quiver instead of a shield. Along the extreme edge of the parapet externally was a narrow border thickly set with rosettes. [PLATE XLIII., Fig. 2.] Next, in the long spaces between the central stairs and those on either side of them, the spandrels contain repetitions of the lion and bull sculpture, while between them and the central stairs the face of the wall is divided horizontally into three bands, each of which has been ornamented with a continuous row of figures. The highest row of the three is unfortunately mutilated, the upper portion of all the bodies being lost in consequence of their having been sculptured upon a parapet wall built originally to protect the edge of the terrace, but now fallen away. The middle and lowest rows are tolerably perfect, and possess considerable interest, as well as some artistic merit. The entire scene represented on the right side seems to be the bringing of tribute or presents to the monarch by the various nations under his sway. On the left-hand side this subject was continued to a certain extent; but the greater part of the space was occupied by representations of guards and officers of the court, the guards being placed towards the centre, and, as it were, keeping the main stairs, while the officers were at a greater distance. The three rows of figures were separated from one another by narrow bands, thickly set with rosettes.

Vol. II.   Plate XLIII.

Fig. 1.

Parapet Wall of Staircase, Persepolis (restored)   Interior View.

Fig. 2.

Parapet Wall of the same (restored).
Exterior view.

PLATE XLIII

The builder of this magnificent work was not content to leave it to history or tradition to connect his name with his construction, but determined to make the work itself the means of perpetuating his memory. In three conspicuous parts of the staircase, slabs were left clear of sculpture, undoubtedly to receive inscriptions commemorative of the founder. The places selected were the front of the middle staircase, the exact centre of the whole work, and the space adjoining the spandrels to the extreme right and the extreme left. In one instance alone, however, was this part of the work completed. On the right hand, or western extremity of the staircase, an inscription of thirty lines in the old Persian language informs us that the constructor was "Xerxes, the Great King, the King of Kings, the son of King Darius, the Achaemenian." The central and left-hand tablets, intended probably for Babylonian and Scythic translations of the Persian legend, were never inscribed, and remain blank to the present day.

The remaining staircases will not require very lengthy or elaborate descriptions. They are six in number, and consist, in most instances, of a double flight of steps, similar to the central portion of the staircase which has been just described. Two of them (e and f) belonged to the building marked as the "Palace of Darius" on the plan, and gave entrance to it from the central platform above which it is elevated about fourteen or fifteen feet. Two others (c and d) belonged to the "Palace of Xerxes." These led up to a broad paved space in front of that building, which formed a terrace, elevated about ten feet above the general level of the central platform. Their position was at the two ends of the terrace, opposite to one another; but in other respects they cannot be said to have matched. The eastern, which consisted of two double flights, was similar in general arrangement to the staircase by which the platform was mounted from the plain, excepting that it was not recessed, but projected its full breadth beyond the line of the terrace. It was decidedly the more elegant of the two, and evidently formed the main approach. It was adorned with the usual bull and lion combats, with figures of guardsmen, and with attendants carrying articles needed for the table or the toilet. The inscriptions upon it declare it to be the work of Xerxes. [PLATE XLIV.] The western staircase was composed merely of two single flights, facing one another, with a narrow landing-place between them. It was ornamented like the eastern, but somewhat less elaborately.

East Stairs of Palace of Xerxes. From Fergusson.

PLATE XLIV

A staircase, very similar to this last, but still one with certain peculiarities, was built by Artaxerxes Ochus, at the west side of the Palace of Darius, in order to give it a second entrance. [PLATE XLV., Fig. 1.] There the spandrels have the usual figures of the lion and bull; but the intermediate space is somewhat unusually arranged. It is divided vertically and horizontally into eight squared compartments, three on either side, and two in the middle. The upper of these two contains nothing but a winged circle, the emblem of Divinity being thus placed reverently by itself. Below, in a compartment of double size, is an inscription of Ochus, barbarous in language, but very religious in tone. The six remaining compartments had each four figures, representing tribute-bearers introduced to the royal presence by a court officer.

Fig. 1.

Staircase of Artaxerxes, Persepolis.   Existing condition.

Fig. 2.

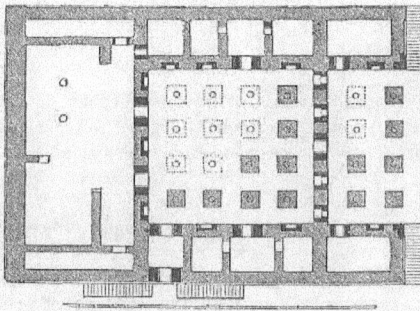

Ground Plan of the Palace of Darius.   50 ft. to 1 inch.

Fig. 3.

King and Attendants,
Persepolis.

PLATE XLV

The other, and original, staircase to this palace (f on the plan) was towards the north, and led up to the great portico, which was anciently its sole entrance. Two flights of steps, facing each other, conducted to a paved space of equal extent with the portico and projecting in front of it about five feet. On the base of the staircase were sculptures in a single line—the lion and bull in either spandrel—and between the spandrels eighteen colossal guardsmen, nine facing either way towards a central inscription, which was repeated in other languages on slabs placed between the guardsmen and the bulls. Above the spandrels, on the parapet which fenced the stairs, was a line of figures representing attendants bringing into the palace materials for the banquet. A similar line adorned the inner wall of the staircase.

Opposite to this, at the distance of about thirty-two yards, was another very similar staircase, leading up to the portico of another building, erected (apparently) by Artaxerxes Ochus, which occupied the south-western corner of the upper platform. The sculptures here seem to have been of the usual character but they are so mutilated that no very decided opinion can be passed upon them.

Last of all, a staircase of a very peculiar character, (h on the plan) requires notice. This is a flight of steps cut in the solid rock, which leads up from the southern terrace to the upper one, at a point intervening between the south-western edifice, or palace of Artaxerxes, and the palace of Xerxes, or central southern edifice. These steps are singular in facing the terrace to which they lead, instead of being placed sideways to it. They are of rude construction, being without a parapet, and wholly devoid of sculpture or other ornamentation. They furnish the only communication between the southern and central terraces.

It is a peculiarity of the Persepolitan ruins that they are not continuous, but present to the modern inquirer the appearance, at any rate, of a number of distinct buildings. Of these the platform altogether contains ten, five of which are of large size, while the remainder are comparatively insignificant.

Of the five large buildings four stand upon the central or upper terrace, while one lies east of that terrace, between it and the mountains. The four upon the central terrace comprise three buildings made up of several sets of chambers, together with one great open pillared hall, to which are attached no subordinate apartments. The three complex edifices will be here termed "palaces," and will take the names of their respective founders, Darius, Xerxes, and Artaxerxes Ochus: the fourth will be called the "Great Hall of Audience." The building between the upper terrace and the mountains will be termed the "Great Eastern Edifice."

The "Palace of Darius," which is one of the most interesting of the Persepolitan buildings, stands near the western edge of the platform, midway between the "Great Hall of Audience" and the "Palace of Artaxerxes Ochus." [PLATE XLVI., Fig. 1.] It is a building about one hundred and thirty five feet in length, and in breadth a little short of a hundred. Of all the existing buildings on the platform it occupies the most exalted position, being elevated from fourteen to fifteen feet above the general level of the central terrace, and being thus four or five feet higher than the "Palace of Xerxes." It fronted towards the south, where it was approached by a double staircase of the usual character, which led up to a deep portico of eight pillars arranged in two rows. On either side of the portico were guard-rooms, which opened upon it, in length twenty-three feet, and in breadth thirteen. Behind the portico lay the main chamber, which was a square of fifty feet, having a roof supported by sixteen pillars, arranged in four rows of four, in line with the pillars of the portico. [PLATE XLV., Fig. 2.] The bases for the pillars alone remain; and it is thus uncertain whether their material was stone or wood. They were probably light and slender, not greatly interrupting the view. The hall was surrounded on all sides by walls from four to five feet in thickness, in which were doors, windows, and recesses, symmetrically arranged. The entrance from the portico was by a door in the exact centre of the front wall, on either side of which were two windows, looking into the portico. The opposite, or back, wall was pierced by two doors, which faced the intercolumniations of the side rows of pillars, as the front door faced the intercolumniation of the central rows. Between the two doors which pierced the back wall was a squared recess, and similar recesses ornamented the same wall on either side of the doors. The side walls were each pierced originally by a single doorway, between which and the front wall was a squared recess, while beyond, between the doorways and the back wall, were two recesses of the same character. Curiously enough, these side doorways and recesses fronted the pillars, not the intercolumniations.

Plate XLVI.

Fig. 1.

Façade of the Palace of Darius, Persepolis. (From Fergusson.)

Fig. 2

South Front of the Palace of Darius, Persepolis, restored (after Flandin)

PLATE XLVI

No sculpture, so far as appears, adorned this apartment, excepting in the doorways, which however had in every case this kind of ornamentation. The doorways in the back wall exhibited on their jambs figures of the king followed by two attendants, one holding a cloth, and the other a fly-chaser. [PLATE XLV., Fig. 3.] These figures had in every case their faces turned towards the apartment. The front doorway showed on its jambs the monarch followed by the parasol-bearer and the bearer of the fly-chaser, with his back turned to the apartment, issuing forth, as it were, from it. On the jambs of the doors of the side apartments was represented the king in combat with a lion or a monster, the king here in every case facing outwards, and seeming to guard the entrances to the side chambers.

At the back of the hall, and at either side, were chambers of very moderate dimensions. The largest were to the rear of the building, where there seems to have been one about forty feet by twenty-three, and another twenty-eight feet by twenty. The doorways here had sculptures, representing attendants bearing napkins and perfumes. The side chambers, five in number, were considerably smaller than those behind the great hall, the largest not exceeding thirty-four feet by thirteen.

It seems probable that this palace was without any second story. There is no vestige in any part of it of a staircase—no indication of its height having ever exceeded from twenty-two to twenty-five feet.

It was a modest building, simple and regular, covering less than half the space of an ordinary palace in Assyria. [PLATE XLV., Fig. 2.] Externally, it must have presented an appearance not very dissimilar to that of the simpler Greek temples; distinguished from them by peculiarities of ornamentation, but by no striking or important feature, excepting the grand and elaborately sculptured staircase. Internally, it was remarkable for the small number of its apartments, which seem not to have been more than twelve or thirteen, and for the moderate size of most of them. Even the grand central hall covered a less area than three out of the five halls in the country palace of Sargon. The effect of this room was probably fine, though it must have been somewhat over-crowded with pillars. If these were, however (as is probable), light wooden posts, plated with silver or with gold, and if the ceiling consisted (as it most likely did) of beams, crossing each other at right angles, with square spaces between them, all likewise coated with the precious metals; if moreover the cold stone walls, excepting where they were broken by a doorway, or a window, were similarly decked; if curtains of brilliant hues hung across the entrances; if the pavement was of many-colored stones, and in places covered with magnificent carpets; if an elevated golden throne, under a canopy of purple, adorned the upper end of the room, standing against the wall midway between the two doors—if this were in truth the arrangement and ornamentation of the apartment, we can well understand that the coup d'oeil must have been effective, and the impression made on the spectator highly pleasing. A room fifty feet square, and not much more than twenty high, could not be very grand; but elegance of form, combined with richness of material and splendor of coloring, may have more than compensated for the want of that grandeur which results from mere size.

If it be inquired how a palace of the dimensions described can have sufficed even for one of the early Persian kings, the reply must seemingly be that the building in question can only have contained the public apartments of the royal residence—the throne-room, banqueting-rooms, guard-rooms, etc.,—and that it must have been supplemented by at least one other edifice of a considerable size, the Gynaeceum or "House of the Women." There is ample room on the platform for such a building, either towards the east, where the ground is now occupied by a high mound of rubbish, or on the west, towards the edge of the platform, where traces of a large edifice were noted by Niebuhr. On the whole, this latter situation seems to be the more probable; and the position of the Gynaeceum in this quarter may account for the alteration made by Artaxerxes Ochus in the palace of Darius, which now seriously interferes with its symmetry. Artaxerxes cut a doorway in the outer western wall, and another opposite to it in the western wall of the great hall, adding at the same time a second staircase to the building, which thus became accessible from the west no less than from the south. It has puzzled the learned in architecture to assign a motive for this alteration. May we not find an adequate one in the desire to obtain a ready and comparatively private access to the Gynaeceum, which must have been somewhere on the platform, and which may well have lain in this direction?

The minute account which has been now given of this palace will render unnecessary a very elaborate description of the remainder. Two grand palatial edifices seem to have been erected on the platform by later kings—one by Xerxes and the other by Artaxerxes Ochus; but the latter of these is in so ruined a condition, and the former is so like the palace of Darius, that but few remarks need be made upon either. The palace of Xerxes is simply that of Darius on a larger scale, the pillars in the portico being increased from two rows of four to two rows of six, and the great hall behind being a square of eighty instead of a square of fifty feet, with thirty-six instead of sixteen pillars to support its roof. On either side of the hall, and on either side of the portico, were apartments like those already described as abutting on the same portions of the older palace, differing from them chiefly in being larger and more numerous. The two largest, which were thirty-one feet square, had roofs supported on pillars, the numbers of such supports being in each case four. The only striking difference in the plans of the two buildings consisted in the absence from the palace of Xerxes of any apartments to the rear of the great hall. In order to allow space for an ample terrace in front, the whole edifice was thrown back so close to the edge of the upper platform that no room was left for any chambers at the back, since the hall itself was here brought almost to the very verge of the sheer descent from the central to the low southern terrace. In ornamentation the palaces also very closely resembled each other, the chief difference being that the combats of the king with lions and mythological monsters, which form the regular ornamentation of the side-chambers in the palace of Darius, occur nowhere in the residence of his son, where they are replaced by figures of attendants bringing articles for the toilet or the table, like those which adorn the main staircase of the older edifice. Figures of the same kind also ornament all the windows in the palace of Xerxes. A tone of mere sensual enjoyment is thus given to the later edifice, which is very far from characterizing the earlier; and the decline of morals at the Court, which history indicates as rapid about this period, is seen to have stamped itself, as such changes usually do, upon the national architecture.

A small building, at the distance of about twenty or twenty-five yards from the eastern wall of the palace of Xerxes, possesses a peculiar interest, in consequence of its having some claims to be considered the most ancient structure upon the platform. It consists of a hall and portico, in size, proportions, and decoration almost exactly resembling the corresponding parts of Darius's palace, but unaccompanied by any trace of circumjacent chambers, and totally devoid of inscriptions. The building is low, on the level of the northern, rather than on that of the central terrace, and is indeed half buried in the rubbish which has accumulated at its base. Its fragments are peculiarly grand and massive, while its sculptures are in strong and bold relief. There can be little doubt but that it was originally, like the hall and portico of Darius, surrounded on three sides by chambers. These, however, have entirely disappeared, having probably been pulled down to furnish materials for more recent edifices. Like the palaces of Xerxes and Artaxerxes Ochus, and unlike the palace of Darius, the building faces to the north, which is the direction naturally preferred in such a climate. We may suppose it to have been the royal residence of the earlier times, the erection of Cyrus or Cambyses, and to have been intended especially for summer use, for which its position well fitted it. Darius, wishing for a winter palace at Persepolis, as well as a summer one, took probably this early palace for his model, and built one as nearly as possible resembling it, except that, for the sake of greater warmth, he made his new erection face southwards. Xerxes, dissatisfied with the size of the old summer palace, built a new one at its side of considerably larger dimensions, using perhaps some of the materials of the old palace in his new building. Finally, Artaxerxes Ochus made certain additions to the palace of Xerxes on its western side, and at the same time added a staircase and a doorway to the winter residence of Darius. Thus the Persepolitan palace, using the word in its proper sense of royal residence, attained its full dimensions, occupying the southern half of the great central platform, and covering with its various courts and buildings a space 500 feet long by 375 feet wide, or nearly the space covered by the less ambitious of the palaces of Assyria.

Besides edifices adapted for habitation, the Persepolitan platform sustained two other classes of buildings. These were propylaea, or gateways—places commanding the approach to great buildings, where a guard might be stationed to stop and examine all comers—and halls of a vast size, which were probably throne-rooms, where the monarch held his court on grand occasions, to exhibit himself in full state to his subjects. The propylaea upon the platform appear to have been four in number. One, the largest, was directly opposite the centre of the landing-place at the top of the great stairs which gave access to the platform from the plain. This consisted of a noble apartment, eighty-two feet square, with a roof supported by four magnificent columns, each between fifty and sixty feet high. The walls of the apartment were from sixteen to seventeen feet thick. Two grand portals, each twelve feet wide by thirty-six feet high, led into this apartment, one directly facing the head of the stairs, and the other opposite to it, towards the east. Both were flanked with colossal bulls, those towards the staircase being conventional representations of the real animal, while the opposite pair are almost exact reproductions of the winged and human-headed bulls, with which the Assyrian discoveries have made us so familiar. The accompanying illustration [PLATE XLVII., Fig. 1.], which is taken from a photograph, exhibits this inner pair in their present condition. The back of one of the other pair is also visible. Two of the pillars—which alone are still standings appear in their places, intervening between the front and the back gateway.

Fig. 1.

Great Propylæa of Xerxes (from a photograph).

Fig 2.

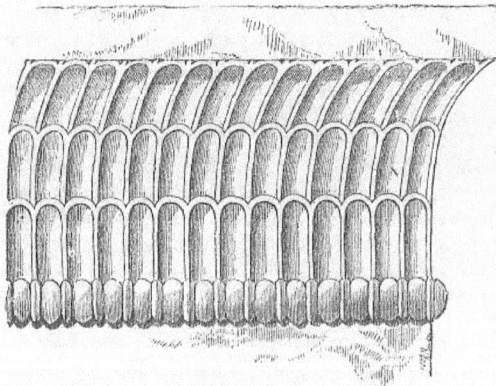

Ornament over Windows, Persepolis.

PLATE XLVII

The walls which enclosed this chamber, notwithstanding their immense thickness, have almost entirely disappeared. On the southern side alone, where there seems to have been a third doorway, unornamented, are there any traces of them. We must conclude that they were either of burnt brick or of small blocks of stone, which the natives of the country in later times found it convenient to use as material for their own buildings.

An edifice, almost exactly similar to this, but of very inferior dimensions, occupied a position due east of the palace of Darius, and a little to the north of the main staircase leading to the terrace in front of the palace of Xerxes. The bases of two pillars and the jambs of three doorways remain, from which it is easy to reconstruct the main building. Its position seems to mark it as designed to give entrance to the structure, whatever it was, which occupied the site of the great mound (M on the Plan) east of Darius's palace, and north of the palace of his son. The ornamentation, however, would rather connect it with the more eastern of the two great pillared halls, which will have to be described presently.

A third edifice of the same kind stood in front of the great eastern hall, at the distance of about seventy yards from its portico. This building is more utterly ruined than either of the preceding, and its dimensions are open to some doubt. On the whole, it seems probable that it resembled the great propylaea at the head of the stairs leading from the plain rather than the central propylaea just described. Part of its ornamentation was certainly a colossal bull, though whether human-headed or not cannot be determined.

The fourth of the propylaea was on the terrace whereon stood the palace of Xerxes, and directly fronting the landing-place at the head of its principal stairs, just as the propylaea first described fronted the great stairs leading up from the plain. Its dimensions were suited to those of the staircase which led to it, and of the terrace on which it was placed. It was less than one fourth the size of the great propylaea, and about half that of the propylaea which stood the nearest to it. The bases of the four pillars alone remain in situ; but, from the proportions thus obtained, the position of the walls and doorways is tolerably certain.

We have now to pass to the most magnificent of the Perse-politan buildings—the Great Pillared Halls—which constitute the glory of Arian architecture, and which, even in their ruins, provoke the wonder and admiration of modern Europeans, familiar with all the triumphs of Western art, with Grecian temples, Roman baths and amphitheatres, Moorish palaces, Turkish mosques, and Christian cathedrals. Of these pillared halls, the Persepolitan platform supports two, slightly differing in their design, but presenting many points of agreement. They bear the character of an earlier and a later building—a first effort in the direction which circumstances compelled the architecture of the Persians to take, and the final achievement of their best artists in this kind of building.

Nearly midway in the platform between its northern and its southern edges, and not very far from the boundary of rocky mountain on which the platform abuts towards the east, is the vast edifice which has been called with good reason the "Hall of a Hundred Columns," since its roof was in all probability supported by that number of pillars. This building consisted of a single magnificent chamber, with a portico, and probably guard-rooms, in front, of dimensions quite unequalled upon the platform. The portico was 183 feet long by 52 feet deep, and was sustained by sixteen pillars, about 33 feet high, arranged in two rows of eight. The great chamber behind was a square of 227 feet, and had therefore an area of about 51,000 feet. Over this vast space were distributed, at equal distances from one another, one hundred columns, each 35 feet high, arranged in ten rows of ten each, every pillar thus standing at a distance of nearly 20 feet from any other. The four walls which enclosed this great hall had a uniform thickness of 10 1/2 feet, and were each pierced at equal intervals by two doorways, the doorways being thus exactly opposite to one another, and each looking down an avenue of columns. In the spaces of wall on either side of the doorways, eastward, westward, and southward, were three niches, all square-topped, and bearing the ornamentation which is universal in the case of all niches, windows, and doorways in the Persepolitan ruins. [PLATE XLVII., Fig. 2.] In the northern, or front, wall, the niches were replaced by windows looking upon the portico, excepting towards the angles of the building, where niches were retained, owing to a peculiarity in the plan of the edifice which has now to be noticed.

Plate XLVIII.

Vol. II

Fig. 1.

Fig. 3.   Gateway to Hall of a Hundred Columns (from a Photograph).

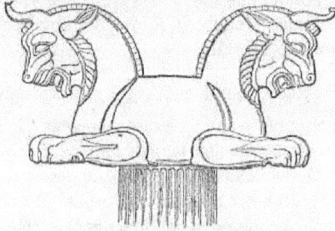

Double Griffin Capital, Persepolis.

Fig. 2.

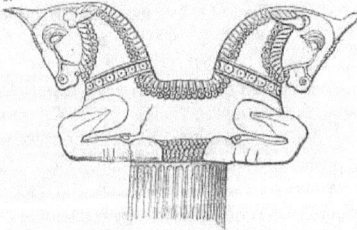

Double Bull Capital, Persepolis.

PLATE XLVIII

The portico, instead of being, as in every other Persian instance, of the same width with the building which it fronted, was 44 feet narrower, its antce projecting from the front wall, not at either extremity, but at the distance of 11 feet from the corner. While the porch was thus contracted, so that the pillars had to be eight in each row instead of ten, space was left on either side for a narrow guard-room opening on to the porch, indications of which are seen in the doorways placed at right angles to the front wall, which are ornamented with the usual figures of soldiers armed with spear and shield. It has been suggested that the hall was, like the smaller pillared chambers upon the platform, originally surrounded on three sides by a number of lesser apartments; and this is certainly possible: but no trace remains of any such buildings. The ornamentation which exists seems to show that the building was altogether of a public character. Instead of exhibiting attendants bringing articles for the toilet or the banquet, it shows on its doors the monarch, either engaged in the art of destroying symbolical monsters, or seated on his throne under a canopy, with the tiara on his head, and the golden sceptre in his right hand. The throne representations are of two kinds. On the jambs of the great doors leading out upon the porch, we see in the top compartment the monarch seated under the canopy, accompanied by five attendants, while below him are his guards, arranged in five rows of ten each, some armed with spears and shields, others with spears, short swords, bows and quivers. Thus the two portals together exhibit the figures of 200 Persian guardsmen in attendance on the person of the king. The doors at the back of the building present us with a still more curious sculpture. On these the throne appears elevated on a lofty platform, the stages of which, three in number, are upheld by figures in different costumes, representing apparently the natives of all the different provinces of the Empire. It is a reasonable conjecture that this great hall was intended especially for a throne-room, and that in the representations on these doorways we have figured a structure which actually existed under its roof (probably at t in the plan)—a platform reached by steps, whereon, in the great ceremonies of state, the royal throne was placed, in order that the monarch might be distinctly seen at one and the same time by the whole Court.

The question of the lighting of this huge apartment presents some difficulties. On three sides, as already observed, the hall had (so far as appears) no windows—the places where windows might have been expected to occur being occupied by niches. The apparent openings are consequently reduced to some fifteen, viz., the eight doorways, and seven windows, which looked out upon the portico, and were therefore overhung and had a north aspect. It is clear that sufficient light could not have entered the apartment from these—the only visible—apertures. We must therefore suppose either that the walls above the niches were pierced with windows, which is quite possible, or else that light was in some way or other admitted from the roof. The latter is the supposition of those most competent to decide. M. Flandin conjectures that the roof had four apertures, placed at the points where the lines drawn from the northern to the southern, and those drawn from the eastern to the western, doors would intersect one another. He seems to suppose that these openings were wholly unprotected, in which case they would have admitted, in a very inconvenient way, both the sun and the rain. May we not presume that, if such openings existed, they were guarded by louvres such as have been regarded as probably lighting the Assyrian halls, and of which a representation has already been given?

The portico of the Hall of a Hundred Columns was flanked on either side by a colossal bull, standing at the inner angle of the antes, and thus in some degree narrowing the entrance. Its columns were fluted, and had in every case the complex capital, which occurs also in the great propylaea and in the Hall of Xerxes. It was built of the same sort of massive blocks as the south-eastern edifice, or Ancient Palace—blocks often ten feet square by seven feet thick, and may be ascribed probably to the same age as that structure. Like that edifice, it is situated somewhat low; it has no staircase, and no inscription. We may fairly suppose it to have been the throne-room or great hall of audience of the early king who built the South-eastern Palace.

We have now to describe the most remarkable of all the Persepolitan edifices—a building the remains of which stretch nearly 350 feet in one direction, while in the other they extend 246 feet. Its ruins consist almost entirely of pillars, which are divided into four groups. The largest of these was a square of thirty-six pillars, arranged in six rows of six, all exactly equidistant from one another, and covering an area of above 20,000 square feet. On three sides of this square, eastward, northward, and westward, were magnificent porches, each consisting of twelve columns, arranged in two rows, in line with the pillars of the central cluster. These porches stood at the distance of seventy feet from the main building, and have the appearance of having been entirely separate from it. They are 143 feet long, by thirty broad, and thus cover each an area of 4260 feet. The most astonishing feature in the whole building is the height of the pillars. These, according to the measurements of M. Flandin, had a uniform altitude throughout the building of sixty-four feet. Even in their ruin, they tower over every other erection upon the platform, retaining often, in spite of the effects of time, an elevation of sixty feet.

The capitals of the pillars were of three kinds. Those of the side colonnades were comparatively simple: they consisted, in each case, of a single member, formed, in the eastern colonnade, of two half-griffins, with their heads looking in opposite directions [PLATE XLVII, Fig. 2]; and, in the western colonnade, of two half-bulls, arranged in the same manner [PLATE XLVII., Fig. 3]. The capitals of the pillars in the northern colonnade, which faced the great sculptured staircase, and constituted the true front of the building, were of a very complex character. They may be best viewed as composed of three distinct members—first, a sort of lotos-bud, accompanied by pendent leaves; then, above that, a member, composed of volutes like those of the Ionic order, but placed in a perpendicular instead of a horizontal direction; and at the top, a member composed of two half-bulls, exactly similar to that which forms the complete capital of the western group of pillars. The pillars of the groat central cluster had capitals exactly like those of the northern colonnade.

The bases of the colonnade pillars are of singular beauty. Bell-shaped, and ornamented with a double or triple row of pendent lotus-leaves, some rounded, some narrowed to a point; they are as graceful as they are rare in their forms, and attract the admiration of all beholders. Above them rise the columns, tapering gently as they ascend, but without any swell or entasis. They consist of several masses of stone, carefully joined together, and secured at the joints by an iron cramp in the direction of the column's axis. All are beautifully fluted along their entire length, the number of the incisions or flutings being from forty-eight to fifty-two in each pillar. They are arcs of circles smaller than semicircles, thus resembling those of the Doric, rather than those of the Ionic or Corinthian order. The cutting of all is very exact and regular.

There can be little doubt but that both the porches, and the great central pillar-cluster, were roofed in. The double-bull and double-griffin capital are exactly suited to receive the ends of beams, which would stretch from pillar to pillar, and support a roof and an entablature. [PLATE L., Fig.1.] We may see in the entrances to the royal tombs the true use of pillars in a Persian building, and the character of the entablature which, they were intended to sustain, Assuming, then, that both the great central pillar phalanx and the three detached colonnades supported a roof, the question arises, were the colonnades in any way united with the main building, or did they stand completely detached from it? It has been supposed that they were all porticos in antis, connected with the main building by solid walls—that the great central column-cluster was surrounded on all sides by a wall of a very massive description, from the four corners of which similar barriers were carried down to the edge of the terrace, abutting in front upon the steps of the great sculptured staircase, and extending eastward and westward, so as to form the antce of an eastern and a western portico. In the two corners between the northern in antae of the side porticos and the antae of the portico in front are supposed to have been large guard-rooms, entirely filling up the two angles. The whole building is thus brought into close conformity with the "Palace of Xerxes," from which it is distinguished only by its superior size, its use of stone pillars, and the elongation of the tetrastyle chambers at the sides of that edifice into porticos of twelve pillars each.

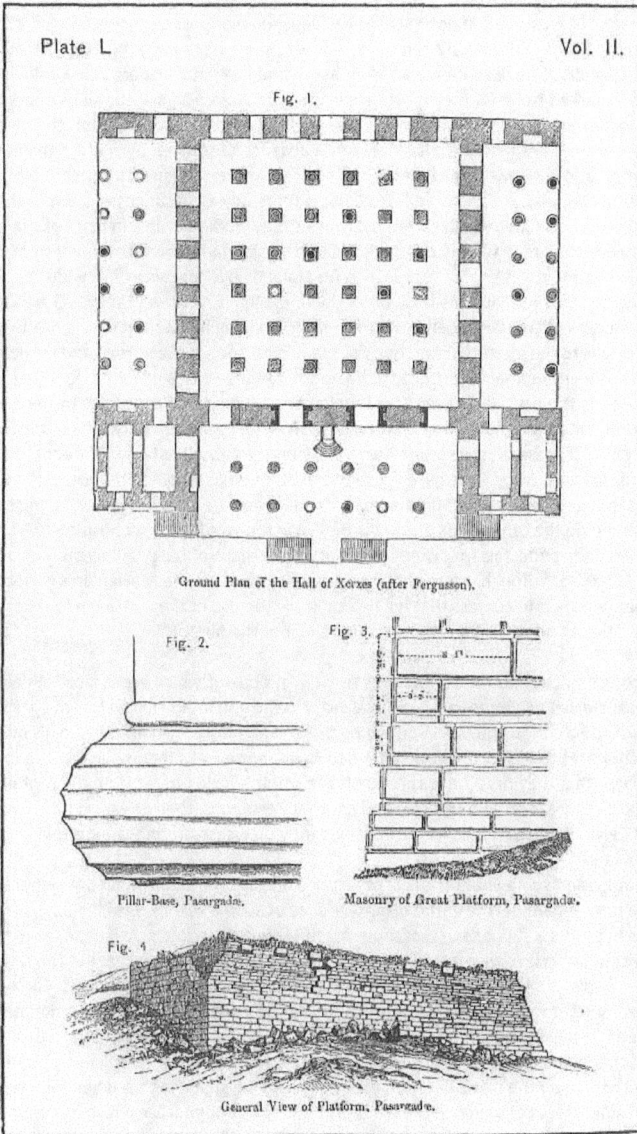

Plate L   Vol. II.

Fig. 1.

Ground Plan of the Hall of Xerxes (after Fergusson).

Fig. 2.

Fig. 3.

Pillar-Base, Pasargadæ.

Masonry of Great Platform, Pasargadæ.

Fig. 4

General View of Platform, Pasargadæ.

PLATE L

The ingenuity of this conception is unquestionable; and one is tempted at first sight to accept a solution which removes so much that is puzzling, and establishes so remarkable a harmony between works whose outward aspect is so dissimilar. It seems like the inspiration of genius to discern so clearly the like in the unlike, and one inclines at first to believe that what is so clever cannot but be true. But a rigorous examination of the evidence leads to an opposite conclusion, and if it does not absolutely disprove Mr. Fergusson's theory, at any rate shows it to be in the highest degree doubtful. Such walls as he describes, with their antae and their many doors and windows, should have left very marked traces of their existence in great squared pillars at the sides of porticos, in huge door-frames and window-frames, or at least in the foundations of walls, or, the marks of them, on some part of the paved terrace. Now the entire absence of squared pillars for the ends of antce, of door-frames, and window-frames, or even of such sculptured fragments as might indicate their former existence, is palpable and is admitted; nor is there any even supposed trace of the walls, excepting in one of the lines which by the hypothesis they would occupy. In front of the building, midway between the great pillar-cluster and the north colonnade, are the remains of four stone bases, parallel to one another, each seventeen feet long by five feet six inches wide. Mr. Fergusson regards these bases as marking the position of the doors in his front wall; and they are certainly in places where doors might have been looked for, if the building had a front wall, since the openings are exactly opposite the inter-columniations of the pillars, both in the portico and in the main cluster. But there are several objections to the notion of these bases being the foundations of the jambs of doors. In the first place, they are too wide apart, being at the distance from one another of seventeen feet, whereas no doorway on the platform exceeds a width of twelve or thirteen feet. In the second place, if these massive stone bases were prepared for the jambs of doors, it could only have been for massive stone jambs like those of the other palaces; but in that case, the jambs could not have disappeared. Thirdly, if the doorways on this side were thus marked, why were they not similarly marked on the other sides of the building? On the whole, the supposition of M. Flandin, that the bases were pedestals for ornamental statues, perhaps of bulls, seems more probable than that of Mr. Fergusson; though, no doubt, there are objections also to M. Flandin's hypothesis, and it would be perhaps best to confess that we do not know the use of these strange foundations, which have nothing that at all resembles them upon the rest of the platform.

Another strong objection to Mr. Fergusson's theory, and one of which he, to a certain extent, admits the force, is the existence of drains, running exactly in the line of his side walls, which, if such walls existed, would be a curious provision on the part of the architect for undermining his own work. Mr. Fergusson supposes that they might be intended to drain the walls themselves and keep them dry. But as it is clear that they must have carried off the whole surplus water from the roof of the building, and as there is often much rain and snow at Persepolis, their effect on the foundations of such a wall as Mr. Fergusson imagines would evidently be disastrous in the extreme.

To these minute and somewhat technical objections may be added the main one, whereof all alike can feel the force—namely, the entire disappearance of such a vast mass of building as Mr. Fergusson's hypothesis supposes. To account for this, Mr. Fergusson is obliged to lay it down, that in this magnificent structure, with its solid stone staircase, its massive pavement of the same material, and its seventy-two stone pillars, each sixty-four feet high, the walls were of mud. Can we believe in this incongruity? Can we imagine that a prince, who possessed an unbounded command of human labor, and an inexhaustible supply of stone in the rocky mountains close at hand, would have had recourse to the meanest of materials for the walls of an edifice which he evidently intended to eclipse all others upon the platform. And, especially, can we suppose this, when the very same prince used solid blocks of stone, in the walls of the very inferior edifice which he constructed in this same locality? Mr. Fergusson, in defence of his hypothesis, alleges the frequent combination of meanness with magnificence in the East, and softens down the meanness in the present case by clothing his mud walls with enamelled tiles, and painting them with all the colors of the rainbow. But here again the hypothesis is wholly unsupported by fact. Neither at Persepolis, nor at Pasargadae, nor at any other ancient Persian site, has a single fragment of an enamelled tile or brick been discovered. In Babylonia and Assyria, where the employment of such an ornamentation was common, the traces of it which remain are abundant. Must not the entire absence of such traces from all exclusively Persian ruins be held to indicate that this mode of adorning edifices was not adopted in Persia?

If then we resign the notion of this remarkable building having been a walled structure, we must suppose that it was a summer throne-room, open to all the winds of heaven, except so far as it was protected by curtains. For the use of these by the Persians in pillared edifices, we have important historical authority in the statement already quoted from the Book of Esther. The Persian palace, to which that passage directly refers, contained a structure almost the exact counterpart of this at Persepolis; and it is probable that at both places the interstices between the outer pillars of, at any rate, the great central colonnade, were filled with "hangings of white and green and blue, fastened with cords of white and purple to silver rings," which were attached to the "pillars of marble;" and that by these means an undue supply of light and air, as well as an unseemly publicity, were prevented. A traveller in the country well observes, in allusion to this passage from Esther: Nothing could be more appropriate than this method at Susa and Persepolis, the spring residences of the Persian monarchs. It must be considered that these columnar halls were the equivalents of the modern throne-rooms, that here all public business was dispatched, and that here the king might sit and enjoy the beauties of the landscape. With the rich plains of Susa and Persepolis before him, he could well, after his winter's residence at Babylon, dispense with massive walls, which would only check the warm fragrant breeze from those verdant prairies adorned with the choicest flowers. A massive roof, covering the whole expanse of columns, would be too cold and dismal, whereas curtains around the central group would serve to admit both light and warmth. Nothing can be conceived better adapted to the climate or the season.

If the central cluster of pillars was thus adapted to the purposes of a throne-room, equally well may the isolated colonnades have served as ante-chambers or posts for guards. Protected, perhaps, with curtains or awnings of their own, of a coarser material than those of the main chamber, or at any rate casting, when the sun was high, a broad and deep shadow, they would give a welcome shelter to those who had to watch over the safety of the monarch, or who were expecting but had not yet received their summons to the royal presence. Except in the very hottest weather, the Oriental does not love to pass his day within doors. Seated on the pavement in groups, under the deep shadows of these colonnades, which commanded a glorious view of the vast fertile plain of the Bendamir, of the undulating mountain-tract beyond, and of the picturesque hills known now as Koh-Istakhr, or Koh-Rhamgherd, the subjects of the Great King, who had business at Court, would wait, agreeably enough, till their turn came to approach the throne.

Our survey of the Persepolitan platform is now complete; but, before we entirely dismiss the subject of Persian palaces, it seems proper to say a few words with respect to the other palatial remains of Achasmenian times, remains which exist in three places—at Murgab or Pasargadse, at Istakr, and at the great mound of Susa. The Murgab and Istakr ruins were carefully examined by MM. Coste and Flandin; while General Williams and Mr. Loftus diligently explored, and completely made out, the plan of the Susian edifice.

The ruins at Murgab, which are probably the most ancient in Persia, comprise, besides the well-known "Tomb of Cyrus," two principal buildings. The largest of these was of an oblong-square shape, about 147 feet long by 116 wide. It seems to have been surrounded by a lofty wall, in which were huge portals, consisting of great blocks of stone, partially hollowed out, to render them portable. There was an inscription on the jambs of each portal, containing the words, "I am Cyrus the King, the

Achaemenian." Within the walled enclosure which may have been skirted internally by a colonnade was a pillared building, of much greater height than the surrounding walls, as is evident from the single column which remains. This shaft, which is perfectly plain, and shows no signs of a capital, has an altitude of thirty-six feet, with a diameter of three feet four inches at the base. On the area around, which was carefully paved, are the bases of seven other similar pillars, arranged in lines, and so situated as apparently to indicate an oblong hall, supported by twelve pillars, in three rows of four each.

Vol. II

Plate XLIX.

Fig. 1.

Single volute Capital, Persepolis.

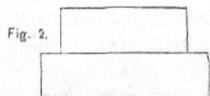

Fig. 2.

Base of Pillars forming central Cluster.

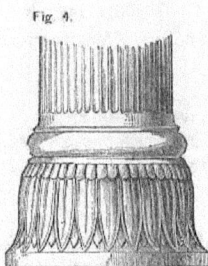

Fig. 3.

Fig. 4.

Another Pillar-Base in the same.

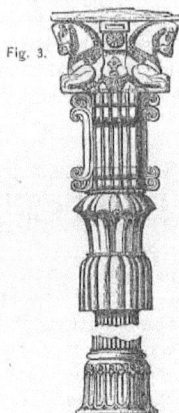

Complex Capital and Base of Pillars in the Great Hall of Xerxes (Persepolis)

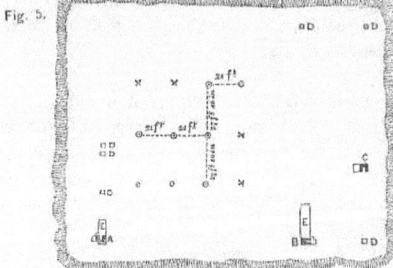

Fig. 5.

Plan of Palace, Pasargadæ.
A, B, C. Pillars with inscriptions.   D D. Pillar Bases.   E E. Remains of Pavement.

PLATE XLIX

The chief peculiarity of the arrangement is, a variety in the width of the intercolumniations, which measure twenty-seven feet ten inches in one direction, but twenty-one feet only in the other. The smaller building, which is situated at only a short distance from the larger one, covers a space of 125 feet by fifty. It consists of twelve pillar bases, arranged in two rows of six each, the pillars being somewhat thicker than those of the other building, and placed somewhat closer together. [PLATE XLIX., Fig. 5.] The form of the base is very singular. It exhibits at the side a semicircular bulge, ornamented with a series of nine flutings, which are carried entirely round the base in parallel horizontal circles. [PLATE L., Fig. 2.] In front of the pillar bases, at the distance of about twenty-three feet from the nearest, is a square column, still upright, on which is sculptured a curious mythological figure, together with the same curt legend, which appears on the larger building—"I am Cyrus, the King, the Achaemenian."

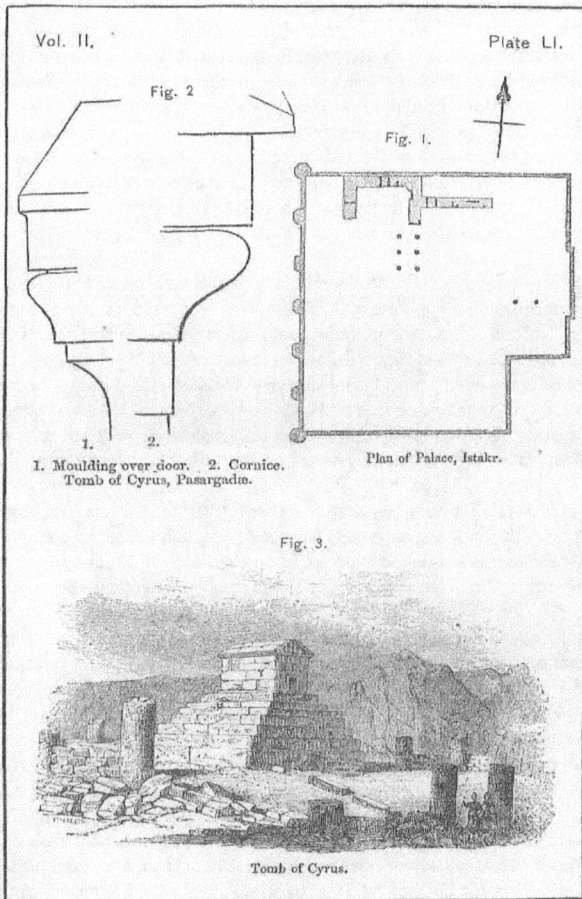

Vol. II.　　　　　　　　　　　　　　　Plate LI.

Fig. 2

Fig. I.

1.　　2.
1. Moulding over door.　2. Cornice.
Tomb of Cyrus, Pasargadæ.

Plan of Palace, Istakr.

Fig. 3.

Tomb of Cyrus.

PLATE LI

There are two other buildings at Murgab remarkable for their masonry. One is a square tower, with slightly projecting corners, built of hewn blocks of stone, very regularly laid, and carried to a height of forty-two feet. The other is a platform, exceedingly massive and handsome, composed entirely of squared stone, and faced with blocks often eight or ten feet long, laid in horizontal courses, and rusticated throughout in a manner that is highly ornamental. [PLATE L. Fig. 3.] The style resembles that of the substructions of the Temple of Jerusalem. It occurs occasionally, though somewhat rarely, in Greece; but there is said to exist nowhere so extensive and beautiful a specimen of it as that of the platform at this ancient site. [PLATE L., Fig. 4.]

The palace at Istakr is in better preservation than either of the two pillared edifices at Murgab; but still, it is not in such a condition as to enable us to lay down with any certainty even its ground-plan. [PLATE LI., Fig. 1.] One pillar only remains erect; but the bases of eight others have been found in situ; the walls are partly to be traced, and the jambs of several doorways and niches are still standing. These remains show that in many respects, as in the character of the pillars, which were fluted and had capitals like those already described, in the massiveness of the door and window jambs, and in the thickness of the walls, the Istakr Palace resembled closely the buildings on the Persepolitan platform; but at the same time they indicate that its plan was wholly different, and thus our knowledge of the platform buildings in no degree enables us to complete, or even to carry forward to any appreciable extent, the ground-plan of the edifice derived from actual research. The height of the columns, which is inferior to that of the lowest at the great platform, would seem to indicate, either that the building was the first in which stone pillars were attempted, or that it was erected at a time when the Persians no longer possessed the mechanical skill required to quarry, transport, and raise into place the enormous blocks used in the best days of the nation.

The palace of Susa, exhumed by Mr. Loftus and General Williams, consisted of a great Hall or Throne-room, almost exactly a duplicate of the Chehl Minar at Persepolis, and of a few other very inferior buildings. It stood at the summit of the great platform, a quadrilateral mass of unburnt brick, which from a remote antiquity had supported the residence of the old Susian kings. It fronted a little west of north, and commanded a magnificent view over the Susianian plains to the mountains of Lauristan. An inscription, repeated on four of its pillar-bases, showed that it was originally built by Darius Hystaspis, and afterwards repaired by Artaxerxes Longimanus. As it was so exactly a reproduction of an edifice already minutely described, no further account of it need be here given.

From the palaces of the Persian kings we may now pass to their tombs, remarkable structures which drew the attention of the ancients, and which have been very fully examined and represented in modern times. These tombs are eight in number, but present only two types, so that it will be sufficient to give in this place a detailed account of two tombs—one of each description.

The most ancient, and, on the whole, the most remarkable of the tombs, is almost universally allowed to be that of the Great Cyrus. It is unique in design, totally different from all the other royal sepulchres; and, though it has been often described, demands, and must receive, notice in any account that is given of the ancient Persian constructions. The historian Arrian calls it "a house upon a pedestal;" and this brief description exactly expresses its general character. On a base, composed of huge blocks of the most beautiful white marble,1 which rises pyramidically in seven steps of different heights, there stands a small "house" of similar material, crowned with a stone roof, which is formed in front and rear into a pediment resembling that of a Greek temple. [PLATE LI., Fig.3.] The "house" has no window, but one of the end walls was pierced by a low and narrow doorway, which led into a small chamber or cell, about eleven feet long, seven broad, and seven high. Here, as ancient writers inform us, the body of the Great Cyrus was deposited in a golden coffin. Internally the chamber is destitute of any inscription, and indeed seems to have been left perfectly plain. Externally, there is a cornice of some elegance below the pediment, a good molding over the doorway, which is also doubly recessed—and two other very slight moldings, one at the base of the "house," and the other at the bottom of the second step. [PLATE LI., Fig. 2.] Except for these, the whole edifice is perfectly plain. Its present height above the ground is thirty-six feet, and it may originally have been a foot or eighteen inches higher, for the top of the roof is worn away. It measures at the base forty-seven feet by forty-three feet nine inches.

1. Ground-plan of Tomb of Darius, Nakhsh-i-Rustam.

2. Ground-plan of another Royal Tomb.

PLATE LII

The tomb stands within a rectangular area, marked out by pillars, the bases or broken shafts of which are still to be seen. They appear to have been twenty-four in number; all of them circular and smooth, not fluted; six pillars occupied each side of the rectangle, and they stood distant from each other about fourteen feet. It is probable that they originally supported a colonnade, which skirted internally a small walled court, within which the tomb was placed. The capitals of the pillars, if they had any, have wholly disappeared; and the researches conducted on the spot have failed to discover any trace of them.

The remainder of the Persian royal sepulchres are rock-tombs, excavations in the sides of mountains, generally at a considerable elevation, so placed as to attract the eye of the beholder, while they are extremely difficult of approach. Of this kind of tomb there are four in the face of the mountain which bounds the Pulwar Valley on the north-west, while there are three others in the immediate vicinity of the Persepolitan platform, two in the mountain which overhangs it, and one in the rocks a little further to the south. The general shape of the excavations, as it presents itself to the eye of the spectator, resembles a Greek cross. [PLATE LII., Fig. 1.] This is divided by horizontal lines into three portions, the upper one (corresponding with the topmost limb of the cross) containing a very curious sculptured representation of the monarch worshipping Ormazd; the middle one, which comprises the two side limbs, together with the space between them, being carved architecturally so as to resemble a portico; and the third compartment (corresponding with the lowest limb of the cross) being left perfectly plain. In the centre of the middle compartment is sculptured on the face of the rock the similitude of a doorway, closely resembling those which still stand on the great platform; that is to say, doubly recessed, and ornamented at the top with lily-work. The upper portion of this doorway is filled with the solid rock, smoothed to a flat surface and crossed by three horizontal bars. The lower portion, to the height of four or five feet, is cut away; and thus entrance is given to the actual tomb, which is hollowed out in the rock behind.

Thus far the rock tombs, are, with scarcely an exception, of the same type. The excavations, however, behind their ornamental fronts, present some curious differences. In the simplest case of all, we find, on entering, an arched chamber, thirteen feet five inches long by seven feet two inches wide, from which there opens out, opposite to the door and at the height of about four feet from the ground, a deep horizontal recess, arched, like the chamber. Near the front of this recess is a further perpendicular excavation, in length six feet ten inches, in width three feet three inches, and in depth the same. This was the actual sarcophagus, and was covered, or intended to be covered, by a slab of stone. In the deeper part of the recess there is room for two other such sarcophagi; but in this case they have not been excavated, one burial only having, it would seem, taken place in this tomb. Other sepulchres present the same general features, but provide for a much greater number of interments. In that of Darius Hystaspis the sepulchral chamber contains three distinct recesses, in each of which are three sarcophagi, so that the tomb would hold nine bodies. It has, apparently, been cut originally for a single recess, on the exact plan of the tomb described above, but has afterwards been elongated towards the left. [PLATE LIII., Fig. 1.] Two of the tombs show a still more elaborate ground-plan—one in which curved lines take to some extent the place of straight ones. [PLATE LII., Fig. 2.] The tombs above the platform of Persepolis are more richly ornamented than the others, the lintels and sideposts of the doorways being covered with rosettes, and the entablature above the cornice bearing a row of lions, facing on either side towards the centre. [PLATE LIII., Fig. 2.]

Fig. 2.

Fig. 1.

1.   2.

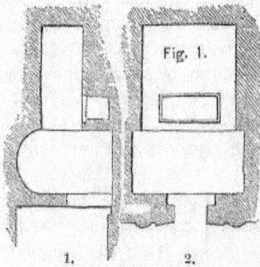

1. Section of Tomb, Persepolis.
2. Ground plan of the same.

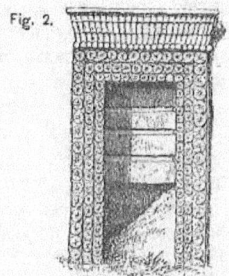

Entrance to a Royal Tomb,
Persepolis.

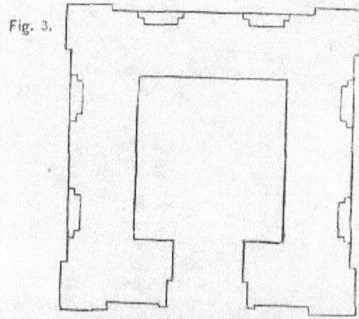

Fig. 3.

1. Section of Tower, Nakhsh-i-Rustam.

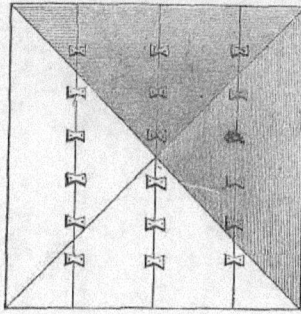

2. Roof of the same.

PLATE LIII

A curious edifice, belonging probably to the later Achaemenian times, stands immediately in front of the four royal tombs at Nakhsh-i-Eustam. This is a square tower, composed of large blocks of marble, cut with great exactness, and joined together without mortar or cement of any kind. The building is thirty-six feet high; and each side of it measures, as near as possible, twenty-four feet. It is ornamented with pilasters at the corners and with six recessed niches, or false windows, in three ranks, one over the other, on three out of its four faces. On the fourth face are two niches only, one over the other; and below them is a doorway with a cornice. The surface of the walls between the pilasters is also ornamented with a number of rectangular depressions, resembling the sunken ends of beams. The doorway, which looks north, towards the tombs, is not at the bottom of the building, but half-way up its side, and must have been reached either by a ladder or by a flight of steps. It leads into a square chamber, twelve feet wide by nearly eighteen high, extending to the top of the building, and roofed in with four large slabs of stone, which reach entirely across from side to side, being rather more than twenty-four feet long, six feet wide, and from eighteen inches to three feet in thickness. [PLATE LIII., Fig. 3.] On the top these slabs are so cut that the roof has every way a slight incline; at their edges they are fashioned between the pilasters, into a dentated cornice, like that which is seen on the tomb. Externally they were clamped together in the same careful way which we find to have been in use both at Persepolis and Parsargadae. The building seems to have been closed originally by two ponderous stone doors. [PLATE LIV., Fig. 1.]

Plate LIV.   Vol II-

Fig. 1

Front View of the Tower, showing excavation.

Fig. 2.

Massive Gateway (Istakr).

PLATE LIV

Another remarkable construction, which must belong to a very ancient period in the history of the country, is a gateway composed of enormous stones, which forms a portion of the ruins of Istakr. [PLATE LIV., Fig. 2.] It has generally been regarded as one of the old gates of the city; but its position in the gorge between the town wall and the opposite mountain, and the fact that it lies directly across the road from Pasargadae into the plain of Merdasht, seem rather to imply that it was one of those fortified "gates," which we know to have been maintained by the Persians, at narrow points along their great routes, for the purpose of securing them, and stopping the advance of an enemy. On either side were walls of vast thickness, on the one hand abutting upon the mountain, on the other probably connected with the wall of the town, while between them were three massive pillars, once, no doubt, the supports of a tower, from which the defenders of the gate would engage its assailants at a great advantage.

We have now described (so far as our data have rendered it possible) all the more important of the ancient edifices of the Persians, and may proceed to consider the next branch of the present inquiry, namely, their skill in the mimetic arts. Before, however, the subject of their architecture is wholly dismissed, a few words seem to be required on its general character and chief peculiarities.

First, then, the simplicity and regularity of the style are worthy of remark. In the ground-plans of buildings the straight line only is used; all the angles are right angles; all the pillars fall into line; the intervals between pillar and pillar are regular, and generally equal; doorways are commonly placed opposite intercolumniations; where there is but one doorway, it is in the middle of the wall which it pierces; where there are two, they correspond to one another. Correspondence is the general law. Not only does door correspond to door, and pillar to pillar, but room to room, window to window, and even niche to niche. Most of the buildings are so contrived that one half is the exact duplicate of the other; and where this is not the case, the irregularity is generally either slight, or the result of an alteration, made probably for convenience sake. Travellers are impressed with the Grecian character of what they behold, though there is an almost entire absence of Greek forms. The regularity is not confined to single buildings, but extends to the relations of different edifices one to another. The sides of buildings standing on one platform, at whatever distance they may be, are parallel. There is, however, less consideration paid than we should have expected to the exact position, with respect to a main building, in which a subordinate one shall be placed. Propylaea, for instance, are not opposite the centre of the edifice to which they conduct, but slightly on one side of the centre. And generally, excepting in the parallelism of their sides, buildings seem placed with but slight regard to neighboring ones.

For effect, the Persian architecture must have depended, firstly, upon the harmony that is produced by the observance of regularity and proportion; and, secondly, upon two main features of the style. These were the grand sculptured staircases which formed the approaches to all the principal buildings, and the vast groves of elegant pillars in and about the great halls. The lesser buildings were probably ugly, except in front. But such edifices as the Chehl Minar at Persepolis, and its duplicate at Susa—where long vistas of columns met the eye on every side, and the great central cluster was supported by lighter detached groups, combining similarity of form with some variety of ornament, where richly colored drapings contrasted with the cool gray stone of the building, and a golden roof overhung a pavement of many hues—must have been handsome, from whatever side they were contemplated, and for general richness and harmony of effect may have compared favorably with any edifices which, up to the time of their construction, had been erected in any country or by any people. If it may seem to some that they were wanting in grandeur, on account of their comparatively low height—a height which, including that of the platform, was probably in no case much more than a hundred feet—it must be remembered that the buildings of Greece and (except the Pyramids) those of Egypt, had the same defect, and that, until the constructive powers of the arch came to be understood, it was almost impossible to erect a building that should be at once lofty and elegant. Height, moreover, if the buildings are for use, implies inconvenience, a waste of time and power being involved in the ascent and descent of steps. The ancient architects, studying utility more than effect, preferred spreading out their buildings to piling them up, and rarely, unless in thickly-peopled towns, even introduced a second story.

The spectator, however, was impressed with a sense of grandeur in another way. The use of huge blocks of stone, not only in platforms, but in the buildings themselves, in the shafts of pillars, the antae of porticos, the jambs of doorways, occasionally in roofs, and perhaps in epistylia, produced the same impression of power, and the same feeling of personal insignificance in the beholder, which is commonly effected by great size in the edifice, and particularly by height. The mechanical skill required to transport and raise into place the largest of these blocks must have been very considerable, and their employment causes not merely a blind admiration of those who so built on the part of ignorant persons, but a profound respect for them on the part of those who are by their studies and tastes best qualified for pronouncing on the relative and absolute merits of architectural masterpieces.

Among the less pleasing peculiarities of the Persian architecture may be mentioned a general narrowness of doors in proportion to their height, a want of passages, a thickness of walls, which is architecturally clumsy, but which would have had certain advantages in such a climate, an inclination to place the doors of rooms near one corner, an allowance of two entrances into a great hall from under a single portico, a peculiar position of propylaea, and the very large employment of pillars in the interior of buildings. In many of these points, and also in the architectural use which was made of sculpture, the style of building resembled, to some extent, that of Assyria; the propylaea, however, were less Assyrian than Egyptian; while in the main and best features of the architecture, it was (so far as we can tell) original. The solid and handsome stone platforms, the noble staircases, and the profusion of light and elegant stone columns, which formed the true glory of the architecture—being the features on which its effect chiefly depended—have nowhere been discovered in Assyria; and all the evidence is against their existence. The Arians found in Mesopotamia an architecture of which the pillar was scarcely an element at all—which was fragile and unenduring—and which depended for its effect on a lavish display of partially colored sculpture and more richly tinted enamelled brick. Instead of imitating this, they elaborated for themselves, from the wooden buildings of their own mountain homes, a style almost exactly the reverse of that with which their victories had brought them into contact. Adopting, of main features, nothing but the platform, they imparted even to this a new character, by substituting in its construction the best for the worst of materials, and by further giving to these stone structures a massive solidity, from the employment of huge, blocks, which made them stand in the strongest possible contrast to the frail and perishable mounds of Babylonia and Assyria. Having secured in this way a firm and enduring basis, they proceeded to erect upon it buildings where the perpendicular line was primary and the horizontal secondary—buildings of almost, the same solid and massive character as the platform itself—forests of light but strong columns, supporting a wide-spreading roof, sometimes open to the air, sometimes enclosed by walls, according as they were designed for summer or winter use, or for greater or less privacy. To edifices of this character elaborate ornamentation was unnecessary; for the beauty of the column is such that nothing more is needed to set off a building. Sculpture would thus be dispensed with, or reserved for mere occasional use, and employed not so much on the palace itself as on its outer approaches; while brick enamelling could well be rejected altogether, as too poor and fragile a decoration for buildings of such strength and solidity.

The origination of this columnar architecture must be ascribed to the Medes, who, dwelling in or near the more wooden parts of the Zagros range, constructed, during the period of their empire, edifices of considerable magnificence, whereof wooden pillars were the principal feature, the courts being surrounded by colonnades, and the chief buildings having porticos, the pillars in both cases being of wood. A wooden roof rested on these supports, protected externally by plates of metal. We do not know if the pillars had capitals, or if they supported an entablature; but probability is in favor of both these arrangements having existed. When the Persians succeeded the Medes in the sovereignty of Western Asia, they found Arian architecture in this condition. As stone, however, was the natural material of their country, which is but scantily wooded and is particularly barren towards the edge of the great plateau, where their chief towns were situated, and as they had from the first a strong desire of fame and a love for the substantial and the enduring, they almost immediately substituted for the cedar and cypress pillars of the Medes, stone shafts, plain or fluted, which they carried to a surprising height, and fixed with such firmness that many of them have resisted the destructive powers of time, of earthquakes, and of vandalism for more than three-and-twenty centuries, and still stand erect and nearly as perfect as when they received the last touch from the sculptor's hand more than 2000 years ago. It is the glory of the Persians in art to have invented this style, which they certainly did not learn from the Assyrians, and which they can scarcely be supposed to have adopted from Egypt, where the conception of the pillar and its ornamentation were wholly different. We can scarcely doubt that Greece received from this quarter the impulse which led to the substitution of the light and elegant forms which distinguish the architecture of her best period from the rude and clumsy work of the more ancient times.

Of the mimetic art of the Persians we do not possess any great amount, or any great variety, of specimens. The existing remains consist of reliefs, either executed on the natural rock or on large slabs of hewn stone used in building, of impressions upon coins, and of a certain number of intaglios cut upon gems. We possess no Persian statues, no modelled figures, no metal castings, no carvings in ivory or in wood, no enamellings, no pottery even. The excavations on Persian sites have been singularly barren of those minor results which flowed so largely from the Mosopotamian excavations, and have yielded no traces of the furniture, domestic implements, or wall-ornamentation of the people; have produced, in fact, no small objects at all, excepting a few cylinders and some spear and arrow heads, thus throwing scarcely any light on the taste or artistic genius of the people.

The nearest approach to statuary which we meet with among the Persian remains are the figures of colossal bulls, set to guard portals, or porticos, which are not indeed sculptures in the round, but are specimens of exceedingly high relief, and which, being carved in front as well as along the side, do not fall very far short of statues. Of such figures, we find two varieties—one representing the real animal, the other a monster with the body and legs of a bull, the head of a man, and the wings of an eagle. There is considerable merit in both representations. They are free from the defect of flatness, or want of breadth in comparison with the length, which characterizes the similar figures of Assyrian artists; and they are altogether grand, massive, and imposing. The general proportions of the bulls are good, the limbs are accurately drawn, the muscular development is well portrayed, and the pose of the figure is majestic. Even the monstrous forms of human-headed bulls have a certain air of quiet dignity, which is not without its effect on the beholder; and, although implying no great artistic merit, since they are little more than reproductions of Assyrian models, indicate an appreciation of some of the best qualities of Assyrian art—the combination of repose with strength, of great size with the most careful finish, and of strangeness with the absence of any approach to grotesqueness or absurdity. The other Persian reliefs may be divided under four heads:

(1) Mythological representations of a man—the king apparently—engaged in combat with a lion, a bull, or a monster; (2) Processions of guards, courtiers, attendants, or tribute-bearers; (3) Representations of the monarch walking, seated upon his throne, or employed in the act of worship; and (4) Representations of lions and bulls, either singly or engaged in combat.

On the jambs of doorways in three of the Persepolitan buildings, a human figure, dressed in the Median robe, but with the sleeve thrown back from the right arm, is represented in the act of killing either a lion, a bull, or a grotesque monster. In every case the animal is rampant, and assails his antagonist with three of his feet, while he stands on the fourth. The lion and bull have nothing about them that is very peculiar; but the monsters present most strange and unusual combinations. One of them has the griffin head, which we have already seen in use in the capitals of columns, a feathered crest and neck, a bird's wings, a scorpion's tail, and legs terminating in the claws of an eagle. The other has an eagle's head, ears like an ass, feathers on the neck, the breast, and the back, with the body, legs, and tail of a lion. [PLATE LV., Fig. 1.] Figures of equal grotesqueness, some of which possess certain resemblances to these, are common in the mythology of Assyria, and have been already represented in these volumes; but the Persian specimens are no servile imitations of these earlier forms. The idea of the Assyrian artist has, indeed, been borrowed; but Persian fancy has worked it out in its own way, adding, modifying, and subtracting in such a manner as to give to the form produced a quite peculiar, and (so to speak) native character.

Fig. 1.

Fig. 2.   King killing a Monster, Persepolis. (From a photograph.)

Persian subjects bringing tribute to the King, Persepolis. (From a Photograph.)

PLATE LV

Persian gems abound with monstrous forms, of equal, or even superior grotesqueness. As the Gothic architects indulged their imagination in the most wonderful combinations to represent evil spirits or the varieties of vice and sensualism, so the Persian gem-engravers seem to have allowed their fancy to run riot in the creation of monsters, representative of the Powers of Darkness or of different kinds of evil, The stones exhibit the king in conflict with a vast variety of monsters, some nearly resembling the Persepolitan, while others have strange shapes unseen elsewhere. Winged lions, with two tails and with the horns of a ram or an antelope, sphinxes and griffins of half a dozen different kinds, and various other nondescript creatures, appear upon the Persian gems and cylinders, furnishing abundant evidence of the quaint and prolific fancy of the designers.

The processional subjects represented by the Persian artists are of three kinds. In the simplest and least interesting the royal guards, or the officers of the court, are represented in one or more lines of very similar figures, either moving in one direction, or standing in two bodies, one facing the other, in the attitude of quiet expectation. In these subjects there is a great sameness, and a very small amount of merit. The proportion of the forms is, indeed, fairly good, the heads and hands are well drawn, and there is some grace in certain of the figures, but the general effect is tame and somewhat heavy; the attitudes are stiff, and present little variety, while, nevertheless, they are sometimes impossible; there is a monotonous repetition of identically the same figure, which is tiresome, and a want of grouping which is very inartistic. If Persia had produced nothing better than this in sculpture, she would have had to be placed not only behind Assyria, but behind Egypt, as far as the sculptor's art is concerned.

Processional scenes of a more attractive character are, however, tolerably frequent. Some exhibit to us the royal purveyors arriving at the palace with their train of attendants, and bringing with them the provisions required for the table of the monarch. Here we have some varieties of costume which are curious, and some representations of Persian utensils, which are not without a certain interest. Occasionally, too, we are presented with animal forms, as kids, which have considerable merit.

But by far the most interesting of the processional scenes, are those which represent the conquered nations bringing to the monarch those precious products of their several countries which the Lord of Asia expected to receive annually, as a sort of free gift from his subjects, in addition to the fixed tribute which was exacted from them. Here we have a wonderful variety of costume and equipment, a happy admixture of animal with human forms, horses, asses, chariots, sheep, cattle, camels, interspersed among men, and the whole divided into groups by means of cypress-trees, which break the series into portions, and allow the eye to rest in succession upon a number of distinct pictures. Processions of this kind occurred on several of the Persepolitan staircases; but by far the most elaborate and complete is that on the grand steps in front of the Chehl Minar, or Great Hall of Audience, where we see above twenty such groups of figures, each with it own peculiar features, and all finished with the utmost care and delicacy. The illustration [PLATE LV., Fig. 2], which is taken from a photograph, will give a tolerable idea of the general character of this relief; it shows the greater portion of six groups, whereof two are much injured by the fall of the parapet-wall on which they were represented, while the remaining four are in good preservation. It will be noticed that the animal forms—the Bactrian camel and the humped ox—are superior to the human, and have considerable positive merit as works of art. This relative superiority is observable throughout the entire series, which contains, besides several horses (some of which have been already represented in these volumes), a lioness, an excellent figure of the wild ass, and two tolerably well-drawn sheep. [PLATE LVI., Fig. 2 and 3.]

Plate LVI.

Fig. 1.

Fig. 2.

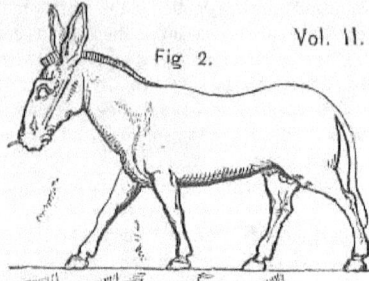

Wild Ass, Persepolis.

Attendant bringing a kid
to the palace. (Perse-
polis.)

Fig. 3

Horned Sheep, Persepolis.

Fig. 4.

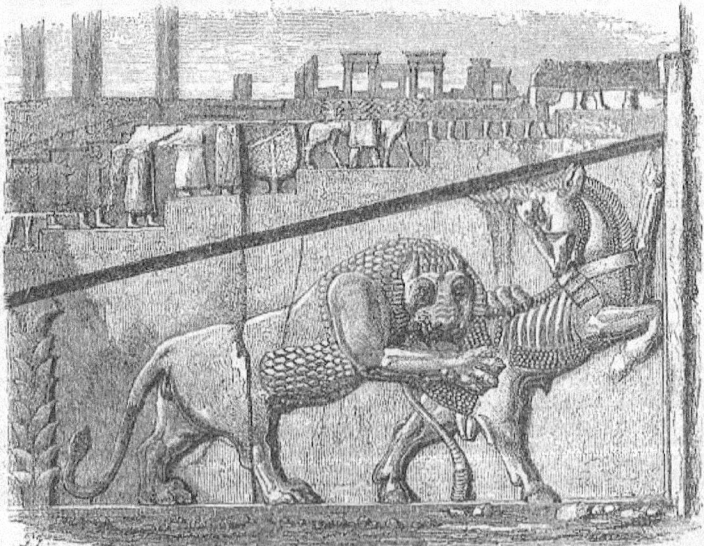

Lion devouring a Bull, Persepolis. (From a Photograph.)

PLATE LVI

The representations of the monarch upon the reliefs are of three kinds. In the simplest, he is on foot, attended by the parasol-bearer and the napkin-bearer, or by the latter only, apparently in the act of proceeding from one part of the palace to another. In the more elaborate he is either seated on an elevated throne, which is generally supported by numerous caryatid figures, or he stands on a platform similarly upheld, in the act of worship before an altar. This latter is the universal representation upon tombs, while the throne scenes are reserved for palaces. In both representations the supporting figures are numerous; and it is here chiefly that we notice varieties of physiognomy, which are evidently intended to recall the differences in the physical type of the several races by which the Empire was inhabited. In one case, we have a negro very well portrayed; in others we trace the features of Scyths or Tatars. It is manifest that the artist has not been content to mark the nationality of the different figures by costume alone, but has aimed at reproducing upon the stone the physiognomic peculiarities of each race.

The purely animal representations which the bas-reliefs bring before us are few in number, and have little variety of type. The most curious and the most artistic is one which is several times repeated at Persepolis, where it forms the usual ornamentation of the triangular spaces on the facades of stairs. This is a representation of a combat between a lion and a bull, or (perhaps, we should rather say) a representation of a lion seizing and devouring a bull; for the latter animal is evidently powerless to offer any resistance to the fierce beast which has sprung upon him from behind, and has fixed both fangs and claws in his body. [PLATE LVI., Fig. 4.] In his agony the bull rears up his fore-parts, and turns his head feebly towards his assailant, whose strong limbs and jaws have too firm a hold to be dislodged by such struggles as his unhappy victim is capable of making. In no Assyrian drawing is the massiveness and strength of the king of beasts more powerfully rendered than in this favorite group, which the Persian sculptors repeated without the slightest change from generation to generation. The contour of the lion, his vast muscular development, and his fierce countenance are really admirable, and the bold presentation of the face in full, instead of in profile, is beyond the ordinary powers of Oriental artists.

Drawings of bulls and lions in rows, where each animal is the exact counterpart of all the others, are found upon the friezes of some of the tombs, and upon the representations of canopies over the royal throne. These drawings are fairly spirited, but have not any extraordinary merit. They reproduce forms well known in Assyria. A figure of a sitting lion seems also to have been introduced occasionally on the facades of staircases, occurring in the central compartment of the parapet-wall at top. These figures, in no case, remain complete; but enough is left to show distinctly what the attitude was, and this appears not to have resembled very closely any common Assyrian type. [PLATE LVII., Fig. 1.]

Fig. I. Fig 2 Plate. LVII.

Fragment of a sitting Lion, Persepolis.

Persian Portrait.
(From a Gem.)

Fig. 3.

Fig. 4 Persian cylinders.

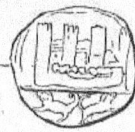

1 2

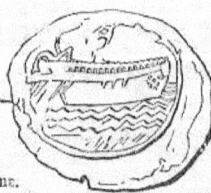

3
Persian Coins.

PLATE LVII

The Persian gem-engravings have considerable merit, and need not fear a comparison with those of any other Oriental nation. They occur upon hard stones of many different kinds, as cornelian, onyx, rock-crystal, sapphirine, sardonyx, chalcedony, etc., and are executed for the most part with great skill and delicacy. The designs which they embody are in general of a mythological character; but sometimes scenes of real life occur upon them, and then the drawing is often good, and almost always spirited. In proof of this, the reader may be referred to the hunting-scenes already given, which are derived wholly from this source, as well as to the gems figured [PLATE LVI., Fig. 3], one of which is certainly, and the other almost certainly, of Persian workmanship. In the former we see the king, not struggling with a mythological lion but engaged apparently in the actual chase of the king of beasts Two lions have been roused from their lairs, and the monarch hastily places an arrow on the string, anxious to despatch one of his foes before the other can come to close quarters The eagerness of the hunter and the spirit and boldness of the animals are well represented. In the other gem, while there is less of artistic excellence, we have a scene of peculiar interest placed before us. A combat between two Persians and two Cythians seems to be represented. The latter marked by their peaked cap and their loose trousers, fight with the bow and the battle-axe, the former with the bow and the sword One Scyth is receiving his death-wound, the other is about to let loose a shaft, but seems at the same time half inclined to fly The steady confidence of the warriors on the one side contrasts well with the timidity and hesitancy of their weaker and smaller rivals. [PLATE LVII., Fig. 3.]

The vegetable forms represented on the gems are sometimes graceful and pleasing. This is especially the case with palm-trees, a favorite subject of the artists, who delineated with remarkable success the feathery leaves, the pendant fruit and the rough bark of the stem. [PLATE LVIII., Fig 1.] The lion-hunter represented on the signet-cylinder of Darius Hystaspis takes place in a palm-grove, and furnishes the accompanying example of this form of vegetable life.

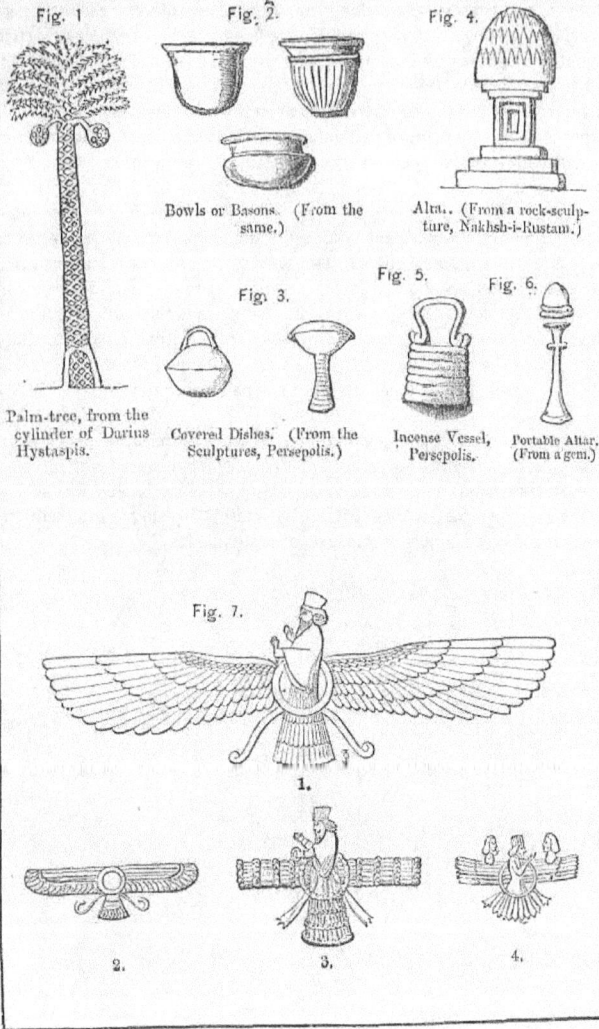

Plate LVIII.   Vol. II.

Fig. 1   Fig. 2.   Fig. 4.

Bowls or Basons. (From the   Altar.. (From a rock-sculp-
          same.)   ture, Nakhsh-i-Rustam.)

                          Fig. 5.   Fig. 6.
                Fig. 3.

Palm-tree, from the
cylinder of Darius   Covered Dishes. (From the   Incense Vessel,   Portable Altar.
Hystaspis.   Sculptures, Persepolis.)   Persepolis.   (From a gem.)

Fig. 7.

1.

2.   3.   4.

PLATE LVIII

One gem, ascribed on somewhat doubtful grounds to the Persians of Achaemenian times, contains what appears to be a portrait. It is thought to be the bust of a satrap of Salamis in Cyprus, and is very carefully executed. If really of Persian workmanship, it would indicate a considerable advance in the power of representing the human countenance between the time of Darius Hystaspis and that of Alexander [PLATE LVII. Fig. 2.]

Persian coins are of three principal types. The earliest have on the one side the figure of a monarch bearing the diadem and armed with the bow and javelin, while on the other there is an irregular indentation of the same nature with the quadratum incusum of the Greeks. This rude form is replaced in later times by a second design, which is sometimes a horseman, sometimes the forepart of a ship, sometimes the king drawing an an arrow from his quiver. Another type exhibits on the obverse the monarch in combat with a lion while the reverse shows a galley, or a towered and battlemented city with two lions standing below it, back to back. The third common type has on the obverse the king in his chariot, with his charioteer in front of him, and (generally) an attendant carrying a fly-chaser behind. The reverse has either the trireme or the battlemented city. A specimen of each type is given. [PLATE LVII., Fig. 4.]

The artistic merit of these medals is not great. The relief is low, and the drawing generally somewhat rude. The head of the monarch in the early coins is greatly too large. The animal forms are, however, much superior to the human, and the horses which draw the royal chariot, the lions placed below the battlemented city, and the bulls which are found occasionally in the same position, must be pronounced truthful and spirited.

Of the Persian taste in furniture, utensils, personal ornaments and the like, we need say but little. The throne and footstool of the monarch are the only pieces of furniture represented in the sculptures, and these, though sufficiently elegant in their forms, are not very remarkable. Costliness of material seems to have been more prized than beauty of shape; and variety appears to have been carefully eschewed, one single uniform type of each article occurring in all the representations. The utensils represented are likewise few in number, and limited to certain constantly repeated forms. The most elaborate is the censer, which has been already given. With this is usually seen a sort of pail or basket, shaped like a lady's reticule, in which the aromatic gums for burning were probably kept. [PLATE LVIII., Fig. 5.] A covered dish, and a goblet with an inverted saucer over it, are also forms of frequent occurrence in the hands of the royal attendants; and the tribute-bearers frequently carry, among their other offerings, bowls or basons, which, though not of Persian manufacture, were no doubt left at the court, and took their place among the utensils of the palace. [PLATE LVIII., Figs. 2 and 3.]

In the matter of personal ornaments the taste of the Persians seems to have been peculiarly simple. Earrings were commonly plain rings of gold; bracelets mere bands of the same metal. Collars were circlets of gold twisted in a very inartificial fashion. There was nothing artistic in the sheaths or hilts of swords, though spear-shafts were sometimes adorned with the representation of an apple or a pomegranate. Dresses seem not to have been often patterned, but to have depended generally for their effect on make and color. In all these respects we observe a remarkable contrast between the Arian and the Semitic races, extreme simplicity characterizing the one, while the most elaborate ornamentation was affected by the other.

Persia was not celebrated in antiquity for the production of any special fabrics. The arts of weaving and dyeing were undoubtedly practised in the dominant country, as well as in most of the subject provinces, and the Persian dyes seem even to have had a certain reputation; but none of the productions of their looms acquired a name among foreign nations. Their skill, indeed, in the mechanical arts generally was, it is probable, not more than moderate. It was their boast that they were soldiers, and had won a position by their good swords which gave them the command of all that was most exquisite and admirable, whether in the natural world or among the products of human industry. So long as the carpets of Babylon and Sardis, the shawls of Kashmir and India, the fine linen of Borsippa and Egypt, the ornamental metal-work of Greece, the coverlets of Damascus, the muslins of Babylonia, the multiform manufactures of the Phoenician towns, poured continually into Persia Proper in the way of tribute, gifts, or merchandise, it was needless for the native population to engage largely in industrial enterprise.

To science the ancient Persians contributed absolutely nothing. The genius of the nation was adverse to that patient study and those laborious investigations from which alone scientific progress ensues. Too light and frivolous, too vivacious, too sensuous for such pursuits, they left them to the patient Babylonians, and the thoughtful, many-sided Greeks. The schools of Orchoe, Borsippa, and Miletus flourished under their sway, but without provoking their emulation, possibly without so much as attracting their attention. From first to last, from the dawn to the final close of their power, they abstained wholly from scientific studies. It would seem that they thought it enough to place before the world, as signs of their intellectual vigor, the fabric of their Empire and the buildings of Susa and Persepolis.

CHAPTER VI

RELIGION

The original form of the Persian religion has been already described under the head of the third or Median monarchy. It was identical with the religion of the Medes in its early shape, consisting mainly in the worship of Ahura-Mazda, the acknowledgment of a principle of evil—Angro-Mainyus, and obedience to the precepts of Zoroaster. When the Medes, on establishing a wide-spread Empire, chiefly over races by whom Magism had been long professed, allowed the creed of their subjects to corrupt their own belief, accepted the Magi for their priests, and formed the mixed religious system of which an account has been given in the second volume of this work, the Persians in their wilder country, less exposed to corrupting influences, maintained their original faith in undiminished purity, and continued faithful to their primitive traditions. The political dependence of their country upon Media during the period of the Median sway made no difference in this respect; for the Medes were tolerant, and did not seek to interfere with the creed of their subjects. The simple Zoroastrian belief and worship, overlaid by Magism in the now luxurious Media, found a refuge in the rugged Persian uplands, among the hardy shepherds and cultivators of that unattractive region, was professed by the early Achaemenian princes, and generally acquiesced in by the people.

The main feature of the religion daring this first period was the acknowledgment and the worship of a single supreme God—"the Lord God of Heaven"—"the giver (i.e. maker) of heaven and earth"— the disposer of thrones, the dispenser of happiness. The foremost place in inscriptions and decrees was assigned, almost universally, to the "great god, Ormazd." Every king, of whom we have an inscription more than two lines in length, speaks of Ormazd as his upholder; and the early monarchs mention by name no other god. All rule "by the grace of Ormazd." From Ormazd come victory, conquest, safety, prosperity, blessings of every kind. The "law of Ormazd" is the rule of life. The protection of Ormazd is the one priceless blessing for which prayer is perpetually offered.

While, however, Ormazd holds this exalted and unapproachable position, there is still an acknowledgment made, in a general way, of "other gods." Ormazd is "the greatest of the gods" (mathista baganam). It is a usual prayer to ask for the protection of Ormazd, together with that of these lesser powers (hada bagaibish). Sometimes the phrase is varied, and the petition is for the special protection of a certain class of Deities—the Dii familiares—or "deities who guard the house."

The worship of Mithra, or the Sun, does not appear in the inscriptions until the reign of Artaxerxes Mnemon, the victor of Cunaxa. It is, however, impossible to doubt that it was a portion of the Persian religion, at least as early as the date of Herodotus. Probably it belongs, in a certain sense, to primitive Zoroastrianism, but was kept in the background during the early period, when a less materialistic worship prevailed than suited the temper of later times.

Nor can it be doubted that the Persians held during this early period that Dualistic belief which has been the distinguishing feature of Zoroastrianism from a time long anterior to the commencement of the Median Empire down to the present day. It was not to be expected that this belief would show itself in the inscriptions, unless in the faintest manner; and it can therefore excite no surprise that they are silent, or all but silent, on the point in question. Nor need we wonder that this portion of their creed was not divulged by the Persians to Herodotus or to Xenophon, since it is exactly the sort of subject on which reticence was natural and might have been anticipated. Neither the lively Halicarnassian, nor the pleasant but somewhat shallow Athenian, had the gift of penetrating very deeply into the inner mind of a foreign people; added to which, it is to be remembered that they were unacquainted with Persia Proper, and drew their knowledge of Persian opinions and customs either from hearsay or from the creed and practices of the probably mixed garrisons which held Asia Minor, Syria, and Egypt.

Persian worship, in these early times, was doubtless that enjoined by the Zendavesta, comprising prayer and thanksgiving to Ormazd and the good spirits of his creation, the recitation of Gathas or hymns, the performance of sacrifice, and participation in the Soma ceremony. Worship seems to have taken place in temples, which are mentioned (according to the belief of most cuneiform scholars) in the Behistun inscription. Of the character of these buildings we can say nothing. It has been thought that those two massive square towers so similar in construction, which exist in a more or less ruined condition at Murgab and Nakhsh-i-Rustam, are Persian temples of the early period, built to contain an altar on which the priests offered victims. But the absence of any trace of an altar from both, the total want of religious emblems, and the extremely small size of the single apartment which each tower contains, make strongly against the temple theory; not to mention that a much more probable use may be suggested for the buildings.

With respect to the altars upon which sacrifice was offered, we are not left wholly without evidence. The Persian monarchs of the early period, including Darius Hystaspis, represented themselves on their tombs in the act of worship. Before them, at the distance of a few feet, stands an altar, elevated on three steps, and crowned with the sacrificial fire. Its form is square, and its only ornaments are a sunken squared recess, and a strongly projecting cornice at top. The height of the altar, including the steps, was apparently about four and a half feet. [PLATE LVIII., Fig. 4.]

The Persians' favorite victim was the horse; but they likewise sacrificed cattle, sheep, and goats. Human sacrifices seem to have been almost, if not altogether, unknown to them, and were certainly alien to the entire spirit of the Zoroastrian system. The flesh of the victim was probably merely shown to the sacred fire, after which it was eaten by the priests, the sacrificer, and those whom the latter associated with himself in the ceremony.

The spirit of the Zendavesta is wholly averse to idolatry, and we may fully accept the statement of Herodotus that images of the gods were entirely unknown to the Persians. Still, they did not deny themselves a certain use of symbolic representations of their deities, nor did they even scruple to adopt from idolatrous nations the forms of their religious symbolism. The winged circle, with or without the addition of a human figure, which was in Assyria the emblem of the chief Assyrian deity, Asshur, became with the Persians the ordinary representation of the Supreme God, Ormazd, and, as such, was placed in most conspicuous positions on their rock tombs and on their buildings. [PLATE

LVIII., Fig. 7.] Nor was the general idea only of the emblem adopted, but all the details of the Assyrian model were followed, with one exception. The human figure of the Assyrian original wore the close-fitting tunic, with short sleeves, which was the ordinary costume in Assyria, and had on its head the horned cap which marked a god or a genius. In the Persian counterpart this costume was exchanged for the Median robe, and a tiara, which was sometimes that proper to the king,23 sometimes that worn with the Median robe by court officers. [PLATE LVIII., Fig. 7.]

Mithra, or the Sun, is represented in Persian sculptures by a disk or orb, which is not four-rayed like the Assyrian, but perfectly plain and simple. In sculptures where the emblems of Ormazd and Mithra occur together, the position of the former is central, that of the latter towards the right hand of the tablet. The solar emblem is universal on sculptured tombs, but is otherwise of rare occurrence.

Vol II.   Plate LIX.

Figure of a Good Genius, Pasargadæ.

PLATE LIX

Spirits of good and evil, the Ahuras and Devas of the mythology, were represented by the Persians under human, animal, or monstrous forms. There can be little doubt that it is a good genius—

perhaps the "well-formed, swift, tall Serosh"—who appears on one of the square pillars set up by Cyrus at Pasargadae. This figure is that of a colossal man, from whose shoulders issue four wings, two of which spread upwards above his head, while the other two droop and reach nearly to his feet. [PLATE LIX.] It stands erect, in profile, with both arms raised and the hands open. The costume of the figure is remarkable. It consists of a long fringed robe reaching from the neck to the ankles—apparently of a stiff material, which conceals the form—and of a very singular head-dress. This is a striped cap, closely fitting the head, overshadowed by an elaborate ornament, of a character purely Egyptian. First there rise from the top of the cap two twisted horns, which, spreading right and left, become a sort of basis for the other forms to rest upon. These consist of two grotesque human-headed figures, one at either side, and of a complex triple ornament between them, clumsily imitated from a far more elegant Egyptian model. [PLATE LX., Fig. 1.]

The winged human-headed bulls, which the Persians adopted from the Assyrians, with very slight modifications, were also, it is probable, regarded as emblems of some god or good genius. They would scarcely otherwise have been represented on Persian cylinders as upholding the emblem of Ormazd in the same way that human-headed bulls uphold the similar emblem of Asshur on Assyrian cylinders. [PLATE LX., Fig. 2.] Their position, too, at Persepolis, where they kept watch over the entrance to the palace, accords with the notion that they represented guardian spirits, objects of the favorable regard of the Persians. Yet this view is not wholly free from difficulty. The bull appears in the bas-reliefs of Persepolis among the evil, or at any rate hostile, powers, which the king combats and slays; and though in these representations the animal is not winged or human-headed, yet on some cylinders apparently Persian, the monarch contends with bulls of exactly the same type as that which is assigned in other cylinders to the upholders of Ormazd. It would seem therefore that in this case the symbolism was less simple than usual, the bull in certain combinations and positions representing a god or a good spirit, while in others he was the type of a deva or evil genius.

Plate LX.

Vol. II.

Fig 1.

Figure with curious head dress (Egyptian).

Fig 2.

No. 1.

No. 2.

Persian Cylinders.

Fig. 3.

No. 1.

No. 2.

Fig. 4

Monsters, probably representing evil spirits, from Persian gems or cylinders.

PLATE LX

The most common representatives of the Evil Powers of the mythology were lions, winged or unwinged, and monsters of several different descriptions. At Persepolis the lions which the king stabs or strangles are of the natural shape, and this type is found also upon gems and cylinders; but on these last the king's antagonist is often a winged, while sometimes he is a winged and horned, lion. [PLATE LX., Fig. 3.] The monsters are of two principal types. In both the forms of a bird and a beast are commingled; but in the one the bird, and in the other the beast predominates. Specimens are given [PLATE LX., Fig. 4] taken from Persian gems and cylinders.

Such seems to have been, in outline, the purer and more ancient form of the Persian religion. During its continuance a fierce iconoclastic spirit animated the princes of the Empire, who took every opportunity of showing their hatred and contempt for the idolatries of the neighboring nations, burning temples, confiscating or destroying images, scourging or slaying idolatrous priests, putting a stop to festivals, disturbing tombs, smiting with the sword animals believed to be divine incarnations. Within their own dominions the fear of stirring up religious wars compelled them to be moderately tolerant, unless it were after rebellion, when a province lay at their mercy; but when they invaded foreign countries, they were wont to exhibit in the most open and striking way their aversion to materialistic religions. In Greece, during the great invasion, they burned every temple that they came near; in Egypt, on their first attack, they outraged every religious feeling of the people.

It was during this time of comparative purity, when the anti-idolatrous spirit was in full force, that a religious sympathy seems to have drawn together the two nations of the Persians and the Jews. Cyrus evidently identified Jehovah with Ormazd, and, accepting as a divine command the prophecy of Isaiah, undertook to rebuild their temple for a people who, like his own, allowed no image of God to defile the sanctuary. Darius, similarly, encouraged the completion of the work, after it had been interrupted by the troubles which followed the death of Cambyses. The foundation was thus laid for that friendly intimacy between the two peoples, of which we have abundant evidence in the books of Ezra, Nehemiah, and Esther, a friendly intimacy which caused the Jews to continue faithful to Persia to the last, and to brave the conqueror of Issus rather than desert masters who had shown them kindness and sympathy.

The first trace that we have of a corrupting influence being brought to bear on the Persian religion is connected with the history of the pseudo-Smerdis. According to Herodotus, Cambyses, when he set out on his Egyptian expedition, left a Magus, Patizeithes, at the capital, as comptroller of the royal household. The conferring of an office of such importance on the priest of an alien religion is the earliest indication which we have of a diminution of zeal for their ancestral creed on the part of the Achaemenian kings, and the earliest historical proof of the existence of Magism beyond the limits of Media. Magism was really, it is probable, an older creed than Zoroastrianism in the country where the Persians were settled; but it now, for the first time since the Persian conquest, began to show itself, to thrust itself into high places, and to attract general notice. From being the religion of the old Scythic tribes whom the Persians had conquered and whom they held in subjection, it had passed into being the religion of great numbers of the Persians themselves. The same causes which had corrupted Zoroastrianism in Media soon after the establishment of the Empire, worked also, though more slowly, in Persia, and a large section of the nation was probably weaned from its own belief, and won over to Magism, before Cambyses went into Egypt. His prolonged absence in that country brought matters to a crisis. The Magi took advantage of it to attempt a substitution of Magism for Zoroastrianism as the religion of the state. When this attempt failed, there was no doubt a reaction for a time, and Zoroastrianism thought itself triumphant. But a foe is generally most dangerous when he is despised. Magism, repulsed in its attempt to oust the rival religion, derived wisdom from the lesson, and thenceforth set itself to sap the fortress which it could not storm. Little by little it crept into favor, mingling itself with the old Arian creed, not displacing it, but only adding to it. In the later Persian system the Dualism of Zoroaster and the Magian elemental worship were jointly professed—the Magi were accepted as the national priests—the rights and ceremonies of the two religions were united—a syncretism not unusual in the ancient world blended into one two creeds originally quite separate and distinct, but in few respects antagonistic—and the name of Zoroaster being still fondly cherished in the memory of the nation, while in their practical religion Magian rites predominated, the mixed religion acquired the name, by which it was known to the later Greeks, of "the Magism of Zoroaster."

The Magian rites have been described in the chapter on the Median Religion. Their leading feature was the fire-worship, which is still cherished among those descendants of the ancient Persians who did not submit to the religion of Islam. On lofty spots in the high mountain-chain which traversed both Media and Persia, fire-altars were erected, on which burnt a perpetual flame, watched constantly lest it should expire, and believed to have been kindled from heaven. Over the altar in most instances a shrine or temple was built; and on these spots day after day the Magi chanted their incantations, displayed their barsoms or divining-rods, and performed their choicest ceremonies. Victims were not offered on these fire-altars. When a sacrifice took place, a fire was laid hard-by with logs of dry wood, stript of their bark, and this was lighted from the flame which burned on the altar. On the fire thus kindled was consumed a small part of the fat of the victim; but the rest was cut into joints, boiled, and eaten or sold by the worshipper. The true offering, which the god accepted, was, according to the Magi, the soul of the animal.

If human victims were ever really offered by the Persians as sacrifices, it is to Magian influence that the introduction of this horrid practice must be attributed, since it is utterly opposed to the whole spirit of Zoroaster's teaching. An instance of the practice is first reported in the reign of Xerxes, when Magism, which had been sternly repressed by Darius Hystaspis, began once more to lift its head, crept into favor at Court, and obtained a status which it never afterwards forfeited. According to Herodotus, the Persians, on their march into Greece, sacrificed, at Ennea Hodoi on the Strymon river, nine youths and nine maidens of the country, by burying them alive. Herodotus seems to have viewed the act as done in propitiation of a god resembling the Grecian Pluto; but it is not at all certain that he interpreted it correctly. Possibly he mistook a vengeance for a religious ceremony. The Brygi, who dwelt at this time in the vicinity of Ennea Hodoi, had given Mardonius a severe defeat on a former occasion; and the Persians were apt to treasure up such wrongs, and visit them, when occasion offered, with extreme severity.

When the Persians had once yielded to the syncretic spirit so far as to unite the Magian tenets and practices with their primitive belief, they were naturally led on to adopt into their system such portions of the other religions, with which they were brought into close contact, as possessed an attraction for them. Before the date of Herodotus they had borrowed from the Babylonians the worship of a Nature-Goddess, whom the Greeks identified at one time with Aphrodite, at another with Artemis, at another (probably) with Here, and had thus made a compromise with one of the grossest of the idolatries which, theoretically, they despised and detested. The Babylonian Venus, called in the original dialect of her native country Nana, was taken into the Pantheon of the Persians, under the name of Nansea, Anaea, Anaitis, or Tanata, and became in a little while one of the principal objects of Persian worship. At first idolatry, in the literal sense, was avoided; but Artaxerxes Mnemon, the conqueror of Cunaxa, an ardent devotee of the goddess, not content with the mutilated worship which he found established, resolved to show his zeal by introducing into all the chief cities of the Empire the image of his patroness. At Susa, at Persepolis, at Babylon, at Ecbatana, at Damascus, at Sardis, at Bactra, images of Anaitis were set up by his authority for the adoration of worshippers. It is to be feared that at this time, if not before, the lascivious rites were also adopted, which throughout the East constituted the chief attraction of the cult of Venus.

With the idolatry thus introduced, another came soon to be joined. Mithra, so long an object of reverence, if not of actual worship, to the Zoroastrians, was in the reign of Artaxerxes Mnemon, honored, like Anaitis, with a statue, and advanced into the foremost rank of deities. The exact form which the image took is uncertain; but probability is in favor of the well-known type of a human figure slaying a prostrate bull, which was to the Greeks and Romans the essential symbol of the

Mithraic worship. The intention of this oft-repeated group has been well explained by Hyde, who regards it as a representation of the Sun quitting the constellation of Taurus, the time when in the East his fructifying power is the greatest. The specimens which we possess of this group belong to classical art and to times later than Alexander; but we can scarcely suppose the idea to have been Occidental. The Western artists would naturally adopt the symbolism of those from whom they took the rites, merely modifying its expression in accordance with their own aesthetic notions.

Towards the close of the Empire two other gods emerged from the obscurity in which the lower deities of the Zoroastrian system were shrouded during the earlier and purer period. Vohu-manu, or Bah-man, and Amerdat, or Amendat, two of the councillors of Ormazd, became the objects of a worship, which was clearly of an idolatrous character. Shrines were built in their honor, and were frequented by companies of Magi, who chanted their incantations, and performed their rites of divination in these new edifices as willingly as in the old Fire-temples. The image of Bah-man was of wood, and was borne in procession on certain occasions.

Thus as time went on, the Persian religion continually assimilated itself more and more to the forms of belief and worship which prevailed in the neighboring parts of Asia. Idolatries of several kinds came into vogue, some adopted from abroad, others developed out of their own system. Temples, some of which had a character of extraordinary magnificence, were erected to the honor of various gods; and the degenerate descendants of pure Zoroastrian spiritualists bowed down to images, and entangled themselves in the meshes of a sensualistic and most debasing Nature-worship. Still, amid whatsoever corruptions, the Dualistic faith was maintained. The supremacy of Ormazd was from first to last admitted. Ahriman retained from first to last the same character and position, neither rising into an object of worship, nor sinking into a mere personification of evil. The inquiries which Aristotle caused to be made, towards the very close of the Empire, into the true nature of the Persian Religion, showed him Ormazd and Ahriman still recognized as Principles, still standing in the same hostile and antithetical attitude, one towards the other, which they occupied when the first Fargard of the Vendidad was written, long anterior to the rise of the Persian Power.

CHAPTER VII

CHRONOLOGY AND HISTORY

"I saw the man pushing westward, and northward, and southward; so that no beast might stand before him, neither was there any that could deliver out of his hand; but he did according to his will, and became great."—Daniel, viii. 4.

The history of the Persian Empire dates from the conquest of Astyages by Cyrus, and therefore commences with the year B.C. 558. But the present inquiry must be carried considerably further back, since in this, as in most other cases, the Empire grew up out of a previously existing monarchy. Darius Hystaspis reckons that there had been eight Persians kings of his race previously to himself; and though it is no doubt possible that some of the earlier names may be fictitious, yet we can scarcely suppose that he was deceived, or that he wished to deceive, as to the fact that long anterior to his own reign, or that of his elder contemporary, Cyrus, Persia had been a monarchy, governed by a line of princes of the same clan, or family, with himself. It is our business in this place, before entering upon the brilliant period of the Empire, to cast a retrospective glance over the earlier ages of obscurity, and to collect therefrom such scattered notices as are to be found of the Persians and their princes or kings before they suddenly attracted the general attention of the civilized world by their astonishing achievements under the great Cyrus.

The more ancient of-the sacred books of the Jews, while distinctly noticing the nation of the Medes, contain no mention at all of Persia or the Persians. The Zendavesta, the sacred volume of the people themselves, is equally silent on the subject. The earliest appearance of the Persians in history is in the inscriptions of the Assyrian kings, which begin to notice them about the middle of the ninth century B.C. At this time Shalmaneser II. found them in south-western Armenia, where they were in close contact with the Medes, of whom, however, they seem to have been wholly independent. Like the modern Kurds in this same region, they owned no subjection to a single head, but were under the government of numerous petty chieftains, each the lord of a single town or of a small mountain district. Shalmaneser informs us that he took tribute from twenty-five such chiefs. Similar tokens of submission were paid also to his son and grandson. After this the Assyrian records are silent as to the Persians for nearly a century, and it is not until the reign of Sennacherib that we once more find them brought into contact with the power which aspired to be mistress of Asia. At the time of their reappearance they are no longer in Armenia, but have descended the line of Zagros and reached the districts which lie north and north-east of Susiana, or that part of the Bakhtiyari chain which, if it is not actually within Persia Proper, at any rate immediately adjoins upon it. Arrived thus far, it was easy for them to occupy the region to which they have given permanent name; for the Bakhtiyari mountains command it and give a ready access to its valleys and plains.

The Persians would thus appear not to have completed their migrations till near the close of the Assyrian period, and it is probable that they did not settle into an organized monarchy much before the fall of Nineveh. At any rate we hear of no Persian ruler of note or name in the Assyrian records, and the reign of petty chiefs would seem therefore to have continued at least to the time of Asshur-bani-pal, up to which date we have ample records. The establishment, however, about the year B.C. 660, or a little later, of a powerful monarchy in the kindred and neighboring Media, could not fail to attract attention, and might well provoke imitation in Persia; and the native tradition appears to have been that about this time. Persian royalty began in the person of a certain Achaemenes (Hakhamanish), from whom all their later monarchs, with one possible exception, were proud to trace their descent.

The name Achaemenes cannot fail to arouse some suspicion. The Greek genealogies render us so familiar with heroes eponymi—imaginary personages, who owe their origin to the mere fact of the existence of certain tribe or race names, to account for which they were invented—that whenever, even in the history of other nations, we happen upon a name professedly personal, which stands evidently in close connection with a tribal designation, we are apt at once to suspect it of being fictitious. But in the East tribal and even ethnic names were certainly sometimes derived from actual persons; and it may be questioned whether the Persians, or the Iranic stock generally, had the notion of inventing personal eponyms. The name Achaemenes, therefore, in spite of its connection with the royal clan name of Achaemenidae, may stand as perhaps that of a real Persian king, and, if so, as probably that of the first king, the original founder of the monarchy, who united the scattered tribes in one, and thus raised Persia into a power of considerable importance.

The immediate successor of Achaemenes appears to have been his son, Teispes. Of him and of the next three monarchs, the information that we possess is exceedingly scanty. The very names of one or two in the series are uncertain. One tradition assigns either to the second or the fourth king of the list the establishment of friendly relations with a certain Pharnaces, King of Cappadocia, by an intermarriage between a Persian princess, Atossa, and the Cappadocian monarch. The existence of communication at this time between petty countries politically unconnected, and placed at such a distance from one another as Cappadocia and Persia, is certainly what we should not have expected; but our knowledge of the general condition of Western Asia at the period is too slight to justify us in a positive rejection of the story, which indicates, if it be true, that even during this time of comparative obscurity, the Persian monarchs were widely known, and that their alliance was thought a matter of importance.

The political condition of Persia under these early monarchs is a more interesting question than either the names of the kings or the foreign alliances which they attracted. According to Herodotus, that condition was one of absolute and unqualified subjection to the sway of the Medes, who conquered Persia and imposed their yoke upon the people before the year B.C. 634. The native records, however, and the accounts which Xenophon preferred, represent Persia as being at this time a separate and powerful state, either wholly independent of Media, or, at any rate, held in light bonds of little more than nominal dependence. On the whole, it appears most probable that the true condition of the country was that which this last phrase expresses. It maybe doubted whether there had ever been a conquest; but the weaker and less developed of the two kindred states owned the suzerainty of the stronger, and though quite unshackled in her internal administration, and perhaps not very much interfered with in her relations towards foreign countries, was, formally, a sort of Median fief, standing nearly in the position in which Egypt now stands to Turkey. The position was irksome to the sovereigns rather than unpleasant to the people. It detracted from the dignity of the Persian monarchs, and injured their self-respect; it probably caused them occasional inconvenience, since from time to time they would have to pay their court to their suzerain; and it seems towards the close of the Median period to have involved an obligation which must have been felt, if not as degrading, at any rate as very disagreeable. The monarch appears to have been required to send his eldest son as a sort of hostage to the Court of his superior, where he was held in a species of honorable captivity, not being allowed to quit the Court and return home without leave, but being otherwise well treated. The fidelity of the father was probably supposed to be in this way secured while it might be hoped that the son would be conciliated, and made an attached and willing dependent.

When Persian history first fairly opens upon us in the pages of Xenophon and of Nicolaus Damascenus, this is the condition of things which we find existing. Cambyses, the father of Cyrus the Great—called Atradates by the Syrian writer—is ruler of Persia, and resides in his native country, while his son Cyrus is permanently, or at any rate usually, resident at the Median Court, where he is in high favor with the reigning monarch, Astyages. According to Xenophon, who has here the support of Herodotus, he is Astyages' grandson, his father, Cambyses, being married to Mandane, that monarch's daughter. According to Nicolaus, who in this agrees with Ctesias, he is no way related to Astyages, who retains him at his court because he is personally attached to him. In the narrative of the latter writer, which has already been preferred in these volumes, the young prince, while at the Court, conceives the idea of freeing his own country by a revolt, and enters into secret communication with his father for the furtherance of his object. His father somewhat reluctantly assents, and preparations are made, which lead to the escape of Cyrus and the commencement of a war of independence. The details of the struggle, as they are related by Nicolaus, have been already given. After repeated defeats, the Persians finally make a stand at Pasargadae, their capital, where in two great battles they destroy the power of Astyages, who himself remains a prisoner in the hands of his adversary.

In the course of the struggle the father of Cyrus had fallen, and its close, therefore, presented Cyrus himself before the eyes of the Western Asiatics as the undisputed lord of the great Arian Empire which had established itself on the ruins of the Semitic. Transfers of sovereignty are easily made in the East, where independence is little valued, and each new conqueror is hailed with acclamations from millions. It mattered nothing to the bulk of Astyages' subjects whether they were ruled from Ecbatana or Pasargadae, by Median or Persian masters. Fate had settled that a single lord was to bear sway over the tribes and nations dwelling between the Persian Gulf and the Euxine; and the arbitrament of the sword had now decided that this single lord should be Cyrus. We may readily believe the statement of Nicolaus that the nations previously subject to the Medes vied with each other in the celerity and zeal with which they made their submission to the Persian conqueror. Cyrus succeeded at once to the full inheritance of which he had dispossessed Astyages, and was recognized as king by all the tribes between the Halys and the desert of Khorassan.

He was at this time, if we may trust Dino, exactly forty years of age, and was thus at that happy period in life when the bodily powers have not yet begun to decay, while the mental are just reaching their perfection. Though we may not be able to trust implicitly the details of the war of independence which have come down to us, yet there can be no doubt that he had displayed in its course very remarkable courage and conduct. He had intended, probably, no more than to free his country from the Median yoke; by the force of circumstances he had been led on to the destruction of the Median power, and to the establishment of a Persian Empire in its stead. With empire had come an enormous accession of wealth. The accumulated stores of ages, the riches of the Ninevite kings—the "gold," the "silver," and the "pleasant furniture" of those mighty potentates, of which there was "none end"—together with all the additions made to these stores by the Median monarchs, had fallen into his hands, and from comparative poverty he had come per saltum into the position of one of the wealthiest—if not of the very wealthiest—of princes. An ordinary Oriental would have been content with such a result, and have declined to tempt fortune any more. But Cyrus was no ordinary Oriental. Confident in his own powers, active, not to say restless, and of an ambition that nothing could satiate, he viewed, the position which he had won simply as a means of advancing himself to higher eminence. According to Ctesias, he was scarcely seated upon the throne, when he led an expedition to the far north-east against the renowned Bactrians and Sacans; and at any rate, whether this be true or no—and most probably it is an anticipation of later occurrences—it is certain that, instead of folding his hands, Cyrus proceeded with scarcely a pause on a long career of conquest, devoting his whole life to the carrying out of his plans of aggression, and leaving a portion of his schemes, which were too extensive for one life to realize, as a legacy to his successor. The quarter to which he really first turned his attention seems to have been the north-west. There, in the somewhat narrow but most fertile tract between the river Halys and the Egean Sea, was a state which seemed likely to give him trouble—a state which had successfully resisted all the efforts of the Medes to reduce it, and which recently, under a warlike prince, had shown a remarkable power of expansion. An instinct of danger warned the scarce firmly-settled monarch to fix his eye at once upon Lydia; in the wealthy and successful Croesus, the Lydian king, he saw one whom dynastic interests might naturally lead to espouse the quarrel of the conquered Mede, and whose power and personal qualities rendered him a really formidable rival.

The Lydian monarch, on his side, did not scruple to challenge a contest. The long strife which his father had waged with the great Cyaxares had terminated in a close alliance, cemented by a marriage, which made Croesus and Astyages brothers. The friendship of the great power of Western Asia, secured by this union, had set Lydia free to pursue a policy of self-aggrandizement in her own immediate, neighborhood. Rapidly, one after another, the kingdoms of Asia Minor had been reduced; and, excepting the mountain districts of Lycia and Cilicia, all Asia within the Halys now owned the sway of the Lydian king. Contented with his successes, and satisfied that the tie of relationship secured him from attack on the part of the only power which he had need to fear, Croesus had for some years given himself up to the enjoyment of his gains and to an ostentatious display of his magnificence. It was a rude shock to the indolent and self-complacent dreams of a sanguine optimism, which looked that "to-morrow should be as to-day, only much more abundant," when tidings came that revolution had raised its head in the far south-east, and that an energetic prince, in the full vigor of life, and untrammelled by dynastic ties, had thrust the aged Astyages from his throne, and girt his own brows with the Imperial diadem. Croesus, according to the story, was still in deep grief on account of the untimely death of his eldest son, when the intelligence reached him. Instantly rousing himself from his despair, he set about his preparations for the struggle, which his sagacity saw to be inevitable. After consultation of the oracles of Greece, he allied himself with the Grecian community, which appeared to him on the whole to be the most powerful. At the same time he sent ambassadors to Babylon and Memphis, to the courts of Labynetus and Amasis, with proposals for an alliance offensive and defensive between the three secondary powers of the Eastern world against that leading power whose superior strength and resources were felt to constitute a common danger. His representations were effectual. The kings of Babylon and Egypt, alive to their own peril, accepted his proposals; and a joint league was formed between the three monarchs and the republic of Sparta for the purpose of resisting the presumed aggressive spirit of the Medo-Persians.

Cyrus, meanwhile, was not idle. Suspecting that a weak point in his adversary's harness would be the disaffection of some of his more recently conquered subjects, he sent emissaries into Asia Minor to sound the dispositions of the natives. These emissaries particularly addressed themselves to the Asiatic Greeks, who, coming of a freedom-loving stock, and having been only very lately subdued, would it was thought, be likely to catch at an opportunity of shaking off the yoke of their conqueror. But, reasonable as such hopes must have seemed, they were in this instance doomed to disappointment. The Ionians, instead of hailing Cyrus as a liberator, received his overtures with suspicion. They probably thought that they were sure not to gain, and that they might possibly lose, by a change of masters. The yoke of Croesus had not, perhaps, been very oppressive; at any rate it seemed to them preferable to "bear the ills they had," rather than "fly to others" which might turn out less tolerable.

Disappointed in this quarter, the Persian prince directed his efforts to the concentration of a large army, and its rapid advance into a position where it would be excellently placed both for defence and attack. The frontier province of Cappadocia, which was only separated from the dominions of the Lydian monarch by a stream of moderate size, the Halys, was a most defensible country, extremely fertile and productive, abounding in natural fastnesses, and inhabited by a brave and warlike population. Into this district Cyrus pushed forward his army with all speed, taking, as it would seem, not the short route through Diarbekr, Malatiyah, and Gurun, along which the "Royal Road" afterwards ran, but the more circuitous one by Erzerum, which brought him into Northern Cappadocia, or Pontus, as it was called by the Romans. Here, in a district named Pteria, which cannot have been very far from the coast, he found his adversary, who had crossed the Halys, and taken several Cappadocian towns, among which was the chief city of the Pterians. Perceiving that his troops considerably outnumbered those of Crcesus, he lost no time in giving him battle. The action was fought in the Pterian country, and was stoutly contested, terminating at nightfall without any decisive advantage to either party. The next day neither side made any movement; and Crcesus, concluding from his enemy's inaction that, though he had not been able to conquer him, he had nothing to fear from his desire of vengeance or his spirit of enterprise, determined on a retreat. He laid the blame of his failure, we are told, on the insufficient number of his troops, and purposed to call for the contingents of his allies, and renew the war with largely augmented forces in the ensuing spring.

Cyrus, on his part, allowed the Lydians to retire unmolested, thus confirming his adversary in the mistaken estimate which he had formed of Persian courage and daring. Anticipating the course which Croesus would adopt under the circumstances, he kept his army well in hand, and, as soon as the Lydians were clean gone, he crossed the Halys, and marched straight upon Sardis. Croesus, deeming himself safe from molestation, had no sooner reached his capital than he had dismissed the bulk of his troops to their homes for the winter, merely giving them orders to return in the spring, when he hoped to have received auxiliaries from Sparta, Babylon, and Egypt. Left thus almost without defence, he suddenly heard that his audacious foe had followed on his steps, had ventured into the heart of his dominions, and was but a short distance from the capital. In this crisis he showed a spirit well worthy of admiration. Putting himself at the head of such an army of native Lydians as he could collect at a few hours' notice, he met the advancing foe in the rich plain a little to the east of Sardis, and gave him battle immediately. It is possible that even under these disadvantageous circumstances he might in fair fight have been victorious, for the Lydian cavalry were at this time excellent, and decidedly superior to the Persian. But Cyrus, aware of their merits, had recourse to stratagem, and by forming his camels in front, so frightened the Lydian horses that they fled from the field. The riders dismounted and fought on foot, but their gallantry was unavailing. After a prolonged and bloody combat the Lydian army was defeated, and forced to take refuge behind the walls of the capital.

Croesus now in hot haste sent off fresh messengers to his allies, begging them to come at once to his assistance. He had still a good hope of maintaining himself till their arrival, for his city was defended by walls, and was regarded by the natives as impregnable. An attempt to storm the defences failed; and the siege must have been turned into a blockade but for an accidental discovery. A Persian soldier had approached to reconnoitre the citadel on the side where it was strongest by nature, and therefore guarded with least care, when he observed one of the garrison descend the rock after his helmet, which had fallen from his head, pick it up, and return with it. Being an expert climber, he attempted the track thus pointed out to him, and succeeded in reaching the summit. Several of his comrades followed in his steps; the citadel was surprised, and the town taken and plundered.

Thus fell the greatest city of Asia Minor after a siege of fourteen days. The Lydian monarch, it is said, narrowly escaped with his life from the confusion of the sack; but, being fortunately recognized in time, was made prisoner, and brought before Cyrus. Cyrus at first treated him with some harshness, but soon relented, and, with that clemency which was a common characteristic of the earlier Persian kings, assigned him a territory for his maintenance, and gave him an honorable position at Court, where he passed at least thirty years, in high favor, first with Cyrus, and then with Cambyses. Lydia itself was absorbed at once into the Persian Empire, together with most of its dependencies, which submitted as soon as the fall of Sardis was known. There still, however, remained a certain amount of subjugation to be effected. The Greeks of the coast, who had offended the Great King by their refusal of his overtures, were not to be allowed to pass quietly into the condition of tributaries; and there were certain native races in the south-western corner of Asia Minor which declined to submit without a struggle to the new conqueror. But these matters were not regarded by Cyrus as of sufficient importance to require his own personal superintendence. Having remained at Sardis for a few weeks, during which time he received an insulting message from Sparta, whereto he made a menacing reply, and having arranged for the government of the newly-conquered province and the transmission of its treasures to Ecbatana, he quitted Lydia for the interior, taking Croesus with him, and proceeded towards the Median capital. He was bent on prosecuting without delay his schemes of conquest in other quarters—schemes of a grandeur and a comprehensiveness unknown to any previous monarch.

Scarcely, however, was he departed when Sardis became the scene of an insurrection. Pactyas, a Lydian, who had been entrusted with the duty of conveying the treasures of Croesus and his more wealthy subjects to Ecbatana, revolted against Tabalus, the Persian commandant of the town, and being joined by the native population and numerous mercenaries, principally Greeks, whom he hired with the treasure that was in his hands, made himself master of Sardis, and besieged Tabalus in the citadel. The news reached Cyrus while he was upon his march; but, estimating the degree of its importance aright, he did not suffer it to interfere with his plans. He judged it enough to send a general with a strong body of troops to put down the revolt, and continued his own journey eastward. Mazares, a Mede, was the officer selected for the service. On arriving before Sardis, he found that Pactyas had relinquished his enterprise and fled to the coast, and that the revolt was consequently at an end. It only remained to exact vengeance. The rebellious Lydians were disarmed.

Pactyas was pursued with unrelenting hostility, and demanded, in succession, of the Cymaeans, the Mytilenseans, and the Chians, of whom the last-mentioned surrendered him. The Greek cities which had furnished Pactyas with auxiliaries were then attacked, and the inhabitants of the first which fell, Priene, were one and all sold as slaves.

Mazares soon afterwards died, and was succeeded by Ha-pagus, another Mede, who adopted a somewhat milder policy towards the unfortunate Greeks. Besieging their cities one by one, and taking them by means of banks or mounds piled up against the walls, he, in some instances, connived at the inhabitants escaping in their ships, while, in others, he allowed them to take up the ordinary position of Persian subjects, liable to tribute and military service, but not otherwise molested. So little irksome were such terms to the Ionians of this period that even those who dwelt in the islands off the coast, with the single exception of the Samians—though they ran no risk of subjugation, since the Persians did not possess a fleet—accepted voluntarily the same position, and enrolled themselves among the subjects of Cyrus.

One Greek continental town alone suffered nothing during this time of trouble. When Cyrus refused the offers of submission, which reached him from the Ionian and AEolian Greeks after his capture of Sardis, he made an exception in favor of Miletus, the most important of all the Grecian cities in Asia. Prudence, it is probable, rather than clemency, dictated this course, since to detach from the Grecian cause the most powerful and influential of the states was the readiest way of weakening the resistance they would be able to make. Miletus singly had defied the arms of four successive Lydian kings, and had only succumbed at last to the efforts of the fifth, Croesus. If her submission had been now rejected, and she had been obliged to take counsel of her despair, the struggle between the Greek cities and the Persian generals might have assumed a different character.

Still more different might have been the result, if the cities generally had had the wisdom to follow a piece of advice which the great philosopher and statesman of the time, Thales, the Milesian, is said to have given them. Thales suggested that the Ionians should form themselves into a confederation, to be governed by a congress which should meet at Teos, the several cities retaining their own laws and internal independence, but being united for military purposes into a single community. Judged by the light which later events, the great Ionian revolt especially, throw upon it, this advice is seen to have been of the greatest importance. It is difficult to say what check, or even reverse, the arms of Persia might not have at this time sustained, if the spirit of Thales had animated his Asiatic countrymen generally; if the loose Ionic Amphictyony, which in reality left each state in the hour of danger to its own resources, had been superseded by a true federal union, and the combined efforts of the thirteen Ionian communities had been directed to a steady resistance of Persian aggression and a determined maintenance of their own independence. Mazares and Harpagus would almost certainly have been baffled, and the Great King himself would probably have been called off from his eastern conquests to undertake in person a task which after all he might have failed to accomplish.

The fall of the last Ionian town left Harpagus free to turn his attention to the tribes of the south-west which had not yet made their submission—the Carians, the Dorian Greeks, the Caunians, and the people of Lycia. Impressing the services of the newly-conquered Ionians and AEolians, he marched first against Caria, which offered but a feeble resistance. The Dorians of the continent, Myndians, Halicarnassians, and Cnidians. submitted still more tamely, without any struggle at all; but the Caunians and Lycians showed a different spirit. These tribes, which were ethnically allied, and of a very peculiar type, had never yet, it would seem, been subdued by any conqueror. Prizing highly the liberty they had enjoyed so long, they defended themselves with desperation. When they were defeated in the field they shut themselves up within the walls of their chief cities, Caunus and Xanthus, where, finding resistance impossible, they set fire to the two places with their own hands, burned their wives, children, slaves, and valuables, and then sallying forth, sword in hand, fell on the besiegers' lines, and fought till they were all slain.

Meanwhile Cyrus was pursuing a career of conquest in the far east. It was now, according to Herodotus, who is, beyond all question, a better authority than Ctesias for the reign of Cyrus, that the reduction of the Bactrians and the Sacans, the chief nations of what is called by moderns Central Asia, took place. Bactria was a country which enjoyed the reputation of having been great and glorious at a very early date. In one of the most ancient portions of the Zendavesta it was celebrated as "Bahhdi eredhwo-drafsha," or "Bactria" with the lofty banner; and traditions not wholly to be despised made it the native country of Zoroaster. There is good reason to believe that, up to the date of Cyrus, it had maintained its independence, or at any rate that it had been untouched by the great monarchies which for above seven hundred years had borne sway in the western parts of Asia. Its people were of the Iranic stock, and retained in their remote and somewhat savage country the simple and primitive habits of the race. Though their arms were of indifferent character, they were among the best soldiers to be found in the East, and always showed themselves a formidable enemy. According to Ctesias, when Cyrus invaded them, they fought a pitched battle with his army, in which the victory was with neither party. They were not, he said, reduced by force of arms at all, but submitted voluntarily when they found that Cyrus had married a Median princess. Herodotus, on the contrary, seems to include the Bactrians among the nations which Cyrus subdued, and probability is strongly in favor of this view of the matter. So warlike a nation is not likely to have submitted unless to force; nor is there any ground to believe that a Median marriage, had Cyrus contracted one, would have made him any the more acceptable to the Bactrians.

On the conquest of Bactria followed, we may be tolerably sure, an attack upon the Sacae. This people, who must certainly have bordered on the Bactrians, dwelt probably either on the Pamir Steppe, or on the high plain of Chinese Tartary, east of the Bolar range—the modern districts of Kashgar and Yarkand. They were reckoned excellent soldiers. They fought with the bow, the dagger, and the battle-axe, and were equally formidable on horseback and on foot. In race they were probably Tatars or Turanians, and their descendants or their congeners are to be seen in the modern inhabitants of these regions. According to Ctesias, their women took the field in almost equal numbers with their men; and the mixed army which resisted Cyrus amounted, including both sexes, to half a million. The king who commanded them was a certain Amorges, who was married to a wife called Sparethra. In an engagement with the Persians he fell into the enemy's hands, whereupon Sparethra put herself at the head of the Sacan forces, defeated Cyrus, and took so many prisoners of importance that the Persian monarch was glad to release Amorges in exchange for them. The Sacse, however, notwithstanding this success, were reduced, and became subjects and tributaries of Persia.

Among other countries subdued by Cyrus in this neighborhood, probably about the same period, may be named Hyrcania, Parthia, Chorasmia, Sogdiana, Aria (or Herat), Drangiana, Arachosia, Sattagydia, and Gandaria. The brief epitome which we possess of Ctesias omits to make any mention of these minor conquests, while Herodotus sums them all up in a single line; but there is reason to believe that the Cnidian historian gave a methodized account of their accomplishment, of which scattered notices have come down to us in various writers. Arrian relates that there was a city called Cyropolis, situated on the Jaxartes, a place of great strength defended by very lofty walls, which had been founded by the Great Cyrus. This city belonged to Sogdiana. Pliny states that Capisa, the chief city of Capisene, which lay not far from the upper Indus, was destroyed by Cyrus. This place is probably Kafshan, a little to the north of Kabul. Several authors tell us that the Ariaspse, a people of Drangiana, assisted Cyrus with provisions when he was warring in their neighborhood, and received from him in return a new name, which the Greeks rendered by "Euergetse"—"Benefactors." The Ariaspae must have dwelt near the Hamoon, or Lake of Seistan. We have thus traces of the conqueror's presence in the extreme north on the Jaxartes, in the extreme east in Affghanistan, and towards the south as far as Seistan and the Helmend; nor can there be any reasonable doubt that he overran and reduced to subjection the whole of that vast tract which lies between the Caspian on the west, the Indus valley and the desert of Tartary towards the east, the Jaxartes or Sir Deria on the north, and towards the south the Great Deserts of Seistan and Khorassan.

More uncertainty attaches to the reduction of the tract lying south of these deserts. Tradition said that Cyrus had once penetrated into Gedrosia on an expedition against the Indians, and had lost his entire army in the waterless and trackless desert; but there is no evidence at all that he reduced the country. It appears to have been a portion of the Empire in the reign of Darius Hystaspis, but whether that monarch, or Cambyses, or the great founder of the Persian power conquered it, cannot at present be determined.

The conquest of the vast tract lying between the Caspian and the Indus, inhabited (as it was) by a numerous, valiant, and freedom-loving population, may well have occupied Cyrus for thirteen or fourteen years. Alexander the Great spent in the reduction of this region, after the inhabitants had in a great measure lost their warlike qualities, as much as five years, or half the time occupied by his whole series of conquests. Cyrus could not have ventured on prosecuting his enterprises, as did the Macedonian prince, continuously and without interruption, marching straight from one country to another without once revisiting his capital. He must from time to time have returned to Ecbatana or Pasargadae; and it is on the whole most probable that, like the Assyrian monarchs, he marched out from home on a fresh expedition almost every year. Thus it need cause us no surprise that fourteen years were consumed in the subjugation of the tribes and nations beyond the Iranic desert to the north and the north-east, and that it was not till B.C. 539, when he was nearly sixty years of age, that the Persian monarch felt himself free to turn his attention to the great kingdom of the south.

The expedition of Cyrus against Babylon has been described already. Its success added to the Empire the rich and valuable provinces of Babylonia, Susiana, Syria, and Palestine, thus augmenting its size by about 240,000 or 250,000 square miles. Far more important, however, than this geographical increase was the removal of the last formidable rival—the complete destruction of a power which represented to the Asiatics the old Semitic civilization, which with reason claimed to be the heir and the successor of Assyria, and had a history stretching back for a space of nearly two thousand years. So long as Babylon, "the glory of kingdoms," "the praise of the whole earth," retained her independence, with her vast buildings, her prestige of antiquity, her wealth, her learning, her ancient and grand religious system, she could scarcely fail to be in the eyes of her neighbors the first power in the world, if not in mere strength, yet in honor, dignity, and reputation. Haughty and contemptuous herself to the very last, she naturally imposed on men's minds, alike by her past history and her present pretensions; nor was it possible for the Persian monarch to feel that he stood before his subjects as indisputably the foremost man upon the earth until he had humbled in the dust the pride and arrogance of Babylon. But, with the fall of the Great City, the whole fabric of Semitic greatness was shattered. Babylon became "an astonishment and a hissing"—all her prestige vanished—and Persia stepped manifestly into the place, which Assyria had occupied for so many centuries, of absolute and unrivalled mistress of Western Asia.

The fall of Babylon was also the fall of an ancient, widely spread, and deeply venerated religious system. Not of course, that the religion suddenly disappeared or ceased to have votaries, but that, from a dominant system, supported by all the resources of the state, and enforced by the civil power over a wide extent of territory, it became simply one of many tolerated beliefs, exposed to frequent rebuffs and insults, and at all times overshadowed by a new and rival system—the comparatively pure creed of Zoroastrianism, The conquest of Babylon by Persia was, practically, if not a death-blow, at least a severe wound, to that sensuous idol-worship which had for more than twenty centuries been the almost universal religion in the countries between the Mediterranean and the

Zagros mountain range. The religion never recovered itself—was never reinstated. It survived, a longer or a shorter time, in places. To a slight extent it corrupted Zoroastrianism; but, on the whole, from the date of the fall of Babylon it declined. "Bel bowed down; Nebo stooped;" "Merodach was broken in pieces." Judgment was done upon the Babylonian graven images; and the system, of which they formed a necessary part, having once fallen from its proud pre-eminence, gradually decayed and vanished.

Parallel with the decline of the old Semitic idolatry was the advance of its direct antithesis, pure spiritual Monotheism. The same blow which laid the Babylonian religion in the dust struck off the fetters from Judaism. Purified and refined by the precious discipline of adversity, the Jewish system, which Cyrus, feeling towards it a natural sympathy, protected, upheld, and replaced in its proper locality, advanced from this time in influence and importance, leavening little by little the foul mass of superstition and impurity which came in contact with it. Proselytism grew more common. The Jews spread themselves wider. The return from, the captivity, which Cyrus authorized almost immediately after the capture of Babylon, is the starting point from which we may trace a gradual enlightenment of the heathen world by the dissemination of Jewish beliefs and practices—such dissemination being greatly helped by the high estimation in which the Jewish system was held by the civil authority, both while the empire of the Persians lasted, and when power passed to the Macedonians.

On the fall of Babylon its dependencies seem to have submitted to the conqueror, with a single exception. Phoenicia, which had never acquiesced contentedly either in Assyrian or in Babylonian rule, saw, apparently, in the fresh convulsion that was now shaking the East, an opportunity for recovering autonomy. It was nearly half a century since her last struggle to free herself had terminated unsuccessfully. A new generation had grown up since that time—a generation which had seen nothing of war, and imperfectly appreciated its perils. Perhaps some reliance was placed on the countenance and support of Egypt, which, it must have been felt, would view with satisfaction any obstacle to the advance of a power wherewith she was sure, sooner or later, to come into collision. At any rate, it was resolved to make the venture. Phoenicia, on the destruction of her distant suzerain, quietly resumed her freedom; abstained from making any act of submission to the conqueror; while, however, at the same time, she established friendly relations for commercial purposes with one of the conqueror's vassals, the prince who had been sent into Palestine to re-establish the Jews at Jerusalem.

It might have been expected that Cyrus, after his conquest of Babylon, would have immediately proceeded towards the south-west. The reduction of Egypt had, according to Herodotus, been embraced in the designs which he formed fifteen years earlier. The non-submission of Phoenicia must have been regarded as an act of defiance which deserved signal chastisement. It has been suspected that the restoration of the Jews was prompted, at least in part, by political motives, and that Cyrus, when he re-established them in their country, looked to finding them of use to him in the attack which he was meditating upon Egypt. At any rate it is evident that their presence would have facilitated his march through Palestine, and given him a point d'appui, which could not but have been of value. These considerations make it probable that an Egyptian expedition would have been determined on, had not circumstances occurred to prevent it.

What the exact circumstances were, it is impossible to determine. According to Herodotus, a sudden desire seized Cyrus to attack the Massagetae, who bordered his Empire to the north-east. He led his troops across the Araxes (Jaxartes?), defeated the Massagetae by stratagem in a great battle, but was afterwards himself defeated and slain, his body falling into the enemy's hands, who treated it with gross indignity. According to Ctesias, the people against whom he made his expedition were the Derbices, a nation bordering upon India, Assisted by Indian allies, who lent them a number of elephants, this people engaged Cyrus, and defeated him in a battle, wherein he received a mortal wound. Reinforced, however, by a body of Sacae, the Persians renewed the struggle, and gained a complete victory, which was followed by the submission of the nation. Cyrus, however, died of his wound on the third day after the first battle.

This conflict of testimony clouds with uncertainty the entire closing scene of the life of Cyrus. All that we can lay down as tolerably well established is, that instead of carrying out his designs against Egypt, he engaged in hostilities with one of the nations on his north-eastern frontier, that he conducted the war with less than his usual success, and in the course of it received a wound of which he died (B.C. 529), after he had reigned nine-and-twenty years. That his body did not fall into the enemy's hands appears, however, to be certain from the fact that it was conveyed into Persia Proper, and buried at Pasargadae.

It may be suspected that this expedition, which proved so disastrous to the Persian monarch, was not the mere wanton act which it appears to be in the pages of our authorities. The nations of the north-east were at all times turbulent and irritable, with difficulty held in check by the civilized power that bore rule in the south and west. The expedition of Cyrus, whether directed against the Massagetae or the Derbices, was probably intended to strike terror into the barbarians of these regions, and was analogous to those invasions which were undertaken under the wisest of the Roman Emperors, across the Rhine and Danube, against Germans, Goths, and Sarmatae. The object of such inroads was not to conquer, but to alarm—it was hoped by an imposing display of organized military force to deter the undisciplined hordes of the prolific North from venturing across the frontier and carrying desolation through large tracts of the Empire. Defensive warfare has often an aggressive look. It may have been solely with the object of protecting his own territories from attack that Cyrus made his last expedition across the Jaxertes, or towards the upper Indus.

The character of Cyrus, as represented to us by the Greeks, is the most favorable that we possess of any early Oriental monarch. Active, energetic, brave, fertile in stratagems, he has all the qualities required to form a successful military chief. He conciliates his people by friendly and familiar treatment, but declines to spoil them by yielding to their inclinations when they are adverse to their true interests. He has a ready humor, which shows itself in smart sayings and repartees, that take occasionally the favorite Oriental turn of parable or apologue. He is mild in his treatment of the prisoners that fall into his hands, and ready to forgive even the heinous crime of rebellion. He has none of the pride of the ordinary eastern despot, but converses on terms of equality with those about him. We cannot be surprised that the Persians, contrasting him with their later monarchs, held his memory in the highest veneration, and were even led by their affection for his person to make his type of countenance their standard of physical beauty.

The genius of Cyrus was essentially that of a conqueror, not of an administrator. There is no trace of his having adopted anything like a uniform system for the government of the provinces which he subdued. In Lydia he set up a Persian governor, but assigned certain important functions to a native; in Babylon he gave the entire direction of affairs into the hands of a Mede, to whom he allowed the title and style of king; in Judaea he appointed a native, but made him merely "governor" or "deputy;" in Sacia he maintained as tributary king the monarch who had resisted his arms. Policy may have dictated the course pursued in each instance, which may have been suited to the condition of the several provinces; but the variety allowed was fatal to consolidation, and the monarchy, as Cyrus left it, had as little cohesion as any of those by which it was preceded.

Though originally a rude mountain-chief, Cyrus, after he succeeded to empire, showed himself quite able to appreciate the dignity and value of art. In his constructions at Pasargadae he combined massiveness with elegance, and manifested a taste at once simple and refined. He ornamented his buildings with reliefs of an ideal character. It is probably to him that we owe the conception of the light tapering stone shaft, which is the glory of Persian architecture. If the more massive of the Persepolitan buildings are to be ascribed to him, we must regard him as having fixed the whole plan and arrangement which was afterwards followed in all Persian palatial edifices.

In his domestic affairs Cyrus appears to have shown the same moderation and simplicity which we observe in his general conduct. He married, as it would seem, one wife only, Cassandane, the daughter of Pharnaspes, who was a member of the royal family. By her he had issue two sons and at least three daughters. The sons were Cambyses and Smerdis; the daughters Atossa, Artystone, and one whose name is unknown to us. Cassandane died before her husband, and was deeply mourned by him. Shortly before his own death he took the precaution formally to settle the succession. Leaving the general inheritance of his vast dominions to his elder son, Cambyses, he declared it to be his will that the younger should be entrusted with the actual government of several large and important provinces. He thought by this plan to secure the well-being of both the youths, never suspecting that he was in reality consigning both to untimely ends, and even preparing the way for an extraordinary revolution.

The ill effect of the unfortunate arrangement thus made appeared almost immediately. Cambyses was scarcely settled upon the throne before he grew jealous of his brother, and ordered him to be privately put to death. His cruel orders were obeyed, and with so much secrecy that neither the mode of the death, nor even the fact, was known to more than a few. Smerdis was generally believed to be still alive; and thus an opportunity was presented for personation—a form of imposture very congenial to Orientals, and one which has often had very disastrous consequences. We shall find in the sequel this opportunity embraced, and results follow of a most stirring and exciting character.

It required time, however, to bring to maturity the fruits of the crime so rashly committed. Cambyses, in the meanwhile, quite unconscious of danger, turned his attention to military matters, and determined on endeavoring to complete his father's scheme of conquest by the reduction of Egypt. Desirous of obtaining a ground of quarrel less antiquated than the alliance, a quarter of a century earlier, between Amasis and Croesus, he demanded that a daughter of the Egyptian king should be sent to him as a secondary wife. Amasis, too timid to refuse, sent a damsel named Nitetis, who was not his daughter; and she, soon after her arrival, made Cambyses acquainted with the fraud. A ground of quarrel was thus secured, which might be put forward when it suited his purpose; and meanwhile every nerve was being strained to prepare effectually for the expedition. The difficulty of a war with Egypt lay in her inaccessibility. She was protected on all sides by seas or deserts; and, for a successful advance upon her from the direction of Asia, it was desirable both to obtain a quiet passage for a large army through the desert of El-Tij, and also to have the support of a powerful fleet in the Mediterranean. This latter was the paramount consideration. An army well supplied with camels might carry its provisions and water through the desert, and might intimidate or overpower the few Arab tribes which inhabited it; but, unless the command of the sea was gained and the navigation of the Nile closed, Memphis might successfully resist attack. Cambyses appears to have perceived with sufficient clearness the conditions on which victory depended, and to have applied himself at once to securing them. He made a treaty with the Arab Sheikh who had the chief influence over the tribes of the desert; and at the same time he set to work to procure the services of a powerful naval force. By menaces or negotiations he prevailed upon the Phoenicians to submit themselves to his yoke, and having thus obtained a fleet superior to that of Egypt, he commenced hostilities by robbing her of a dependency which possessed considerable naval strength, in this way still further increasing the disparity between his own fleet and that of his enemy. Against the combined ships of Phoenicia, Cyprus, Ionia, and AEolis, Egypt was powerless, and her fleets seem to have quietly yielded the command of the sea. Cambyses was thus able to give his army the support of a naval force, as it marched along the coast, from Carmel probably to Pelusium; and when, having defeated the Egyptians at the last-named place, he proceeded against Memphis, he was able to take possession of the Nile, and to blockade the Egyptian capital both by land and water.

It appears that four years were consumed by the Persian monarch in his preparations for his Egyptian expedition. It was not until B.C. 525 that he entered Egypt at the head of his troops, and fought the great battle which decided the fate of the country. The struggle was long and bloody. Psammenitus, who had succeeded his father Amasis, had the services, not only of his Egyptian subjects, but a large body of mercenaries besides, Greeks and Carians. These allies were zealous in his cause, and are said to have given him a horrible proof of their attachment. One of their body had deserted to the Persians some little time before the expedition, and was believed to have given important advice to the invader. He had left his children behind in Egypt; and these his former comrades now seized, and led out in front of their lines, where they slew them before their father's eyes, and, having so done, mixed their blood in a bowl with water and wine, and drank, one and all, of the mixture. The battle followed immediately after; but, in spite of their courage and fanaticism, the Egyptian army was completely defeated. According to Ctesias, fifty thousand fell on the vanquished side, while the victors lost no more than seven thousand. Psammenitus, after his defeat, threw himself into Memphis, but, being blockaded by land and prevented from receiving supplies from the sea, after a stout resistance, he surrendered. The captive monarch received the respectful treatment which Persian clemency usually accorded to fallen sovereigns. Herodotus even goes so far as to intimate that, if he had abstained from conspiracy, he would probably have been allowed to continue ruler of Egypt, exchanging, of course, his independent sovereignty for a delegated kingship held at the pleasure of the Lord of Asia.

The conquest of Egypt was immediately followed by the submission of the neighboring tribes. The Libyans of the desert tract which borders the Nile valley to the west, and even the Greeks of the more remote Barca and Cyrene, sent gifts to the conqueror and consented to become his tributaries. But Cambyses placed little value on such petty accessions to his power. Inheriting the grandeur of view which had characterized his father, he was no sooner master of Egypt than he conceived the idea of a magnificent series of conquests in this quarter, whereby he hoped to become Lord of Africa no less than of Asia, or at any rate to leave himself without a rival of any importance on the vast continent which his victorious arms had now opened to him. Apart from Egypt, Africa possessed but two powers capable, by their political organization and their military strength, of offering him serious resistance. These were Ethiopia and Carthage—the one the great power of the South, the equal, if not even the superior, of Egypt—the other the great power of the West—remote, little known, but looming larger for, the obscurity in which she was shrouded, and attractive from her reputed wealth. The views of Cambyses comprised the reduction of both these powers, and also the conquest of the oasis of Ammon. As a good Zoroastrian, he was naturally anxious to exhibit the superiority of Ormazd to all the "gods of the nations;" and, as the temple of Ammon in the oasis had the greatest repute of all the African shrines, this design would be best accomplished by its pillage and destruction. It is probable that he further looked to the subjugation of all the tribes on the north coast between the Nile valley and the Carthaginian territory; for he would undoubtedly have sent an army along the shore to act in concert with his fleet, had he decided ultimately on making the expedition. An unexpected obstacle, however, arose to prevent him. The Phoenicians, who formed the main strength of his navy, declined to take any part in an attack on Carthage, since the Carthaginians were their colonists, and the relations between the two people had always been friendly. Cambyses did not like to force their inclinations, on account of their recent voluntary submission; and as, without their aid, his navy was manifestly unequal to the proposed service, he felt obliged to desist from the undertaking.

While the Carthaginian scheme was thus nipped in the bud, the enterprises which Cambyses attempted to carry out led to nothing but disaster. An army, fifty thousand strong, despatched from Thebes against Ammon, perished to a man amid the sands of the Libyan desert. A still more numerous force, led by Cambyses himself towards the Ethiopian frontier, found itself short of supplies on its march across Nubia, and was forced to return, without glory, after suffering considerable loss. It became evident that the abilities of the Persian monarch were not equal to his ambition—that he insufficiently appreciated the difficulties and dangers of enterprises—while a fatal obstinacy prevented him from acknowledging and retrieving an error while retrieval was possible. The Persians, we may be sure, grew dispirited under such a leader; and the Egyptians naturally took heart. It seems to have been shortly after the return of Cambyses from his abortive expedition against Ethiopia that symptoms of an intention to revolt began to manifest themselves in Egypt. The priests declared an incarnation of Apis, and the whole country burst out into rejoicings. It was probably now that Psammenitus, who had hitherto been kindly treated by his captor, was detected in treasonable intrigues, condemned to death, and executed. At the same time, the native officers who had been left in charge of the city of Memphis were apprehended and capitally punished. Such stringent measures had all the effect that was expected from them; they wholly crushed the nascent rebellion; they left, however, behind them a soreness, felt alike by the conqueror and the conquered, which prevented the establishment of a good understanding between the Great King and his new subjects. Cambyses knew that he had been severe, and that his severity had made him many enemies; he suspected the people, and still more suspected the priests, their natural leaders; he soon persuaded himself that policy required in Egypt a departure from the principles of toleration which were ordinarily observed towards their subjects by the Persians, and a sustained effort on the part of the civil power to bring the religion, and its priests, into contempt. Accordingly, he commenced a serious of acts calculated to have this effect. He stabbed the sacred calf, believed to be incarnate Apis; he ordered the body of priests who had the animal in charge to be publicly scourged; he stopped the Apis festival by making participation in it a capital offence; he opened the receptacles of the dead, and curiously examined the bodies contained in them, he intruded himself into the chief sanctuary at Memphis, and publicly scoffed at the grotesque image of Phtha; finally, not content with outraging in the same way the inviolable temple of the Cabeiri, he wound up his insults by ordering that their images should be burnt. These injuries and indignities rankled in the minds of the Egyptians, and probably had a large share in producing that bitter hatred of the Persian yoke which shows itself in the later history on so many occasions; but for the time the policy was successful: crushed beneath the iron heel of the conqueror—their faith in the power of their gods shaken, their spirits cowed, their hopes shattered—the Egyptian subjects of Cambyses made up their minds to submission. The Oriental will generally kiss the hand that smites him, if it only smite hard enough. Egypt became now for a full generation the obsequious slave of Persia, and gave no more trouble to her subjugator than the weakest or the most contented of the provinces.

The work of subjection completed, Cambyses, having been absent from his capital longer than was at all prudent, prepared to return home. He had proceeded on his way as far as Syria, when intelligence reached him of a most unexpected nature. A herald suddenly entered his camp and proclaimed, in the hearing of the whole army, that Cambyses, son of Cyrus, had ceased to reign, and that the allegiance of all Persian subjects was henceforth to be paid to Smerdis, son of Cyrus. At first, it is said, Cambyses thought that his instrument had played him false, and that his brother was alive and had actually seized the throne; but the assurances of the suspected person, and a suggestion which he made, convinced him of the contrary, and gave him a clue to the real solution of the mystery. Prexaspes, the nobleman inculpated, knew that the so-called Smerdis must be an impostor, and suggested his identity with a certain Magus, whose brother had been intrusted by Cambyses with the general direction of his household and the care of the palace. He was probably led to make the suggestion by his knowledge of the resemblance borne by this person to the murdered prince, which was sufficiently close to make personation possible. Cambyses was thus enabled to appreciate the gravity of the crisis, and to consider whether he could successfully contend with it or no. Apparently, he decided in the negative. Believing that he could not triumph over the conspiracy which had decreed his downfall, and unwilling to descend to a private station—perhaps even uncertain whether his enemies would spare his life—he resolved to fly to the last refuge of a dethroned king, and to end all by suicide. Drawing his short sword from its sheath, he gave himself a wound, of which he died in a few days.

It is certainly surprising that the king formed this resolution. He was at the head of an army, returning from an expedition, which, if not wholly successful, had at any rate added to the empire an important province. His father's name was a tower of strength; and if he could only have exposed the imposture that had been practised on them, he might have counted confidently on rallying the great mass of the Persians to his cause. How was it that he did not advance on the capital, and at least strike one blow for empire? No clear and decided response can be made to this inquiry; but we may indistinctly discern a number of causes which may have combined to produce in the monarch's mind the feeling of despondency whereto he gave way. Although he returned from Egypt a substantial conqueror, his laurel wreath was tarnished by ill-success; his army, weakened by its losses, and dispirited by its failures, was out of heart; it had no trust in his capacity as a commander, and could not be expected to fight with enthusiasm on his behalf. There is also reason to believe that he was generally unpopular on account of his haughty and tyrannical temper, and his contempt of law and usage, where they interfered with the gratification of his desires. Though we should do wrong to accept as true all the crimes laid to his charge by the Egyptians, who detested his memory, we cannot doubt the fact of his incestuous marriage with his sister, Atossa, which was wholly repugnant to the religious feelings of his nation. Nor can we well imagine that there was no foundation at all for the stories of the escape of Croesus, the murder of the son of Prexaspes, and the execution in Egypt on a trivial charge of twelve noble Persians. His own people called Cambyses a "despot" or "master," in contrast with Cyrus, whom they regarded as a "father," because, as Herodotus says, he was "harsh and reckless," whereas his father was mild and beneficent. Further, there was the religious aspect of the revolution, which had taken place, in the background. Cambyses may have known that in the ranks of his army there was much sympathy with Magism, and may have doubted whether, if the whole conspiracy were laid bare, he could count on anything like a general adhesion of his troops to the Zoroastrian cause. These various grounds, taken together, go far towards accounting for a suicide which at first sight strikes us as extraordinary, and is indeed almost unparalleled.

Of the general character of Cambyses little more need be said. He was brave, active, and energetic, like his father: but he lacked his father's strategic genius, his prudence, and his fertility in resources. Born in the purple, he was proud and haughty, careless of the feelings of others, and impatient of admonition or remonstrance. His pride made him obstinate in error; and his contempt of others led on naturally to harshness, and perhaps even to cruelty. He is accused of "habitual drunkenness," and was probably not free from the intemperance which was a common Persian failing; but there is not sufficient ground for believing that his indulgence was excessive, much less that it proceeded to the extent of affecting his reason. The "madness of Cambyses," reported to and believed in by Herodotus, was a fiction of the Egyptian priests, who wished it to be thought that their gods had in this way punished his impiety. The Persians had no such tradition, but merely regarded him as unduly severe and selfish. A dispassionate consideration of all the evidence on the subject leads to the conclusion that Cambyses lived and died in the possession of his reason, having neither destroyed it through inebriety nor lost it by the judgment of Heaven.

The death of Cambyses (B.C. 522) left the conspirators, who had possession of the capital, at liberty to develop their projects, and to take such steps as they thought best for the consolidation and perpetuation of their power. The position which they occupied was one of peculiar delicacy. On the one hand, the impostor had to guard against acting in any way which would throw suspicion on his being really Smerdis, the son of Cyrus. On the other, he had to satisfy the Magian priests, to whom he was well known, and on whom he mainly depended for support, if his imposture should be detected. These priests must have desired a change of the national religion, and to effect this must have been the true aim and object of the revolution. But it was necessary to proceed with the utmost caution. An open proclamation that Magism was to supersede Zoroastrianism would have seemed a strange act in an Achaemenian prince, and could scarcely have failed to arouse doubts which might easily terminate in discovery. The Magian brothers shrank from affronting this peril, and resolved, before approaching it, to obtain for the new government an amount of general popularity which would make its overthrow in fair fight difficult. Accordingly the new reign was inaugurated by a general remission of tribute and military service for the space of three years—a measure which was certain to give satisfaction to all the tribes and nations of the Empire, except the Persians. Persia Proper was at all times exempt from tribute, and was thus, so far, unaffected by the boon granted, while military service was no doubt popular with the ruling nation, for whose benefit the various conquests were effected. Still Persia could scarcely take umbrage at an inactivity which was to last only three years, while to the rest of the Empire the twofold grace accorded must have been thoroughly acceptable.

Further to confirm his uncertain hold upon the throne, the Pseudo-Smerdis took to wife all the widows of his predecessor. This is a practice common in the East; and there can be no doubt that it gives a new monarch a certain prestige in the eyes of his people. In the present case, however, it involved a danger. The wives of the late king were likely to be acquainted with the person of the king's brother; Atossa, at any rate, could not fail to know him intimately. If the Magus allowed them to associate together freely, according to the ordinary practice, they would detect his imposture and probably find a way to divulge it. He therefore introduced a new system into the seraglio. Instead of the free intercourse one with another which the royal consorts had enjoyed previously, he established at once the principle of complete isolation. Each wife was assigned her own portion of the palace; and no visiting of one wife by another was permitted. Access to them from without was altogether forbidden, even to their nearest relations; and the wives were thus cut off wholly from the external world, unless they could manage to communicate with it by means of secret messages. But precautions of this kind, though necessary, were in themselves suspicious; they naturally suggested an inquiry into their cause and object. It was a possible explanation of them that they proceeded from an extreme and morbid jealousy; but the thought could not fail to occur to some that they might be occasioned by the fear of detection.

However, as time went on, and no discovery was actually made, the Magus grew bolder, and ventured to commence that reformation of religion which he and his order had so much at heart. He destroyed the Zoroastrian temples in various places, and seems to have put down the old worship, with its hymns in praise of the Zoroastrian deities. He instituted Magian rites in lieu of the old ceremonies, and established his brother Magians as the priest-caste of the Persian nation. The changes introduced were no doubt satisfactory to the Medes, and to many of the subject races throughout the Empire. They were even agreeable to a portion of the Persian people, who leant towards a more material worship and a more gorgeous ceremonial than had contented their ancestors. If the faithful worshippers of Ormazd saw them with dismay, they were too timid to resist, and tacitly acquiesced in the religious revolution.

In one remote province the change gave a fresh impulse to a religious struggle which was there going on, adding strength to the side of intolerance. The Jews had now been engaged for fifteen or sixteen years in the restoration of their temple, according to the permission granted them by Cyrus. Their enterprise was distasteful to the neighboring Samaritans, who strained every nerve to prevent its being brought to a successful issue, and as each new king mounted the Persian throne, made a fresh effort to have the work stopped by authority. Their representations had had no effect upon Cambyses; but when they were repeated on the accession of the Pseudo-Smerdis, the result was different. An edict was at once sent down to Palestine, reversing the decree of Cyrus, and authorizing the inhabitants of Samaria to interfere forcibly in the matter, and compel the Jews to desist from building. Armed with this decree, the Samaritan authorities hastened to Jerusalem, and "made the Jews to cease by force and power."

These revelations of a leaning towards a creed diverse from that of the Achaemenian princes, combined with the system of seclusion adopted in the palace—a system not limited to the seraglio, but extending also to the person of the monarch, who neither quitted the palace precincts himself, nor allowed any of the Persian nobles to enter them—must have turned the suspicions previously existing into a general belief and conviction that the monarch seated on the throne was not Smerdis the son of Cyrus, but an impostor. Yet still there was for a while no outbreak. It mattered nothing to the provincials who ruled them, provided that order was maintained, and that the boons granted them at the opening of the new reign were not revoked or modified. Their wishes were no doubt in favor of the prince who had remitted their burthens; and in Media a peculiar sympathy would exist towards one who had exalted Magism. Such discontent as was felt would be confined to Persia, or to Persia and a few provinces of the north-east, where the Zoroastrian faith may have maintained itself.

At last, among the chief Persians, rumors began to arise. These were sternly repressed at the outset, and a reign of terror was established, during which men remained silent through fear. But at length some of the principal nobles, convinced of the imposture, held secret council together, and discussed the measures proper to be adopted under the circumstances. Nothing, however, was done until the arrival at the capital of a personage felt by all to be the proper leader of the nation in the existing crisis. This was Darius, the son of Hystaspes, a prince of the blood royal who probably stood in the direct line of the succession, failing the issue of Cyrus. At the early age of twenty he had attracted the attention of that monarch, who suspected him even then of a design to seize the throne. He was now about twenty-eight years of age, and therefore at a time of life suited for vigorous enterprise; which was probably the reason why his father, Hystaspes, who was still alive, sent him to the capital, instead of proceeding thither in person. Youth and vigor were necessary qualifications for success in a struggle against the holders of power; and Hystaspes no longer possessed those advantages. He therefore yielded to his son that headship of the movement to which his position would have entitled him; and, with the leadership in danger, he yielded necessarily his claim to the first place, when the time of peril should be past and the rewards of victory should come to be apportioned.

Darius, on his arrival at the capital, was at once accepted as head of the conspiracy, and with prudent boldness determined on pushing matters to an immediate decision. Overruling the timidity of a party among the conspirators, who urged delay, he armed his partisans, and proceeded, without a moment's pause, to the attack. According to the Greek historians, he and his friends entered the palace in a body, and surprised the Magus in his private apartments, where they slew him after a brief struggle. But the authority of Darius discredits the Greek accounts, and shows us, though with provoking brevity, that the course of events must have been very different. The Magus was not slain in the privacy of his palace, at Susa or Ecbatana, but met his death in a small and insignificant fort in the part of Media called "the Maesan plain," or, more briefly, "Nisaea," whither he appears to have fled with a band of followers. Whether he was first attacked in the capital, and escaping threw himself into this stronghold, or receiving timely warning of his danger withdrew to it before the outbreak occurred, or merely happened to be at the spot when the conspirators decided to make their attempt, we have no means of determining. We only know that the scene of the last struggle was Sictachotes, in Media; that Darius made the attack accompanied by six Persian nobles of high rank; and that the contest terminated in the slaughter of the Magus and of a number of his adherents, who were involved in the fall of their master.

Nor did the vengeance of the successful conspirators stop here. Speeding to the capital, with the head of the Magus in their hands, and exhibiting everywhere this proof at once of the death of the late king and of his imposture, they proceeded to authorize and aid in carrying out, a general massacre of the Magian priests, the abettors of the later usurpation. Every Magus who could be found was poniarded by the enraged Persians; and the caste would have been well-nigh exterminated, if it had not been for the approach of night. Darkness brought the carnage to an end; and the sword, once sheathed, was not again drawn. Only, to complete the punishment of the ambitious religionists who had insulted and deceived the nation, the day of the massacre was appointed to be kept annually as a solemn festival, under the name of the Magophonia; and a law was passed that on that day no Magus should leave his house.

The accession of Darius to the vacant throne now took place (Jan. 1, B.C. 521). According to Herodotus it was preceded by a period of debate and irresolution, during which the royal authority was, as it were, in commission among the Seven; and in this interval he places not only the choice of a king, but an actual discussion on the subject of the proper form of government to be established. Even his contemporaries, however, could see that this last story was unworthy of credit and it may be questioned whether any more reliance ought to be placed on the remainder of the narrative. Probably the true account of the matter is, that, having come to a knowledge of the facts of the case, the heads of the seven great Persian clans or families met together in secret conclave and arranged all their proceedings beforehand. No government but the monarchical could be thought of for a moment, and no one could assert any claim to be king but Darius. Darius went into the conspiracy as a pretender to the throne: the other six were simply his "faithful men," his friends and well-wishers. While, however, the six were far from disputing Darius's right, they required and received for themselves a guarantee of certain privileges, which may either have belonged to them previously, by law or custom, as the heads of the great clans, or may have been now for the first time conceded. The king-bound himself to choose his wives from among the families of the conspirators only, and sanctioned their claim to have free access to his person at all times without asking his permission. One of their number, Otanes, demanded and obtained even more. He and his house were to remain "free," and were to receive yearly a magnificent kaftan, or royal present. Thus, something like a check on unbridled despotism was formally and regularly established; an hereditary nobility was acknowledged; the king became to some extent dependent on his grandees; he could not regard himself as the sole fountain of honor; six great nobles stood round the throne as its supports; but their position was so near the monarch that they detracted somewhat from his prestige and dignity.

The guarantee of these privileges was, we may be sure, given, and the choice of Darius as king made, before the attack upon the. Magus began. It would have been madness to allow an interval of anarchy. When Darius reached the capital, with the head of the Pseudo-Smerdis in his possession, he no doubt proceeded at once to the palace and took his seat upon the vacant throne. No opposition was offered to him. The Persians gladly saw a scion of their old royal stock installed in power. The provincials were too far off to interfere. Such malcontents as might be present would be cowed by the massacre that was going on in the streets. The friends and intimates of the fallen monarch would be only anxious to escape notice. The reign of the new king no doubt commenced amid those acclamations which are never wanting in the East when a sovereign first shows himself to his subjects.

The measures with which the new monarch inaugurated his reign had for their object the re-establishment of the old worship. He rebuilt the Zoroastrian temples which the Magus had destroyed, and probably restored the use of the sacred chants and the other accustomed ceremonies. It may be suspected that his religious zeal proceeded often to the length of persecution, and that the Magian priests were not the only persons who, under the orders which he issued, felt the weight of the secular arm. His Zoroastrian zeal was soon known through the provinces; and the Jews forthwith resumed the building of their temple, trusting that their conduct would be consonant with his wishes. This trust was not misplaced: for, when the Samaritans once more interfered and tried to induce the new king to put a stop to the work, the only result was a fresh edict, confirming the old decree of Cyrus, forbidding interference, and assigning a further grant of money, cattle, corn, etc., from the royal stores, for the furtherance of the pious undertaking. Its accomplishment was declared to be for the advantage of the king and his house, since, when the temple was finished, sacrifices would be offered in it to "the God of Heaven," and prayer would be made "for the life of the king and of his sons." Such was the sympathy which still united pure Zoroastrianism with the worship of Jehovah. But the reign, which, so far, might have seemed to be auspiciously begun, was destined ere long to meet opposition, and even to encounter armed hostility, in various quarters. In the loosely organized empires of the early type, a change of sovereign, especially if accompanied by revolutionary violence, is always regarded as an opportunity for rebellion. Doubt as to the condition of the capital paralyzes the imperial authority in the provinces; and bold men, taking advantage of the moment of weakness, start up in various places, asserting independence, and seeking to obtain for themselves kingdoms out of the chaos which they see around them. The more remote provinces are especially liable to be thus affected, and often revolt successfully on such an occasion. It appears that the circumstances under which Darius obtained the throne were more than usually provocative of the spirit of disaffection and rebellion. Not only did the governors of remote countries, like Egypt and Lydia, assume an attitude incompatible with their duty as subjects, but everywhere, even in the very heart of the Empire, insurrection raised its head; and for six long years the new king was constantly employed in reducing one province after another to obedience. Susiana, Babylonia, Persia itself, Media, Assyria, Armenia, Hyrcania, Parthia, Margiana, Sagartia, and Sacia, all revolted during this space, and were successively chastised and recovered. It may be suspected that the religious element entered into some of these struggles, and that the unusual number of the revolts and the obstinate character of many of them were connected with the downfall of Magism and the restoration of the pure Zoroastrian faith, which Darius was bent on effecting. But this explanation can only be applied partially. We must suppose, besides, a sort of contagion of rebellion—an awakening of hopes, far and wide, among the subject nations, as the rumor that serious troubles had broken out reached them, and a resolution to take advantage of the critical state of things, spreading rapidly from one people to another.

A brief sketch of these various revolts must now be given. They commenced with a rising in Susiana, where a certain Atrines assumed the name and state of king, and was supported by the people. Almost simultaneously a pretender appeared in Babylon, who gave out that he was the son of the late king, Nabonidus, and bore the world-renowned name of Nebuchadnezzar. Darius, regarding this second revolt as the more important of the two, while he dispatched a force to punish the Susianians, proceeded in person against the Babylonian pretender. The rivals met at the river Tigris, which the Babylonians held with a naval force, while their army was posted on the right bank, ready to dispute the passage. Darius, however, crossed the river in their dispute, and, defeating the troops of his antagonist, pressed forward against the capital. He had nearly reached it, when the pretender gave him battle for the second time at a small town on the banks of the Euphrates. Fortune again declared in favor of the Persians, who drove the host of their enemy into the water and destroyed great numbers. The soi-disant Nebuchadnezzar escaped with a few horsemen and threw himself into Babylon; but the city was ill prepared for a siege, and was soon taken, the pretender falling into the hands of his enemy, who caused him to be executed.

Meanwhile, in Susiana, Atrines, the original leader of the rebellion, had been made prisoner by the troops sent against him, and, being brought to Darius while he was on his march against Babylon, was put to death. But this severity had little effect. A fresh leader appeared in the person of a certain Martes, a Persian who, taking example from the Babylonian rebel, assumed a name which connected him with the old kings of the country, and probably claimed to be their descendant, but the hands of Darius were now free by the termination of the Babylonian contest, and he was able to proceed towards Susiana himself. This movement, apparently, was unexpected; for when the Susianians heard of it they were so alarmed that they laid hands on the pretender and slew him.

A more important rebellion followed. Three of the chief provinces of the empire, Media, Armenia, and Assyria, revolted in concert. A Median monarch was set up, who called himself Xathrites, and claimed descent from the great Oyaxares; and it would seem that the three countries immediately acknowledged his sway. Darius, seeing how formidable the revolt was, determined to act with caution. Settling himself at the newly-conquered city of Babylon, he resolved to employ his generals against the rebels, and in this way to gauge the strength of the outbreak, before adventuring his own person into the fray. Hydarnes, one of the Seven conspirators, was sent into Media with an army, while Dadarses, an Armenian, was dispatched into Armenia, and Vomises, a Persian, was ordered to march through Assyria into the same country. All three generals were met by the forces of the pretender, and several battles were fought, with results that seem not to have been very decisive. Darius claims the victory on each occasion for his own generals; but it is evident that his arms made little progress, and that, in spite of several small defeats, the rebellion maintained a bold front, and was thought not unlikely to be successful. So strong was this feeling that two of the eastern provinces, Hyrcania and Parthia, deserted the Persian cause in the midst of the struggle, and placed themselves under the rule of Xathrites. Either this circumstance, or the general position of affairs, induced Darius at length to take the field in person. Quitting Babylon, he marched into Media, and being met by the pretender near a town called Kudrus, he defeated him in a great battle. This is no doubt the engagement of which Herodotus speaks, and which he rightly regards as decisive. The battle of Kudrus gave Ecbatana into the hands of Darius, and made the Median prince an outcast and a fugitive. He fled towards the East, probably intending to join his partisans in Hyrcania and Parthia, but was overtaken in the district of Rhages and made prisoner by the troops of Darius. The king treated his captive with extreme severity. Having cut off his nose, ears, and tongue, he kept him for some time chained to the door of his palace, in order that there might be no doubt of his capture. When this object had been sufficiently secured, the wretched sufferer was allowed to end his miserable existence. He was crucified in his capital city, Ecbatana, before the eyes of those who had seen his former glory.

The rebellion was thus crushed in its original seat, but it had still to be put down in the countries whereto it had extended itself. Parthia and Hyrcania, which had embraced the cause of the pretender, were still maintaining a conflict with their former governor, Hystaspes, Darius's father. Darius marched as far as Rhages to his father's assistance, and dispatched from that point a body of Persian troops to reinforce him. With this important aid Hystaspes once more gave the rebels battle, and succeeded in defeating them so entirely that they presently made their submission.

Troubles, meanwhile, had broken out in Sagartia. A native chief, moved probably by the success which had for a while attended the Median rebel who claimed to rule as the descendant and representative of Cyaxares, came forward with similar pretensions, and was accepted by the Sargartians as their monarch. This revolt, however, proved unimportant. Darius suppressed it with the utmost facility by means of a mixed army of Persians and Medes, whom he placed under a Median leader, Tachamaspates. The pretender was captured and treated almost exactly in the same way as the Mede whose example he had followed. His nose and ears were cut off; he was chained for a while at the palace door; and finally he was crucified at Arbela.

Another trifling revolt occurred about the same time in Margiana. The Margians rebelled and set up a certain Phraates, a native, to be their king. But the satrap of Bactria, within whose province Margiana lay, quelled the revolt almost immediately.

Hitherto, however thickly troubles had come upon him, Darius could have the satisfaction of feeling that he was contending with foreigners, and that his own nation at any rate was faithful and true. But now this consolation was to be taken from him. During his absence in the provinces of the north-east Persia itself revolted against his authority, and acknowledged for king an impostor, who, undeterred by the fate of Gomates, and relying on the obscurity which still hung over the end of the real Smerdis, assumed his name, and claimed to be the legitimate occupant of the throne. The Persians at home were either deceived a second time, or were willing to try a change of ruler; but the army of Darius, composed of Persians and Medes, adhered to the banner under which they had so often marched to victory, and enabled Darius, after a struggle of some duration, to re-establish his sway. The impostor suffered two defeats at the hands of Artabardes, one of Darius's generals, while a force which he had detached to excite rebellion in Arachosia was engaged by the satrap of that province and completely routed. The so-called Smerdis was himself captured, and suffered the usual penalty of unsuccessful revolt, crucifixion.

Before, however, these results were accomplished—while the fortune of war still hung in the balance—a fresh danger threatened. Encouraged by the disaffection which appeared to be so general, and which had at length reached the very citadel of the Empire, Babylon revolted for the second time. A man, named Aracus, an Armenian by descent, but settled in Babylonia, headed the insurrection, and, adopting the practice of personation so usual at the time, assumed the name and style of "Nebuchadnezzar, son of Nabonidus." Less alarmed on this occasion than at the time of the first revolt, the king was content to send a Median general against the new pretender. This officer, who is called Intaphres, speedily chastised the rebels, capturing Babylon, and taking Aracus prisoner. Crucifixion was again the punishment awarded to the rebel leader.

A season of comparative tranquillity seems now to have set in; and it may have been in this interval that Darius found time to chastise the remoter governors, who without formally declaring themselves independent, or assuming the title of king, had done acts savoring of rebellion. Oroetes, the governor of Sardis, who had comported himself strangely even under Cambyses, having ventured to entrap and put to death an ally of that monarch's, Polycrates of Samos, had from the time of the Magian revolution assumed an attitude quite above that of a subject. Having a quarrel with Mitrobates, the governor of a neighboring province, he murdered him and annexed his territory. When Darius sent a courier to him with a message the purport of which he disliked, he set men to waylay and assassinate him. It was impossible to overlook such acts; and Darius must have sent an army into Asia Minor, if one of his nobles had not undertaken to remove Oroetes in another way. Arming himself with several written orders bearing the king's seal, he went to Sardis, and gradually tried the temper of the guard which the satrap kept round his person. When he found them full of respect for the royal authority and ready to do whatever the king commanded, he produced an order for the governor's execution, which they carried into effect immediately.

The governor of Egypt, Aryandes, had shown a guilty ambition in a more covert way. Understanding that Darius had issued a gold coinage of remarkable purity, he, on his own authority and without consulting the king, issued a silver coinage of a similar character. There is reason to believe that he even placed his name upon his coins; an act which to the Oriental mind distinctly implied a claim of independent sovereignty. Darius taxed him with a design to revolt, and put him to death on the charge, apparently without exciting any disturbance.

Still, however, the Empire was not wholly tranquillized. A revolt in Susiana, suppressed by the conspirator Gobryas, and another among the Sacae of the Tigris, quelled by Darius in person, are recorded on the rock of Behistun, in a supplementary portion of the Inscription. We cannot date, unless it be by approximation, these various troubles; but there is reason to believe that they were almost all contained within a space not exceeding five or six years. The date of the Behistun Inscription is fixed by internal evidence to about B.C. 516-515—in other words, to the fifth or sixth year of the reign of Darius. Its erection seems to mark the termination of the first period of the reign, or that of disturbance, and the commencement of the second period, or that of tranquillity, internal progress, and patronage of the fine arts by the monarch.

It was natural that Darius, having with so much effort and difficulty reduced the revolted provinces to obedience, should proceed to consider within himself how the recurrence of such a time of trouble might be prevented. His experience had shown him how weak were the ties which had hitherto been thought sufficient to hold the Empire together, and how slight an obstacle they opposed to the tendency, which all great empires have, to disruption. But, however natural it might be to desire a remedy for the evils which afflicted the State, it was not easy to devise one. Great empires had existed in Western Asia for above seven hundred years, and had all suffered more or less from the same inherent weakness; but no one had as yet invented a cure, or even (so far as appears) conceived the idea of improving on the rude system of imperial sway which the first conqueror had instituted. It remained for Darius, not only to desire, but to design—not only to design, but to bring into action—an entirely new form and type of government. He has been well called "the true founder of the Persian state." He found the Empire a crude and heterogeneous mass of ill-assorted elements, hanging loosely together by the single tie of subjection to a common head; he left it a compact and regularly organized body, united on a single well-ordered system, permanently established everywhere.

On the nature and details of this system it will be necessary to speak at some length. It was the first, and probably the best, instance of that form of government which, taking its name from the Persian word for provincial ruler, is known generally as the system of "satrapial" administration. Its main principles were, in the first place, the reduction of the whole Empire to a quasi-uniformity by the substitution of one mode of governing for several; secondly, the substitution of fixed and definite burthens on the subject in lieu of variable and uncertain calls; and thirdly, the establishment of a variety of checks and counterpoises among the officials to whom it was necessary that the crown should delegate its powers, which tended greatly to the security of the monarch and the stability of the kingdom. A consideration of the modes in which these three principles were applied will bring before us in a convenient form the chief points of the system.

Uniformity, or a near approach to it, was produced, not so much by the abolition of differences as by superadding one and the same governmental machinery in all parts of the Empire. It is an essential feature of the satrapial system that it does not aim at destroying differences, or assimilating to one type the various races and countries over which it is extended. On the contrary, it allows, and indeed encourages, the several nations to retain their languages, habits, manners, religion, laws, and modes of local government. Only it takes care to place above all these things a paramount state authority, which is one and the same everywhere, whereon the unity of the kingdom is dependent. The authority instituted by Darius was that of his satraps. He divided the whole empire into a number of separate governments—a number which must have varied at different times, but which seems never to have fallen short of twenty. Over each government he placed a satrap, or supreme civil governor, charged with the collection and transmission of the revenue, the administration of justice, the maintenance of order, and the general supervision of the territory. These satraps were nominated by the king at his pleasure from any class of his subjects, and held office for no definite term, but simply until recalled, being liable to deprivation or death at any moment, without other formality than the presentation of the royal firman. While, however, they remained in office they were despotic—they represented the Great King, and were clothed with a portion of his majesty—they had palaces, Courts, body-guards, parks or "paradises," vast trains of eunuchs and attendants, well-filled, seraglios. They wielded the power of life and death. They assessed the tribute on the several towns and villages within their jurisdiction at their pleasure, and appointed deputies—called sometimes, like themselves, satraps—over cities or districts within their province, whose office was regarded as one of great dignity. They exacted from the provincials, for their own support and that of their Court, over and above the tribute due to the crown, whatever sum they regarded them as capable of furnishing. Favors, and even justice, had to be purchased from them by gifts. They were sometimes guilty of gross outrages on the persons and honor of their subjects. Nothing restrained their tyranny but such sense of right as they might happen to possess, and the fear of removal or execution if the voice of complaint reached the monarch.

Besides this uniform civil administration, the Empire was pervaded throughout by one and the same military system. The services of the subject nations as soldiers were, as a general rule, declined, unless upon rare and exceptional cases. Order was maintained by large and numerous garrisons of foreign troops—Persians and Medes—quartered on the inhabitants, who had little sympathy with those among whom they lived, and would be sure to repress sternly any outbreak. All places of much strength were occupied in this way; and special watch was kept upon the great capitals, which were likely to be centres of disaffection. Thus a great standing army, belonging to the conquering race, stood everywhere on guard throughout the Empire, offending the provincials no doubt by their pride, their violence, and their contemptuous bearing, but rendering a native revolt under ordinary circumstances hopeless.

Some exceptions to the general uniformity had almost of necessity to be made in so vast and heterogeneous an empire as the Persian. Occasionally it was thought wise to allow the continuance of a native dynasty in a province; and the satrap had in such a case to share with the native prince a divided authority. This was certainly the case in Cilicia, and probably in Paphlagonia and Phoenicia. Tribes also, included within the geographical limits of a satrapy, were sometimes recognized as independent; and petty wars were carried on between these hordes and their neighbors. Robber bands in many places infested the mountains, owing no allegiance to any one, and defied alike the satrap and the standing army.

The condition of Persia Proper was also purely exceptional. Persia paid no tribute, and was not counted as a satrapy. Its inhabitants were, however, bound, when the king passed through their country, to bring him gifts according to their means. This burthen may have been felt sensibly by the rich, but it pressed very lightly on the poor, who, if they could not afford an ox or a sheep, might bring a little milk or cheese, a few dates, or a handful of wild fruit. On the other hand, the king was bound, whenever he visited Pasargadae, to present to each Persian woman who appeared before him a sum equal to twenty Attic drachmas, or about sixteen shillings of our money. This custom commemorated the service rendered by the sex in the battle wherein Cyrus first repulsed the forces of Astyages.

The substitution of definite burthens on the subject in lieu of variable and uncertain charges was aimed at, rather than effected, by the new arrangement of the revenue which is associated with the name of Darius. This arrangement consisted in fixing everywhere the amount of tribute in money and in kind which each satrapy was to furnish to the crown. A definite money payment, varying, in ordinary satrapies, from 170 to 1000 Babylonian silver talents,330 or from L42,000. to L250,000. of our money, and amounting, in the exceptional case of the Indian satrapy, to above a million sterling, was required annually by the sovereign, and had to be remitted by the satrap to the capital. Besides this, a payment, the nature and amount of which was also fixed, had to be made in kind, each province being required to furnish that commodity, or those commodities, for which it was most celebrated. This latter burthen must have pressed very unequally on different portions of the Empire, if the statement of Herodotus be true that Babylonia and Assyria paid one-third of it. The payment seems to have been very considerable in amount. Egypt had to supply grain sufficient for the nutriment of 120,000 Persian troops quartered in the country. Media had to contribute 100,000 sheep, 4000 mules, and 3000 horses; Cappadocia, half the above number of each kind of animal; Armenia furnished 20,000 colts; Cilicia gave 360 white horses and a sum of 140 talents (L35,000.) in lieu of further tribute in kind. Babylonia, besides corn, was required to furnish 500 boy eunuchs. These charges, however, were all fixed by the crown, and may have been taken into consideration in assessing the money payment, the main object of the whole arrangement evidently being to make the taxation of each province proportionate to its wealth and resources.

The assessment of the taxation upon the different portions of his province was left to the satrap. We do not know on what principles he ordinarily proceeded, or whether any uniform principles at all were observed throughout the Empire. But we find some evidence that, in places at least, the mode of exaction and collection was by a land-tax. The assessment upon individuals, and the actual collection from them, devolved, in all probability, on the local authorities, who distributed the burthen imposed upon their town, village, or district as they thought proper. Thus the foreign oppressor did not come into direct contact with the mass of the conquered people, who no doubt paid the calls made upon them with less reluctance through the medium of their own proper magistrates.

If the taxation of the subject had stopped here, he would have had no just ground of complaint against his rulers. The population of the Empire cannot be estimated at less than forty millions of souls. The highest estimate of the value of the entire tribute, both in money and kind, will scarcely place it at more than ten millions sterling. Thus far, then, the burthen of taxation would certainly not have exceeded five shillings a head per annum. Perhaps it would not have reached half that amount. But, unhappily, neither was the tribute the sole tax which the crown exacted from its subjects, nor had the crown the sole right of exacting taxation. Persian subjects in many parts of the Empire paid, besides their tribute, a water-rate, which is expressly said to have been very productive. The rivers of the Empire were the king's; and when water was required for irrigation, a state officer superintended the opening of the sluices, and regulated the amount of the precious fluid which might be drawn off by each tribe or township. For the opening of the sluices a large sum was paid to the officer, which found its way into the coffers of the state. Further, it appears that such things as fisheries—and if so, probably salt-works, mines, quarries, and forests—were regarded as crown property, and yielded large sums to the revenue. They appear to have been farmed to responsible persons, who undertook to pay at a certain fixed rate, and made what profit they could by the transaction. The price of commodities thus farmed would be greatly enhanced to the consumer.

By these means the actual burthen of taxation upon the subject was rendered to some extent uncertain and indefinite, and the benefits of the fixed tribute system were diminished. But the chief drawback upon it has still to be mentioned. While the claims of the crown upon its subjects were definite and could not be exceeded, the satrap was at liberty to make any exactions that he pleased beyond them. There is every reason to believe that he received no stipend, and that, consequently, the burthen of supporting him, his body-guard, and his Court was intended to fall on the province which had the benefit of his superintendence. Like a Roman proconsul, he was to pay himself out of the pockets of his subjects; and, like that class of persons, he took care to pay himself highly. It has been calculated that one satrap of Babylon drew from his province annually in actual coin a sum equal to L100,000. of our money. We can scarcely doubt that the claims made by the provincial governors were, on the average, at least equal to those of the crown; and they had the disadvantage of being irregular, uncertain, and purely arbitrary.

Thus, what was gained by the new system was not so much the relief of the subject from uncertain taxation as the advantage to the crown of knowing beforehand what the revenue would be, and being able to regulate its expenditure accordingly. Still a certain amount of benefit did undoubtedly accrue to the provincials from the system; since it gave them the crown for their protector. So long as the payments made to the state were irregular, it was, or at least seemed to be, for the interest of the crown to obtain from each province as much as it could anyhow pay. When the state dues were once fixed, as the crown gained nothing by the rapacity of its officers, but rather lost, since the province became exhausted, it was interested in checking greed, and seeing that the provinces were administered by wise and good satraps.

The control of its great officers is always the main difficulty of a despotic government, when it is extended over a large space of territory and embraces many millions of men. The system devised by Darius for checking and controlling his satraps was probably the best that has ever yet been brought into operation. His plan was to establish in every province at least three officers holding their authority directly from the crown, and only responsible to it, who would therefore act as checks one upon another. These were the satrap, the military commandant, and the secretary. The satrap was charged with the civil administration, and especially with the department of finance. The commandant was supreme over the troops. The office of the secretary is less clearly defined; but it probably consisted mainly in keeping the Court informed by despatches of all that went on in the province. Thus, if the satrap were inclined to revolt, he had, in the first place, to persuade the commandant, who would naturally think that, if he ran the risk, it might as well be for himself; and, further, he had to escape the lynx eyes of the secretary, whose general right of superintendence gave him entrance everywhere, and whose prospects of advancement would probably depend a good deal upon the diligence and success with which he discharged the office of "King's Eye" and "Ear." So, if the commandant were ambitious of independent sway, he must persuade the satrap, or he would have no money to pay his troops; and he too must blind the secretary, or else bribe him into silence. As for the secretary, having neither men nor money at his command, it was impossible that he should think of rebellion.

But the precautions taken against revolt did not end here. Once a year, according to Xenophon, or more probably at irregular intervals, an officer came suddenly down from the Court with a commission to inspect a province. Such persons were frequently of royal rank, brothers or sons of the king. They were accompanied by an armed force, and were empowered to correct whatever was amiss in the province, and in case of necessity to report to the crown the insubordination or incompetency of its officers. If this system had been properly maintained, it is evident that it would have acted as a most powerful check upon misgovernment, and would have rendered revolt almost impossible.

Another mode by which it was sought to secure the fidelity of the satraps and commandants was by choosing them from among the king's blood relations, or else attaching them to the crown by marriage with one of the princesses. It was thought that the affection of sons and brothers would be a restraint upon their ambition, and that even connections by marriage would feel that they had an interest in upholding the power and dignity of the great house with which they had been thought worthy of alliance. This system, which was entensively followed by Darius, had on the whole good results, and was at any rate preferable to that barbarous policy of prudential fratricide which has prevailed widely in Oriental governments.

The system of checks, while it was effectual for the object at which it specially aimed, had one great disadvantage. It weakened the hands of authority in times of difficulty. When danger, internal or external, threatened, it was an evil that the powers of government should be divided, and the civil authority lodged in the hands of one officer, the military in those of another. Concentration of power is needed for rapid and decisive action, for unity of purpose, and secrecy both of plan and of execution. These considerations led to a modification of the original idea of satrapial government, which was adopted partially at first—in provinces especially exposed to danger, internal or external—but which ultimately became almost universal. The offices of satrap, or civil administrator, and commandant, or commander of the troops, were vested in the same person, who came in this way to have that full and complete authority which is possessed by Turkish pashas and modern Persian khans or beys—an authority practically uncontrolled. This system was advantageous for the defence of a province against foes; but it was dangerous to the stability of the Empire, since it led naturally to the occurrence of formidable rebellions.

Two minor points in the scheme of Darius remain to be noticed, before this account of his governmental system can be regarded as complete. These are his institution of posts, and his coinage of money.

In Darius's idea of government was included rapidity of communication. Regarding it as of the utmost importance that the orders of the Court should be speedily transmitted to the provincial governors, and that their reports and those of the royal secretaries should be received without needless delay, he established along the lines of routes already existing between the chief cities of the Empire a number of post-houses, placed at regular intervals, according to the estimated capacity of a horse to gallop at his best speed without stopping. At each post-house were maintained, at the cost of the state, a number of couriers and several relays of horses. When a despatch was to be forwarded it was taken to the first post-house along the route, where a courier received it, and immediately mounting on horseback galloped with it to the next station. Here it was delivered to a new courier, who, mounted on a fresh horse, took it the next stage on its journey; and thus it passed from hand to hand till it reached its destination. According to Xenophon, the messengers travelled by night as well as by day; and the conveyance was so rapid that some even compared it to the flight of birds. Excellent inns or caravanserais were to be found at every station; bridges or ferries were established upon all the streams; guard-houses occurred here and there, and the whole route was kept secure from the brigands who infested the Empire. Ordinary travellers were glad to pursue so convenient a line of march; it does not appear, however, that they could obtain the use of post-horses even when the government was in no need of them. The coinage of Darius consisted, it is probable, both of a gold and silver issue. It is not perhaps altogether certain that he was the first king of Persia who coined money; but, if the term "daric" is really derived from his name, that alone would be a strong argument in favor of his claim to priority. In any case, it is indisputable that he was the first Persian king who coined on a large scale, and it is further certain that his gold coinage was regarded in later times as of peculiar value on account of its purity. His gold darics appear to have contained, on an average, not quite 124 grains of pure metal, which would make their value about twenty two shillings of our money. They were of the type usual at the time both in Lydia and in Greece—flattened lumps of metal, very thick in comparison with the size of their surface, irregular, and rudely stamped. The silver darics were similar in general character, but exceeded the gold in size. Their weight was from 224 to 230 grains, and they would thus have been worth not quite three shillings of our money. It does not appear that any other kinds of coins besides these were ever issued from the Persian mint. They must, therefore, it would seem, have satisfied the commercial needs of the people.

From this review of the governmental system of Darius we must now return to the actions of his later life. The history of an Oriental monarchy must always be composed mainly of a series of biographies; for, as the monarch is all in all in such communities, his sayings, doings, and character, not only determine, but constitute, the annals of the State. In the second period of his reign, that which followed on the time of trouble and disturbance, Darius (as has been already observed) appears to have pursued mainly the arts of peace. Bent on settling and consolidating his Empire, he set up everywhere the satrapial form of government, organized and established his posts, issued his coinage, watched over the administration of justice, and in various ways exhibited a love of order and method, and a genius for systematic arrangement. At the same time he devoted considerable attention to ornamental and architectural works, to sculpture, and to literary composition. He founded the royal palace at Susa, which was the main residence of the later kings. At Persepolis he certainly erected one very important building; and it is on the whole most probable that he designed—if he did not live to execute—the Chehl Minor itself—the chief of the magnificent structures upon the great central platform. The massive platform itself, with its grand and stately steps, is certainly of his erection, for it is inscribed with his name. He gave his works all the solidity and strength that is derivable from the use of huge blocks of a good hard material. He set the example of ornamenting the stepped approached to a palace with elaborate bas-reliefs. He designed and caused to be constructed in his own lifetime the rock-tomb at Nakhsh-i-Rustam, in which his remains were afterwards laid. The rock-sculpture at Behistun was also his work. In attention to the creation of permanent historical records he excelled all the Persian kings, both before him and after him. The great Inscription of Behistun has no parallel in ancient times for length, finish, and delicacy of execution, unless it be in Assyria or in Egypt. The only really historical inscription at Persepolis is one set up by Darius. He was the only Persian king, except perhaps one, who placed an inscription upon his tomb. The later monarchs in their records do little more than repeat certain religious phrases and certain forms of self-glorification which occur in the least remarkable inscriptions of their great predecessor. He alone oversteps those limits, and presents us with geographical notices and narratives of events profoundly interesting to the historian.

During this period of comparative peace, which may have extended from about B.C. 516 to B.C. 508 or 507, the general tranquillity was interrupted by at least one important expedition. The administrational merits of Darius are so great that they have obscured his military glories, and have sent him down to posterity with the character of an unwarlike monarch—if not a mere "peddler," as his subjects said, yet, at any rate, a mere consolidator and arranger. But the son of Hystaspes was no carpet prince. He had not drawn the sword against his domestic foes to sheath it finally and forever when his triumph over them was completed. On the contrary, he regarded it as incumbent on him to carry on the aggressive policy of Cyrus and Cambyses, his great predecessors, and like them to extend in one direction or another the boundaries of the Empire. Perhaps he felt that aggression was the very law of the Empire's being, since if the military spirit was once allowed to become extinct in the conquering nation, they would lose the sole guarantee of their supremacy. At any rate, whatever his motive, we find him, after he had snatched a brief interval of repose, engaging in great wars both towards his eastern and his western frontier—wars which in both instances had results of considerable importance.

The first grand expedition was towards the East. Cyrus, as we have seen, had extended the Persian sway over the mountains of Affghanistan and the highlands from which flow the tributaries of the Upper Indus. From these eminences the Persian garrisons looked down on a territory possessing every quality that could attract a powerful conqueror. Fertile, well-watered, rich in gold, peopled by an ingenious yet warlike race, which would add strength no less than wealth to its subjugators, the Punjab lay at the foot of the Sufeid Koh and Suliman ranges, inviting the attack of those who could swoop down when they pleased upon the low country. It was against this region that Darius directed his first great aggressive effort. Having explored the course of the Indus from Attock to the sea by means of boats, and obtained, we may suppose, in this way some knowledge of the country and its inhabitants, he led or sent an expedition into the tract, which in a short time succeeded in completely reducing it. The Punjab, and probably the whole valley of the Indus, was annexed, and remained subject till the later times of the Empire. The results of this conquest were the acquisition of a brave race, capable of making excellent soldiers, an enormous increase of the revenue, a sudden and vast influx of gold into Persia, which led probably to the introduction of the gold coinage, and the establishment of commercial relations with the natives, which issued in a regular trade carried on by coasting-vessels between the mouths of the Indus and the Persian Gulf.

The next important expedition—one probably of still greater magnitude—took exactly the opposite direction. The sea which bounded the Persian dominion to the west and the north-west narrowed in two places to dimensions not much exceeding those of of the greater Asiatic rivers. The eye which looked across the Thracian Bosphorus or the Hellespont seemed to itself to be merely contemplating the opposite bank of a pretty wide stream. Darius, consequently being master of Asia Minor, and separated by what seemed to him so poor a barrier from fertile tracts of vast and indeed indefinite extent, such as were nowhere else to be found on the borders of his empire, naturally turned his thoughts of conquest to this quarter. His immediate desire was, probably, to annex Thrace; but he may have already entertained wider views, and have looked to embracing in his dominions the lovely isles and coasts of Greece also, so making good the former threats of Cyrus. The story of the voyage and escape of Democedes, related by Herodotus with such amplitude of detail, and confirmed to some extent from other sources, cannot be a mere myth without historical foundation. Nor is it probable that the expedition was designed merely for the purpose of "indulging the exile with a short visit to his native country," or of collecting "interesting information." If by the king's orders a vessel was fitted out at Sidon to explore the coasts of Greece under the guidance of Democedes, which proceeded as far as Crotona in Magna Grsecia, we may be tolerably sure that a political object lay at the bottom of the enterprise. It would have exactly the same aim and end as the eastern voyage of Scylax, and would be intended, like that, to pave the way for a conquest. Darius was therefore, it would seem, already contemplating the reduction of Greece Proper, and did not require to have it suggested to him by any special provocation. Mentally, or actually, surveying the map of the world, so far as it was known to him, he saw that in this direction only there was an attractive country readily accessible. Elsewhere his Empire abutted on seas, sandy deserts, or at best barren steppes; here, and here only, was there a rich prize close at hand and (as it seemed) only waiting to be grasped.

But if the aggressive force of Persia was to be turned in this direction, if the stream of conquest was to be set westward along the flanks of Rhodope and Haemus, it was essential to success, and even to safety, that the line of communication with Asia should remain intact. Now, there lay on the right flank of an army marching into Europe a vast and formidable power, known to be capable of great efforts, which, if allowed to feel itself secure from attack, might be expected at any time to step in, to break the line of communication between the east and west, and to bring the Persians who should be engaged in conquering Pseonia, Macedonia, and Greece, into imminent danger. It is greatly to the credit of Darius that he saw this peril—saw it and took effectual measures to guard against it. The Scythian expedition was no insane project of a frantic despot, burning for revenge, or ambitious of an impossible conquest. It has all the appearance of being a well-laid plan, conceived by a moderate and wise prince, for the furtherance of a great design, and the permanent advantage of his empire. The lord of South-Western Asia was well aware of the existence beyond his northern frontier of a standing menace to his power. A century had not sufficed to wipe out the recollection of that terrible time when Scythian hordes had carried desolation far and wide over the fairest of great regions that were now under the Persian dominion. What had occurred once might recur. Possibly, as a modern author suggests, "the remembrance of ancient injuries may have been revived by recent aggressions." It was at any rate essential to strike terror into the hordes of the Steppe Region in order that Western Asia might attain a sense of security. It was still more essential to do so if the north-west was to become the scene of war, and the Persians were to make a vigorous effort to establish themselves permanently in Europe. Scythia, it must be remembered, reached to the banks of the Danube. An invader, who aspired to the conquest even of Thrace, was almost forced into collision with her next neighbor.

Darius, having determined on his course, prefaced his expedition by a raid, the object of which was undoubtedly to procure information. He ordered Ariaramnes, satrap of Cappadocia, to cross the Euxine with a small fleet, and, descending suddenly upon the Scythian coast, to carry off a number of prisoners. Ariaramnes executed the commission skilfully, and was so fortunate as to make prize of a native of high rank, the brother of a Scythian chief or king. From this person and his companions the Persian monarch was able to obtain all the information which he required. Thus enlightened, he proceeded to make his preparations. Collecting a fleet of 600 ships, chiefly from the Greeks of Asia, and an army estimated at from 700,000 to 800,000 men, which was made up of contingents from all the nations under his rule, he crossed the Bosphorus by a bridge of boats constructed by Mandrocles a Samian; marched through Thrace along the line of the Little Balkan, receiving the submission of the tribes as he went; crossed the Great Balkan; conquered the Getae, who dwelt between that range and the Danube; passed the Danube by a bridge, which the Ionian Greeks had made with their vessels just above the apex of the Delta; and so invaded Scythia. The natives had received intelligence of his approach, and had resolved not to risk a battle. They retired as he advanced, and endeavored to bring his army into difficulties by destroying the forage, driving off the cattle, and filling in the wells. But the commissariat of the Persians was, as usual, well arranged. Darius remained for more than two months in Scythia without incurring any important losses. He succeeded in parading before the eyes of the whole nation the immense military power of his empire. He no doubt inflicted considerable damage on the hordes, whose herds he must often have captured, and whose supplies of forage he curtailed. It is difficult to say how far he penetrated. Herodotus was informed that he marched east to the Tanais (Don), and thence north to the country of the Budini, where he burnt the staple of Gelonus, which cannot well have been below the fiftieth parallel, and was probably not far from Voronej. It is certainly astonishing that he should have ventured so far inland, and still more surprising that, having done so, he should have returned with his army well-nigh intact. But we can scarcely suppose the story that he destroyed the staple of the Greek trade a pure fiction. He would be glad to leave his mark in the country, and might make an extraordinary effort to reach the only town that was to be found in the whole steppe region. Having effected his purpose by its destruction, he would retire, falling back probably upon the coast, where he could obtain supplies from his fleet. It is beyond dispute that he returned with the bulk of his army, having suffered no loss but that of a few invalid troops whom he sacrificed. Attempts had been made during his absence to induce the Greeks, who guarded the bridge over the Danube, to break it, and so hinder his return; but they were unsuccessful. Darius recrossed the river after an interval of somewhat more than two months, victorious according to his own notions, and regarded himself as entitled thenceforth to enumerate among the subject races of his empire "the Scyths beyond the sea." On his return march through Thrace, he met, apparently, with no opposition. Before passing the Bosphorus, he gave a commission to one of his generals, a certain Megabazus, to complete the reduction of Thrace, and assigned him for the purpose a body of 80,000 men, who remained in Europe while Darius and the rest of his army crossed into Asia.

Megabazus appears to have been fully worthy of the trust reposed in him. In a single campaign (B.C. 506) he overran and subjugated the entire tract between the Propontis and the Strymon, thus pushing forward the Persian dominion to the borders of Macedonia. Among the tribes which he conquered were the Perinthians, Greeks; the Pseti, Cicones, Bistones, Sapaei, Dersaei and Edoni, Thracians; and the Paeoplae and Siripasones, Pseonians. These last, to gratify a whim of Darius, were transported into Asia. The Thracians who submitted were especially those of the coast, no attempt, apparently, being made to penetrate the mountain fastnesses and bring under subjection the tribes of the interior.

The first contact between Persia and Macedonia possesses peculiar interest from the circumstances of the later history. An ancestor of Alexander the Great sat upon the throne of Macedon when the general of Darius was brought in his career of conquest to the outskirts of the Macedonian power. The kingdom was at this time comparatively small, not extending much beyond Mount Bermius on the one hand, and not reaching very far to the east of the Axius on the other. Megabazus saw in it, we may be sure, not the fated destroyer of the Empire which he was extending, but a petty state which the mere sound of the Persian name would awe into subjection. He therefore, instead of invading the country, contented himself with sending an embassy, with a demand for earth and water, the symbols, according to Persian custom, of submission. Amyntas, the Macedonian king, consented, to the demand at once; and though, owing to insolent conduct on the part of the ambassadors, they were massacred with their whole retinue, yet this circumstance did not prevent the completion of Macedonian vassalage. When a second embassy was sent to inquire into the fate of the first, Alexander, the son of Amyntas, who had arranged the massacre, contrived to have the matter hushed up by bribing one of the envoys with a large sum of money and the hand of his sister, Gygsea. Macedonia took up the position of a subject kingdom, and owned for her true lord the great monarch of Western Asia.

Megabazus, having accomplished the task assigned him, proceeded to Sardis, where Darius had remained almost, if not quite, a full year His place was taken by Otanes, the son of Sisamnes, a different person from the conspirator, who rounded off the Persian conquests in these parts by reducing, probably in B.C. 505, the cities of Byzantium, Chalcedon, Antandrus, and Lamponium, with the two adjacent islands of Letnnos and Imbrus. The inhabitants of all were, it appears, taxable, either with having failed to give contingents towards the Scythian expedition, or with having molested it on its return—crimes these, which Otanes thought it right to punish by their general enslavement.

Darius, meanwhile, had proceeded to the seat of government, which appears at this time to have been Susa. He had perhaps already built there the great palace, whose remains have been recently disinterred by English enterprise; or he may have wished to superintend the work of construction. Susa, which was certainly from henceforth the main Persian capital, possessed advantages over almost any other site. Its climate was softer than that of Ecbatana and Persepolis, less sultry than that of Babylon. Its position was convenient for communicating both with the East and with the West. Its people were plastic, and probably more yielding and submissive than the Medes or the Persians. The king, fatigued with his warlike exertions, was glad for a while to rest and recruit himself at Susa, in the tranquil life of the Court. For some years he appears to have conceived no new aggressive project; and he might perhaps have forgotten his designs upon Greece altogether, had not his memory been stirred by a signal and extraordinary provocation.

The immediate circumstances which led to the Ionian Revolt belong to Greek rather than to Persian history, and have been so fully treated of by the historians of the Hellenic race that a knowledge of them may be assumed as already possessed by the reader. What is chiefly remarkable about them is, that they are so purely private and personal. A chance quarrel between Aristagoras of Miletus and the Persian Megabates, pecuniary difficulties pressing on the former, and the natural desire of Histiseus, father-in-law of Aristagoras, to revisit his native place, were undoubtedly the direct and immediate causes of what became a great national outbreak. That there must have been other and wider predisposing causes can scarcely be doubted. Among them two may be suggested. The presence of Darius in Asia Minor, and his friendliness towards the tyrants who bore sway in most of the Greek cities, were calculated to elate those persons in their own esteem, and to encourage in them habits and acts injurious or offensive to their subjects. Their tyranny under these circumstances would become more oppressive and galling. At the same time the popular mind could not fail to associate together the native despot and the foreign lord, who (it was clear to all) supported and befriended each other. If the Greeks of Asia, like so many of their brethren in Europe, had grown weary of their tyrants and were desirous of rising against them, they would be compelled to contemplate the chances of a successful resistance to the Persians. And here there were circumstances in the recent history calculated to inspirit them and give them hopes. Six hundred Greek ships, manned probably by 120,000 men, had been lately brought together, and had formed a united fleet. The fate of the Persian land-army had depended on their fidelity. It is not surprising that a sense of strength should have been developed, and something like a national spirit should have grown up in such a condition of things.

If this were the state of feeling among the Greeks, the merit of Aristagoras would be, that he perceived it, and, regardless of all class prejudices, determined to take advantage of the chance which it gave him of rising superior to his embarrassments. Throwing himself on the popular feeling, the strength of which he had estimated aright, he by the same act gave freedom to the cities, and plunged his nation into a rebellion against Persia. It was easy for reason to show, when the matter was calmly debated, that the probabilities of success against the might of Darius were small. But the arrest of the tyrants by Aristagoras, and his deliverance of them into the hands of their subjects, was an appeal to passion against which reason was powerless. No state could resist the temptation of getting rid of the tyranny under which it groaned. But the expulsion of the vassal committed those who took part in it to resist in arms the sovereign lord.

In the original revolt appear to have been included only the cities of Ionia and AEolis. Aristagoras felt that some further strength was needed, and determined to seek it in European Greece. Repulsed from Sparta, which was disinclined to so distant an expedition, he applied for aid to cities on which he had a special claim. Miletus counted Athens as her mother state; and Eretria was indebted to her for assistance in her great war with Chalcis. Applying in these quarters Aristagoras succeeded better, but still obtained no very important help. Athens voted him twenty ships, Eretria five and with the promise of these succors he hastened back to Asia.

The European contingent soon afterwards arrived; and Aristagoras, anxious to gain some signal success which should attract men to his cause, determined on a most daring enterprise. This was no less than an attack on Sardis, the chief seat of the Persian power in these parts, and by far the most important city of Asia Minor. Sailing to Ephesus, he marched up the valley of the Cayster, crossed Mount Tmolus, and took the Lydian capital at the first onset. Artaphernes, the satrap, was only able to save the citadel; the invaders began to plunder the town, and in the confusion it caught fire and was burnt. Aristagoras and his troops hastily retreated, but were overtaken before they could reach Ephesus by the Persians quartered in the province, who fell upon them and gave them a severe defeat. The expedition then broke up; the Asiatic Greeks dispersed among their cities; the Athenians and Eretrians took ship and sailed home.

Results followed that could scarcely have been anticipated. The failure of the expedition was swallowed up in the glory of its one achievement. It had taken Sardis—it had burnt one of the chief cities of the Great King. The news spread like wildfire on every side, and was proclaimed aloud in places where the defeat of Ephesus was never even whispered. Everywhere revolt burst out. The Greeks of the Hellespont—not only those of Asia but likewise those of Europe—the Carians and Caunians of the south-western coast—even the distant Cyprians broke into rebellion; the Scythians took heart and made a plundering raid through the Great King's Thracian territories;4 vassal monarchs, like Miltiades, assumed independence, and helped themselves to some of the fragments of the Empire that seemed falling to pieces. If a great man, a Miltiades or a Leondias, had been at the head of the movement, and if it had been decently supported from the European side, a successful issue might probably have been secured.

But Aristagoras was unequal to the occasion; and the struggle for independence, which had promised so fair, was soon put down. Despite a naval victory gained by the Greeks over the

Phoenician fleet off Cyprus, that island was recovered by the Persians within a year. Despite a courage and a perseverance worthy of a better fate, the Carians were soon afterwards forced to succumb. The reduction of the Hellespontine Greeks and of the AEolians followed. The toils now closed around Ionia, and her cities began to be attacked one by one; whereupon the incapable Aristagoras, deserting the falling cause, betook himself to Europe, where a just Nemesis pursued him: he died by a Thracian sword. After this the climax soon arrived. Persia concentrated her strength upon Miletus, the cradle of the revolt, and the acknowledged chief of the cities; and though her sister states came gallantly to her aid, and a fleet was collected which made it for a while doubtful which way victory might incline, yet all was of no avail. Laziness and insubordination began and treachery completed the work which all the force of Persia might have failed to accomplish; the combined Ionian fleet was totally defeated in the battle of Lade; and soon after Miletus herself fell. The bulk of her inhabitants were transported into inner Asia and settled upon the Persian Gulf. The whole Ionian coast was ravaged, and the cities punished by the loss of their most beautiful maidens and youths. The islands off the coast were swept of their inhabitants. The cities on the Hellespont and Sea of Marmora were burnt. Miltiades barely escaped from the Chersonese with the loss of his son and his kingdom. The flames of rebellion were everywhere ruthlessly trampled out; and the power of the Great King was once more firmly established over the coasts and islands of the Propontis and the Egean Sea.

It remained, however, to take vengeance upon the foreigners who had dared to lend their aid to the king's revolted subjects, and had borne a part in the burning of Sardis. The pride of the Persians felt such interference as an insult of the grossest kind: and the tale may well be true that Darius, from the time that he first heard the news, employed an officer to bid him daily "remember Athens." The schemes which he had formerly entertained with respect to the reduction of Greece recurred with fresh force to his mind; and the task of crushing the revolt was no sooner completed than he proceeded to attempt their execution. Selecting Mardonius, son of Gobryas the conspirator, and one of his own sons-in-law, for general, he gave him the command of a powerful expedition, which was to advance by way of Thrace, Macedonia, and Thessaly, against Eretria and Athens. At the same time, with a wisdom which we should scarcely have expected in an Oriental, he commissioned him, ere he quitted Asia, to depose the tyrants who bore rule in the Greek cities, and to allow the establishment of democracies in their stead. Such a measure was excellently calculated to preserve the fidelity of the Hellenic population and to prevent any renewal of disturbance. It gave ample employment to unquiet spirits by opening to them a career in their own states—and it removed the grievance which, more than anything else, had produced the recent rebellion.

Mardonius having effected this change proceeded into Europe. He had a large land force and a powerful navy, and at first was successful both by land and sea. The fleet took Thasos, an island valuable for its mines; and the army forced the Macedonians to exchange their position of semi-independence for that of full Persian subjects, liable to both tribute and military service. But this fair dawn was soon overcast. As the fleet was rounding Athos a terrible tempest arose which, destroyed 300 triremes and more than 20,000 men, some of whom were devoured by sea-monsters, while the remainder perished by drowning. On shore, a night attack of the Brygi, a Thracian tribe dwelling in the tract between the Strymon and the Axius, brought disaster upon the land force, numbers of which were slain, while Mardonius himself received a wound. This disgrace, indeed, was retrieved by subsequent operations, which forced the Brygi to make their submission; but the expedition found itself in no condition to advance further, and Mardonius retreated into Asia.

Darius, however, did not allow failure to turn him from his purpose. The attack of Mardonius was followed within two years by the well-known expedition under Datis (B.C. 490), which, avoiding the dangers of Athos, sailed direct to its object, crossing the Egean by the line of the Cyclades, and falling upon Eretria and Attica. Eretria's punishment warned the Athenians to resist to the uttermost; and the skill of Miltiades, backed by the valor of his countrymen, gave to Athens the great victory of Marathon. Datis fell back upon Asia, having suffered worse disasters than his predecessor, and bore to the king the melancholy tidings that his vast force of from 100,000 to 200,000 men had been met and worsted by 20,000 Athenians and Plataeans.

Still Darius was not shaken in his resolution. He only issued fresh orders for the collection of men, ships, and materials. For three years Asia resounded with the din of preparation; and it is probable that in the fourth year a fresh expedition would have been led into Greece, had not an important occurrence prevented it. Egypt, always discontented with its subject position under a race which despised its religion, and perhaps occasionally persecuted it, broke out into open revolt (B.C. 487). Darius, it seems, determined to divide his forces, and proceed simultaneously against both enemies; he even contemplated leading one of the two expeditions in person; but before his preparations were completed his vital powers failed. He died in the year following the Egyptian revolt (B.C. 486), in the sixty-third year of his age, and the thirty-sixth of his reign, leaving his crown to his eldest son by Atossa, Xerxes.

The character of Darius will have revealed itself with tolerable clearness in the sketch which has been here given of the chief events of his reign. But a brief summary of some of its main points may not be superfluous. Darius Hystaspis was, next to Cyrus, the greatest of the Persian kings; and he was even superior to Cyrus in some particulars. His military talent has been underrated. Though not equal to the founder of the Empire in this respect, he deserves the credit of energy, vigor, foresight, and judicious management in his military expeditions, of promptness in resolving and ability in executing, of discrimination in the selection of generals, and of a power of combination not often found in Oriental commanders. He was personally brave, and quite willing to expose himself, even in his old age, to dangers and hardships. But he did not unnecessarily thrust himself into peril. He was content to employ generals, where the task to be accomplished did not seem to be beyond their powers; and he appears to have been quite free from an unworthy jealousy of their successes. He was a man of kindly and warm feeling—strongly attached to his friends; he was clement and even generous towards conquered foes. When he thought the occasion required it, he could be severe but his inclination was towards mildness and indulgence. He excelled all the other Persian kings in the arts of peace. To him, and him alone, the Empire owed its organization. He was a skilful administrator, a good financier, and a wise and far-seeing ruler. Of all the Persian princes he is the only one who can be called "many-sided." He was organizer, general, statesman, administrator, builder, patron of arts and literature, all in one. Without him Persia would probably have sunk as rapidly as she rose, and would be known to us only as one of the many meteor powers which have shot athwart the horizon of the East.

Xerxes, the eldest son of Darius by Atossa, succeeded his father by virtue of a formal act of choice. It was a Persian custom that the king, before he went out of his dominions on an expedition, should nominate a successor. Darius must have done this before his campaign in Thrace and Scythia; and if Xerxes was then, as is probable, a mere boy, it is impossible that he should have received the appointment. Artobazanes, the eldest of all Darius's sons, whose mother, a daughter of Gobryas, was married to Darius before he became king, was most likely then nominated, and was thenceforth regarded as the heir-apparent. When, however, towards the close of his reign Darius again proposed to head a foreign expedition, an opportunity occurred of disturbing this arrangement, of which Atossa, Darius's favorite wife, whose influence over her husband was unbounded, determined to take advantage. According to the law, a fresh signification of the sovereign's will was now requisite; and Atossa persuaded Darius to make it in favor of Xerxes. The pleas put forward were, first, that he was the eldest son of the king, and secondly, that he was descended from Cyrus. This latter argument could not fail to have weight. Backed by the influence of Atossa, it prevailed over all other considerations; and hence Xerxes obtained the throne.

If we may trust the informants of Herodotus, it was the wish of Xerxes on his accession to discontinue the preparations against Greece, and confine his efforts to the re-conquest of Egypt. Though not devoid of ambition, he may well have been distrustful of his own powers; and, having been nurtured in luxury, he may have shrunk from the perils of a campaign in unknown regions. But he was surrounded by advisers who had interests opposed to his inclinations, and who worked on his facile temper till they prevailed on him to take that course which seemed best calculated to promote their designs. Mardonius was anxious to retrieve his former failure, and expected, if Greece were conquered, that the rich prize would become his own satrapy. The refugee princes of the family of Pisistratus hoped to be reinstated under Persian influence as dependent despots of Athens. Demaratus of Sparta probably cherished a similar expectation with regard to that capital. The Persian nobles generally, who profited by the spoils of war, and who were still full of the military spirit, looked forward with pleasure to an expedition from which they anticipated victory, plunder, and thousands of valuable captives. The youthful king was soon persuaded that the example of his predecessors required him to undertake some fresh conquest, while the honor of Persia absolutely demanded that the wrongs inflicted upon her by Athens should be avenged. Before, however, turning his arms against Greece, two revolts required his attention. In the year B.C. 485—the second of his reign—he marched into Egypt, which he rapidly reduced to obedience and punished by increasing its burthens. Soon afterwards he seems to have provoked a rebellion of the Babylonians by acts which they regarded as impious, and avenged by killing their satrap, Zopyrus, and proclaiming their independence. Megabyzus, the son of Zopyrus, recovered the city, which was punished by the plunder and ruin of its famous temple and the desolation of many of its shrines.

Xerxes was now free to bend all his efforts against Greece, and, appreciating apparently to the full the magnitude and difficulty of the task, resolved that nothing should be left undone which could possibly be done in order to render success certain. The experience of former years had taught some important lessons. The failure of Datis had proved that such an expedition as could be conveyed by sea across the Egean would be insufficient to secure the object sought, and that the only safe road for a conqueror whose land force constituted his real strength was along the shores of the European continent. But if a large army took this long and circuitous route, it must be supported by a powerful fleet; and this involved a new danger. The losses of Mardonius off Athos had shown the perils of Egean navigation, and taught the lesson that the naval force must be at first far more than proportionate to the needs of the army, in order that it might still be sufficient notwithstanding some considerable disasters. At the same time they had indicated one special place of danger, which might be avoided, if proper measures were taken. Xerxes, in the four years which followed on the reduction of Egypt, continued incessantly to make the most gigantic preparations for his intended attack upon Greece, and among them included all the precautions which a wise foresight could devise in order to ward off every conceivable peril. A general order was issued to all the satraps throughout the Empire, calling on them to levy the utmost force of their province for the new war; while, as the equipment of Oriental troops depends greatly on the purchase and distribution of arms by their commander, a rich reward was promised to the satrap whose contingent should appear at the appointed place and time in the most gallant array. Orders for ships and transports of different kinds were given to the maritime states, with such effect that above 1200 triremes and 3000 vessels of an inferior description were collected together. Magazines of corn were formed at various points along the intended line of route. Above all, it was determined to bridge the Hellespont by a firm and compact structure, which it was thought would secure the communication of the army from interruption by the elements; and at the same time it was resolved to cut through the isthmus which joined Mount Athos to the continent, in order to preserve the fleet from disaster at that most perilous part of the proposed voyage. These remarkable works, which made a deep impression on the minds of the Greeks, have been ascribed to a mere spirit of ostentation on the part of Xerxes; the vain-glorious monarch wished, it is supposed, to parade his power, and made a useless bridge and an absurd cutting merely for the purpose of exhibiting to the world the grandeur of his ideas and the extent of his resources. But there is no necessity for travelling beyond the line of ordinary human motive in order to discover a reason for the works in question. The bridge across the Hellespont was a mere repetition of the construction by which Darius had passed into Europe when he made his Scythian expedition, and probably seemed to a Persian not a specially dignified or very wonderful way of crossing so narrow a strait, but merely the natural mode of passage. The only respect in which the bridge of Xerxes differed from constructions with which the Persians were thoroughly familiar, was in its superior solidity and strength. The shore-cables were of unusual size and weight, and apparently of unusual materials; the formation of a double line—of two bridges, in fact, instead of one—was almost without a parallel; and the completion of the work by laying on the ordinary plank-bridge a solid causeway composed of earth and brushwood, with a high bulwark on either side, was probably, if not unprecedented, at any rate very uncommon. Boat-bridges were usually, as they are even now in the East, somewhat rickety constructions, which animals unaccustomed to them could with difficulty be induced to cross. The bridge of Xerxes was a high-road, as AEschylus calls it along, which men, horses, and vehicles might pass with as much comfort and facility as they could move on shore.

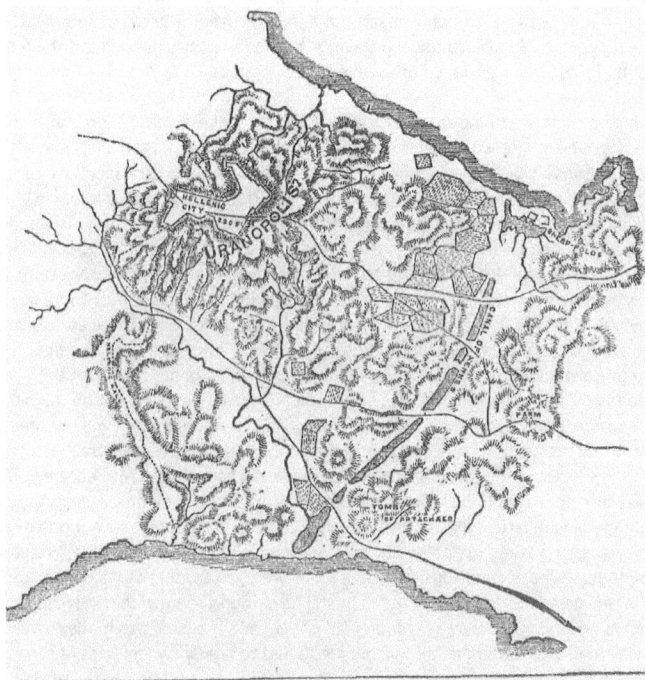

Plan of Canal.

PLATE LXI

The utility of such a work is evident. Without it Xerxes must have been reduced to the necessity of embarking in ships, conveying across the strait, and disembarking, not only his entire host, but all its stores, tents, baggage, horses, camels, and sumpter-beasts. If the numbers of his army approached even the lowest estimate that has been formed of them, it is not too much to say that many weeks must have been spent in this operation. As it was, the whole expedition marched across in seven days. In the case of ship conveyance, continual accidents would have happened: the transport would from time to time have been interrupted by bad weather; and great catastrophes might have occurred. By means of the bridge the passage was probably effected without any loss of either man or beast. Moreover, the bridge once established, there was a safe line of communication thenceforth between the army in Europe and the headquarters of the Persian power in Asia, along which might pass couriers, supplies, and reinforcements, if they should be needed. Further, the grandeur, massiveness, and apparent stability of the work was calculated to impose upon the minds of men, and to diminish their power of resistance by impressing them strongly with a sense of the irresistible greatness and strength of the invader.

The canal of Athos was also quite a legitimate and judicious undertaking. [PLATE LXI.] No portion of the Greek coast is so dangerous as that about Athos. Greek boatmen even at the present day refuse to attempt the circumnavigation; and probably any government less apathetic than that of the Turks would at once re-open the old cutting. The work was one of very little difficulty, the breadth of the isthmus being less than a mile and a half, the material sand and marl, and the greatest height of the natural ground above the level of the sea about fifty feet. The construction of a canal in such a locality was certainly better than the formation of a ship-groove or Diolcus—the substitute for it proposed by Ferodotus, [PLATE LXI.] not to mention that it is doubtful whether at the time that this cutting was made ship-grooves were known even to the Greeks.

Xerxes, having brought his preparations into a state of forwardness, having completed his canal and his bridge—after one failure with the latter, for which the constructors and the sea were punished—proceeded, in the year B.C. 481, along the "Royal Road" from Susa to Sardis, and wintered at the Lydian capital. His army is said to have accompanied him; but more probably it joined him in the spring, flocking in, contingent after contingent, from the various provinces of his vast Empire. Forty-nine nations, according to Herodotus, served under his standard; and their contingents made up a grand total of eighteen hundred thousand men. Of these, eighty thousand were cavalry, while twenty thousand rode in chariots or on camels; the remainder served on foot. There are no sufficient means of testing these numbers. Figures in the mouth of an Oriental are vague and almost unmeaning; armies are never really counted: there is no such thing as a fixed and definite "strength" of a division or a battalion. Herodotus tells us that a rough attempt at numbering the infantry of the host was made on this occasion; but it was of so rude and primitive a description that little dependence can be placed on the results obtained by it. Ten thousand men were counted, and were made to stand close together; a line was then drawn round them, and a wall built on the line to the height of a man's waist; within the enclosure thus made all the troops in turn entered, and each time that the enclosure appeared to be full, ten thousand were supposed to be within it. Estimated in this way, the infantry was regarded as amounting to 1,700,000. It is clear that such mode of counting was of the roughest kind, and might lead to gross exaggeration. Each commander would wish his troops to be thought more numerous than they really were, and would cause the enclosure to appear full when several thousands more might still have found room within it. Nevertheless there would be limits beyond which exaggeration could not go; and if Xerxes was made to believe that the land force which he took with him into Europe amounted to nearly two millions of men, it is scarcely doubtful but that it must have exceeded one million.

The motley composition of such a host has been described in a former chapter. Each nation was armed and equipped after its own fashion, and served in a body, often under a distinct commander. The army marched through Asia in a single column, which was not, however, continuous, but was broken into three portions. The first portion consisted of the baggage animals and about half of the contingents of the nations; the second was composed wholly of native Persians, who preceded and followed the emblems of religion and the king; the third was made up of the remaining national contingents. The king himself rode alternately in a chariot and in a litter. He was preceded immediately by ten sacred horses, and a sacred chariot drawn by eight milk-white steeds. Round him and about him were the choicest troops of the whole army, twelve thousand horse and the same number of foot, all Persians, and those too not taken at random, but selected carefully from the whole mass of the native soldiery. Among them seem to have been the famous "Immortals"—a picked body of 10,000 footmen, always maintained at exactly the same number, and thence deriving their appellation.

The line of march from Sardis to Abydos was only partially along the shore. The army probably descended the valley of the Hermus nearly to its mouth, and then struck northward into the Caicus vale, crossing which it held on its way, with Mount Kara-dagh (Cane) on the left, across the Atarnean plain, and along the coast to Adramytium (Adramyti) and Antandros, whence it again struck inland, and, crossing the ridge of Ida, descended into the valley of the Scamander. Some losses were incurred from the effects of a violent thunderstorm amid the mountains; but they cannot have been of a any great consequence. On reaching the Scamander the army found its first difficulty with respect to water. That stream was probably low, and the vast host of men and animals were unable to obtain from it a supply sufficient for their wants. This phenomenon, we are told, frequently recurred afterwards; it surprises the English reader, but is not really astonishing, since, in hot countries, even considerable streams are often reduced to mere threads of water during the summer.

Rounding the hills which skirt the Scamander valley upon the east, the army marched past Rhoeteum, Ophrynium, and Dardanus to Abydos. Here Xerxes, seated upon a marble throne, which the people of Abydos had erected for him on the summit of a hill, was able to see at one glance his whole, armament, and to feast his eyes with the sight. It is not likely that any misgivings occurred to him at such a moment. Before him lay his vast host, covering with its dense masses the entire low ground between the hills and the sea; beyond was the strait, and to his left the open sea, white with the sails of four thousand ships; the green fields of the Chersonese smiled invitingly a little further on; while, between him and the opposite shore, the long lines of his bridges lay darkling upon the sea, like a yoke placed upon the neck of a captive. Having seen all, the king gave his special attention to the fleet, which he now perhaps beheld in all its magnitude for the first time. Desirous of knowing which of his subjects were the best sailors, he gave orders for a sailing-match, which were at once carried out. The palm was borne off by the Phoenicians of Sidon, who must have beaten not only their own countrymen of Tyre, but the Greeks of Asia and the islands.

On the next day the passage took place. It was accompanied by religious ceremonies. Waiting for the sacred hour of sunrise, the leader of the host, as the first rays appeared, poured a libation from a golden goblet into the sea, and prayed to Mithra that he might effect the conquest of Europe. As he prayed he cast into the sea the golden goblet, and with it a golden bowl and a short Persian sword. Meanwhile the multitude strewed all the bridge with myrtle boughs, and perfumed it with clouds of incense. The "Immortals" crossed first, wearing garlands on their heads. The king, with the sacred chariot and horses passed over on the second day. For seven days and seven nights the human stream flowed on without intermission across one bridge, while the attendants and the baggage-train made use of the other. The lash was employed to quicken the movements of laggards. At last the whole army was in Europe, and the march resumed its regularity.

It is unnecessary to follow in detail the advance of the host along the coast of Thrace, across Chalcidice, and round the Thermaic Gulf into Pieria. If we except the counting of the fleet and army at Doriscus no circumstances of much interest diversified this portion of the march, which lay entirely through territories that had previously submitted to the Great King. The army spread itself over a wide tract of country, marching generally in three divisions, which proceeded by three parallel lines—one along the coast, another at some considerable distance inland, and a third, with which was Xerxes himself, midway between them. At every place where Xerxes stopped along his line of route the natives had, besides furnishing corn for his army, to entertain him and his suite at a great banquet, the cost of which was felt as a heavy burthen. Contributions of troops or ships were also required from all the cities and tribes; and thus both fleet and army continually swelled as they advanced onward. In crossing the track between the Strymon and the Axius some damage was suffered by the baggage-train from lions, which came down from the mountains during the night and devoured many of the camels; but otherwise the march was effected without loss, and the fleet and army reached the borders of Thessaly intact, and in good condition. Here it was found that there was work for the pioneers, and a reconnaissance of the enemy's country before entering it was probably also thought desirable. The army accordingly halted some days in Pieria, while preparations were being made for crossing the Olympic range into the Thessalian lowland.

During the halt intelligence arrived which seemed to promise the invader an easy conquest. Xerxes, while he was staying at Sardis, had sent heralds to all the Grecian states, excepting Athens and Sparta, with a demand for earth and water, the recognized symbols of submission. His envoys now returned, and brought him favorable replies from at least one-third of the continental Greeks—from the Perrhaebians, Thessalians, Dolopians, Magnetians, Achaeans of Phthiotis, Enianians, Malians, Locrians, and from most of the Boeotians. Unless it were the insignificant Phocis, no hostile country seemed to intervene between the place where his army lay and the great object of the expedition, Attica. Xerxes, therefore, having first viewed the pass of Tempe, and seen with his own eyes that no enemy lay encamped beyond, passed over the Olympic range by a road cut through the woods by his army, and proceeded southwards across Thessaly and Achaea Phthiotis into Malis, the fertile plain at the mouth of the Spercheius river. Here, having heard that a Greek force was in the neighborhood, he pitched his camp not far from the small town of Trachis.

Thus far had the Greeks allowed the invader to penetrate their country without offering him any resistance. Originally there had been an intention of defending Thessaly, and an army under Evsenetus, a Spartan polemarch, and Themistocles, the great Athenian, had proceeded to Tempe, in order to cooperate with the Thessalians in guarding the pass. But the discovery that the Olympic range could be crossed in the place where the army of Xerxes afterwards passed it had shown that the position was untenable; and it had been then resolved that the stand should be made at the next defensible position, Thermopylae. [PLATE LXII.] Here, accordingly, a force was found—small, indeed, if it be compared with the number of the assailants, but sufficient to defend such a position as that where it was posted against the world in arms. Three hundred Spartans, with their usual retinue of helots, 700 Lacedaemonians, other Peloponnesians to the number of 2800, 1000 Phocians, the same number of Locrians, 700 Thespians, and 400 Thebans, formed an army of 9000 men—quite as numerous a force as could be employed with any effect in the defile they were sent to guard. The defile was a long and narrow pass shut in between a high mountain, Callidromus, and the sea, and crossed at one point by a line of wall in which was a single gateway. Unless the command of the sea were gained, or another mode of crossing the mountains discovered, the pass could scarcely be forced.

Plate LXII
Vol II

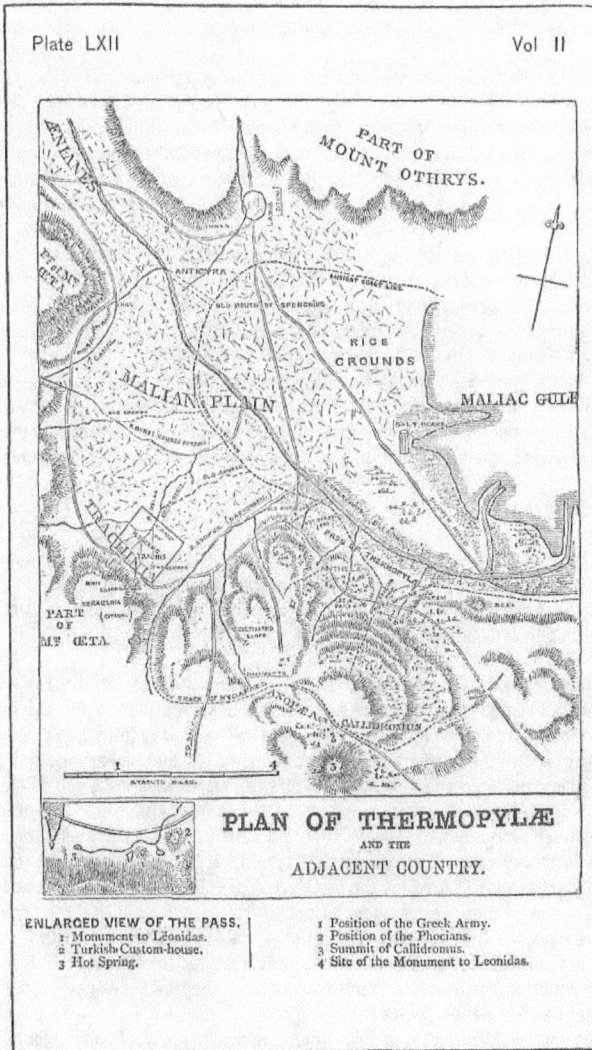

PLAN OF THERMOPYLÆ
AND THE
ADJACENT COUNTRY.

ENLARGED VIEW OF THE PASS.
1 Monument to Léonidas.
2 Turkish Custom-house.
3 Hot Spring.

1 Position of the Greek Army.
2 Position of the Phocians.
3 Summit of Callidromus.
4 Site of the Monument to Leonidas.

PLATE LXII

Xerxes, however, confident in his numbers—after waiting four days at Trachis, probably in the hope that his fleet would join him—proceeded on the fifth day to the assault. First the Medes and Cissians, then the famous "Immortals" were sent into the jaws of the pass against the immovable foe; but neither detachment could make any impression. The long spears, large shields, and heavy armor of the Greeks, their skilful tactics, and steady array, were far more than a match for the inferior equipments and discipline of the Asiatics. Though the attack was made with great gallantry, both on this day and the next, it failed to produce the slightest effect. Very few of the Greeks were either slain or wounded; and it seemed as if the further advance of a million of men was to be stopped by a force less than a hundredth part of their number.

But now information reached Xerxes which completely changed the face of affairs. There was a rough mountain-path leading from Trachis up the gorge of the Asopus and across Callidromus to the rear of the Greek position, which had been unknown to the Greeks when they decided on making their first stand at Thermopylae, and which they only discovered when their plans no longer admitted of alteration. It was, perhaps, not much more than a goat-track, and apparently they had regarded it as scarcely practicable, since they had thought its defence might be safely entrusted to a thousand Phocians. Xerxes, however, on learning the existence of the track, resolved at once to make trial of it. His Persian soldiers were excellent mountaineers. He ordered Hydarnes to take the "Immortals," and, guided by a native, to proceed along the path by night, and descend with early dawn into the rear of the Greeks, who would then be placed between two fires. The operation was performed with complete success. The Phocian guard, surprised at the summit, left the path free while they sought a place of safety. The Greeks in the pass below, warned during the night of their danger, in part fled, in part resolved on death. When morning came, Leonidas, at the head of about half his original army, moved forward towards the Malian plain, and there met the advancing Persians. A bloody combat ensued, in which the Persians lost by far the greater number; but the ranks of the Greeks were gradually thinned, and they were beaten back step by step into the narrowest part of the pass, where finally they all perished, except the four hundred Thebans, who submitted and were made prisoners.

So terminated the first struggle on the soil of Greece, between the invaders and the invaded. It seemed to promise that, though at vast cost, Persia would be victorious. If her loss in the three days' combat was 20,000 men, as Herodotus states, yet, as that of her enemy was 4000, the proportionate advantage was on her side.

But, for the conquest of such a country as Greece, it was requisite, not only that the invader should succeed on land, but also that he should be superior at sea. Xerxes had felt this, and had brought with him a fleet, calculated, as he imagined, to sweep the Greek navy from the Egean. As far as the Pagasaean Gulf, opposite the northern extremity of Euboea, his fleet had advanced without meeting an enemy. It had encountered one terrible storm off the coast of Magnesia, and had lost 400 vessels; but this loss was scarcely felt in so vast an armament. When from Aphetse, at the mouth of the gulf, the small Greek fleet, amounting to no more than 271 vessels, was seen at anchor off Artemisium, the only fear which the Persian commanders entertained was lest it should escape them. They at once detached 200 vessels to sail round the Coast coast of Euboea, and cut off the possibility of retreat. When, however, these vessels were all lost in a storm, and when in three engagements on three successive days, the Greek fleet showed itself fully able to contend against the superior numbers of its antagonist, the Persians themselves could not fail to see that their naval supremacy was more than doubtful. The fleet at Artemisium was not the entire Greek naval force; on another occasion it might be augumented, while their own could scarcely expect to receive reinforcements. The fights at Artemisium foreshadowed a day when the rival fleets would no longer meet and part on equal terms, but Persia would have to acknowledge herself inferior.

Meanwhile, however, the balance of advantage rested with the invaders. The key of Northern Greece was won, and Phocis, Locris, Boeotia, Attica, and the Megarid lay open to the Persian army. The Greek fleet could gain nothing by any longer maintaining the position of Artemisium, and fell back towards the south, while its leaders anxiously considered where it should next take up its station. The Persians pressed on both by land and sea. A rapid march through Phocis and Boeotia brought Xerxes to Athens, soon after the Athenians, knowing that resistance would be vain, had evacuated it. The Acropolis, defended by a few fanatics, was taken and burnt. One object of the expedition was thus accomplished. Athens lay in ruins; and the whole of Attica was occupied by the conqueror. The Persian fleet, too, finding the channel of the Euripus clear, sailed down it, and rounding Sunium, came to anchor in the bay of Phalerum.

In the councils of the Greeks all was doubt and irresolution. The army, which ought to have mustered in full force at Thermopylae and Callidromus, and which, after those passes were forced, might have defended Cithaeron and Parnes, had never ventured beyond the Isthmus of Corinth, and was there engaged in building a wall across the neck of land from sea to sea. The fleet lay off Salamis, where it was detained by the entreaties of the Athenians, who had placed in that island the greater part of the non-combatant population; but the inclination was strong on the part of many to withdraw westward and fight the next battle, if a battle must be fought, in the vicinity of the land force, which would be a protection in case of defeat. Could Xerxes have had patience for a few days, the combined fleet would have broken up. The Peloponnesian contingents would have withdrawn to the isthmus; and the Athenians, despairing of success, would probably have sailed away to Italy. But the Great King, when he saw the vast disproportion between his own fleet and that of the enemy, could not believe in the possibility of the Greeks offering a successful resistance. Like a modern emperor, who imagined that, if only he could have been with his fleet, all would necessarily have gone well, Xerxes supposed that by having the sea-fight under his own eye he would be sure of victory. Thus again, as at Artemisium, the only fear felt was lest the Greeks should fly, and in that way escape chastisement. Orders were therefore issued to the Persian fleet to close up at once, and blockade the eastern end of the Salaminian strait, while a detachment repeated the attempted manoeuvre at Euboea, and sailed round the island to guard the channel at its western outlet.

These movements were executed late in the day on which the Persian fleet arrived at Phalerum. During the night intelligence reached the commanders that the retreat of the Greeks was about to commence at once; whereupon the Persian right wing was pushed forward into the strait, and carried beyond the Greek position so as to fill the channel where it opens into the bay of Eleusis. The remainder of the night passed in preparations for the battle on both sides. At daybreak both fleets advanced from their respective shores, the Persians being rather the assailants. Their thousand vessels were drawn up in three lines, and charged their antagonists with such spirit that the general inclination on the part of the Greeks was at first to retreat. Some of their ships had almost touched the shore, when the bold example of one of the captains, or a cry of reproach from unknown lips, produced a revulsion of feeling, and the whole line advanced in good order. The battle was for a short time doubtful; but soon the superiority of Greek naval tactics began to tell. The Persian vessels became entangled one with another, and crashing together broke each other's oars. The triple line increased their difficulties. If a vessel, overmatched, sought to retreat, it necessarily came into collision with the ships stationed in its rear. These moreover pressed too eagerly forward, since their captains were anxious to distinguish themselves in order to merit the approval of Xerxes. The Greeks found themselves able to practice with good effect their favorite manoeuvre of the periplus, and thus increased the confusion. It was not long before the greater part of the Persian fleet became a mere helpless mass of shattered or damaged vessels. Five hundred are said to have been sunk—the majority by the enemy, but some even by their own friends. The sea was covered with wrecks, and with wretches who clung to them, till the ruthless enemy slew them or forced them to let go their hold.

This defeat was a death-blow to the hopes of Xerxes, and sealed the fate of the expedition. From the moment that he realized to himself the fact of the entire inability of his fleet to cope with that of the Greeks, Xerxes made up his mind to return with all haste to Asia. From over-confidence he fell into the opposite extreme of despair, and made no effort to retrieve his ill fortune. His fleet was ordered to sail straight for the Hellespont, and to guard the bridges until he reached them with his army. He himself retreated hastily along the same road by which he had advanced, his whole army accompanying him as far as Thessaly, where Marnonius was left with 260,000 picked men, to prevent pursuit, and to renew the attempt against Greece in the ensuing year. Xerxes pressed on to the Hellespont, losing vast numbers of his troops by famine and sickness on the way, and finally returned into Asia, not by his magnificent bridge, which a storm had destroyed, but on board a vessel, which, according to some, narrowly escaped shipwreck during the passage. Even in Asia disaster pursued him. Between Abydos and Sardis his army suffered almost as much from over-indulgence as it had previously suffered from want; and of the mighty host which had gone forth from the Lydian capital in the spring not very many thousands can have re-entered it in the autumn.

Still, however, there was a possibility that the success which his own arms had failed to achieve might reward the exertions of his lieutenants. Mardonius had expressed himself confident that with 300,000 picked soldiers he could overpower all resistance, and make Greece a satrapy of Persia. Xerxes had raised his forces to that amount by sending Artabazus back from Sestos at the head of a corps d'armee numbering 40,000 men. The whole army of 300,000 wintered in Thessaly; and Mardonius, when spring came, having vainly endeavored to detach the Athenians from the Grecian ranks, marched through Boeotia in Attica, and occupied Athens for the second time. Hence he proceeded to menace the Peloponnese, where he formed an alliance with the Argives, who promised him that they would openly embrace the Persian cause. At the same time the Athenians, finding that Sparta took no steps to help them, began to waver in their resistance, and to contemplate accepting the terms which Mardonius was still willing to grant them. The fate of Greece trembled in the balance, and apparently was determined by the accident of a death and a succession, rather than by any wide-spread patriotic feeling or any settled course of policy. Cleombrotus, regent for the young son of Leonidas, died, and his brother Pausanias—a brave, clever, and ambitious man—took his place. We can scarcely be wrong in ascribing—at least in part—to this circumstance the unlooked-for change of policy, which electrified the despondent ambassadors of Athens almost as soon as Pausanias was installed in power. It was suddenly announced that Sparta would take the offensive. Ten thousand hoplites and 400,000 light-armed—the largest army that she ever levied—took the field, and, joined at the isthmus by above 25,000 Peloponnesians, and soon afterwards by almost as many Athenians and Megarians, proceeded to seek the foreigners, first in Attica, and then in the position to which they had retired in Boeotia. On the skirts of Citheeron, near Platsea, a hundred and eight thousand Greeks confronted more than thrice their number of Persians and Persian subjects; and now at length the trial was to be made whether, in fair and open fight on land, Greece or Persia would be superior. A suspicion of what the result would be might have been derived from Marathon. But there the Persians had been taken at a disadvantage, when the cavalry, their most important arm, was absent. Here the error of Datis was not likely to be repeated. Mardonius had a numerous and well-armed cavalry, which he handled with no little skill. It remained to be seen, when the general engagement came, whether, with both arms brought fully into play, the vanquished at Marathon would be the victors.

The battle of Plataea was brought on under circumstances very unfavorable to the Greeks. Want of water and a difficulty about provisions had necessitated a night movement on their part. The cowardice of all the small contingents, and the obstinacy of an individual Spartan, disconcerted the whole plan of the operation, and left the Lacedaemonians and the Athenians at daybreak separated from each other, and deserted by the whole body of their allies. Mardonius attacked at once, and prevented the junction of the two allies, so that two distinct and separate engagements went on at the same time. In both the Greeks were victorious. The Spartans repulsed the Persian horse and foot, slew Mardonius and were the first to assail the Persian camp. The Athenians defeated the medizing Greeks, and effected a breach in the defences of the camp, on which the Spartans had failed to make any impression. A terrible carnage followed. The contingent of 40,000 troops under Artabazus alone drew off in good order.

The remainder were seized with panic, and were either slaughtered like sheep or fled in complete disarray. Seventy thousand Greeks not only defeated but destroyed the army of 300,000 barbarians, which melted away and disappeared making no further stand anywhere. The disaster of Marathon was repeated on a larger scale, and without the resource of an embarkation. Henceforth the immense superiority of Greek troops to Persian was well known on both sides; and nothing but the distance from Greece of her vital parts, and the quarrels of the Greek states among themselves, preserved for nearly a century and a half the doomed empire of Persia.

The immediate result of the defeats of Salamis and Platsea was a contraction of the Persian boundary towards the west. Though a few Persian garrisons maintained themselves for some years on the further side of the straits, soothing thereby the wounded vanity of the Great King, who liked to think that he had still a hold on Europe; yet there can be no doubt that, after the double flight of Xerxes and Artabazus, Macedonia, Pseonia, and Thrace recovered their independence. Persia lost her European provinces, and began the struggle to retain those of Asia. Terminus receded, and having once receded never advanced again in this quarter. The Greeks took the offensive. Sailing to Asia, they not only liberated from their Persian bondage the islands which lay along the coast, but landing their men on the continent, attacked and defeated an army of 60,000 Persians at Mycale, and destroyed the remnant of the ships that had escaped from Salamis. Could they have made up their minds to maintain a powerful fleet permanently on the coast of Asia, they might at once have deprived Persia of her whole sea-hoard on the Propontis and the Egean; but neither of the two great powers of Greece was prepared for such a resolve. Sparta disliked distant expeditions; and Athens did not as yet see her way to undertaking the protection of the continental Greeks. She had much to do at home, and had not yet discovered those weak points in her adversary's harness, which subsequently enabled her to secure by treaty the freedom of the Greek cities upon the mainland. For the present, therefore, Persia only lost the bulk of her European possessions, and the islands of the Propontis and the Egean.

The circumstances which caused a renewal of Greek agressions upon Asia towards the close of the reign of Xerxes are not very clearly narrated by the authors who speak of them. It appears, however, that after twelve years of petty operations, during which Eion was recovered, and Doriscus frequently attacked, but without effect, the Athenians resolved, in B.C. 466, upon a great expedition to the eastward. Collecting a fleet of 300 vessels, which was placed under the command of Cimon, the son of Miltiades, they sailed to the coast of Caria and Lycia, where they drove the Persian garrisons out of the Greek towns, and augmenting their navy by fresh contingents at every step, proceeded along the shores of Pamphylia as far as the mouth of the river Eurymedon, where they found a Phoenician fleet of 340 vessels, and a Persian army, stationed to protect the territory. Engaging first the fleet they defeated it, and drove it ashore, after which they disembarked and gained a victory over the Persian army. As many as two hundred triremes were taken or destroyed. They then sailed on towards Cyprus, where they met and destroyed a squadron of eighty ships, which was on its way to reinforce the fleet at the Eurymedon. Above a hundred vessels, 20,000 captives, and a vast amount of plunder were the prize of this war; which had, however, no further effect on the relations of the two powers.

In the following year the reign of Xerxes came to an end abruptly. With this monarch seems to have begun those internal disorders of the seraglio, which made the Court during more than a hundred and forty years a perpetual scene of intrigues, assassinations, executions, and conspiracies. Xerxes, who appears to have only one wife, Amestris, the daughter (or grand-daughter) of the conspirator, Otanes, permitted himself the free indulgence of illicit passion among the princesses of the Court, the wives of his own near relatives. The most horrible results followed. Amestris vented her jealous spite on those whom she regarded as guilty of stealing from her the affections of her husband; and to prevent her barbarities from producing rebellion, it was necessary to execute the persons whom she had provoked, albeit they were near relations of the monarch. The taint of incontinence spread among the members of the royal family; and a daughter of the king, who was married to one of the most powerful nobles, became notorious for her excesses. Eunuchs rose into power, and fomented the evils which prevailed. The king made himself bitter enemies among those whose position was close to his person. At last, Artabanus, chief of the guard, a courtier of high rank, and Aspamitres, a eunuch, who held the office of chamberlain, conspired against their master, and murdered him in his sleeping apartment, after he had reigned twenty years.

The character of Xerxes falls below that of any preceding monarch. Excepting that he was not wholly devoid of a certain magnanimity, which made him listen patiently to those who opposed his views or gave him unpalatable advice and which prevented him from exacting vengeance on some occasions, he had scarcely a trait whereon the mind can rest with any satisfaction. Weak and easily led, puerile in his gusts of passion and his complete abandonment of himself to them—selfish, fickle, boastful, cruel, superstitious, licentious—he exhibits to us the Oriental despot in the most contemptible of all his aspects—that wherein the moral and the intellectual qualities are equally in defect, and the career is one unvarying course of vice and folly. From Xerxes we have to date at once the decline of the Empire in respect of territorial greatness and military strength, and likewise its deterioration in regard to administrative vigor and national spirit. With him commenced the corruption of the Court—the fatal evil, which almost universally weakens and destroys Oriental dynasties. His expedition against Greece exhausted and depopulated the Empire; and though, by abstaining from further military enterprises, he did what lay in his power to recruit its strength, still the losses which his expedition caused were certainly not repaired in his lifetime.

As a builder, Xerxes showed something of the same grandeur of conception which is observable in his great military enterprise and in the works by which it was accompanied. His Propylaea, and the sculptured staircase in front of the Chebl Minar, which is undoubtedly his work, are among the most magnificent erections upon the Persepolitan platform; and are quite sufficient to place him in the foremost rank of Oriental builders. If we were to ascribe the Chehl Minar itself to him, we should have to give him the palm above all other kings of Persia; but on the whole it is most probable that that edifice and its duplicate at Susa were conceived, and in the main, constructed, by Darius.

Xerxes left behind him three sons—Darius, Hystaspes, and Artaxerxes—and two daughters, Amytis and Rhodogune. Hystaspes was satrap of Bactria, and at the time of their father's death, only Darius and Artaxerxes were at the Court.

Fearing the eldest son most, Artabanus persuaded Artaxerxes that the assassination of Xerxes was the act of his brother, whereupon Artaxerxes caused him to be put to death, and himself ascended the throne (B.C. 465).

Troubles, as usual, accompanied this irregular accession. Artabanus, not content with exercising an influence under Artaxerxes such as has caused some authors to speak of him as king, aimed at removing the young prince, and making himself actual monarch. But his designs being betrayed to Artaxerxes by Megabyzus, and at the same time his former crimes coming to light, he was killed, together with his tool Aspamitres, seven months after the murder of Xerxes. The sons of Artabanus sought to avenge his death, but were defeated by Megabyzus in an engagement, wherein they lost their lives.

Meanwhile, in Bactria, Hystaspes, who had a rightful claim to the throne, raised the standard of revolt. Artaxerxes marched against him in person, and engaged him in two battles, the first of which was indecisive, while in the second the Bactrians suffered defeat, chiefly (according to Ctesias) because the wind blew violently in their faces. So signal was victory, that Bactria at once submitted. Hystaspes' fate is uncertain.

Not long after the reduction of Bactria, Egypt suddenly threw off the Persian yoke (B.C. 460). Inarus, a king of the wild African tribes who bordered the Nile valley on the west, but himself perhaps a descendant of the old monarchs of Egypt, led the insurrection, and, in conjunction with an Egyptian, named Amyrtseus, attacked the Persian troops stationed in the country, who were commanded by Achaemenes, the satrap. A battle was fought near Papremis in the Delta, wherein the Persians were defeated, and Achaemenes fell by the hand of Inarus himself. The Egyptians generally now joined in the revolt; and the remnant of the Persian army was shut up in Memphis. Inarus had asked the aid of Athens; and an Athenian fleet of 200 sail was sent to his assistance. This fleet sailed up the Nile, defeated a Persian squadron, and took part in the capture of Memphis and the siege of its citade (White Castle). When the Persian king first learned what had happened, he endeavored to rid himself of his Athenian enemies by inducing the Spartans to invade their country; but, failing in his attempt, he had recourse to arms, and, levying a vast host, which he placed under the command of Megabyzus, sent that officer to recover the revolted province. Megabyzus marched upon Memphis, defeated the Egyptians and their allies in a great battle, relieved the citadel of Memphis from its siege, and recovered the rest of the town. The Athenians fled to the tract called Prosopitis, which was a a portion of the Delta, completely surrounded by two branch streams of the Nile. Here they were besieged for eighteen months, till Megabyzus contrived to turn the water from one of the two streams, whereby the Athenian ships were stranded, and the Persian troops were able to march across the river bed, and overwhelm the Athenians with their numbers. A few only escaped to Cyrene. The entire fleet fell into the enemy's hands; and a reinforcement of fifty more ships, arriving soon after the defeat, was attacked unawares after it had entered the river, and lost more than half its number. Inarus was betrayed by some of his own men, and, being carried prisoner to Persia, suffered death by crucifixion. Amyrtseus fled to the fens, where for a while he maintained his independence. Egypt, however, was with this exception recovered to the Empire (B.C. 455); and Athens was taught that she could not always invade the dominions of the Great King with impunity.

Six years after this, the Athenians resolved on another effort. A fleet of 200 ships was equipped and placed under the command of the victor of the Eurymedon, Cimon, with orders to proceed into the Eastern Mediterranean, and seek to recover the laurels lost in Egypt. Cimon sailed to Cyprus, where he received a communication from Amyrtseus, which induced him to dispatch sixty ships to Egypt, while with the remaining one hundred and forty he commenced the siege of Citium. Here he died, either of disease or from the effects of a wound; and his armament, pressed for provisions, was forced soon afterwards to raise the siege, and address itself to some other enterprise. Sailing past Salamis, it found there a Cilician and Phoenician fleet, consisting of 300 vessels, which it immediately attacked and defeated, notwithstanding the disparity of number. Besides the ships which were sunk, a hundred triremes were taken; and the sailors then landed and gained a victory over a Persian army upon the shore. Artaxerxes, upon this, fearing lest he should lose Cyprus altogether, and thinking that, if Athens became mistress of this important island, she would always be fomenting insurrection in Egypt, made overtures for peace to the generals who were now in command. His propositions were favorably received. Peace was made on the following terms:—Athens agreed to relinquish Cyprus, and recall her squadron from Egypt; while the king consented to grant freedom to all the Greek cities on the Asiatic continent, and not to menace them either by land or water. The sea was divided between the two powers, Persian ships of war were not to sail to the west of Phaselis in the Levant, or of the Cyanean islands in the Euxine; and Greek war-ships, we may assume, were not to show themselves east of those limits. On these conditions there was to be peace and amity between the Greeks and the Persians, and neither nation was to undertake any expeditions against the territories of the other. Thus terminated the first period of hostility between Greece and Persia, a period of exactly half a century, commencing B.C. 499 and. ending B.C. 449, in the seventeenth year of Artaxerxes.

It was probably not many years after the conclusion of this peace that a rebellion broke out in Syria. Megabyzus, the satrap of that important province, offended at the execution of Inarus, in violation of the promise which he had himself made to him, raised a revolt against his sovereign, defeated repeatedly the armies sent to reduce him to obedience, and finally treated with Artaxerxes as to the terms on which he would consent to be reconciled. Thus was set an example, if not of successful insurrection, yet at any rate of the possibility of rebelling with impunity—an example which could not fail to have a mischievous effect on the future relations of the monarch with his satraps. It would have been better for the Empire had Megabyzus suffered the fate of Oroetes, instead of living to a good old age in high favor with the monarch whose power he had weakened and defied.

Artaxerxes survived the "Peace of Callias" twenty-four years. His relations with the Greeks continued friendly till his demise, though, on the occasion of the revolt of Samos (B.C. 440), Pissuthnes, satrap of Sardis, seems to have transgressed the terms of the treaty, and to have nearly brought about a renewal of hostilities. It was probably in retaliation for the aid given to the revolted Samians, that the Athenians, late in the reign of Artaxerxes, made an expedition against Caunus, which might have had important consequences, if the Caunians had not been firm in their allegiance. A revolt of Lycia and Caria under Zopyrus, the son of Megabyzus, assisted by the Greeks, might have proved even more difficult to subdue than the rebellion of Syria under his father. Persia, however, escaped this danger; and Artaxerxes, no doubt, saw with pleasure a few years later the Greeks turn their arms against each other—Athens, his great enemy, being forced into a contest for existence with the Peloponnesian confederacy under Sparta.

The character of Artaxerxes, though it receives the approval of Plutarch and Diodorus, must be pronounced on the whole poor and contemptible. His ready belief of the charge brought by Artabanus against his brother, Darius, admits perhaps of excuse, owing to his extreme youth; but his surrender of Inarus to Amestris on account of her importunity, his readiness to condone the revolt of Megabyzus, and his subjection throughout almost the whole of his life to the evil influence of Amytis, his sister, and Amestris, his mother—both persons of ill-regulated lives—are indications of weakness and folly quite unpardonable in a monarch. That he was mild in temperament, and even kind and good-natured, is probable. But he had no other quality that deserves the slightest commendation. In the whole course of his long reign he seems never once to have adventured himself in the field against an enemy. He made not a single attempt at conquest in any direction. We have no evidence that he patronized either literature or the arts. His peace with Athens was necessary perhaps, but disgraceful to Persia. The disorders of the Court increased under his reign, from the license (especially) which he allowed the Queen-mother, who sported with the lives of his subjects. The decay of the Empire received a fatal impulse from the impunity which he permitted to Megabyzus.

Like his father, Artaxerxes appears to have had but one legitimate wife. This was a certain Damaspia, of whom nothing is known, except that she died on the same day as her husband, and was the mother of his only legitimate son, Xerxes. Seventeen other sons, who survived him, were the issue of various concubines, chiefly—it would appear—Babylonians. Xerxes II. succeeded to the throne on the death of his father (B.C. 425), but reigned forty-five days only, being murdered after a festival, in which he had indulged too freely, by his half-brother, Secydianus or Sogdianus. Secydianus enjoyed the sovereignty for little more than half a year, when he was in his turn put to death by another, brother, Ochus, who on ascending the throne took the name of Darius, and became known to the Greeks as Darius Nothus.

Darius Nothus had in his father's lifetime been made satrap of Hyrcania, and had married his aunt, Parysatis, a daughter of Xerxes. He had already two children at his accession,—a daughter, Amestris, and a son, Arsaces, who succeeded him as Artaxerxes. His reign, which lasted nineteen years, was a constant scene of insurrections and revolts, some of which were of great importance, since they had permanent and very disastrous consequences. The earliest of all was raised by his full-brother, Arsites, who rebelled in conjunction with a son of Megabyzus, and, obtaining the support of a number of Greek mercenaries, gained two victories over the forces dispatched against him by the king. At last, however, the fortune of war changed. Persian gold was used to corrupt the mercenaries; and the rebels being thus reduced to extremities, were forced to capitulate, yielding themselves on the condition that their lives should be spared. Parysatis induced her husband to disregard the pledges given and execute both Arsites and his fellow-conspirator—thus proclaiming to the world that, unless by the employment of perfidy, the Empire was incapable of dealing with those who rebelled against its authority.

The revolt of Pissuthnes, satrap of Lydia, was the next important outbreak. Its exact date is uncertain; but it seems not to have very long preceded the Athenian disasters in Sicily. Pissuthnes, who had held his satrapy for more than twenty years, was the son of a Hystaspes, and probably a member of the royal family. His wealth—the accumulations of so long a term of office—enabled him to hire the services of a body of Greek mercenaries, who were commanded by an Athenian, called Lycon. On these troops he placed his chief dependence; but they failed him in the hour of need. Tissaphernes, the Persian general sent against him, bribed Lycon and his men, who thereupon quitted Pissuthnes and made common cause with his adversaries. The unfortunate satrap could no longer resist, and therefore surrendered upon terms, and accompanied Tissaphernes to the Court. Darius, accustomed now to disregard the pledged word of his officers, executed him forthwith, and made over his satrapy to Tissaphernes, as a reward for his zeal. Lycon, the Athenian traitor, received likewise a handsome return for his services, the revenues of several towns and districts being assigned him by the Great King.

The rebellion, however, was not wholly crushed by the destruction of its author, Amorges, a bastard son of Pissuthnes, continued to maintain himself in Caria, where he was master of the strong city of Iasus, on the north coast of the Sinus Iasicus, and set the power of Tissaphernes at defiance. Having probably inherited the wealth of his father, he hired a number of Peloponnesian mercenaries, and succeeded in maintaining himself as an independent monarch for some years.

Such was the condition of things in Asia Minor, when intelligence arrived of the fearful disasters which had befallen the Athenians in Sicily—disasters without a parallel since those of Salamis— sudden, unexpected, overwhelming. The news, flying through Asia, awoke everywhere a belief that the power of Athens was broken, and that her hostility need no longer be dreaded. The Persian monarch considered that under the altered circumstances it would be safe to treat the Peace of Callias as a dead letter, and sent down orders to the satraps of Lydia and Bithynia that they were once more to demand and collect the tribute of the Greek cities within their provinces. The satraps began to speculate on the advantages which they might derive from alliance with the enemies of Athens, and looked anxiously to see a Peloponnesian fleet appear off the coast of Asia. Tissaphernes and Pharnabazus vied with each other in the tempting offers which they made to Sparta, and it was not long before a formal treaty was concluded between that state and Persia, by which the two powers bound themselves to carry on war conjointly against Athens.

Thus the contest between Persia and her rival entered upon a new phase. Henceforth until the liberties of Greece were lost, the Great King could always count on having for his ally one of the principal Grecian powers. His gold was found to possess attractions which the Greeks were quite unable to resist. At one time Sparta, at another Athens, at another Thebes yielded to the subtle influence; Greek generals commanded the Persian armies; Greek captains manoeuvered the Persian fleets; the very rank and file of the standing army came to be almost as much Greek as Persian. Acting on the maxim, Divide et impera, Persia prolonged for eighty years her tottering Empire, by the skilful use which she made of the mutual jealousies and divisions of the Hellenic states.

It scarcely belongs to the history of Persia to trace in detail the fortunes of the contending powers during the latter portion of the Peloponnesian war. We need only observe that the real policy of the Court of Susa, well understood, and, on the whole, tolerably well carried out by the satraps, was to preserve the balance of power between Athens and Sparta, to allow neither to obtain too decided a preponderance, to help each in turn, and encourage each to waste the other's strength, but to draw back whenever the moment came for striking a decisive blow against either side. This policy skilfully pursued by Tissaphernes (who had a genius for intrigue and did not require an Alcibiades to give him lessons in state-craft), more clumsily by Pharnabazus, whose character was comparatively sincere and straightforward, prevailed until the younger Cyrus made his appearance upon the scene, when a disturbing force came into play which had disastrous effects both on the fortunes of Greece and on those of Persia. The younger Cyrus had personal views of self-aggrandizement which conflicted with the true interests of his nation, and was so bent on paving the way for his own ascent to sovereign power that he did not greatly care whether he injured his country or no. As the accomplishment of his designs depended mainly on his obtaining a powerful land-force, he regarded a Spartan as preferable to an Athenian alliance; and, having once made his choice, he lent his ally such effectual aid that in two years from the time of his coming down to the coast the war was terminated. Persian gold manned and partly built the fleet which conquered at AEgos-Potami; perhaps it contributed in a still more decisive manner to the victory. Cyrus, by placing his stores at the entire command of Lysander, deserved and acquired the cordial good-will of Sparta and the Peloponnesians generally— an advantage of which we shall find him in the sequel making good use.

The gain to Persia from the dominion which she had reacquired over the Greeks of Asia was more than counter-balanced by a loss of territory in another quarter, which seems to have occurred during the reign of Darius Nothus, though in what exact year is doubtful. The revolt of Egypt is placed by Heeren and Clinton in B.C. 414, by Eusebius in B.C. 411, by Manetho in the last year of Darius Nothus, or B.C. 405. The earlier dates depend on the view that the Amyrtseus of Manetho's twenty-eighth dynasty was the leader of the rebellion, and had a reign of six years at this period—a view which is perhaps unsound. Manetho probably represented Nepherites (Nefaorot) as the leader; and it is quite clear that he placed the re-establishment of the old throne of the Pharaohs in the year that Darius Nothus died. As his authority is the best that we can obtain upon this obscure point, we may regard the last days of the Persian monarch as clouded by news of a rebellion, which had been perhaps for some time contemplated, but which did not break out until he was known to be in a moribund condition.

A few years earlier, B.C. 408 or 409, the Medes had made an unsuccessful attempt to recover their independence. The circumstances of this revolt, which is mentioned by no writer but Xenophon, are wholly unknown, but we may perhaps connect it with the rebellion of Terituchmes, a son-in-law of the king. The story of Terituchmes, which belongs to this period, deserves at any rate to be told, as illustrating, in a very remarkable way, the corruption, cruelty, and dissoluteness of the Persian Court at the time to which we have now come. Terituchmes was the son of Idernes, a Persian noble of high rank, probably a descendant of the conspirator Hydarnes. On the death of his father, he succeeded to his satrapy, as to a hereditary fief, and being high in favor with Darius Nothus, he received in marriage that monarch's daughter, Amestris. Having, however, after his marriage become enamored of his own half-sister, Roxana, and having persuaded her to an incestuous commerce, he grew to detest his wife, and as he could not rid himself of her without making an enemy of the king, he entered into a conspiracy with 300 others, and planned to raise a rebellion. The bond of a common crime, cruel and revolting in its character, was to secure the fidelity of the rebels one to another. Amestris was to be placed in a sack, and each conspirator in turn was to plunge his sword into her body. It is not clear whether this intended murder was executed or no. Hoping to prevent it, Darius commissioned a certain Udiastes, who was in the service of Terituchmes, to save his daughter by any means that might be necessary; and Udiastes, collecting a band, set upon Terituchmes and slew him after a strenuous resistance. After this, his mother, brothers, and sisters were apprehended by the order of Parysatis, the queen, who caused Roxana to be hewn in pieces, and the other unfortunates to be buried alive. It was with great difficulty that Arsaces, the heir-apparent, afterwards Artaxerxes Mnemon, preserved his own wife, Statira, from the massacre. It happened that she was sister to Terituchmes, and, though wholly innocent of his offence, she would have been involved in the common destruction of her family had not her husband with tears and entreaties begged her life of his parents. The son of Terituchmes maintained himself for a while in his father's government; but Parysatis succeeded in having him taken off by poison.

The character of Darius Nothus is seen tolerably clearly in the account of his reign which has been here given. He was at once weak and wicked. Contrary to his sworn word, he murdered his brothers, Secydianus and Arsites. He broke faith with Pissuthnes. He sanctioned the wholesale execution of Terituchmes' relatives. Under him the eunuchs of the palace rose to such power that one of them actually ventured to aspire to the sovereignty. Parysatis, his wife, one of the most cruel and malignant even of Oriental women, was in general his chosen guide and counsellor. His severities cannot, however, in all eases be ascribed to her influence, for he was anxious that she should put the innocent Statira to death, and, when she refused, reproached her with being foolishly lenient. In his administration of the Empire he was unsuccessful; for, if he gained some tracts of Asia Minor, he lost the entire African satrapy. Under him we trace a growing relaxation of the checks by which the great officers of the state were intended to have been held under restraint. Satraps came to be practically uncontrolled in their provinces, and the dangerous custom arose of allowing sons to succeed, almost as a matter of course, to the governments of their fathers. Powers unduly large were lodged in the hands of a single officer, and actions, that should have brought down upon their perpetrators sharp and signal punishment, were timorously or negligently condoned by the supreme authority. Cunning and treachery were made the weapons wherewith Persia contended with her enemies. Manly habits were laid aside, and the nation learned to trust more and more to the swords of mercenaries.

Shortly before the death of Darius there seems to have been a doubt raised as to the succession. Parysatis, who preferred her second son to her first-born, imagined that her influence was sufficient to induce her husband to nominate Cyrus, instead of Arsaces, to succeed him; and Cyrus is said to have himself expected to be preferred above his brother. He had the claim, if claim it can be called, that he was the first son born to his father after he became king; but his main dependence was doubtless on his mother. Darius, however, proved less facile in his dying moments than he had been during most of his life, and declined to set aside the rights of the eldest son on the frivolous pretence suggested to him. His own feelings may have inclined him towards Arsaces, who resembled him far more than Cyrus did in character; and Cyrus, moreover, had recently offended him, and been summoned to court, to answer a very serious charge. Arsaces, therefore, was nominated, and took the name of Artaxerxes—as one of a king who had reigned long, and, on the whole, prosperously.

An incident of ill omen accompanied the commencement of the new reign (B.C. 405). The inauguration of the monarch was a religious ceremony, and took place in a temple at Pasargadae, the old capital, to which a peculiar sanctity was still regarded as attaching. Artaxerxes had proceeded to this place, and was about to engage in the ceremonies, when he was interrupted by Tissaphernes, who informed him that his life was in danger. Cyrus, he said, proposed to hide himself in the temple, and assassinate him as he changed his dress, a necessary part of the formalities. One of the officiating priests—a Magus, as it would seem—confirmed the charge. Cyrus was immediately arrested, and would have been put to death on the spot, had not his mother interfered, and, embracing him in her arms, made it impossible for the executioner to perform his task. With some difficulty she persuaded Artaxerxes to spare his brother's life and allow him to return to his government, assuring him, and perhaps believing, that the charges made against her favorite were without foundation.

Cyrus returned to Asia Minor with the full determination of attacking his brother at the earliest opportunity. He immediately began the collection of a mercenary force, composed wholly of Greeks, on whose arms he was disposed to place far more reliance than on those of Orientals. As Tissaphernes had returned to the coast with him, and was closely watching all his proceedings, it was necessary to exercise great caution, lest his intentions should become known before he was ready to put them into execution. He therefore had recourse to three different devices. Having found a cause of quarrel with Tissaphernes in the ambiguous terms of their respective commissions, he pressed it on to an actual war, which enabled him to hire troops openly, as against this enemy; and in this way he collected from 5000 to 6000 Greeks—chiefly Peloponnesians. He further gave secret commissions to Greek officers, whose acquaintance he had made when he was previously in these parts, to collect men for him, whom they were to employ in their own quarrels until he needed their services. From 3000 to 4000 troops were gathered for him by these persons. Finally, when he found himself nearly ready to commence his march, he discovered a new foe in the Pisidians of the Western Taurus, and proceeded to levy a force against them, which amounted to some thousands more. In all, he had in readiness 11,000 heavy-armed and about 2000 light-armed Greeks before his purpose became so clear that Tissaphernes could no longer mistake it, and therefore started off to carry his somewhat tardy intelligence to the capital.

The aims of Cyrus were different from those of ordinary rebel satraps; and we must go back to the times of Darius Hystaspis in order to find a parallel to them. Instead of seeking to free a province from the Persian yoke, or to carve out for himself an independent sovereignty in some remote corner of the Empire, his intention was to dethrone his brother, and place on his own brows the diadem of his great namesake. It was necessary for him therefore to assume the offensive. Only by a bold advance, and by taking his enemy to some extent unprepared, and so at a disadvantage, could he hope to succeed in his audacious project. It is not easy to see that he could have had any considerable party among the Persians, or any ground for expecting to be supported by any of the subject nations. His following must have been purely personal; and though it may be true that he was of a character to win more admiration and affection than his brother, yet Artaxerxes himself was far from being unpopular with his subjects, whom he pleased by a familiarity and a good-nature to which they were little accustomed. Cyrus knew that his principal dependence must be on himself, on his Greeks, and on the carelessness and dilatoriness of his adversary, who was destitute of military talent and was even thought to be devoid of personal bravery.

Thus it was important to advance as soon as possible. Cyrus therefore quitted Sardis before all his troops were collected (B.C. 401), and marched through Lydia and Phrygia, by the route formally followed in the reverse direction by the army of Xerxes, as far as Celsense, where the remainder of his mercenaries joined him. With his Greek force thus raised to 13,000 men, and with a native army not much short of 100,000, he proceeded on through Phrygia and Lycaonia to the borders of Cilicia, having determined on taking the shortest route to Babylon, through the Cilician and Syrian passes, and then along the course of the Euphrates. At Caystrupedion he was met by Epyaxa, consort of Syennesis, the tributary king of Cilicia, who brought him a welcome supply of money, and probably assured him of the friendly disposition of her husband, who was anxious to stand well with both sides. In Lycaonia, Cyrus divided his forces, and sending a small body of troops under Menon to escort Epyaxa across the mountains and enter Cilicia by the more western of the two practicable passes he proceeded himself with the bulk of his troops to the famous Pylae Cilicias, where he probably knew that Syennesis would only make a feint of resistance. He found the pass occupied; but it was evacuated the next day, on the receipt of intelligence that Menon had already entered the country and that the fleet of Cyrus—composed partly of his own ships, partly of a squadron furnished to him by Sparta—had appeared off the coast and threatened a landing. Cyrus thus crossed the most difficult and dangerous of all the passes that separated him from the heart of the Empire, without the loss of a man.

Thus far it would appear that Cyrus had to a certain extent masked his plans. The Greek captains must have guessed, if they had not actually learnt, his intentions; but to the bulk of the soldiery they had been hitherto absolutely unknown. It was only in Cilicia that the light broke in upon them, and they began to suspect that they were being marched into the interior of Asia, there to engage in a contest with the entire power of the Great King. Something of the horror which is ascribed to Cleomenes, when it was suggested to him a century earlier that he should conduct his Spartans the distance of a three months' journey from the sea, appears to have taken possession of the minds of the mercenaries on their awaking to this conviction. They at once refused to proceed. It was only by the most skilful management on the part of their captains, joined to a judicious liberality on the part of Cyrus, that they were induced to forego their intention of returning home at once, and so breaking up the expedition. A perception of the difficulty of effecting a retreat, together with an increase of pay, extorted a reluctant assent to continue the march, of which the real term and object were even now not distinctly avowed. Cyrus said he proposed to attack the army of Abrocomas, which he believed to be posted on the Euphrates. If he did not find it there, a fresh consultation might be held to consider any further movement.

The march now proceeded rapidly. The gates of Syria—a narrow pass on the east coast of the Gulf of Issus, shut in, like Thermopylae, between the mountains and the sea, and strengthened moreover by fortifications—were left unguarded by Abrocomas; and the army, having traversed them without loss, crossed the Amanus range by the pass of Beilan, and in twenty-nine days from Tarsus reached Thapsacus on the Euphrates. The forces of Artaxerxes had nowhere made their appearance— Abrocomas, though he had 300,000 men at his disposal, had weakly or treacherously abandoned all these strong and easily defensible positions; he does not seem even to have wasted the country; but, having burnt the boats at Thapsacus, he was content to fall back upon Phoenicia, and left the way to Babylon and Susa open. At Thapsacus there was little difficulty in persuading the Greeks, who had no longer the sea before their eyes, to continue the march; they only stipulated for a further increase of pay, which was readily promised them by the sanguine prince, who believed himself on the point of obtaining by their aid the inexhaustible treasures of the Empire. The river, which happened to be unusually low for the time of year, was easily forded. Cyrus entered Mesopotamia, and continued his march down the left bank of the Euphrates at the quickest rate that it was possible to move a hundred thousand Orientals. In thirty-three days he had accomplished above 600 miles, and had approached within 120 miles of Babylon without seeing any traces of an enemy. His only difficulties were from the nature of the country, which, after the Khabour is passed, becomes barren, excepting close along the river. From want of fodder there was a great mortality among the baggage-animals; the price of grain rose; and the Greeks had to subsist almost entirely upon meat. At last, when the Babylonian alluvium was reached, with its abundance of fodder and corn, signs of the enemy began to be observed. Artaxerxes, who after some doubts and misgivings had finally determined to give his enemy battle in the plain, was already on his way from Babylon, with an army reckoned at 900,000 men and had sent forward a body of horse, partly to reconnoitre, partly to destroy the crops, in order to prevent Cyrus and his troops from benefiting by them. Cyrus now advanced slowly and cautiously, at the rate of about fourteen miles a day, expecting each morning to fight a general engagement before evening came. On the third night, believing the battle to be imminent, he distributed the commands and laid down a plan of operations. But morning brought no appearance of the enemy, and the whole day passed tranquilly. In the course of it, he came upon a wide and deep trench cut through the plain for a distance of above forty miles—a recent work, which Artaxerxes had intended as a barrier to stop the progress of his enemy. But the trench was undefended and incomplete, a space of twenty feet being left between its termination and the Euphrates. Cyrus, having passed it, began to be convinced that his brother would not risk a battle in the plain, but would retreat to the mountains and make his stand at Persepolis or Ecbatana. He therefore continued his march negligently. His men piled their arms on the wagons or laid them, across the beasts of burthen; while he himself exchanged the horse which he usually rode for a chariot, and proceeded on his way leisurely, having about his person a small escort, which preserved their ranks, while all the rest of the troops were allowed to advance in complete disarray.

Suddenly, as the army was proceeding in this disorderly manner through the plain, a single horseman was perceived advancing at full gallop from the opposite quarter, his steed all flecked with foam. As he drew near, he shouted aloud to those whom he met, addressing some in Greek, others in Persian, and warning them that the Great King, with his whole force, was close at hand, and rapidly approaching in order of battle. The news took every one by surprise, and at first all was hurry and confusion. The Greeks, however, who were on the right, rapidly marshalled their line, resting it upon the river; while Cyrus put on his armor, mounted his horse, and arranged the ranks of his Asiatics. Ample time was given for completing all the necessary dispositions; since three hours, at the least, must have elapsed from the announcement of the enemy's approach before he actually appeared. Then a white cloud of dust arose towards the verge of the horizon, below which a part of the plain began soon to darken; presently gleams of light were seen to flash out from the dense mass which was advancing, the serried lines of spears came into view, and the component parts of the huge army grew to be discernible. On the extreme left was a body of horsemen with white cuirasses, commanded by Tissaphernes; next came infantry, carrying the long wicker shield, or gerrhum then a solid square of Egyptians, heavily armed, and bearing wooden shields that reached to the feet; then the contingents of many different nations, some on foot, some on horseback, armed with bows and other weapons. The line stretched away to the east further than the Greeks, who were stationed on the right, could see, extending (as it would seem) more than twice the distance which was covered by the army of Cyrus. Artaxerxes was in the centre of his line, on horseback, surrounded by a mounted guard of 6000 Persians. In front of the line, towards the river, were drawn up at wide intervals a hundred and fifty scythed chariots, which were designed to carry terror and confusion into the ranks of the Greeks.

On the other side, Cyrus had upon the extreme right a thousand Paphlagonian cavalry with the more lightly armed of the Greeks; next, the Greek heavy-armed, under Clearchus; and then his Asiatics, stretching in a line to about the middle of his adversary's army, his own special command being in the centre; and his left wing being led by the satrap, Ariaeus. With Ariseus was posted the great mass of the cavalry; but a band of six hundred, clad in complete armor, with their horses also partially armed, waited on Cyrus himself, and accompanied him wherever he went. As the enemy drew near, and Cyrus saw how much he was outflanked upon the left, he made an attempt to remedy the evil by ordering Clearchus to move with his troops from the extreme right to the extreme left of the line, where he would be opposite to Artaxerxes himself. This, no doubt, would have been a hazardous movement to make in the face of a superior enemy; and Clearchus, feeling this, and regarding the execution of the order as left to his discretion, declined to move away from the river. Cyrus, who trusted much to the Greek general's judgment, did not any further press the change, but prepared to fight the battle as he stood.

The combat began upon the right. When the enemy had approached within six or seven hundred yards, the impatience of the Greeks to engage could not be restrained. They sang the paean and started forwards at a pace which in a short time became a run. The Persians did not await their charge. The drivers leaped from their chariots, the line of battle behind them wavered, and then turned and fled without striking a blow. One Greek only was wounded by an arrow. As for the scythed chariots, they damaged their own side more than the Greeks; for the frightened horses in many cases, carried the vehicles into the thick of the fugitives, while the Greeks opened their ranks and gave passage to such as charged in an opposite direction. Moderating their pace so as to preserve their tactical arrangement, but still advancing with great rapidity, the Greeks pressed on the flying enemy, and pursued him a distance of two or three miles, never giving a thought to Cyrus, who, they supposed, would conquer those opposed to him with as much ease as themselves.

But the prince meanwhile was in difficulties. Finding himself outnumbered and outflanked, and fearing that his whole army would be surrounded, and even the victorious Greeks attacked in the rear, he set all upon one desperate cast and charged with his Six Hundred against the six thousand horse who protected his brother. Artagerses, their commander, who met him with a Homeric invective, he slew with his own hand. The six thousand were routed and took to flight; the person of the king was exposed to view; and Cyrus, transported at the sight, rushed forward shouting, "I see the man," and hurling his javelin, struck him straight upon the breast, with such force that the cuirass was pierced and a slight flesh-wound inflicted. The king fell from his horse; but at the same moment Cyrus received a wound beneath the eye from the javelin of a Persian, and in the melee which followed he was slain with eight of his followers. The Six Hundred could lend no effectual aid, because they had rashly dispersed in pursuit of the flying enemy.

As the whole contest was a personal one, the victory was now decided. Fighting, however, continued till nightfall. On learning the death of their leader, the Asiatic troops under Ariseus fled—first to their camp, and then, when Artaxerxes attacked them there, to the last night's station. The Grecian camp was assaulted by Tissaphernes, who at the beginning of the battle had charged through the Greek light-armed, without however, inflicting on them any loss, and had then pressed on, thinking to capture the Grecian baggage. But the guard defended their camp with success, and slew many of the assailants. Tissaphernes and the king drew off after a while, and retraced their steps, in order to complete the victory by routing the troops of Clearchus. Clearchus was at the same time returning from his pursuit, having heard that his camp was in danger, and as the two bodies of troops approached, he found his right threatened by the entire host of the enemy, which might have lapped round it and attacked it in front, in flank, and in rear. To escape this peril he was about to wheel his line and make it rest alone its whole extent upon the river, when the Persians passed him and resumed the position which they had occupied at the beginning of the battle. They were then about to attack, when once more the Greeks anticipated them and charged. The effect was again ludicrous. The Persians would not abide the onset, but fled faster than before. The Greeks pursued them to a village, close by which was a knoll or mound, whither the fugitives had betaken themselves. Again the Greeks made a movement in advance, and immediately the flight recommenced. The last rays of the setting sun fell on scattered masses of Persian horse and foot flying in all directions over the plain from the little band of Greeks.

The battle of Cunaxa was a double blow to the Persian power. By the death of Cyrus there was lost the sole chance that existed of such a re-invigoration of the Empire as might have enabled it to start again on a new lease of life, with ability to held its own, and strength to resume once more the aggressive attitude of former times. The talents of Cyrus have perhaps been overrated, but he was certainly very superior to most Orientals; and there can be no doubt that the Empire would have greatly gained by the substitution of his rule for that of his brother. He was active, energetic, prompt indeed, ready in speech, faithful in the observance of his engagements, brave, liberal—he had more foresight and more self-contro than most Asiatics; he knew how to deal with different classes of men; he had a great power of inspiring affection and retaining it; he was free from the folly of national prejudice, and could appreciate as they deserved both the character and the institutions of foreigners. It is likely that he would have proved a better administrator and ruler than any king of Persia since Darius Hystaspis. He would, therefore, undoubtedly have raised his country to some extent. Whether he could really have arrested its decline, and enabled it to avenge the humiliations of Marathon, Salamis, and the peace of Callias, is, however, exceedingly doubtful. For Cyrus, though he had considerable merits, was not without great and grievous defects. As the Tartar is said always to underlie the Russ, so the true Oriental underlay that coating of Grecian manners and modes of thought and act, with which a real admiration of the Hellenic race induced Cyrus to conceal his native barbarism. When he slew his cousins for an act which he chose to construe as disrespect, and when he executed Orontes for contemplated desertion, secretly and silently, so that no one knew his fate, when transported with jealous rage he rushed madly upon his brother, exposing to hazard the success of all his carefully formed plans, and in fact ruining his cause, the acquired habits of the Phil-Hellene gave way, and the native ferocity of the Asiatic came to the surface. We see Cyrus under favorable circumstances, while conciliation, tact, and self-restraint were necessities of his position, without which he could not possibly gain his ends—we do not know what effect success and the possession of supreme power might have had upon his temper and conduct; but from the acts above-mentioned we may at any rate suspect that the result would have been very injurious.

Again, intellectually, Cyrus is only great for an Asiatic. He has more method, more foresight, more power of combination, more breadth of mind than the other Asiatics of his day, or than the vast mass of Asiatics of any day. But he is not entitled to the praise of a great administrator or of a great general. His three years' administration of Asia Minor was chiefly marked by a barbarous severity towards criminals, and by a lavish expenditure of the resources of his government, which left him in actual want at the moment when he was about to commence his expedition. His generalship failed signally at the battle of Cunaxa, for the loss of which he is far more to be blamed than Clearchus. As he well knew that Artaxerxes was sure to occupy the centre of his line of battle, he should have placed his Greeks in the middle of his own line, not at one extremity. When he saw how much his adversary outflanked him on the left—a contingency which was so probable that it ought to have occurred to him beforehand—he should have deployed his line in that direction, instead of ordering such a movement as Clearchus, not unwisely, declined to execute. He might have trusted the Greeks to fight in line, as they had fought at Marathon; and by expanding their ranks, and moving off his Asiatics to the left, he might have avoided the danger of being outflanked and surrounded. But his capital error was the wildness and abandon of his charge with the Six Hundred—a charge which it was probably right to make under the circumstances, but which required a combination of coolness and courage that the Persian prince evidently did not possess when his feelings were excited. Had he kept his Six Hundred well in hand, checked their pursuit, and abstained from thrusting his own person into unnecessary danger, he might have joined the Greeks as they returned from their first victory and participated in their final triumph. At the same time, Clearchus cannot but be blamed for pushing his suit too far. If, when the enemy in his front fled, he had at once turned against those who were engaging Cyrus, taking them on their left flank, which must have been completely uncovered, he might have been in time to prevent the fatal results of the rash charge made by his leader.

Thus the death of Cyrus, though a calamity to Persia, was scarcely the great loss which it has been represented. A far worse result of the Cyreian expedition was the revelation which it made of the weakness of Persia, and of the facility with which a Greek force might penetrate to the very midst of the Empire, defeat the largest army that could be brought against it, and remain, or return, as it might think proper. Hitherto Babylon and Susa had been, even to the mind of a Greek statesman, remote localities, which it would be the extreme of rashness to attempt to reach by force of arms, and from which it would be utter folly to suppose that a single man could return alive except by permission of the Great King. Henceforth these towns were looked upon as prizes quite within the legitimate scope of Greek ambition, and their conquest came to be viewed as little more than a question of time. The opinion of inaccessibility, which had been Persia's safeguard hitherto, was gone, and in its stead grew up a conviction that the heart of the Empire might be reached with very little difficulty.

It required, however, for the production of this whole change, not merely that the advance to Cunaxa should have been safely made, and the immeasurable superiority of Greek to Asiatic soldiers there exhibited, but also that the retreat should have been effected, as it was effected, without disaster. Had the Ten Thousand perished under the attacks of the Persian horse, or even under the weapons of the Kurds, or amid the snows of Armenia, the opinion of Persian invulnerability would have been strengthened rather than weakened by the expedition. But the return to Greece of ten thousand men, who had defeated the hosts of the Great King in the centre of his dominions, and fought their way back to the sea without suffering more than the common casualties of war, was an evidence of weakness which could not but become generally known, and of which all could feel the force. Hence the retreat was as important as the battle. If in late autumn and mid-winter a small Greek army, without maps or guides, could make its way for a thousand miles through Asia, and encounter no foe over whom it could not easily triumph, it was clear that the fabric of Persian power was rotten, and would collapse on the first serious attack.

Still, it will not be necessary to trace in detail the steps of the retreat. It was the fact of the return, rather than the mode of its accomplishment, which importantly affected the subsequent history of Persia. We need only note that the retreat was successfully conducted in spite, not merely of the military power of the Empire, but of the most barefaced and cruel treachery—a fact which showed clearly the strong desire that there was to hinder the invaders' escape. Persia did not set much store by her honor at this period; but she would scarcely have pledged her word and broken it, without the slightest shadow of excuse, unless she had regarded the object to be accomplished as one of vast importance, and seen no other way which offered any prospect of the desired result. Her failure, despite the success of her treachery, places her military weakness in the strongest possible light. The Greeks, though deprived of their leaders, deceived, surprised, and hemmed in by superior numbers, amid terrific mountains, precipices, and snows, forced their way by sheer dogged perseverance through all obstacles, and reached Trebizond with the loss of not one fourth of their original number.

There was also another discovery made during the return which partly indicated the weakness of the Persian power, and partly accounted for it. The Greeks had believed that the whole vast space enclosed between the Black Sea, Caucasus, Caspian, and Jaxartes on the one hand, and the Arabian Desert, Persian Gulf, and Indian Ocean on the other, was bound together into one single centralized monarchy, all the resources of which were wielded by a single arm. They now found that even towards the heart of the empire, on the confines of Media and Assyria, there existed independent tribes which set the arms of Persia at defiance; while towards the verge of the old dominion whole provinces, once certainly held in subjection, had fallen away from the declining State, and succeeded in establishing their freedom. The nineteenth satrapy of Herodotus existed no more; in lieu of it was a mass of warlike and autonomous tribes—Chalybes, Taochi, Chaldeans, Macronians, Scythians, Colchians, Mosynoecians, Tibarenians—whose services, if he needed them, the King of Persia had to buy, while ordinarily their attitude towards him was one of distrust and hostility. Judging of the unknown from the known, the Greeks might reasonably conclude that in all parts of the Empire similar defections had occurred, and that thus both the dimensions and the resources of the state had suffered serious diminution, and fell far below the conception which they had been accustomed to form of them.

The immediate consequence of the Cyreian expedition was a rupture between Persia and Sparta. Sparta had given aid to Cyrus, and thus provoked the hostility of the Great King. She was not inclined to apologize or to recede. On the contrary, she saw in the circumstances of the expedition strong grounds for anticipating great advantages to herself from a war with so weak an antagonist. Having, therefore, secured the services of the returned Ten Thousand, she undertook the protection of the Asiatic Greeks against Persia, and carried on a war upon the continent against the satraps of Lydia and Phrygia for the space of six years (B.C. 399 to B.C. 394). The disorganization of the Persian Empire became very manifest during this period. So jealous were the two satraps of each other, that either was willing at any time to make a truce with the Spartans on condition that they proceeded to attack the other; and, on one occasion, as much as thirty silver talents was paid by a satrap on the condition that the war should be transferred from his own government to that, of his rival. At the same time the native tribes were becoming more and more inclined to rebel. The Mysians and Pisidians had for a long time been practically independent. Now the Bithynians showed a disposition to shake off the Persian yoke, while in Paphlagonia the native monarchs boldly renounced their allegiance. Agesilaus, who carried on the war in Asia Minor for three years, knew well how to avail himself of all these advantageous circumstances; and it is not unlikely that he would have effected the separation from Persia of the entire peninsula, had he been able to continue the struggle a few years longer. But the league between Argos, Thebes, and Corinth, which jealousy of Sparta caused and Persian gold promoted, proved so formidable, that Agesilaus had to be summoned home: and after his departure, Conon, in alliance with Pharnabazus, recovered the supremacy of the sea for Athens, and greatly weakened Spartan influence in Asia. Not content with this result, the two friends, in the year B.C. 393, sailed across the Egean, and the portentous spectacle of a Persian fleet in Greek waters was once more seen—this time in alliance with Athens! Descents were made upon the coasts of the Peloponnese, and the island of Cythera were seized and occupied. The long walls of Athens were rebuilt with Persian money, and all the enemies of Sparta were richly subsidized. Sparta was made to feel that if she had been able at one time to make the Great King tremble for his provinces, or even for his throne, the King could at another reach her across the Egean, and approach Sparta as nearly as she had, with the Cyreians, approached Babylon.

The lesson of the year B.C. 393 was not thrown away on the Spartan government. The leading men became convinced that unless they could secure the neutrality of the Persians, Sparta must succumb to the hostility of her Hellenic enemies. Under these circumstances they devised, with much skill, a scheme likely to be acceptable to the Persians, which would weaken their chief rivals in Greece—Athens and Thebes—while it would leave untouched their own power. They proposed a general peace, the conditions of which should be the entire relinquishment of Asia to the Persians, and the complete autonomy of all the Greek States in Europe. The first attempt to procure the acceptance of these terms failed (B.C. 393); but six years later, after Antalcidas had explained them at the Persian Court, Artaxerxes sent down an ultimatum to the disputants, modifying the terms slightly as regarded Athens, extending them as regarded himself so as to include the islands of Clazomenae and Cyprus, and requiring their acceptance by all the belligerents, on pain of their incurring his hostility. To this threat all yielded. A Persian king may be excused if he felt it a proud achievement thus to dictate a peace to the Greeks—a peace, moreover, which annulled the treaty of Callias, and gave back absolutely into his hands a province which had ceased to belong to his Empire more than sixty years previously.

It was the more important to Artaxerxes that his relations with the European Greeks should be put upon a peaceful footing, since all the resources of the Empire were wanted for the repression of disturbances which had some years previously broken out in Cyprus. The exact date of the Cyprian revolt under Evagoras, the Greek tyrant of Salamis, is uncertain; but there is evidence that, at least as early as B.C. 391, he was at open war with the power of Persia, and had made an alliance with the Athenians, who both in that year and in B.C. 388 sent him aid. Assisted also by Achoris, independent monarch of Egypt, and Hecatomnus, vassal king of Caria, he was able to take the offensive, to conquer Tyre, and extend his revolt into Cilicia and Idumaea. An expedition undertaken against him by Autophradates, satrap of Lydia, seems to have failed. It was the first object of the Persians, after concluding the "Peace of Antalcidas," to crush Evagoras. They collected 300 vessels, partly from the Greeks of Asia, and brought together an army of 300,000 men. The fleet of Evagoras numbered 200 triremes, and with these he ventured on an attack, but was completely defeated by Tiribazus, who shut him up in Salamis, and, after a struggle which continued for at least six years, compelled him to submit to terms (B.C. 380 or 379). More fortunate than former rebels, he obtained not merely a promise of pardon, which would probably have been violated, but a recognition of his title, and permission to remain in his government, with the single obligation of furnishing to the Great King a certain annual tribute.

During the continuance of this war, Artaxerxes was personally engaged in military operations in another part of his dominions. The Cadusians, who inhabited the low and fertile tract between the Elburz range and the Caspian, having revolted against his authority, Artaxerxes invaded their territory at the head of an army which is estimated at 300,000 foot and 10,000 horse. The land was little cultivated, rugged, and covered with constant fogs; the men were brave and warlike, and having admitted him into their country, seem to have waylaid and intercepted his convoys. His army was soon reduced to great straits, and forced to subsist on the cavalry horses and the baggage-animals. A most disastrous result must have followed, had not Tiribazus, who had been recalled from Cyprus on charges preferred against him by the commander of the land force, Orontes, contrived very artfully to induce the rebels to make their submission. Artaxerxes was thus enabled to withdraw from the country without serious disaster, having shown in his short campaign that he possessed the qualities of a soldier, but was entirely deficient in those of a general.

A time of comparative tranquillity seems to have followed the Cadusian campaign. Artaxerxes strengthened his hold upon the Asiatic Greeks by razing some of their towns and placing garrisons in others. His satraps even ventured to commence the absorption of the islands off the coast; and there is evidence that Sanaos, at any rate, was reduced and added to the Empire. Cilicia, Phoenicia, and Idumaea were doubtless recovered soon after the great defeat of Evagoras. There remained only one province in this quarter which still maintained its revolt, and enjoyed, under native monarchs, the advantages of independence. This was Egypt, which had now continued free for above thirty years, since it shook off the yoke of Darius Nothus. Artaxerxes, anxious to recover this portion of his ancestral dominions, applied in B.C. 375 to Athens for the services of her great general, Iphicrates. His request was granted, and in the next year a vast armament was assembled at Acre under Iphicrates and Pharnabazus, which effected a successful landing in the Delta at the Mendesian mouth of the Nile, stormed the town commanding this branch of the river, and might have taken Memphis, could the energetic advice of the Athenian have stirred to action the sluggish temper of his Persian colleague. But Pharnabazus declined to be hurried, and preferred to proceed leisurely and according to rule. The result was that the season for hostilities passed and nothing had been done. The Nile rose as the summer drew on, and flooded most of the Delta; the expedition could effect nothing, and had to return. Pharnabazus and Iphicrates parted amid mutual recriminations; and the reduction of Egypt was deferred for above a quarter of a century.

In Greece, however, the Great King still retained that position of supreme arbiter with which he had been invested at the "Peace of Antalcidas." In B.C. 372 Antalcidas was sent by Sparta a second time up to Susa, for the purpose of obtaining an imperial rescript, prescribing the terms on which the then existing hostilities among the Greeks should cease. In B.C. 367 Pelopidas and Ismenias proceeded with the same object from Thebes to the Persian capital. In the following year a rescript, more in their favor than former ones, was obtained by Athens. Thus every one of the leading powers of Greece applied in turn to the Great King for his royal mandate, so erecting him by common consent into a sort of superior, whose decision was to be final in all cases of Greek quarrel.

But this external acknowledgment of the imperial greatness of Persia did not, and could not, check the internal decay and tendency to disintegration, which was gradually gaining head, and threatening the speedy dissolution of the Empire. The long reign of Artaxerxes Mnemon was now verging towards its close. He was advanced in years, and enfeebled in mind and body, suspicious of his sons and of his nobles, especially of such as showed more than common ability. Under these circumstances, revolts on the part of satraps grew frequent. First Ariobarzanes, satrap of Phrygia, renounced his allegiance (B.C. 366), and defended himself with success against Autophradates, satrap of Lydia, and Mausolus, native king of Caria under Persia, to whom the task of reducing him had been entrusted. Then Aspis, who held a part of Cappadocia, revolted and maintained himself by the help of the Pisidians, until he was overpowered by Datames. Next Datames himself, satrap of the rest of Cappadocia, understanding that Artaxerxes' mind was poisoned against him, made a treaty with Ariobarzanes, and assumed an independent attitude in his own province. In this position he resisted all the efforts of Autophradates to reduce him to obedience; and Artaxerxes condescended first to make terms with him and then to remove him by treachery. Finally (B.C. 362), there seems to have been something like a general revolt of the western provinces, in which the satraps of Mysia, Phrygia, and Lydia, Mausolus, prince of Caria, and the people of Lycia, Pamphylia, Cilicia, Syria, and Phoenicia participated. Tachos, king of Egypt, fomented the disturbances, which were also secretly encouraged by the Spartans. A terrible conflict appeared to be imminent; but it was avoided by the ordinary resources of bribery and treachery. Orontes, satrap of Phrygia, and Rheomithras, one of the revolted generals, yielding to the attractions of Persian gold, deserted and betrayed their confederates. The insurrection was in this way quelled, but it had raised hopes in Egypt, which did not at once subside. Tachos, the native king, having secured the services of Agesilaus as general, and of Chabrias, the Athenian, as admiral of his fleet, boldly advanced into Syria, was well received by the Phoenicians, and commenced the siege of some of the Syrian cities. Persia might have suffered considerable loss in this quarter, had not the internal quarrels of the Egyptians among themselves proved a better protection to her than her own armies. Two pretenders to the throne sprang up as soon as Tachos had quitted the country, and he was compelled to return to Egypt in order to resist them. The force intended to strike a vigorous blow against the power of Artaxerxes was dissipated in civil conflicts; and Persia had once more to congratulate herself on the intestine divisions of her adversaries. A few years after this, Artaxerxes died, having reigned forty-six years, and lived, if we may trust Plutarch, ninety-four. Like most of the later Persian kings, he was unfortunate in his domestic relations. To his original queen, Statira, he was indeed fondly attached; and she appears to have merited and returned his love, but in all other respects his private life was unhappy. Its chief curse was Parysatis, the queen-mother. This monster of cruelty held Artaxerxes in a species of bondage during almost the whole of his long reign, and acted as if she were the real sovereign of the country. She encouraged Cyrus in his treason, and brought to most horrible ends all those who had been prominent in frustrating it. She poisoned Statira out of hatred and jealousy, because she had a certain degree of influence over her husband. She encouraged Artaxerxes to contract an incestuous marriage with his daughter Atossa, a marriage which proved a fertile source of further calamities. Artaxerxes had three sons by Statira—Darius, Ariaspes, and Ochus. Of these Darius, as the eldest, was formally declared the heir. But Ochus, ambitious of reigning, intrigued with Atossa, and sought to obtain the succession by her aid. So good seemed to Darius the chances of his brother's success that he took the rash step of conspiring against the life of his father, as the only way of securing the throne. His conspiracy was detected, and he was seized and executed, Ariaspes thereby becoming the eldest son, and so the natural heir. Ochus then persuaded Ariaspes that he had offended his father, and was about to be put to a cruel and ignominious death, whereupon that prince in despair committed suicide. His elder brothers thus removed, there still remained one rival, whom Ochus feared. This was Arsames, one of his half-brothers, an illegitimate son of Artaxerxes, who stood high in his favor. Assassination was the weapon employed to get rid of this rival. It is said that this last blow was too much for the aged and unhappy king, who died of grief on receiving intelligence of the murder.

Artaxerxes was about the weakest of all the Persian monarchs. He was mild in temperament, affable in demeanor, goodnatured, affectionate and well-meaning. But, possessing no strength of will, he allowed the commission of the most atrocious acts, the most horrible cruelties, by those about him, who were bolder and more resolute than himself. The wife and son, whom he fondly loved, were plotted against before his eyes; and he had neither the skill to prevent nor the courage to avenge their fate. Incapable of resisting entreaty and importunity, he granted boons which he ought to have refused, and condoned offences which it would have been proper to punish. He could not maintain long the most just resentment, but remitted punishments even when they were far milder than the crime deserved. He was fairly successful in the management of his relations with foreign countries, and in the suppression of disturbances within his own dominions; but he was quite incapable of anything like a strenuous and prolonged effort to renovate and re-invigorate the Empire. If he held together the territories which he inherited, and bequeathed them to his successor augmented rather than diminished, it is to be attributed more to his good fortune than to his merits, and to the mistakes of his opponents than to his own prudence or sagacity.

Ochus, who obtained the crown in the manner related above, was the most cruel and sanguinary of all the Persian kings. He is indeed the only monarch of the Achaemenian line who appears to have been bloodthirsty by temperament. His first act on finding himself acknowledged king (B.C. 359) was to destroy, so far as he could, all the princes of the blood royal, in order that he might have no rival to fear. He even, if we may believe Justin, involved in this destruction a number of the princesses, whom any but the most ruthless of despots would have spared. Having taken these measures for his own security, he proceeded to show himself more active and enterprising than any monarch since Longimanus. It was now nearly half a century since one of the important provinces of the Empire—Egypt—had successfully asserted its independence and restored the throne of its native kings. General after general had been employed in vain attempts to reduce the rebels to obedience. Ochus determined to attempt the recovery of the revolted province in person. Though a rebellion had broken out in Asia Minor, which being supported by Thebes, threatened to become serious, he declined to be diverted from his enterprise. Levying a vast army, he marched into Egypt, and engaged Noctanebo, the king, in a contest for existence. Nectanebo, however, having obtained the services of two Greek generals, Diophantus, an Athenian, and Lamius, a citizen of Sparta, boldly met his enemy in the field, defeated him, and completely repulsed his expedition. Hereupon the contagion of revolt spread. Phoenicia assumed independence under the leadership of Sidon, expelled or massacred the Persian garrisons, which held her cities, and formed an alliance with Egypt. Her example was followed by Cyprus, where the kings of the nine principal towns assumed each a separate sovereignty.

The chronology of this period is somewhat involved; but it seems probable that the attack and failure of Ochus took place about B.C. 351; that the revolts occurred in the next year, B.C. 350; while it was not till B.C. 346, or four years later, that Ochus undertook his second expedition into these regions. He had, however, in the meanwhile, directed his generals or feudatories, to attack the rebels, and bring them into subjection. The Cyprian war he had committed to Idrieus, prince of Caria, who employed on the service a body of 8000 Greek mercenaries, commanded by Phocion, the Athenian, and Evagoras, son of the former Evagoras, the Cyprian monarch; while he had committed to Belesys, satrap of Syria, and Mezseus, satrap of Cilicia, the task of keeping the Phoenicians in check. Idrieus succeeded in reducing Cyprus; but the two satraps suffered a single defeat at the hands of Tennes, the Sidonian king, who was aided by 40,000 Greek mercenaries, sent him by Nectanebo, and commanded by Mentor the Rhodian. The Persian forces were driven out of Phoenicia; and Sidon had ample time to strengthen its defences and make preparations for a desperate resistance. The approach, however, of Ochus, at the head of an army of 330,000 men, shook the resolution of the Phoenician monarch, who endeavored to purchase his own pardon by treacherously delivering up a hundred of the principal citizens of Sidon into the hands of the Persian king, and then admitting him within the defences of the town. Ochus, with the savage cruelty which was his chief characteristic, caused the hundred citizens to be transfixed with javelins, and when 500 more came out as suppliants to entreat his mercy, relentlessly consigned them to the same fate. Nor did the traitor Tennes derive any advantage from his guilty bargain. Ochus, having obtained from him all he needed, instead of rewarding his desertion, punished his rebellion with death. Hereupon the Sidonians, understanding that they had nothing to hope from submission, formed the dreadful resolution of destroying themselves and their town. They had previously, to prevent the desertion of any of their number, burnt their ships. Now they shut themselves up in their houses, and set fire each to his own dwelling. Forty thousand persons lost their lives in the conflagration; and the city was reduced to a heap of ruins, which Ochus sold for a large sum. Thus ended the Phoenician revolt. Among its most important results was the transfer of his services to the Persian king on the part of Mentor the Rhodian, who appears to have been the ablest of the mercenary leaders of whom Greece at this time produced so many.

The reduction of Sidon was followed closely by the invasion of Egypt. Ochus, besides his 330,000 Asiatics, had now a force of 14,000 Greeks—6000 furnished by the Greek cities of Asia Minor; 4000 under Mentor, consisting of the troops which he had brought to the aid of Tennes from Egypt; 3000 sent by Argos; and 1000 from Thebes. He divided his numerous armament into three bodies, and placed at the head of each two generals—one Persian and one Greek. The Greek commanders were Lacrates of Thebes, Mentor of Rhodes, and Nicostratus of Argos, a man of enormous strength, who regarded himself as a second Hercules, and adopted the traditional costume of that hero—a club and a lion's skin. The Persians were Rhossaces, Aristazanes, and Bagoas, the chief of the eunuchs. Nectanebo was only able to oppose to this vast array an army less than one third of the size. Twenty thousand, however, out of the 100,000 troops at his disposal were Greeks; he occupied the Nile and its various branches with a numerous navy the character of the country, intersected by numerous canals, and full of strongly fortified towns, was in his favor; and he might have been expected to make a prolonged, if not even a successful, resistance. But he was deficient in generals, and over-confident in his own powers of command: the Greek captains out-manoeuvred him; and no sooner did he find one line of his defences forced than his ill-founded confidence was exchanged for an alarm as little reasonable. He hastily fell back upon Memphis, leaving the fortified towns to the defence of their garrisons. These consisted of mixed troops, partly Greek and partly Egyptian; between whom jealousies and suspicions were easily sown by the Persian leaders, who by these means rapidly reduced the secondary cities of Lower Egypt, and were advancing upon Memphis, when Nectanebo in despair quitted the country and fled southwards to Ethiopia. All Egypt submitted to Ochus, who demolished the walls of the cities, plundered the temples, and after amply rewarding his mercenaries, returned to his own capital with an immense booty, and with the glory of having successfully carried through a most difficult and important enterprise.

It has been well observed that "the reconquest of Egypt by Ochus must have been one of the most impressive events of the age," and that it "exalted the Persian Empire in force and credit to a point nearly as high as it had ever occupied before." Ochus not only redeemed by means of it his former failure, but elevated himself in the opinions of men to a pitch of glory such as no previous Persian king had reached, excepting Cyrus, Cambyses, and the first Darius. Henceforth we hear of no more revolts or rebellions. Mentor and Bagoas, the two generals who had most distinguished themselves in the Egyptian campaign, were advanced by the gratitude of Ochus to posts of the highest importance, in which their vigor and energy found ample room to display themselves. Mentor, who was governor of the entire Asiatic sea-board, exerted himself successfully to reduce to subjection the many chiefs who during the recent troubles had assumed an independent authority, and in the course of a few years brought once more the whole coast into complete submission and dependence. Bagoas, carried with him by Ochus to the capital, became the soul of the internal administration, and maintained tranquillity throughout the rest of the Empire. The last six years of the reign of Ochus form an exceptional period of vigorous and successful government, such as occurs nowhere else in the history of the later Persian monarchy. The credit of bringing about such a state of things may be due especially to the king's officers, Bagoas and Mentor; but a portion of it must reflect upon himself, as the person who selected them, assigned them their respective tasks, and permanently maintained them in office.

It was during this period of vigor and renewed life, when the Persian monarchy seemed to have recovered almost its pristine force and strength, that the attention of its rulers was called to a small cloud on the distant horizon, which some were wise enough to see portended storm and tempest. The growing power of Macedon, against which Demosthenes was at this time in vain warning the careless Athenians, attracted the consideration of Ochus or of his counsellors; and orders went forth from the Court that Persian influence was to be used to check and depress the rising kingdom. A force was consequently despatched to assist the Thracian prince, Cersobleptes, to maintain his independence; and such effectual aid was given to the city of Perinthus that the numerous and well-appointed army with which Philip had commenced its siege was completely baffled and compelled to give up the attempt (B.C. 340). The battle of Chseroneia had not yet been fought, and Macedonia was still but one of the many states which disputed for supremacy over Greece; but it is evident that she had already awakened the suspicions of Persia, which saw a rival and a possible assailant in the rapidly growing monarchy.

Greater and more systematic efforts might possibly have been made, and the power of Macedon might perhaps have been kept within bounds, had not the inveterate evil of conspiracy and revolution once more shown itself at the Court, and paralyzed for a time the action of the Empire on communities beyond its borders. Ochus, while he was a vigorous ruler and administrator, was harsh and sanguinary. His violence and cruelty rendered him hateful to his subjects; and it is not unlikely that they caused even those who stood highest in his favor to feel insecure. Bagoas may have feared that sooner or later he would himself be one of the monarch's victims, and have been induced by a genuine alarm to remove the source of his terrors. In the year B.C. 338 he poisoned Ochus, and placed upon the throne his youngest son, Arses, at the same time assassinating all the brothers of the new monarch. It was evidently his aim to exercise the supreme power himself, as counsellor to a prince who owed his position to him, and who was moreover little more than a boy. But Arses, though subservient for a year or two, began, as he grew older, to show that he had a will of his own, and was even heard to utter threats against his benefactor whereupon Bagoas, accustomed now to crime, secured himself by a fresh series of murders. He caused Arses and his infant children to be assassinated, and selected one of his friends, Codomannus, the son of Arsanes, to fill the vacant throne. About the same time (B.C. 336), Philip of Macedon was assassinated by the incensed Pausanias; and the two new monarchs—Codomannus, who took the name of Darius, and Alexander the Great—assumed their respective sceptres almost simultaneously.

Codomannus, the last of the Persian kings, might with some reason have complained, like Plato, that nature had brought him in the world too late. Personally brave, as he proved himself into the Cadusian war, tall and strikingly handsome, amiable in temper, capable of considerable exertion, and not altogether devoid of military capacity, he would have been a fairly good ruler in ordinary times, and might, had he fallen upon such times, have held an honorable place among the Persian monarchs. But he was unequal to the difficulties of such a position as that in which he found himself. Raised to the throne after the victory of Chaeroneia had placed Philip at the head of Greece, and when a portion of the Macedonian forces had already passed into Asia, he was called upon to grapple at once with a danger of the most formidable kind, and had but little time for preparation. It is true that Philip's death soon after his own accession gave him a short breathing-space: but at the same time it threw him off his guard. The military talents of Alexander were untried, and of course unknown; the perils which he had to encounter were patent. Codomannus may be excused if for some months after Alexander's accession he slackened his preparations for defence, uncertain whether the new monarch would maintain himself, whether he would overpower the combinations which were formed against him in Greece, whether he would inherit his father's genius for war, or adopt his ambitious projects. It would have been wiser, no doubt, as the event proved, to have joined heart and soul with Alexander's European enemies, and to have carried the war at once to the other side of the Egean. But no great blame attaches to the Persian monarch for his brief inaction. As soon as the Macedonian prince had shown by his campaigns in Thrace, Illyria, and Boeotia that he was a person to be dreaded, Darius Codomannus renewed the preparations which he had discontinued, and pushed them forward with all the speed that was possible. A fleet was rapidly got ready: the satraps of Asia Minor were reinforced with troops of good quality from the interior of the Empire, and were ordered to raise a strong force of mercenaries; money was sent into Greece to the Lacedaemonians and others in order to induce them to create disturbances in Europe; above all, Memnon the Rhodian, a brother of Mentor, and a commander of approved skill, was sent to the Hellespont, at the head of a body of Greeks in Persian pay, with an authority co-ordinate to that of the satraps.

A certain amount of success at first attended these measures. Memnon was able to act on the offensive in North-Western Asia. He marched upon Cyzicus and was within a little of surprising it, obtaining from the lands and villas without the walls an immense booty. He forced Parmenio to raise the siege of Pitane; and when Callas, one of the Macedonian leaders, endeavored to improve the condition of things by meeting the Persian forces in the open field, he suffered a defeat and was compelled to throw himself into Rhoeteum.

These advantages, however, were detrimental rather than serviceable to the Persian cause; since they encouraged the Persian satraps to regard the Macedonians as an enemy no more formidable than the various tribes of Greeks with whom they had now carried on war in Asia Minor for considerably more than a century. The intended invasion of Alexander seemed to them a matter of no great moment—to be classed with expeditions like those of Thimbron and Agesilaus, not to need, as it really did, to be placed in a category of its own. Accordingly, they made no efforts to dispute the passage of the Hellespont, or to oppose the landing of the expedition on the Asiatic shore. Alexander was allowed to transport a force of 30,000 foot and 4000 or 5000 horse from the Chersonese to Mysia without the slightest interference on the part of the enemy, notwithstanding that his naval power was weak and that of the Persians very considerable. This is one of those pieces of remissness in the Persian conduct of military matters, whereof we have already had to note signal instances, and which constantly caused the failure of very elaborate and judicious preparations to meet a danger. Great efforts had been made to collect and equip a numerous fleet, and a few weeks later it was all-powerful in the Egean. But it was absent exactly at the time when it was wanted. Alexander's passage and landing were unopposed, and the Persians thus admitted within the Empire without a struggle the enemy who was fated to destroy it.

When the Persian commanders heard that Alexander was in Asia, they were anxious to give him battle. One alone, the Rhodian Greek, Memnon, proposed and urged a wholly different plan of operations. Memnon advised that a general engagement should be avoided, that the entire country should be laid waste, and even the cities burnt, while the army should retire, cut off stragglers, and seek to bring the enemy into difficulties. At the same time he recommended that the fleet should be brought up, a strong land force embarked on board it, and an effort made to transfer the war into Europe. But Memnon's colleagues, the satraps and commandants of the north-western portion of Asia Minor, could not bring themselves to see that circumstances required a line of action which they regarded as ignominious. It is not necessary to attribute to them personal or selfish motives. They probably thought honestly that they were a match for Alexander with the troops at their disposal, and viewed retreat before an enemy numerically weaker than themselves as a disgrace not to be endured unless its necessity was palpable. Accordingly they determined to give the invader battle. Supposing that Alexander, having crossed into Asia at Abydos, would proceed to attack Dascyleium, the nearest satrapial capital, they took post on the Granicus, and prepared to dispute the further advance of the Macedonian army. They had collected a force of 20,000 cavalry of the best quality that the Empire afforded, and nearly the same number of infantry, who were chiefly, if not solely, Greek mercenaries. With these they determined to defend the passage of the small stream above mentioned—one of the many which flow from the northern flank of Ida into the Propontis.

The battle thus offered was eagerly accepted by the Macedonian. If he could not defeat with ease a Persian force not greatly exceeding his own, he had miscalculated the relative goodness of the soldiers on either side, and might as well desist from the expedition. Accordingly, he no sooner came to the bank of the river, and saw the enemy drawn up on the other side, than, rejecting the advice of Parmenio to wait till the next day, he gave orders that the whole army should enter the stream and advance across it. The Granicus was in most places fordable; but there were occasional deeper parts, which had to be avoided; and there was thus some difficulty in reaching the opposite bank in line. That bank itself was generally steep and precipitous, but offered also several gentle slopes where a landing was comparatively easy. The Persians had drawn up their cavalry along the line of the river close to the water's edge, and had placed their infantry in the rear. Alexander consequently attacked with his cavalry. The engagement began upon the right. Amytas and Ptolemy, who were the first to reach the opposite bank, met with a strenuous resistance and were driven back into the stream by the forces of Memnon and his sons. The battle, however, on this side was restored by Alexander himself, who gradually forced the Persians back after a long hand-to-hand fight, in which he received a slight wound, and slew with his own hand several noble Persians. Elsewhere the resistance was less determined. Parmenio crossed on the left with comparative ease, by his advance relieving Alexander. The Persians found the long spears of the Macedonians and their intermixture of light-armed foot with heavy-armed cavalry irresistible. The Macedonians seem to have received orders to strike at their adversaries' faces—a style of warfare which was as unpleasant to the Persians as it was to the soldiers of Pompey at Pharsalia. Their line was broken where it was opposed to Alexander and his immediate companions; but the contagion of disorder rapidly spread, and the whole body of the cavalry shortly quitted the field, after having lost a thousand of their number. Only the infantry now remained. Against these the Macedonian phalanx was brought up in front, while the cavalry made repeated charges on either flank with overwhelming effect. Deserted by their horse, vastly outnumbered, and attacked on all sides, the brave mercenaries stood firm, fought with desperation, and were mostly slaughtered where they stood. Two thousand out of the 20,000—probably wounded men—were made prisoners. The rest perished, except a few who lay concealed among the heaps of slain.

The Persians lost by the battle 20,000 of their best footmen, and one or two thousand horse. Among their slain the proportion of men of rank was unusually large. The list included Spithridates, satrap of Lydia, Mithrobarzanes, governor of Cappadocia, Pharnaces, a brother-in-law, and Mithridates, a son-in-law of Darius, Arbupales, a grandson of Artaxerxes Mnemon, Omares, the commander of the mercenaries, Niphates, Petines, and Ehoesaces, generals. The Greek loss is said to have been exceedingly small. Aristobulus made the total number of the slain thirty-four; Arrian gives it as one hundred and fifteen, or a little over. It has been suspected that even the latter estimate is below the truth; but the analogy furnished by the other great victories of the Greeks over the Persians tends rather to confirm Arrian's statement.

The battle of the Granicus threw open to Alexander the whole of Asia Minor. There was no force left in the entire country that could venture to resist him, unless protected by walls. Accordingly, the

Macedonian operations for the next twelve months, or during nearly the whole space that intervened between the battles of the Granicus and of Issus, consist of little more than a series of marches and sieges. The reader of Persian history will scarcely wish for an account of these operations in detail. Suffice it to say that Alexander rapidly overran Lydia, Ionia, Caria, Lycia, Pamphylia, Pisidia, and Phrygia, besieged and took Miletus, Halicarnassus, Marmareis, and Sagalassus, and received the submission of Dascyleium, Sardis, Ephesus, Magnesia, Tralles, the Lycian Telmisseis, Pinara, Xanthus, Patara, Phaselis, Side, Aspendus, Celaenee, and Gordium. This last city was the capital of Phrygia; and there the conqueror for the first time since his landing gave himself and his army a few months' rest during the latter part of the winter.

With the first breath of spring his forces were again in motion. Hitherto anxious with respect to the state of things on the coast and in Greece, he had remained in the western half of Asia Minor, within call of his friends in Macedonia, at no time distant more than about 200 miles from the sea. Now intelligence reached him which made him feel at liberty to advance into the interior of Asia. Memnon the Rhodian fell sick and died in the early spring of B.C. 333. It is strange that so much should have depended on a single life; but it certainly seems that there was no one in the Persian service who, on Memnon's death, could replace him—no one fitted for the difficult task of uniting Greeks and Asiatics together, capable of influencing and managing the one while he preserved the confidence of the other. Memnon's death disconcerted all the plans of the Great King, who till it occurred had fully intended to carry the war into his enemy's country. It induced Darius even to give up the notion of maintaining a powerful fleet, and to transfer to the land service the most efficient of his naval forces. At the same time it set Alexander free to march wherever he liked, liberating him from the keen anxiety, which he had previously felt, as to the maintenance of the Macedonian power in Europe.

It now became the object of the Persian king to confront the daring invader of his Western provinces with an army worthy of the Persian name and proportionate to the vastness of the Empire. He had long been collecting troops from many of the most warlike nations, and had got together a force of several hundred thousand men. Forgetting the lessons of his country's previous history, he flattered himself that the host which he had brought together was irresistible, and became anxious to hurry on a general engagement. Starting from Babylon, probably about the time that Alexander left Gordium in Phrygia, he marched up the valley of the Euphrates, and took up a position at Sochi, which was situated in a large open plain, not far from the modern Lake of Antioch. On his arrival there he heard that Alexander was in Cilicia at no great distance; and the Greeks in his service assured him that it would not be long before the Macedonian monarch would seek him out and accept his offer of battle. But a severe attack of illness detained Alexander at Tarsus, and when he was a little recovered, troubles in Western Cilicia, threatening his communications with Greece, required his presence; so that Darius grew impatient, and, believing that his enemy had no intention of advancing further than Cilicia, resolved to seek him in that country. Quitting the open plain of Sochi, he marched northwards, having the range of Amanus on his left, almost as far as the thirty-seventh parallel, when turning sharply to the west, he crossed the chain, and descended upon Issus, in the inner recess of the gulf which bore the same name. Here he came upon Alexander's hospitals, and found himself to his surprise in the rear of his adversary, who, while Darius was proceeding northwards along the eastern flank of Amanus, had been marching southwards between the western flank of the same range and the sea. Alexander had crossed the Pylse, or narrowest portion of the pass, and had reached Myriandrus—a little beyond Iskonderum—when news reached him that Darius had occupied Issus in his rear, and had put to death all the sick and wounded Macedonians whom he had found in the town. At first he could not credit the intelligence; but when it was confirmed by scouts, whom he sent out, he prepared instantly to retrace his steps, and to fight his first great battle with the Persian king under circumstances which he felt to be favorable beyond anything that he could have hoped. The tract of flat land between the base of the mountains and the sea on the borders of the Gulf of Issus was nowhere broader than about a mile and a half. The range of Amanus on the east rose up with rugged and broken hills, so that on this side the operations of cavalry were impracticable. It would be impossible to form a line of battle containing in the front rank more than about 4000 men,1048 and difficult for either party to bring into action as many as 30,000 of their soldiers. Thus the vast superiority of numbers on the Persian side became in such a position absolutely useless, and even Alexander had more troops than he could well employ. No wonder that the Macedonian should exclaim, that "God had declared Himself on the Grecian side by putting it into the heart of Darius to execute such a movement." It may be that Alexander's superior generalship would have made him victorious even on the open plain of Sochi; but in the defile of Issus success was certain, and generalship superfluous.

Darius had started from Issus in pursuit of his adversary, and had reached the banks of the Pinarus, a small stream flowing westward from Amanus into the Mediterranean, when he heard that Alexander had hastened to retrace his stops, and was coming to meet him. Immediately he prepared for battle. Passing a force of horse and foot across the stream in his front, to keep his adversary in check if he advanced too rapidly, he drew up his best troops along the line of the river in a continuous solid mass, the ranks of which must have been at least twenty deep. Thirty thousand Greek mercenaries formed the centre of the line, while on either side of them were an equal number of Asiatic "braves"—picked probably from the mass of the army. Twenty thousand troops of a lighter and inferior class were placed upon the rough hills on the left, the outskirts of the Amanian range, where the nature of the ground allowed them to encircle the Macedonian right, which, to preserve its ranks unbroken, kept the plain. The cavalry, to the number of 30,000, was massed upon the other wing, near the sea.

The battle began by certain movements of Alexander against the flank force which menaced his right. These troops, assailed by the Macedonian light-armed, retreated at once to higher ground, and by their manifest cowardice freed Alexander from all anxiety on their account. Leaving 300 horse to keep the 20,000 in check, he moved on his whole line at a slow pace towards the Pinarus till it came within bow-shot of the enemy, when he gave the order to proceed at a run. The line advanced as commanded; but before it could reach the river, the Persian horse on the extreme right, unable to restrain themselves any longer, dashed across the shallow stream, and assailed Alexander's left, where they engaged in a fierce battle with the Thessalian cavalry, in which neither attained any decided advantage. The infantry, meanwhile, came into conflict along the rest of the line. Alexander himself, with the right and the right-centre, charged the Asiatic troops on Darius's left, who, like their brethren at Cunaxa, instantly broke and fled. Parmenio, with the left-centre, was less successful. The north bank of the Pinarus was in this part steep and defended by stakes in places; the Greek mercenaries were as brave as the Macedonians, and fought valiantly. It was not till the troops which had routed the Persian right began, to act against their centre, assailing it upon the flank, while it was at the same time engaged in front, that the mercenaries were overpowered and gave way. Seeing their defeat, the horse likewise fled, and thus the rout became general.

It is not quite clear what part Darius took in the battle, or how far he was answerable for its untoward result. According to Arrian, he was struck with a sudden panic on beholding the flight of his left wing, and gave orders to his charioteer instantly to quit the field. But Curtius and Diodorus represent him as engaged in a long struggle against Alexander himself, and as only flying when he was in imminent danger of falling into the enemy's hands. Justin goes further, and states that he was actually wounded. The character gained by Darius in his earlier years makes it improbable that he would under any circumstances have exhibited personal cowardice. On the whole it would seem to be most probable that the flight of the Persian monarch occurred, not when the left wing fled, but when the Greek mercenaries among whom he had placed himself began to give way before the irresistible phalanx and the impetuous charges of Alexander. Darius, not unwisely, accepted the defeat of his best troops as the loss of the battle, and hastily retired across Amanus by the pass which had brought him to Issus, whence he hurried on through Sochi to the Euphrates, anxious to place that obstacle between himself and his victorious enemy. His multitudinous host, entangled in the defiles of the mountains, suffered by its own weight and size, the stronger fugitives treading down the weaker, while at the same time it was ruthlessly slaughtered by the pursuing enemy, so long as the waning light allowed. As many as 100,000—90,000 foot and 10,000 horse—are said to have fallen. The ravines were in places choked with the dead bodies, and Ptolemy the son of Lagus related that in one instance he and Alexander crossed a gully on a bridge of this kind. Among the slain were Sabaces, satrap of Egypt, Bubaces, a noble of high rank, and Arsames, Rheomithres, and Atizyes, three of the commanders at the Granicus. Forty thousand prisoners were made. The whole of the Persian camp and camp-equipage fell into the enemy's hands, who found in the royal pavilion the mother, wife, and sister of the king, an infant son, two daughters, and a number of female attendants, wives of noblemen. The treasure captured amounted to 3000 silver talents. Among the trophies of victory were the chariot, bow, shield, and robe of the king, which he had abandoned in his hurried flight.

The loss on the side of the Macedonians was trivial. The highest estimate places it at 450 killed, the lowest at 182. Besides these, 504 were wounded. Thus Alexander had less than 1000 men placed hors de combat. He himself received a slight wound in the thigh from a sword, which, used a little more resolutely, might have changed the fortunes of the world.

The defeat of the Persians at Issus seems to have been due simply to the fact that, practically, the two adversaries engaged with almost equal numbers, and that the troops of Alexander were of vastly superior quality to those of Darhis. The Asiatic infantry—notwithstanding their proud title of "braves"—proved to be worthless; the Greek mercenaries were personally courageous, but their inferior arms and training rendered them incapable of coping with the Macedonian phalanx. The cavalry was the only arm in which the Persians were not greatly at a disadvantage; and cavalry alone cannot gain, or even save a battle. When Darius put himself into a position where he lost all the advantages derivable from superiority of numbers, he made his own defeat and his adversary's triumph certain.

It remained, therefore, before the Empire could be considered as entirely lost, that this error should be corrected, this false step retrieved. All hope for Persia was not gone, so long as her full force had not been met and defeated in a fair and open field. When Darius fled from Issus, it was not simply to preserve for a few months longer his own wretched life; it was to make an effort to redeem the past—to give his country that last chance of maintaining her independence which she had a right to claim at his hands—to try what the award of battle would be under the circumstances which he had fair grounds for regarding as the most favorable possible to his own side and the most disadvantageous to his adversary. Before the heart of the Empire could be reached from the West, the wide Mesopotamian plain had to be traversed—there, in those vast flats, across which the enemy must come, a position might be chosen where there would be room for the largest numbers that even his enormous Empire could furnish—where cavalry and even chariots would be everywhere free to act—where consequently he might engage the puny force of his antagonist to the greatest advantage, outflank it, envelop it, and perhaps destroy it. Darius would have been inexcusable had he given up the contest without trying this last chance—the chance of a battle in the open field with the full collected force of Persia.

His adversary gave him ample time to prepare for this final struggle. The battle of Issus was fought in November, B.C. 333. It was not till the summer of B.C. 331, twenty months later that the Macedonian forces were set in motion towards the interior of the Empire. More than a year and a half was consumed in the reduction of Phoenicia, the siege of Gaza, and the occupation of Egypt.

Alexander, apparently, was confident of defeating Darius in a pitched battle, whenever and under whatever circumstances they should again meet; and regarded as the only serious dangers which threatened him, a possible interruption of his communications with Greece, and the employment of Persian gold and Persian naval force in the raising of troubles on the European side of the Egean. He was therefore determined, before he plunged into the depth of the Asiatic continent, to isolate Persia from Greece, to destroy her naval power, and to cripple her pecuniary resources. The event showed that his decision was a wise one. By detaching from Persia and bringing under his own sway the important countries of Syria, Phoenicia, Palestine, Idumsea, and Egypt, he wholly deprived Persia of her navy, and transferred to himself the complete supremacy of the sea, he greatly increased his own resources while he diminished those of the enemy, and he shut out Persia altogether from communication with Greece, excepting through his territories. He could therefore commence his march into the interior with a feeling of entire security as to his communications and his rear. No foe was left on the coast capable of causing him a moment's uneasiness. Athens and Sparta might chafe and even intrigue; but without the Persian "archers," it was impossible that any force should be raised which could in the slightest degree imperil his European dominions.

From Babylon, whither Darius proceeded straight from Issus, he appears to have made two ineffectual attempts at negotiating with his enemy. The first embassy was despatched soon after his arrival, and, according to Arrian, was instructed merely to make proposals for peace, and to request the restitution of the Queen, the Queen-mother, Sisygambis, the infant prince, and the two princesses, captured by Alexander. To this Alexander replied, in haughty and contemptuous terms, that if Darius would acknowledge him as Lord of Asia, and deliver himself into his power, he should receive back his relatives: if he intended still to dispute the sovereignty, he ought to come and fight out the contest, and not run away.

The second embassy was sent six or eight months later, while Alexander was engaged in the siege of Tyre. Darius now offered, as a ransom for the members of his family held in captivity by Alexander, the large sum of ten thousand talents (L240,000.), and was willing to purchase peace by the cession of all the provinces lying west of the Euphrates, several of which were not yet in Alexander's possession. At the same time he proposed that Alexander should marry his daughter, Statira, in order that the cession of territory might be represented as the bestowal of a dowry. The reply of Alexander was, if possible, ruder and haughtier than before. "What did Darius mean by offering money and territory? All his treasure and all his territory were Alexander's already. As for the proposed marriage, if he (Alexander) liked to marry a daughter of Darius, he should of course do so, whether her father consented or not. If Darius wanted merciful treatment, he had better come and deliver himself up at once."

The terms of this reply rendered further negotiation impossible. Darius had probably not hoped much from his pacific overtures, and was therefore not greatly concerned at their rejection. He knew that the members of his family were honorably and even kindly treated by their captor, and that, so far at any rate, Alexander had proved himself a magnanimous conqueror. He can scarcely have thought that a lasting peace was possible between himself and his young antagonist, who had only just fleshed his maiden sword, and was naturally eager to pursue his career of conquest. Indeed, he seems from the moment of his defeat at Issus to have looked forward to another battle as inevitable, and to have been unremitting in his efforts to collect and arm a force which might contend, with a good hope of victory, against the Macedonians. He replaced the panoplies lost at Issus with fresh ones; he armed his forces anew with swords and spears longer than the Persians had been previously accustomed to employ, on account of the great length of the Macedonian weapons; he caused to be constructed 200 scythed chariots; he prepared spiked balls to use against his enemy's cavalry; above all, he laid under contribution for the supply of troops all the provinces, even the most remote, of his extensive Empire, and asked and obtained important aid from allies situated beyond his borders. The forces which he collected for the final struggle comprised—besides Persians, Medes, Babylonians, and Susianians from the centre of the Empire—Syrians from the banks of the Orontes, Armenians from the neighborhood of Ararat, Cappadocians and Albanians from the regions bordering on the Euxine, Cadusians from the Caspian, Bactrians from the Upper Oxus, Sogdians from the Jaxartes, Arachosians from Cabul, Arians from Herat, Indians from Punjab, and even Sacse from the country about Kashgar and Yarkand, on the borders of the Great Desert of Gobi. Twenty-five nations followed the standard of the Great King, and swelled the ranks of his vast army, which amounted (according to the best authorities) to above a million of men. Every available resource that the Empire possessed was brought into play. Besides the three arms of cavalry, infantry, and chariots, elephants were, for perhaps the first time in the history of military science, marshalled in the battle-field, to which they added an unwonted element of grotesqueness and savagery.

The field of battle was likewise selected with great care, and artificially prepared for the encounter. Darius, it would seem, had at last become convinced that his enemy would seek him out wherever he might happen to be, and that consequently the choice of ground rested wholly with himself. Leaving, therefore, the direct road to Babylon by the line of the Euphrates undefended, he selected a position which possessed all the advantages of the Mesopotamian plain, being open, level, fertile, and well supplied with water, while its vicinity to the eastern and northern provinces, made it convenient for a rendezvous. This position was on the left or east bank of the Tigris, in the heart of the ancient Assyria, not more than thirty miles from the site of Nineveh. Here, in the region called by the Greeks Adiabene, extended between the Tigris and the river Zab or Lycus, a vast plain broken by scarcely any elevations, and wholly bare of both shrubs and trees. The few natural inequalities which presented themselves were levelled by order of Darius, who made the entire plain in his front practicable not only for cavalry but for chariots. At the same time he planted, in the places where Alexander's cavalry was likely to charge, spiked balls to damage the feet of the horses.

Meanwhile, Alexander had quitted Egypt, and after delaying some months in Syria while his preparations were being completed, had crossed the Euphrates at Thapsacus and marched through northern Mesopotamia along the southern flank of the Mons Masius, a district in which provisions, water, and forage were abundant, to the Tigris, which he must have reached in about lat. 36° 30', thirty or forty miles above the site of Nineveh. No resistance was made to his advance; even the passage of the great rivers was unopposed. Arrived on the east bank of the Tigris, Alexander found himself in Assyria Proper, with the stream upon his right and the mountains of Gordyene Kurdistan at no great distance upon his left. But the plain widened as he advanced, and became, as he drew near the position of his enemy, a vast level, nowhere less than thirty miles in breadth, between the outlying ranges of hills and the great river. Darius, whose headquarters had been at Arbela, south of the Zab, on learning Alexander's approach, had crossed that stream and taken post on the prepared ground to the north, in the neighborhood of a small town or village called Gaugamela. Here he drew up his forces in the order which he thought best, placing the scythed chariots in front, with supports of horse—Scythian, Bactrian, Armenian, and Cappadocian—near to them; then, the main line of battle, divided into a centre and two wings, and composed of horse and foot intermixed; and finally a reserve of Babylonians. Sitaceni, and others, massed in heavy column in the rear. His own post was, according to invariable Persian custom, in the centre; and about him were grouped the best troops—the Household brigade, the Melophori or Persian foot-guards, the Mardian archers, some Albanians and Carians, the entire body of Greek mercenaries, and the Indians with their elephants.

Alexander, on his side, determined to leave nothing to chance. Advancing leisurely, resting his troops at intervals, carefully feeling his way by means of scouts, and gradually learning from the prisoners whom he took, and the deserters who came over to him, all the dispositions and preparations of the enemy, he arrived opposite the position of Darius on the ninth day after his passage of the Tigris. His officers were eager to attack at once; but with great judgment he restrained them, gave his troops a night's rest, and obtained time to reconnoitre completely the whole position of the enemy and the arrangement which he had made of his forces. He then formed his own dispositions. The army with which he was to attack above a million of men consisted of 40,300 foot and 7000 horse. Alexander drew them up in three lines:

The first consisted of light-armed troops, horse and foot, of good quality, which were especially intended to act against the enemy's chariots. The next was the main line of battle, and contained the phalanx with the rest of the heavy infantry in the centre, the heavy cavalry upon the two wings. The third line consisted of light troops, chiefly horse, and was instructed to act against such of the Persians as should outflank the Macedonian main line and so threaten their rear. As at Issus, Alexander took the command of the right wing himself, and assigned the left to Parmenio.

As the two armies drew near, Alexander, who found himself greatly outflanked on both wings, and saw in front of him smooth ground carefully prepared for the operations of chariots and cavalry, began a diagonal movement towards the right, which tended at once to place him beyond the levelled ground, and to bring him in contact with his enemy's left wing rather than with his direct front. The movement greatly disconcerted his adversary, who sought to prevent it by extending and advancing his own left, which was soon engaged with Alexander's right in a fierce hand-to-hand conflict. Alexander still pressed his slanting movement, and in resisting it Darius's left became separated from his centre, while at the same time he was forced to give the signal for launching the chariots against the foe sooner than he had intended, and under circumstances that were not favorable. The effect of the operation was much the same as at Cunaxa. Received by the Macedonian light-armed, the chariots were mostly disabled before the enemy's main line was reached; the drivers were dragged from the chariot-boards; and the horses were cut to pieces. Such as escaped this fate and charged the Macedonian line, were allowed to pass through the ranks, which opened to receive them, and were then dealt with by grooms and others in the rear of the army.

No sooner had the chariot attack failed, and the space between the two lines of battle become clear, than Alexander, with the quick eye of a true general, saw his opportunity: to resist his flank movement, the Bactrians and Sacae with the greater part of the left wing had broken off from the main Persian line, and in pressing towards the left had made a gap between their ranks and the centre. Into this gap the Macedonian king, at the head of the "Companion" cavalry and a portion of the phalanx, plunged. Here he found himself in the near neighborhood of Darius, whereupon he redoubled the vigor of his assault, knowing the great importance of any success gained in this quarter. The Companions rushed on with loud cries, pressing with all their weight, and thrusting their spears into the faces of their antagonists—the phalanx, bristling with its thick array of lances, bore them down. Alexander found himself sufficiently near Darius to hurl a spear at him, which transfixed his charioteer. The cry arose that the king had fallen, and the ranks at once grew unsteady. The more timid instantly began to break and fly; the contagion of fear spread; and Darius was in a little while almost denuded of protection on one side. Seeing this, and regarding the battle as lost, since his line was broken, his centre and left wing defeated, while only his right wing remained firm, the Persian monarch yielded to his alarm, and hastily quitting the field, made his way to Arbela. The centre and left fled with him. The right, which was under the command of the Syrian satrap, Mazeus, made a firmer stand. On this side the chariots had done some damage, and the horse was more than a match for the Thessalian cavalry. Parmenio found himself in difficulties about the time when the Persian king fled. His messengers detained a part of the phalanx, which was about to engage in the pursuit, and even recalled Alexander, who was hastening upon the track of Darius. The careful prince turned back, but before he could make his way through the crowd of fugitives to the side of his lieutenant, victory had declared in favor of the Macedonians in this part of the field also. Mazseus and his troops, learning that the king was fled, regarded further resistance as useless, and quitted the field. The Persian army hurriedly recrossed the Zab, pursued by the remorseless conquerors, who slew the unresisting fugitives till they were weary of slaughter. Arrian says that 300,000 fell, while a still larger number were taken prisoners. Other writers make the loss considerably less. All, however, agree that the army was completely routed and dispersed, that it made no attempt to rally, and gave no further trouble to the conqueror.

The conduct of Darius in this—the crisis of his fate—cannot be approved; but it admits of palliation, and does not compel us to withdraw from him that respectful compassion which we commonly accord to great misfortunes. After Issus, it was his duty to make at least one more effort against the invader. To this object he addressed himself with earnestness and diligence. The number and quality of the troops collected at Arbela attests at once the zeal and success of his endeavors. His choice and careful preparation of the field of battle are commendable; in his disposition of his forces there is nothing with which to find fault. Every arm of the service had full room to act; all were brought into play; if Alexander conquered, it was because he was a consummate general, while at the same time he commanded the best troops in the world. Arbela was not, like Issus, won by mere fighting. It was the leader's victory, rather than the soldiers. Alexander's diagonal advance, the confusion which it caused, the break in the Persian line, and its prompt occupation by some of the best cavalry and a portion of the phalanx, are the turning-points of the engagement. All the rest followed as a matter of course. Far too much importance has been assigned to Darius's flight, which was the effect rather than the cause of victory. When the centre of an Asiatic army is so deeply penetrated that the person of the monarch is exposed and his near attendants begin to fall, the battle is won. Darius did not—indeed he could not—"set the example of flight." Hemmed in by vast masses of troops, it was not until their falling away from him on his left flank at once exposed him to the enemy and gave him room to escape, that he could extricate himself from the melee.

No doubt it would have been nobler, finer, more heroic, had the Persian monarch, seeing that all was lost, and that the Empire of the Persians was over, resolved not to outlive the independence of his country. Had he died in the thick of the fight, a halo of glory would have surrounded him. But, because he lacked, in common with many other great kings and commanders, the quality of heroism, we are not justified in affixing to his memory the stigma of personal cowardice. Like Pompey, like Napoleon, he yielded in the crisis of his fate to the instinct of self-preservation. He fled from the field where he had lost his crown, not to organize a new army, not to renew the contest, but to prolong for a few weeks a life which had ceased to have any public value.

It is needless to pursue further the dissolution of the Empire. The fatal blow was struck at Arbela—all the rest was but the long death-agony. At Arbela the crown of Cyrua passed to the Macedonian; the Fifth Monarchy came to an end. The HE-GOAT, with the notable horn between his eyes, had come from the west to the ram which had two horns, and had run into him with the fury of his power. He had come close to him, and, moved with choler, had smitten the ram and broken his two horns—there was no power in the ram to stand before him, but he had cast him down to the ground and stamped upon him—and there was none to deliver the ram out of his hand.